THE MAKING OF *Modern Japan*

SECOND EDITION

Kenneth B. Pyle
UNIVERSITY OF WASHINGTON

D. C. HEATH AND COMPANY
LEXINGTON, MASSACHUSETTS · TORONTO

Address editorial correspondence to

D. C. Heath and Company
125 Spring Street
Lexington, MA 02173

Acquisitions Editor: James Miller

Development Editor: Pat Wakeley

Production Editor: Karen Wise

Designer: David A. Libby

Photo Researcher: Billie L. Porter

Production Coordinator: Charles Dutton

Permissions Editor: Margaret Roll

Published simultaneously in Canada.

Printed in the United States of America.

International Standard Book Number: 0–669–20020–4

Library of Congress Catalog Number: 95–68947

14-MV-08

The Making of Modern Japan

To Will and Annie
and
to their mother

Preface

The end of the twentieth century is an opportune time to gather our thoughts about modern Japan. The era of Japan's "late development" has drawn to a close. Until recently, the dominant theme of modern Japanese history was the national determination to overtake the advanced industrial countries. By adopting from the West its science and technology, its institutions and knowledge, Japan set out to preserve its sovereignty and catch up with those Western countries that in the middle of the nineteenth century had opened Japan and subjected it to semicolonial restrictions. By the 1980s the achievement of this heroic goal was proclaimed. Japan was recognized as an international leader and at the end of the twentieth century began to reassess its national goals and purpose. In short, looking back, we can now see the modern era whole.

My intention in writing this book is to set forth in rather stark, straightforward fashion some of the main themes in the historical development of modern Japanese society. It is my hope that these themes, culled from three decades of teaching the subject, may prove of value to anyone wishing a broad understanding of the emergence of Japan as a world power in modern times. I have tried, in the course of writing, to avoid overwhelming the reader with the names and details that are characteristic of the "past politics" approach to history, and instead to concentrate on the dynamics of historical change.

How far back in history is it sensible to go in order to describe the emergence of modern Japan? We could begin the story in the middle of the nineteenth century with Commodore Perry's opening of Japan to the Western world. The difficulty with such a starting point is that it leaves the reader with an inadequate understanding of many of the forces that made modern Japan. It tends, in particular, to exaggerate the impact of the West while overlooking those long-term trends in Japanese society and economy already at work before the redoubtable

Yankee arrived, trends that created conditions favorable to industrialization.

By their nature historians are prone to move ever farther back in time to determine the roots of historical movements. "The explanation of the very recent in terms of the remotest past," wrote Marc Bloch, "naturally attractive to [scholars] who have made of this past their chief subject of research, has sometimes dominated our studies to the point of a hypnosis. In its most characteristic aspect, this idol of the historian tribe may be called the obsession with origins."[1] Without wishing to fall under the sway of that idol, I have chosen to begin this book with the far-reaching reshaping of Japanese institutions that occurred at the end of the sixteenth century. Here we may clearly find the roots of modern Japanese development, for the institutions established at that time set in motion the long-run social and economic trends favorable to industrialization. We therefore begin our account with the unification of Japan at the end of the sixteenth century and the establishment, in the decades that followed, of a novel system of territorial control known as the Tokugawa Bakufu. When Japan was governed by the Tokugawa system during the subsequent period, 1600–1868, the warfare and turbulence of previous centuries disappeared, cities grew, agricultural productivity rose, the country was knit together by improved communications, trade prospered, and population stabilized.

All those developments might still not have led to the industrial revolution had there not been a political revolution. The Meiji Restoration of 1868 brought to power new leadership from the old samurai class with a vision of a radically transformed country. A party within the old warrior elite seized power in that year and embarked upon a revolutionary program that saved Japan from national disaster, such as was experienced nearly everywhere else in Asia. To understand fully this new leadership and its receptivity to change and new ideas, we must go back to the origins of the Tokugawa system and to the institutional developments that gradually changed the samurai from a rough, unlettered military class into a bureaucratic ruling elite. Because the samurai officialdom proved so responsive to the challenges of industrialization in the nineteenth century, Japan was able to pursue its modern goals without first enduring the kind of great internal upheaval that most other countries have suffered. Those warrior revolutionaries led Japan through a generation of reforms that changed it from a predominantly agrarian society in 1868 to a nearly industrial economy by the turn of the century. An English resident in Japan during this breathtaking change wrote that its swift pace "makes a man

[1]Marc Bloch, *The Historian's Craft,* trans. Peter Putnam (New York, 1964), p. 29.

feel preternaturally old; for here he is in modern times, . . . and yet he can himself distinctly remember the Middle Ages. . . . Thus does it come about that . . . we ourselves feel well-nigh four hundred years old."[2]

As the title of this book implies, modern Japan was a deliberate creation. It was "made." Because of Japan's late development, much of its modern history has been the product of carefully constructed policies and institutions designed to bring the nation abreast of the power and influence of the advanced industrial nations. In other words, modern Japan did not simply and spontaneously rise or emerge as a nation. It advanced through plans laid first by its leaders and decisively shaped at points by certain groups in society.

The Meiji Restoration was first and foremost a pragmatic nationalist response by a rejuvenated elite to the threat that Western imperial power constituted for the Japanese state. Japanese leaders typically were guided by long-term goals of enhancing the power of the nation-state and overcoming Japan's status as a latecomer in the industrial world. Their pragmatic nationalism was marked by an opportunistic, largely reactive, adaptation to international conditions. From the middle of the nineteenth century, Japanese leaders had a keen sensitivity to the forces controlling the international environment. They tried to operate in accord with these forces and use them to Japan's advantage.

To achieve national power, they were willing to swallow cultural pride and borrow massively from an alien civilization. Taking a long view of the future, they reassessed all their cultural values and institutions. No other people were prepared to sacrifice so much of their own heritage. This turned out to be a painful process that stretched out over a century. The novelist Tanizaki Jun'ichirō (1886–1965) wrote plaintively in 1934:

> How unlucky we have been, what losses we have suffered, in comparison with the Westerner. The Westerner has been able to move forward in ordered steps, while we have met superior civilization and had to surrender to it, and we have had to leave a road we have followed for thousands of years. . . . I am aware of and most grateful for the benefits of the age. No matter what complaints we may have, Japan has chosen to follow the West, and there is nothing for her to do but move bravely ahead and leave us old ones behind. But we must be resigned to the fact that as long as our skin is the color it is the loss we have suffered cannot be remedied.[3]

[2]Basil Hall Chamberlain, *Things Japanese* (London, 1891), pp. 1–2.
[3]Jun'ichirō Tanizaki, *In Praise of Shadows*, trans. Thomas J. Harper and Edward G. Seidensticker (Leete's Island Books, 1977), pp. 8, 42.

No other nation carried out a more sweeping cultural revolution than did the modern Japanese.

Yet despite this receptivity to Western civilization, Japan ultimately devised its own methods for overcoming economic backwardness and closing the gap with the advanced industrial societies. It developed distinctive Japanese policies and institutions designed to spur industrial development. An elite bureaucratic leadership was put in place devoted to the national goals. Education focused on the training of a committed populace. Deferring democracy, the state sought to coopt laborers, women's groups, and tenant associations into the political community. Social policies designed to prevent alienation and upheaval were implemented. The values of the system were overwhelmingly directed at the achievement of the national goals.

Japan's success had its costs. Beyond the loss of cultural traditions, the speedy expansion of national power caused great psychological strain and human suffering. Driven by a peculiar combination of insecurity and ambition, the nation pursued industry and empire at a forced march. Lafcadio Hearn, a sensitive observer of the stress Japan put itself under, wrote in 1894:

> The nation has entered upon a period of intellectual overstrain. Consciously or unconsciously, in obedience to sudden necessity, Japan has undertaken nothing less than the tremendous task of forcing mental expansion up to the highest existing standard; and this means forcing the development of the nervous system. For the desired intellectual change, to be accomplished within a few generations, must involve a physiological change never to be effected without terrible cost. In other words, Japan has attempted too much; yet under the circumstances she could not have attempted less.[4]

In 1911 the novelist Natsume Sōseki, despairing of the pace at which his country was driving itself, prophesied "nervous collapse" and admonished his countrymen not be deluded into thinking of Japan as capable of competition on an equal footing with the great powers.[5] The Christian writer Tokutomi Roka was likewise oppressed by a foreboding of disaster. He urged his country in 1906 to turn away from reliance on military power: "Awake, Japan, our beloved fatherland! Open your eyes and see your true self! Japan, repent!"[6]

But historical circumstance did not make it likely that Japan would change course. Having been prodded to industrialize by the challenge of Western imperialism, Japan found its neighbors in East

[4] *The Writings of Lafcadio Hearn* (Boston, 1923), VI, 367.
[5] *Sōseki zenshū* (Tokyo, 1936), XIII, 352–380.
[6] *Tokutomi Roka shū (Meiji bungaku zenshū)* (Tokyo, 1966), XLII, pp. 366–368.

Asia governed by weak regimes in danger of collapse and of being taken over by the European empires, with consequent jeopardy to Japan's security and economic interests. Accordingly, a fear that China and Korea might fall under the sway of European nations, as well as ambition for equality with the Western imperial powers, drove Japan to territorial expansion. Industrialization and a vast empire were achieved, but in the course of their pursuit the national ideology was continuously reinforced in order to overcome the recurring unrest in Japanese society stirred up by such taxing ambitions. The ultimate price for what Lafcadio Hearn called the national "overstrain" was to blunder into a war that could not be won.

In other words, all did not go according to plan. Although much of modern Japan was "made," contingency, the accidental, the unexpected, the unanticipated result, were an inevitable part of its history. By the 1930s Japan had become virtually a prisoner of its own ideology. It was by no means the first time in history, nor was it the last, that a people were kept from pursuing their own best interests by the narrow way in which they conceived their national ideals. Japan lost nearly 3 million people in World War II, including those first victims of the atomic age. The industry and empire for which it had striven were destroyed. The country was an international outcast, occupied by foreign soldiers for the first time in its history.

Despite defeat, popular revulsion from the prewar ideology, and the Occupation's attempt to revolutionize Japanese values, continuities emerged after the war. Segments of the old leadership survived. The elite bureaucracy was largely unscathed. The postwar system was governed by a rejuvenated conservative leadership: its long-term perspective and pragmatic nationalist approaches, and its careful gauging of international trends and conditions, all reemerged intact. All this—the war, the defeat, and the new conservative leadership—dictated a narrowed focus on economic goals and a renewed struggle to close the economic gap with the West. International conditions proved uniquely favorable to the expansion of trade. A more elaborate industrial policy was underwritten by a firm national consensus in support of economic growth. The Japanese people expended prodigies of effort on behalf of these economic goals, and they went from success to success in their material life. But the postwar period exacted painful cultural and political deprivations. Living under an American-imposed constitutional order and subordinating themselves to the American foreign-policy system required the Japanese again to swallow their national pride and to maintain a low profile in international politics. The rewards lay in finally achieving their catch-up economic goals.

At the end of the twentieth century, the Japanese people confront the challenge of replacing those institutions and policies that made modern Japan and brought them success as a late developing nation. Because their interests are now so deeply entwined with international developments, they face a vastly different set of problems and issues. Their responses to these new challenges, however, will be greatly conditioned by the experiences of the late development era that has now drawn to a close.

For their assistance in reviewing the manuscript for this revised edition and offering many valuable suggestions, I wish to express my thanks to J. Michael Allen, Brigham Young University; Gail Bernstein, University of Arizona; David D. Buck, University of Wisconsin, Milwaukee; Lee A. Butler, Brigham Young University; John W. Dower, Massachusetts Institute of Technology; W. Miles Fletcher III, University of North Carolina, Chapel Hill; Sheldon M. Garon, Princeton University; Sally A. Hastings, Purdue University; Atsuko Hirai, Bates College; Ray A. Moore, Amherst College; Mark Ravina, Emory University; Donald Roden, Rutgers University; Brett Sheppard, University of Pittsburgh; Richard J. Smethurst, University of Pittsburgh; Gregory J. Smits, Eastern Washington University; William M. Tsutsui, University of Kansas; and John A. Tucker, University of North Florida.

K. B. P.

Contents

Reunification of Japan

The first Europeans to arrive in Japan were Portuguese traders who landed on the island of Tanegashima off the southern coast in 1543. This first cultural confrontation between Japan and the West was a bewildering experience for both sides. As one observer at Tanegashima remarked whimsically of the Portuguese:

> These men are traders. . . . They understand to a certain degree the distinction between Superior and Inferior, but I do not know whether they have a proper sense of ceremonial etiquette. They eat with their fingers instead of with chopsticks such as we use. They show their feelings without any self-control. They cannot understand the meaning of written characters. They are people who spend their lives roving hither and yon. They have no fixed abode and barter things which they have for those they do not, but withal they are a harmless sort of people.[1]

Jesuit missionaries began arriving in Japan in 1549 and as part of their proselytizing campaign made a genuine effort to understand Japanese manners and customs. It was no easy matter, and one Jesuit in exasperation finally concluded of the Japanese:

> They have rites and ceremonies so different from those of all the other nations that it seems they deliberately try to be unlike any other people. The things which they do in this respect are beyond imagining and it may truly be said that Japan is a world the reverse of Europe; everything is so different and opposite that they are like us in practically nothing. . . . Now all this would not be surprising if they were like so many barbarians, but what astonishes me is that they behave as very prudent and cultured people in all these matters.[2]

As they became more familiar with the basic organization of society and government, the Jesuits began to discern institutions that were in many respects comparable to ones that had existed in medieval Western Europe: a ruling class composed of military leaders and their followers, practices of vassalage and enfeoffment, a military code of honor, and the fragmentation of political authority. Such similarities came to provide the basis for many subsequent comparisons between the feudalism of Western Europe and of Japan. Karl Marx pushed this comparison perhaps as far as anyone else when he wrote in *Das Kapital:* "Japan, with its purely feudal organization of landed property and its developed *petite culture,* gives a much truer picture of the European middle ages than our own history books. . . ."

The Warring States Period, 1467–1568

When the first Europeans arrived, Japan was in the midst of a full-blown feudal period, marked by continuous, widespread warfare. During this so-called Warring States Period, which lasted from the mid-fifteenth to the mid-sixteenth century, power was fragmented to an extraordinary degree. It was "a world without a center."[3] Not only had the authority of the central government dissolved, but regional powerholders too had lost their positions.

Power, in short, lay at the local level. The most important institution was the small feudal state dominated by the local lord and his band of warriors (*samurai*). The lord's power was based solely on his own military strength, for there were no sources of security and prestige other than raw power. His position depended on the continuing loyalty of his samurai retainers, and thus he rewarded his leading vassals with fiefs, titles, and other preferential treatment.

The normal state of relations among these small feudal states was warfare. This was a period of great instability, and fluctuations in power and in amounts of territory controlled were continuous. If a lord failed to defend his territory he would either lose it to a more powerful neighboring lord or he would be overthrown by one of his own vassals.

Perhaps because betrayal and treachery were frequent, loyalty was the highest virtue. Yet no lord could wholly trust his vassals; they might try to overthrow him, or if they felt he was losing to a neighboring lord they might break away and join that lord. In these conditions of endemic warfare, lords were constantly suspicious of one another. It was not just that they were power mad, but rather, somewhat like nations in modern times, each one was afraid of his neighbor, fearful that if he himself did not expand, he would be conquered. The overriding concern of each lord, therefore, was to maximize his military power. This was a topsy-turvy age in which lords rose and fell not merely from one generation to another, but from one decade to another.

Power could scarcely have been further fragmented. Gradually, however, stabilizing forces began to appear. To overcome the conditions of upheaval and instability new institutions were created in the late 1500s, culminating in the establishment of the Tokugawa hegemony and the reunification of the country.

Consolidation of Local Power

The foundation for this great new unified order was laid in the second half of the sixteenth century with the consolidation of power at the local level. The primary reason for the new stability was the emergence, after a century of warfare, of feudal lords (*daimyo*) throughout the country who were able to impose greater control than their predecessors had over both their fighting men and the economic resources of the territory they controlled.

The local lord gained greater power vis-à-vis his samurai retainers by gradually diminishing the independent power bases that had existed within his domain. He learned that by obliging his vassals to reside close to him he could much more effectively control them. The lord achieved greater subordination of his warriors by organizing them more tightly into a methodical ranking. Similarly he was finding more systematic ways to assess the land tax on the peasantry in his domain.

As the process of consolidation of power at the local level went forward, a lord could associate himself with a more powerful lord in his region who would protect and guarantee his position. If then a lord's vassal rose against him, he could call on that powerful regional lord for help. In this way the daimyo formed regional groupings led by a particularly powerful lord; in turn, the power of each daimyo vis-à-vis his own vassals was enhanced by his belonging to such a grouping.

Castle Towns

This consolidation of power at the local level and the increased strength of the daimyo was dramatically symbolized by the massive castles they built in the latter half of the sixteenth century. In a relatively short space of time (especially in the period from 1580 to 1610) castles sprang up across the Japanese countryside. In all parts of the country the newly emergent daimyo, who numbered in excess of 200, built great stone fortresses at the heart of their domains, where they could assemble their samurai retainers and effectively dominate the strategic and productive resources of the surrounding countryside.

These central citadels with towers soaring above the landscape symbolized the new ascendancy of the daimyo at the local level. To build the great structures they had to be able to mobilize large amounts of labor and to assemble highly skilled craftsmen. Previously, during the Warring States Period, fortifications had been of much smaller proportions and were ordinarily located on mountain tops, but in the new, more stable conditions castles were built in the lowlands and plains. Here, in and about the confines of the citadel, the lord settled his vassals and retainers.

As the warriors moved from the countryside into the castles, merchants and artisans and shrines and temples followed quickly to service the warriors' needs. Across Japan new "castle towns" came into being. Prior to 1550 nearly everyone had lived in farming or fishing villages. There were only two or three population centers that could accurately be called cities. One was Kyoto, the capital, which had about a quarter of a million inhabitants. Another was the nearby port of Sakai, the beneficiary of a flourishing overseas trade; it numbered perhaps 50,000 inhabitants. There were probably no more than a half dozen other towns with as many as 20,000. Edo (present-day Tokyo) was still a fishing village.

Then with dramatic suddenness in the years after 1550, new cities began to spring up as a result of the increasing stability at the local level, the building of castles, and the withdrawal of samurai from the countryside. A period of extraordinary urban growth ensued. John W. Hall has written, "Most of the first-ranking castles and castle towns such as Himeji, Osaka, Kanagawa, Wakayama, Tokushima, Kōchi, Takamatsu, Hiroshima, Edo, Wakamatsu, Okayama, Kōfu, Fushimi, Takasaki, Sendai, Fukuoka, Fukui, Kumamoto, Tottori, Matsuyama, Hikone, Fukushima, Yonezawa, Shizuoka, and Nagoya were founded during the brief span of years between 1580 and 1610. It would be hard to find a parallel period of urban construction in world history."[4] The castle towns became important urban centers in the various regions of Japan and remain so today. Edo grew into the modern metropolis of Tokyo. Two-thirds of the present prefectural capitals were once castle towns.

The building of those castle towns and the events associated with it, particularly the removal of most samurai from the countryside into the city, constitute one of the most important developments in the history of Japan. We may sum up their long-range significance as follows.

1. The result of most immediate historical significance was that these fortresses and the control that they exercised over the local countryside further helped stabilize the local areas and provided the building blocks, the firm base upon which national unification could rest. With the samurai settled closely about the castle keep, the daimyo could the more easily control them and hence overcome the topsy-turvy nature of local politics that had prevailed during the preceding Warring States Period.

2. The gradual withdrawal of the samurai from the countryside set in motion a fundamental change in the nature of the warrior ruling class that had immense long-range significance for Japan. Previously samurai had been scattered over the land in villages, living on fiefs granted them by their lord, where they had been responsible for levying taxes, administering local justice, and keeping the peace. Now, however, living in a castle town, the warrior's ties with the land were soon cut. Instead of being rewarded with a fief from his lord, he was paid a stipend. Gradually, over the course of generations, the warriors ceased to be a landed elite. Instead they became more akin to bureaucrats, for the lord as he became absolute in his domain used his retainers as officials and clerks. Living in the castle town, with their juridical and social ties to the land gone, the warriors staffed the daimyo's bureaucracy. Thomas C. Smith sums up the profound transformation that was taking place:

> The lord, having taken in his hands his vassals' political and judicial functions, now governed an average population of about 100,000. To police so large a population, to collect its taxes and regulate its trade, to give it justice and maintain its roads and irrigation works, required a small army of officials and clerks. The lord, of course, used his vassals to perform these functions, to man the expanding and differentiating bureaucracy under him. The warriors who manned the bureaucracy exercised far more power over the rest of the population than warriors ever had before; but it was a new kind of power. Formerly power was personal and territorial; it pertained to a piece of land and belonged to a man as inherited right. Now it was impersonal and bureaucratic: it pertained to a specialized office to which one must be appointed and from which he might be removed.[5]

As the warrior's legal relationship to the land changed, as he became more akin to a bureaucratic officeholder, he came to lack private economic or political power. This fact had great historical significance. The gradual transformation of the feudal ruling class into a landless bureaucratic elite helps to explain the remarkable responsiveness of Japan in the nineteenth century. When faced with the challenge of undertaking the great political and economic changes required by the industrial revolution, Japan responded quickly, in part because it had no politically powerful landed class, no entrenched land-based gentry such as existed in China, which would bitterly resist those changes. We shall explore this factor later. Here it is sufficient to point out that the movement of samurai from the countryside to the castle town in the sixteenth and seventeenth centuries radically changed the nature of the ruling class, in a way that was to ease economic and political change in the nineteenth century.

3. Another consequence associated with the appearance of castle towns and the consolidation of local power was the development of local administrative practice. As the Warring States Period gave way to peaceful stability in the seventeenth century, the castle towns became concerned less with military matters than with problems of local administration. As Hall has summed up: "The great castles of Japan came to house the central and local administrative headquarters of the nation. From them political authority radiated outward into the countryside. . . . Life in Tokugawa Japan became infinitely more regularized and subject to written law than under earlier feudal regimes, and this in turn was a step in the direction of more modern public administration."[6]

4. The growth of the castle towns helped bring into being a large and vital merchant class during the Tokugawa Period (1600–1868). As samurai gradually settled around the castle, a merchant class to service them sprang up. The emerging castle town became the economic center of its domain. As time went on, the merchants took on greater importance and the samurai depended on them to fulfill vital economic functions. One contemporary Confucianist, lamenting the growing power of the merchants, wrote that the samurai in towns lived "as if in an inn"—dependent on the services of the merchants.

5. Along with the rise of the mercantile class, the Tokugawa Period saw a gradual growth of a market economy and of specialization and commercialization in agriculture. In place of the old self-sufficient pattern, farming tended to become far more specialized as produce was sold in the local market. The peasants more and more grew the special crops for which their climate and land were best suited. What they did not themselves produce, they could buy. One must be careful not to exaggerate the suddenness of this development: it took place gradually over a long period of time and at a different pace in various parts of the country.

6. The growth of castle towns contributed to the improvement of transportation. Roads to and from the castle towns became essential for economic, administrative, and strategic functions.

7. Castle towns contributed to development of an urban culture. The brightest and gaudiest culture existed in Edo and Osaka, but even the smaller castle towns were infected by the tastes and life-style of the townsmen.

In tracing the long-range significance of the castle towns, we have gotten far ahead of our story, for these results unfolded gradually over the course of the Tokugawa Period and were by no means evident in the late sixteenth century when castle towns came into being. We shall pursue each one of these consequences in detail in the succeeding pages.

Toward Unification

The stabilization of power at the local level made available the firm base upon which first regional and then national unity could be built. Gradually daimyo at the regional level joined together, the lesser daimyo pledging loyalty to or being conquered by the strongest daimyo in the region. In warfare that occupied the years from 1570 to 1600 these regional groupings contended with one another for national hegemony. It was three successive daimyo from central Hon-

Osaka castle, built in 1583 by Toyotomi Hideyoshi. *National Archives*

shu, Japan's largest island, who assembled a powerful coalition of forces, one by one gained the submission of other regional clusters of daimyo, and ultimately succeeded in unifying Japan.

These three lords were Oda Nobunaga (1534–1582), his chief vassal Toyotomi Hideyoshi (1536–1598), and Tokugawa Ieyasu (1542–1616). What enabled these three extraordinary men to bring about a new centralization of power? Partly their success was due to their strategic location in central Honshu, where they could control the greatest food-producing plains in Japan and where they had easy access to Kyoto, the capital and traditional symbol of legitimacy for national political power. Partly it was the result of brilliant military strategy. No less important, however, was their demonstrated mastery of two of the main sources of feudal power that had to be controlled and exploited: land and peasants.

Toyotomi Hideyoshi, who succeeded to leadership of the reunification campaign after Oda's death in 1582, was particularly successful in devising measures to strengthen control of the land and peasants under his sway. In the 1580s he ordered a sweeping resurvey of the cultivated land in the countryside to determine the productivity of each piece of land and identify the individual responsible for paying the tax on it. Not only did the land survey tighten collection of the land tax and provide a solid new basis for village organization, but it allowed Toyotomi to assign to his vassal daimyo lands he had conquered with firm knowledge of the value of those lands. At the same time he carried out his so-called sword hunt by an edict that forbade all nonsamurai to keep "swords, sidearms, daggers, spears or any other military equipment." Thus a sharp line of distinction was drawn between the sword-carrying warrior elite and the disarmed commoners. Other edicts sought to freeze society by tying peasants to their villages and occupation. Similarly, samurai were not to return to the villages, nor were they to change masters. Toyotomi's purpose was to eliminate both physical and occupational mobility and to stabilize the social order.

These reforms, occurring as the castle towns were being built throughout Japan, served to enhance the trend toward consolidation of the daimyo's power. The meticulous land survey made it easier to withdraw samurai from the countryside and supervise the tax collection from the castle. The other reforms, which disarmed the commoners and tied them to their occupation and village, made local society more tractable to daimyo rule. Thus, as the coalition of daimyo led by Toyotomi gradually brought the country under its authority, reforms were instituted that strengthened the daimyo vis-à-vis their retainers and that diminished the possibility of disruption at the local level. The basis was laid for the remarkable national social and political order that would endure more than two and a half centuries.

Notes

1. Quoted in C. R. Boxer, *The Christian Century in Japan, 1549–1650* (Berkeley: University of California Press, 1951), 29.
2. Alessandro Valignano, quoted in Michael Cooper, *They Came to Japan* (Berkeley: University of California Press, 1965), 229.
3. Mary Elizabeth Berry, *Hideyoshi* (Cambridge, Mass.: Harvard University Press, 1982), ch. 2.
4. John Whitney Hall, "The Castle Town and Japan's Modern Urbanization," in *Studies in the Institutional History of Early Modern Japan,* ed. John Whitney Hall and Marius B. Jansen (Princeton, N.J.: Princeton University Press, 1968), 176.
5. Thomas C. Smith, *Native Sources of Japanese Industrialization, 1750–1920* (Berkeley: University of California Press, 1988), 138.
6. Hall, "Castle Town," 179, 183.

2

Establishment of the Tokugawa System

Toyotomi Hideyoshi's death in 1598 occasioned an intense two-year power struggle to determine who among the most powerful daimyo should succeed him as overlord of the land. At a decisive battle fought in October 1600 at Sekigahara, near Kyoto, the coalition of daimyo forces led by Tokugawa Ieyasu triumphed over an alliance of daimyo from western Japan. He emerged in a preeminent position, able to dispose of all those daimyo who would not accept his overlordship and in possession of an immense amount of territory acquired as the spoils of war, which he could divide among his loyal followers.

From this position of strength the Tokugawa family spent the next several decades building a new system of government. This was accomplished by institutionalizing the control measures devised by themselves and their predecessors during the march toward national unification. It is extremely important to grasp the basic outlines of this system because it provided the framework of Japanese politics and society from which modern Japan emerged.

The Tokugawa Bakufu

In 1603 Tokugawa Ieyasu was invested by the Emperor with the position of *shogun* (generalissimo), traditionally the highest military office in the land. Although in reality Ieyasu's position depended entirely on his own military power, since he had fought his way to the top of the feudal hierarchy, Ieyasu made much of his investiture: the Emperor, although without real political power or even much private wealth, was regarded as the source of political legitimacy, the locus of sovereignty, and the symbol of national unity. In the seventh and eighth centuries, when the Chinese imperial model had been adopted by the Japanese and the capital was established first at Nara and then at Kyoto, the prestige and influence of the imperial family were at their zenith. Even in that time, however, a tradition of the Emperor reigning but not ruling was beginning to take root. Over the next centuries, political power slipped into the hands of the Kyoto nobility and then, as the central government declined, into the hands of feudal fighting men in the countryside. But even as power fragmented and Japan entered a period of full-blown feudalism, the old imperial system, centered in Kyoto, remained the source of legitimacy. The Tokugawa were careful to observe this tradition, not only by seeking to be appointed shogun by the Emperor, but also by acquiring court titles and establishing family ties with the nobility—and ultimately with the imperial house itself. Thus Tokugawa Ieyasu and his descendants who succeeded him as shogun were technically appointed officials, holding the civil and military functions of government delegated by the Emperor.

While these lines of legitimacy were established through the old imperial system in Kyoto, the reality of Tokugawa power depended on stabilizing the coalition of daimyo through which national unification had been achieved. Ieyasu established his seat of government in Edo (present-day Tokyo), where his new castle was built. Government by the shogun, often referred to as the shogunate or *bakufu* (a term meaning military government), was an extremely complex and intricate mechanism. Basically the shogun administered the country along two lines.

First, roughly one-quarter of the land belonged directly to the Tokugawa family, amassed during their rise to power. These lands, scattered throughout the countryside but mostly concentrated in central Honshu, the Tokugawa administered directly through their own samurai retainers. In this category of direct Tokugawa rule were all the important mines, the major seaports, including Osaka and Nagasaki, and the old capital city of Kyoto. Within these direct holdings the bakufu raised its funds, and its rule was in every way absolute.

Second, the remainder of the country, approximately three-quarters of it, was governed indirectly through the daimyo, all of whom after 1600 swore allegiance to the Tokugawa. It was this second, indirect mechanism of governing the country that gave the Tokugawa their greatest concern. Here their power was by no means absolute; it depended on maintaining the coalition of daimyo. Among the daimyo there were some who were very powerful, and the possibility of an anti-Tokugawa alliance among them was an ever-present danger. Because the Tokugawa were not strong enough fully to subjugate the daimyo, the latter were left largely autonomous within their own domains. The bakufu regulated the external affairs of the daimyo's domain but refrained from interfering in internal affairs so long as the daimyo gave no sign of disloyalty toward the Tokugawa.

During the two and a half centuries of Tokugawa rule, the number of daimyo varied between 240 and 295. A daimyo was officially defined as a lord possessing a *han* (domain) with an assessed productivity of at least 10,000 *koku* of rice (1 koku = 4.96 bushels). The size of daimyo domains varied considerably; the largest was assessed in excess of 1 million koku.

There were three different categories of daimyo:

1. The *shimpan* (related) daimyo were members of Tokugawa branch families. If the main line of the family died out, a shogun would be chosen from among these lords, who came to number twenty-three.

2. The *fudai* (house) daimyo were retainers of the Tokugawa house. Most of them were vassals of the Tokugawa prior to the decisive battle of Sekigahara in 1600. Because they owed their status to the Tokugawa, they were considered trustworthy and they helped staff the central councils of the shogunate. Their domains were relatively small. The largest was the Ii house of Hikone with lands assessed at 250,000 koku. By the eighteenth century the house lords numbered in the neighborhood of 140 daimyo.

3. The *tozama* (outer) daimyo were those who had taken Tokugawa Ieyasu as their overlord only after the battle of Sekigahara. Because their pledge of loyalty was relatively recent, they were generally regarded as less trustworthy and therefore excluded from positions in the shogunate. Indeed, among the outer daimyo were lords who had fought against the Tokugawa coalition at Sekigahara, the two most important of which were the domains of Satsuma and Chōshū. Although they had submitted to the Tokugawa after Sekigahara, they still could not be trusted and had to be kept under constant surveillance. (Eventually, two and a half centuries later, it was those two domains that led the overthrow of the shogunate.) Not all of the outer lords had traditions hostile to the Tokugawa. Kaga domain, for example, had been allied with the Tokugawa at Sekigahara, though it had not yet taken Ieyasu as overlord. Many of the outer daimyo possessed very large domains. Kaga was officially assessed in excess of 1 million koku, Satsuma at 770,000, and Chōshū at 369,000. (Lands held directly by the Tokugawa were assessed in excess of 7 million koku.) The outer lords numbered approximately 100.

In addition to the early allegiance of the daimyo, the size of the han, determined by the amount of rice they were capable of producing annually, was a significant measure of importance. By the early eighteenth century, 20 large domains were in existence and assessed at 200,000 or more koku, 78 middling-size domains assessed between 50,000 and 200,000 koku, and 161 small domains assessed between 10,000 and 50,000 koku. As Harold Bolitho writes,

> It was its size, more than anything else, that determined the range of possibilities and responsibilities of any given han. Large han,

> wherever situated, whenever established, and whatever the original political affiliation of their daimyo, were likely to have greater military authority, more regional influence, and greater economic diversity than small ones. Their responsibilities, too, whether to larger numbers of samurai or peasants, were correspondingly more onerous. This in turn predisposed them to a rather higher degree of assertiveness than would have been the case with smaller han . . . [which] had little control over their destiny.[1]

Tokugawa Control System

To maintain hegemony over this unwieldy feudal coalition, the Tokugawa depended on various control measures:

1. *Rearrangement of domains.* One of the most important control measures was the power the shogun had to rearrange or reassign landed holdings for strategic reasons. In this way the disposition of fiefs could be arranged so that potentially disloyal daimyo would be shunted to remote positions or hedged in by loyal daimyo. The shogun could increase or reduce the size of a han depending upon its loyalty. After the battle of Sekigahara, allies of the Tokugawa were rewarded with larger holdings. In addition, at the outset of the Tokugawa Period, the shogun confiscated many domains and created new ones. During the first century of the period, 200 daimyo lost their domains and 280 han transfers shifted daimyo, their vassals, and their families to another part of the country. Thereafter, as the bakufu felt more secure, the system stabilized, and such changes became less frequent.

2. *Alternate attendance system.* By far the most important method devised for controlling the daimyo was the alternate attendance system. Under this system all daimyo were obliged to alternate their residence periodically between their domains and Edo. Ordinarily this meant residing in Edo every other year. While they were in Edo, the shogunate could maintain surveillance over them. When they returned to their domains, the daimyo were required to leave behind their wives and children as hostages. In theory, sojourns in Edo were arranged so that about half the daimyo would be in attendance at any particular time.

Surveillance was not the only purpose. The system also served as a continuous drain on the economic resources of the daimyo. They had to build and maintain houses in Edo for their families and retainers, a considerable number of whom accompanied them on their biennial trip. While in Edo the daimyo were required to perform certain types of ceremonies as well as guard duty. The bakufu made periodic levies for money and labor. A daimyo might be instructed to repair a castle, a

An early seventeenth-century Japanese portrayal of a European ship arriving.
Courtesy, Museum of Fine Arts, Boston

shrine, or a bridge. It became common for daimyo to spend a substantial portion of their domains' tax income for the costs of the alternate attendance system.

3. *Strict management of foreign relations.* To ensure Japanese security and sovereignty and to enhance its own authority, the bakufu brought the management of Japan's foreign relations under its firm control. The most striking aspect of this effort came to be called the seclusion (*sakoku*) policy. This policy was designed to cut off the lords—particularly the powerful outer lords—from the military and economic sources of strength that foreign trade might offer them. It was also intended to eliminate Christianity as a source of social disruption in the stable order the Tokugawa were trying to establish. The Jesuits in their earlier efforts had succeeded, according to their own estimates, in making hundreds of thousands of converts. How meaningful these estimates are is difficult to say, but they did have some successes. Perhaps what was most disturbing to the Tokugawa was the conversion of several important daimyo. Measures to limit the activities of Western missionaries had already been initiated under Toyotomi Hideyoshi. Under the Tokugawa those measures became more stringent: all missionaries were expelled, converts forced to recant, and fiendish persecutions sanctioned. By 1650 Christianity was almost completely eliminated.

Trade, too, was brought under the tight control of the shogunate. Prior to 1600 strong indications of a quickening expansionist impulse were found. Commercial ties with other parts of East and Southeast Asia had grown; most notably, Toyotomi Hideyoshi with grandiose plans of empire had made an abortive invasion of the Korean peninsula in the 1590s. This expansionist urge, however, had to be suppressed, for the requirements of social stability were paramount.

By three seclusion decrees issued in the 1630s Japanese were prohibited from traveling abroad and the size of ships being built was limited to that necessary for coastal trade within the Japanese archipelago. All trade with Western countries was ended except for commercial ties with the Dutch, who were permitted a small trading station on the tiny island of Deshima in the harbor of Nagasaki. Here the Dutch merchants were virtually prisoners, kept under constant surveillance. Somewhat like the daimyo, the Dutch were compelled to make periodic trips to Edo to pay their respects to the shogun.

Englebert Kaempfer, a German doctor serving with the Dutch trading station, described the ludicrous audiences with the shogun (whom he mistakenly called "the Emperor") in 1691:

> As soon as the [head of the trading company] came thither, [the attendants] cried aloud *Hollanda Captain* which was the signal for him to draw near and make his obeisance. Accordingly he crawled

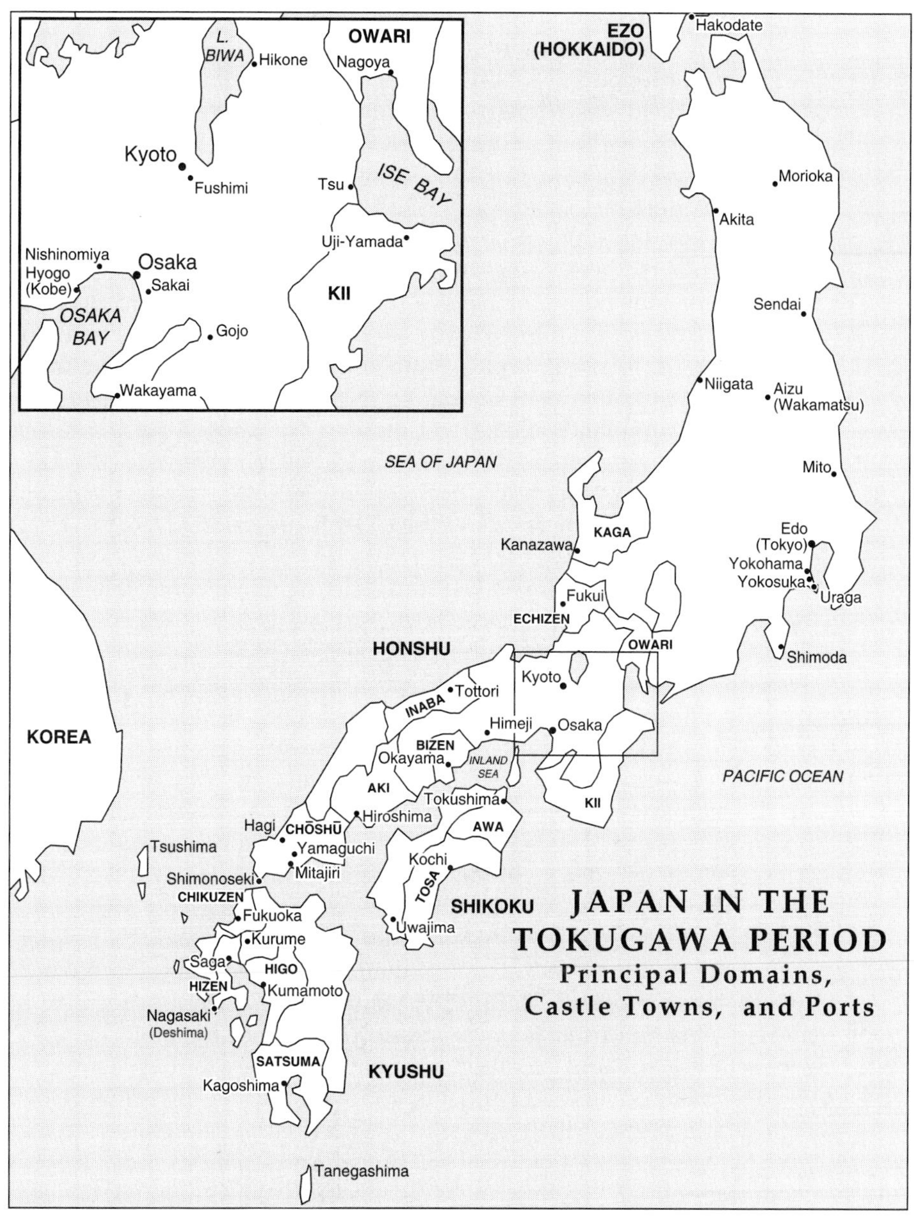

JAPAN IN THE TOKUGAWA PERIOD
Principal Domains, Castle Towns, and Ports

> on his hands and knees to a place showed him between the presents, ranged in due order on one side, and the place where the Emperor [Shogun!] sat on the other, and then, kneeling, he bowed his forehead quite down to the ground, and so crawled backwards like a crab, without uttering one single word. . . . The mutual compliments being over, the succeeding part of this solemnity turned to a perfect farce. We were asked a thousand ridiculous and impertinent questions. The Emperor . . . ordered us to take off our cappas, or cloaks, being our garments of ceremony; then to stand upright that he might have a full view of us; again to walk, to stand still, to compliment each other, to dance, to jump, to play the drunkard, to speak broken Japanese, to read Dutch, to paint, to sing, to put our cloaks on and off. Meanwhile we obeyed the Emperor's commands in the best manner we could, I joining to my dance a love-song in High German. In this manner and with innumerable such other apish tricks, we must suffer ourselves to contribute to the Emperor's and the Court's diversion.[2]

Because the measures taken to restrict Japanese contacts with the Western world were the most striking aspect of the bakufu's strict management of foreign relations, historians have characterized the Tokugawa intentions as negative, reactionary, and xenophobic. More recently, however, some historians have begun to interpret the bakufu's purpose in a more positive light by stressing the shogunate's effort to construct a new system of foreign relations designed to shore up the stability and legitimacy of the Tokugawa government both at home and abroad. They point out that substantial contacts with other parts of Asia continued, although carefully supervised by the Tokugawa. That is, at the same time that the bakufu acted "to restrict those aspects of external affairs deemed inimical to Japan and to the interests of the bakufu, it also strove to build a diplomatic structure which would enhance bakufu legitimacy, assure Japan a sense of security in an East Asia still troubled by war and piracy, and maintain Japanese access to a secure and expanding foreign trade."[3]

The bakufu wanted to enhance its own authority by bringing foreign relations under its strict control. Unlike earlier shoguns who had been willing to adopt a vassal relationship to China in order to promote trade, the Tokugawa shoguns asserted Japan's autonomous status. In its foreign relations, the shogun took the sovereign title "Great Prince of Japan"(*Nihon-koku Taikun*) and, rather than accept a subordinate position in a Sinocentric world order, refused official relations with China. This did not mean isolation from the continent. On the contrary, the bakufu oversaw a burgeoning nonofficial trade with Chinese merchants operating in Nagasaki. The Tokugawa maintained official diplomatic ties with Korea and a substantial trade was conducted through the daimyo of Tsushima, a pair of islands in the straits between Kyushu and the Korean peninsula. The bakufu received numerous tribute missions from the Ryukyu islands and maintained a vigorous trade with the islands through the Satsuma domain in southernmost Kyushu. In sum, the Tokugawa established a "monopoly" on the conduct of external relations as a means to legitimate its new power.

4. *Ideology*. A fourth control directed primarily at the daimyo and their retainers was the use of ideology. To reinforce the dominance of the Tokugawa and of the samurai class, the founders of the regime drew on Confucianism, Shintō, Buddhism, popular religion, and ritual to create an eclectic ideology that would legitimate their rule and provide a philosophical foundation for the social and political order taking shape. Confucianism was not new in Japan. It had been introduced centuries earlier but it had never been so appropriate as it now became. Confucianism held up familial relations as a proper model for government, relations between parent and child being analogous to those between ruler and subject. Because political authority derived its legitimacy from its ethical basis, the ruling elite must by their exemplary moral conduct set an example for the rest of society. Social distinctions were held to be in the natural order of things, and each class, each age, each group had to fulfill its obligations and maintain its proper place if society was to preserve harmony. In sum, Tokugawa society promised to be much more ordered, settled, and regulated than earlier times; and Confucian concepts of a hierarchical society in accord with nature, of benevolent paternalism in government, of an ethical basis for administration, and of a meritorious officialdom, all coincided with Tokugawa purposes.

No less important than the adaptation of neo-Confucianism to the new circumstances, Tokugawa ideology drew on a variety of other sources to exalt and legitimize the new rulers. Shintō mythology was most useful. Ieyasu was rendered a Shintō deity and his burial site at Nikkō, north of Edo, was made into a splendid mausoleum to venerate the founder of the new order. The shrine was built at han expense and daimyo were expected to pay regular homage there. An extraordinary demonstration of the lengths to which the Tokugawa went to establish their supreme status was the arrangement of the marriage of the shogun's daughter to the emperor in 1620. A daughter of this union was crowned empress in 1629, the first time since the eighth century that a woman had ascended the throne. Ideologists both drew upon the imperial court to legitimize the Tokugawa and encroached upon the imperial charisma by refocusing national religious ritual away from the court toward a new center in Edo and Nikkō. Through this syncretic ideology, the Tokugawa "transformed their military power into sacred authority, their rule into an embodiment of the Way of Heaven."[4]

In addition to these controls, other measures were taken to regulate the activities of the daimyo. Many of them were codified. These directives regulated contacts between daimyo, the contracting of marriages between daimyo families, the repair of castles, and so on. Barriers were established on the main highways to monitor the comings and goings of daimyo and their retainers. A system of passports provided further means to check on travel.

Government at the Domain Level

Within their own domains, or han as they came to be called later, the daimyo were left with a great deal of autonomy, free from interference as long as they did not behave in any way regarded as disloyal by the shogunate. The daimyo paid no taxes to the shogunate, although they were subject to periodic exactions of money and labor. Within the han a daimyo was absolute. His position was hereditary, passing ordinarily to his eldest son. When there was no heir, one was adopted. In practice, because the daimyo spent much of his time in Edo, his leading vassals often tended to exercise actual administrative leadership in the han.

The samurai class constituted 6 percent or 7 percent of the population and alone had the right to wear swords and to assume a family surname. It would be a mistake, however, to think of the warriors as a homogeneous group, for there was a great deal of spread or differential within the class. Warriors ranged from the shogun and daimyo at the top, down to the foot soldiers at the bottom. The high-ranking warriors served on the Council of Elders or in some other capacity as advisors to the daimyo. They also acted as heads of guard groups or standing army units, as chiefs of police, as supervisors of financial affairs, and as liaison agents between the daimyo and the shogunate. The middle ranks of samurai served in bureaucratic posts having to do with administration of the castle town, the collection of taxes, and the management of religious and educational affairs. They may also have headed various lesser units of the militia. At the lower levels, warriors served as clerks or as low-ranking military men.

Thus a minute gradation of hierarchy existed within the samurai class with great differences between top and bottom. In Chōshū, for example, Albert Craig tells us that among the 5,675 direct vassals of the daimyo were 40 different ranks. This differential in status was reflected in the annual rice stipend warriors were paid, as the tabulation shows.[5]

Income (koku)	Number of families in the group
More than 100	661
More than 70 and less than 100	202
More than 50 and less than 70	339
More than 40 and less than 50	472
Less than 40	4,001
Total	5,675

Consciousness of rank and observance of status distinctions were maintained throughout society. At the domain school for sons from samurai families in Kaga—to give one interesting example—Ronald P. Dore tells us that regulations provided that any boy from the highest-ranking families was permitted to come to school accompanied by two retainers, as well as one servant to take care of his sandals during school hours and another to hold his umbrella on rainy days. Children from the next rank "could have one retainer, a sandal-minder, and an umbrella-holder. The next, one retainer and a sandal-minder, but they should carry their own umbrella. Younger sons, and those of the lowest rank, should come without servants; the school would provide someone to look after their sandals en masse."[6]

The educator Fukuzawa Yukichi, writing in 1877 after the destruction of the Tokugawa system, looked back with loathing at the status distinctions that were observed in speech, dress, and daily intercourse:

> An *ashigaru* [foot soldier] always had to prostrate himself on the ground in the presence of an upper samurai. If he should encounter an upper samurai on the road in the rain, he had to take off his *geta* [clogs] and prostrate himself by the roadside. . . . Upper samurai rode on horseback, lower samurai went on foot. Upper samurai possessed the privileges of hunting wild boar and fishing; lower samurai had no such privileges. . . . The broad distinction between the upper and lower classes was, however, accepted unquestioningly, almost as though it were a law of nature rather than an invention of man.[7]

Village Government

As a result of the withdrawal of the warriors from the countryside into the castle towns, the actual administration of peasant villages fell into the hands of village headmen. The lord appointed from among his vassals supervisors who would oversee the work of headmen. But within the village itself there was considerable autonomy. Each village, led by its headman, was largely self-governing, and the daimyo would not interfere as long as order was maintained and the taxes were paid to the lord.

The headman came from among the peasants themselves—generally from the old, prestigious, and wealthy families in the village. In many villages the position was hereditary; in others the office was rotated among leading families in the village; and occasionally the headman was elected by propertied villagers. He was responsible for keeping records, settling disputes, maintaining order, and above all for apportioning and collecting the tax that was levied on the village. Often he operated with the help of a village assembly and village codes. By allowing the headman certain visible symbols of status, such as elegant clothing and housing, the lord encouraged the peasants to respect and look up to the headman. The typical village comprised between fifteen and forty clustered houses and was characterized by a strong sense of solidarity, encouraged by centuries of close living and by the cooperative nature of farming. The conformity of everyone in the village to group sentiment was usually ensured by a variety of social pressures, not the least important of which was gossip. The successful headman governed by building up a consensus; and disputes within the village were generally settled by conciliation, compromise, and patient negotiation, in which the headman played the leading role.

Family and the Role of Women

The fundamental institution of all classes of Tokugawa society was the household or family unit. The new sedentary and peaceful life-style of the Tokugawa Period helped to solidify the principle of a society organized around family groups, each pursuing a hereditary "household occupation." This was an important development in Japanese social history. As Bitō Masahide writes, "the research of sociologists and anthropologists has made clear that beginning in the seventeenth century, 'houses' of this kind constituted the basic units of Japanese society, and indeed the house has come to be recognized as a characteristic feature of Japanese society."[8] In general, the ideal family was said to have many distinctive characteristics. First, it was an extended family. It was not simply a nuclear family of husband, wife, and children, but would include several generations. Typically, the core of this extended family group, known as the stem family, was composed of grandparents, their eldest son who was their heir, his wife, and unmarried children. Other sons, when they married, formed branch families that were still part of the larger unit, while daughters left the family at the time of their marriage. The household was more than a biological unit because it often included nonkin such as employees, servants, or an adopted male heir.

Many ties held a large lineage group together, but most important was the economic interdependence of its members, who united in pursuing the family occupation. As Dore describes these economic links, "even in the samurai class . . . the income from the feudal lord's granaries was an endowment of the family rather than of individuals and it did not necessarily vary in amount whether, at any particular time, there was one male from the family in the lord's service or three. . . . A farming family gave the branch family a portion of the family land, a merchant gave the branch family a section of the main family's trade or at least offered all its wholesale buying facilities to help the branch family establish itself in a new area. Similarly, artisan families taught the craft, secured entrance for its branch family into the guild and helped in marketing its products."[9]

A second important characteristic of the Tokugawa household was the emphasis placed on solidarity and continuity through time. The members of this basic unit of social organization were expected to sacrifice personal desires to benefit the group as a whole. Individuals therefore found their identities in the symbols of the family, such as the family property, including the physical house itself, inherited from the ancestors; the traditions of the family, which in upper-class families were sometimes codified in a family constitution; and above all, in the worship of family ancestors. The family name, honor, and status were of constant importance. Anyone's misdoings reflected not only on that individual but on the entire family including the ancestors and descendants. Continuity of the family was regarded as a moral duty: rather than let a family die out, a childless couple would adopt an heir.

A third characteristic of the Tokugawa household was that much greater emphasis was placed on the parent-child relationship than on the husband-wife relationship. For example, in the code of obligations for samurai promulgated in 1684, a man mourned thirteen months for his parents, but only three months for his wife. For a woman, as Dore observes, "marriage is conceived of less as an entry into conjugal relations with a particular man than as entry into another family group. . . . Marriage gives the husband exclusive sexual rights in his wife, but not vice versa. His children by women other than his wife could be adopted into his family. When she enters her new family, the bride goes through a period of explicit training by her mother-in-law in the 'ways of the family.'"[10] A seventeenth-century Confucian treatise entitled *The Great Learning for Women* admonished samurai women to remember that

> it is the chief duty of a girl living in the parental house to practice filial piety towards her father and mother. But after marriage, her chief duty is to honour her father-in-law and mother-in-law—to honour them beyond her own father and mother. . . . Never

> should she be remiss in performing any tasks they may require of her. With all reverence must she carry out, and never rebel against, her father-in-law's commands. . . . A woman has no particular lord. She must look to her husband as her lord and must serve him with all worship and reverence.[11]

A fourth characteristic was the practice of male primogeniture. Ordinarily the eldest direct male descendant inherited the leadership of the household. Succession did not normally await the death of a former head but would occur when the elder son was sufficiently mature to handle family affairs and the father was ready to retire. Widows might succeed to the headship during the minority of their children and, on occasion, daughters might inherit headship, but once married their husbands would replace them.

Fifth, both power and responsibility resided with the househead. In the determination and arrangement of a marriage, the authority of the househead was decisive. Hierarchical relations were maintained throughout family life to inculcate an instinctive respect for relative age and male superiority. On the other hand, in addition to power, responsibility fell on the househead to ensure the well-being of all members of the group. Widowed sisters or unemployed younger brothers could expect the househead to help them.

Many variations on this general pattern of household characteristics existed. Class differences were evident for example in matters of sex, marriage, and divorce. In all these matters more formality was found in the samurai class and greater casualness among peasants. Premarital sex and divorce were more prevalent in the peasant class. Regarding the choice of marriage partner, Dore writes:

> That marriage was arranged by parents was true of all classes of society, but there were variations in the extent to which either the man or the woman concerned had the right to refuse an unattractive mate. Among the samurai, the wedding ceremony was often the occasion of the first meeting of the bride and groom, since the bride often came from a distant part of the country. . . . In the merchant class of the towns, however, an opportunity for the prospective partners to survey each other and to express their personal wishes became an institutionalized part of the marriage process. The *miai*, as this was called, was a deliberately contrived, but by an agreed fiction accidental, meeting arranged by go-betweens for the prospective partners and their families. After the meeting either party could express displeasure with the prospective mate and the negotiations could then be dropped without either side necessarily feeling offended. . . . This system gradually became more general in urban areas, and the modern word for an arranged marriage is a miai-marriage (as opposed to a "love-marriage").[12]

Considerable class and regional differences existed in the power and role of women in the family. In the samurai class, the wife of the househead oversaw the family's domestic matters, exercising control over consumption, the servants, and her daughters-in-law. If widowed, she often increased in power over other important matters such as marriages and disposition of capital. The women of wealthy peasant families were often relatively well off: they could be educated, travel widely, and carry considerable weight in family and village matters. For a poor peasant wife, work was strenuous: "it invariably encompassed planting, cultivating, weeding, and harvesting paddies and vegetable fields; in economically advanced regions women also cultivated cash crops such as vegetables or tobacco, raised silkworms, spun thread, or wove cloth for market."[13] In the average merchant family too the wife kept books and waited on customers. Because commoner women were often integral to the productive work of the family, males had to be more involved than is commonly thought in child rearing and housework. Regional differences were found too. In some parts of the country peasant women had the reputation of ruling the roost and even serving as househeads. In sum, as one scholar who studies the subject concludes, "It is impossible to establish a single portrait of rural women."[14]

The Character of the Tokugawa System

The period of unification culminating in the establishment of the Tokugawa shogunate is one of the great seminal periods in Japanese institutional history, comparable to the founding of the imperial state on the Chinese model around the year 700 and to the creation of the modern nation-state after 1868. It will be useful to conclude this chapter by assessing the nature of the Tokugawa system and the unique form that it took.

Tokugawa institutions were fundamentally shaped by the purpose of ending the turmoil and upheaval of the Warring States Period. In Europe, the modern nation-state was born out of a similarly feudal period as monarchies steadily expanded their power. Japan too achieved a new degree of political unity, but centralization under the Tokugawa stopped short of what was achieved in Europe. As we have seen, the domains survived with a considerable amount of autonomy; the daimyo were preserved as direct vassals of the Tokugawa shogunate. This system is therefore often described as centralized feudalism.

Some historians have wondered why the new rulers did not press unification to its logical conclusion by eliminating the daimyo. To these scholars it appeared that Japan could have followed a course similar to that of Europe, but its progress was arrested midway in its evolution from feudal decentralization to national centralization. The unifiers, as Mary Elizabeth Berry writes, made an aggressive and systematic attack on the roots of social disorder and lawless violence.[15] They instituted policies that would prevent disturbances of the peace. They disarmed the peasantry, removed samurai from the countryside, brought foreign affairs under strict control, eliminated religion as an independent force, and put constraints on daimyo independence. They emphasized the notion of the "common good" or "public interest" and suppressed the possibilities of personal factions and private alliances. In short, they went to great lengths to eliminate the bases of defiance and disturbances of the peace.

But, the Tokugawa did not choose to further consolidate and centralize their power. They did not press on to achieve a monopoly of military power in the shogunate. They did not try to establish a national system of taxation. They did not try to control the production and distribution of the food supply. They did not create a national bureaucracy. Such measures would have moved them in the direction of the centralized monarchies emerging in Europe in this period. Instead they left control over local government, taxation, and military force to the daimyo. The Tokugawa system is therefore known as the *baku-han* system—a combination of bakufu and han rule, a "feudal-central hybrid."[16] It appears that the initial impetus toward centralization stalled. Why?

The comparison with Europe in 1600 may be misleading. Feudalism in Japan was not yet ready to disintegrate at this time. The process of national unification in Japan had to follow its own distinctive course. The unifiers had been dependent on feudal alliances at every step along the way to consolidating national power. The Tokugawa shogunate lacked the independent military and administrative capacity to unite the country; it was dependent on the compliance of the daimyo. Each needed the other. For the daimyo, joining in this system provided a kind of collective security and legitimacy. In other words, given the residual strength of the daimyo in 1600, centralization went as far as it could. It went as far as was necessary to establish order, stability, and peace. The Tokugawa could be satisfied with this degree of centralization. As James W. White writes, "the power of the Tokugawa in 1600 was sufficient to establish political stability and civil order with the acquiescence of the daimyo; elimination of their prerogatives would have entailed further rebellion, and they too had much to gain from the peace that acquiescence entailed."[17] Subsequently, after the Tokugawa system stabilized, the daimyo were subject to central control and supervision. Most important, as we shall see, the vigorous growth of the commercial economy under the Tokugawa system steadily eroded the strength of the daimyo. These developments then created the possibility of greater centralization and the birth of a highly centralized nation-state in the nineteenth century.

Unless we understand the reasons why unification followed this path it will seem as though Japan missed an opportunity to develop as a centralized state in 1600. In fact, for a long time many historians did believe that the Tokugawa system halted progressive trends such as the emergence of a fluid class system, free cities, and vibrant international contacts. To these scholars the Tokugawa system seemed rigid, repressive, and reactionary. This view that the Tokugawa control system was a retrogressive step, a turning back of the clock, is known as the "refeudalization thesis" because it interpreted the Tokugawa system as a "reformulation . . . of the essential components of medieval feudalism in a more politically stable and highly organized form."[18]

This view of the Tokugawa system as essentially feudal, repressive, and outmoded was once widely held. In the aftermath of World War II when the Japanese searched their history to try to understand what had gone wrong, many identified the Tokugawa system as the cause of the national tragedy because it prevented progress toward a more open Japanese society.

In recent decades, many historians have interpreted the Tokugawa system in a more favorable light. Rather than stressing its despotic nature, they have found progressive trends in the Tokugawa society and economy. They have termed the Tokugawa years as Japan's "early modern period" by "drawing attention away from the period's feudal aspects and toward those long-term trends related to the emergence of the modern Japanese state and economy after 1868."[19]

Notes

1. John Whitney Hall, ed., *Early Modern Japan,* vol. 4 of *The Cambridge History of Japan,* ed. John Whitney Hall (Cambridge: Cambridge University Press, 1991), 190.
2. Englebert Kaempfer, *History of Japan* (Glasgow: University of Glasgow Press, 1906), 295–297.
3. Ronald P. Toby, *State and Diplomacy in Early Modern Japan: Asia in the Development of the Tokugawa Bakufu* (Stanford, Calif.: Stanford University Press, 1991), 233.
4. Herman Ooms, *Tokugawa Ideology: Early Constructs, 1570–1680* (Princeton, N.J.: Princeton University Press, 1985), 289.
5. Reprinted by permission of the publishers from *Chōshū in the Meiji Restoration* by Albert M. Craig, Cambridge, Mass.: Harvard University Press, copyright © 1961 by the President and Fellows of Harvard College, p. 113.
6. Ronald P. Dore, *Education in Tokugawa Japan* (Berkeley: University of California Press, 1965), 181–182.

7. Fukuzawa Yukichi, "Kyūhanjō," trans. Carmen Blacker, in *Monumenta Nipponica* 9 (April 1953), 310–311.
8. Hall, *Early Modern Japan,* 373.
9. Ronald P. Dore, *City Life in Japan,* (Berkeley: University of California Press, 1958), 103–104.
10. Ibid., 96–97.
11. Quoted in Basil Hall Chamberlain, *Things Japanese* (London: K. Paul, Trench, Trubner, 1927), 504.
12. Dore, *City Life,* 108.
13. Kathleen S. Uno, "Women and Changes in the Household Division of Labor," in *Recreating Japanese Women, 1600–1945,* ed. Gail Lee Bernstein (Berkeley: University of California Press, 1991), 27.
14. Anne Walthall, "The Life Cycle of Farm Women in Tokugawa Japan," in *Recreating Japanese Women,* ed. Bernstein, 43.
15. Mary Elizabeth Berry, "Public Peace and Private Attachment: The Goals and Conduct of Power in Early Modern Japan," *Journal of Japanese Studies* 12 (summer 1986), 237–272.
16. James W. White, "State Growth and Popular Protest in Tokugawa Japan," *Journal of Japanese Studies* 14 (winter 1988), 1–25.
17. Ibid.
18. Wakita Osamu, "The Social and Economic Consequences of Unification," in *Early Modern Japan,* ed. Hall, 97.
19. Ibid., 98.

3

Growth of Tokugawa Society

The Tokugawa leaders set out to create institutions that would stabilize political and social conditions in the country, thereby preventing a breakup of their coalition and a lapse back into feudal warfare. They succeeded remarkably well; the Tokugawa system endured until 1868. During this period there were very few battles to be fought: the Warring States Period had given way to an era of ordered living. The control measures, instituted to preserve the balance of forces within the coalition that brought the Tokugawa to power, proved effective in inhibiting political change.

Society, while stable, did not remain static. Although on the surface the Tokugawa political system held intact for over two and a half centuries, the entire social and economic basis of that system was quietly transformed. All classes of Japanese—warriors, peasants, merchants—underwent profound change in nature and structure. Tokugawa society grew in unexpected directions until at last a political revolution was inevitable.

Roots of Change

The very success of the Tokugawa system was in the long run responsible for its undoing. Paradoxically, the roots of revolutionary economic and social change lay in the very reforms just discussed, which were carried out in the sixteenth and seventeenth centuries to try to stabilize society. The control measures, especially the alternate attendance system and the removal of samurai from the countryside, effectively maintained the political status quo, but at the same time they promoted economic changes that slowly undermined the Tokugawa order.

Limitations on Japan's external relations might have been expected to retard economic growth, for several of the flourishing cities, such as the ports of Sakai and Hakata, had depended upon foreign trade. The economy now turned in upon itself. It might have stagnated except that the requirements of the Tokugawa system provided a powerful stimulant to new economic activity.

Consider the alternate attendance system. Inadvertently, it was surely one of the most important factors contributing to the rise of a money economy. It was intended as a means to control the daimyo by requiring their periodic attendance at the capital, where the bakufu could keep them under continuous surveillance; by requiring the maintenance of residences in Edo, where families were kept as hostages to deter rebellion; finally, by draining their finances by the heavy cost of journeying to and from the capital and of maintaining residences there.

The expenses of the daimyo for the periodic (ordinarily biennial) sojourns in Edo were very great. The largest of the daimyo proceeded to the capital with as many as several thousand retainers; and costs for food and lodging, for hiring boats and porters to cross the numerous water barriers, and the like became immense. As tastes grew more luxurious the processions became occasions for competitive display. Weapons and equipage were elaborately and expensively decorated, thereby advertising the status of the daimyo. In the capital, consumption tended to be even more conspicuous. Each daimyo normally had several mansions, maintained by a permanent staff that, in the case of the largest daimyo, numbered in excess of 10,000 in the mid-eighteenth century.

To obtain specie for these enormous expenses, a daimyo took a large portion of the tax rice collected from the peasantry in his domain and sold it in Osaka and other market centers. Subsequent use of specie stimulated the growth of commercial transactions and an increased use of money. In Edo (not to mention along the main roads leading into the capital) businesses sprang up to cater to the wants of the warriors and to serve the needs of a growing population. Of negligible size before the battle of Sekigahara, Edo grew to a metropolis of about 1 million by 1720—considerably larger than London or Paris at that time. Teeming with samurai visiting from all parts of the country, it became Japan's chief consumption center. To the southwest Osaka, the chief market for surplus rice of many han, also became a great distribution center, with a powerful merchant class directing its commercial activity. Although it grew less rapidly than Edo, by 1800 Osaka had a population of 400,000, and taken together with nearby Kyoto and Sakai the area comprised an urban population in the neighborhood of 1 million people. Much of the trade of the country converged on the Edo and the Osaka-Kyoto areas.

So the alternate attendance system achieved its purpose of maintaining the political status quo only for a time. In the long run it undermined the political order by stimulating fundamental economic and social change that the Tokugawa system could not accommodate.

In addition to the alternate attendance system, the removal of the samurai from the countryside and their settlement in the castle towns also had ironic and unexpected results in the long run. The original purpose, as we have seen, sprang from the daimyo's determination to diminish the "independence" of his vassals, thereby stabilizing the political system at the domain level. But the settlement of samurai in the castle towns created local consumption centers and brought into being a merchant class that was of considerable size and influence. A market system grew up to supply the wants of the samurai class and in the long run came to occupy a position of great economic importance. At the same time, the growth of a market network around the castle towns fundamentally altered the social order in the countryside. What had been intended as a measure to control the lord's retainers ended by contributing to a vast change in local society.

Transformation of the Samurai Class

The new circumstances of society also immensely changed the nature of the samurai class. As warfare ceased to be a way of life and a sedentary style took its place, the samurai were compelled to adjust to conditions of peace. In essence their transformation was from a feudal military class to a bureaucratic elite, and though warrior traditions were kept alive, the reality of their daily life had little in common with that of their predecessors in the Warring States Period.

Living in the castle towns on stipends paid them by their lord, the warriors manned his expanding and rapidly differentiating bureaucracy. Rules were established, regularizing their behavior in patterns befitting bureaucrats. Codes were issued, standardizing bureaucratic procedure by providing rules for office hours, for procurement and purchase of office supplies, for systems of guard duty, and similar subjects. Gradually the foundations of civil administration were laid, as the daimyo promulgated codes regulating many aspects of political and economic life and as he clarified procedures of government and chains of administrative responsibility. By the end of the seventeenth century, the daimyo's government had become a complex and elaborately structured bureaucratic organization with a finely graded officialdom that had charge of rural, town, financial, temple and shrine, and social affairs.

Under the peaceful conditions that prevailed, effective governance depended upon an orderly civil administration and the rule of public law. The lord therefore had very different expectations of his retainers than was the case earlier. One lord, writing in 1714, "lamented the tendency of officials to ignore administrative precedent; henceforth, he states, they should consult the office diaries kept by predecessors and conduct all business accordingly, calling this strict observance of precedent the 'highest loyalty.'"[1] To samurai of the Warring States Period such a conception of loyalty would have been unimaginable!

The contradictions between their living martial traditions, symbolized by the two swords they wore, and the new position of samurai as a civil administrative elite were not easy to reconcile. The most dramatic illustration of this tension occurred in 1702 when forty-seven masterless samurai (*rōnin*) determined to avenge the death of their lord in accord with the traditional warrior code. Their vendetta, however, transgressed shogunal law, and after anguished controversy—in which they were praised in some quarters for their high ideals and condemned in others for their illegal behavior—they were at last required to commit *seppuku* (ritual suicide).

Confucian scholars, writing on the code of the warrior (*bushidō*), sought to reconcile these tensions by urging the samurai to strike a balance between military training and book learning. The latter, however, tended to loom larger in the warrior's new role as civil administrator. One of the most interesting and important aspects of the transformation was the increasing literacy and education of the samurai. At the beginning of the Tokugawa Period warriors were a rough, unlettered class, but by the end nearly all were literate and schooled. From the outset Tokugawa Ieyasu stressed that pursuit of learning must be given the same consideration as the military arts. Learning was necessary in order to acquire the practical techniques of operating a bureaucracy as well as the moral principles upon which samurai government was founded.

Rule by a hereditary military elite was justified with the assertion that samurai governed by virtue of their ethical example. Therefore study of the Confucian classics was essential. The bakufu led the way in educational development by establishing a Confucian academy in Edo early in the period, and the domains followed this example by also founding schools in the castle towns. Domain-sponsored schools proliferated in the latter half of the Tokugawa Period and by the end there were nearly 200.

Change in Agrarian Society

At the outset of the Tokugawa Period a pattern of self-sufficient, cooperative farming prevailed over nearly all the countryside. Consciousness of individual and class interests tended to be submerged in the cohesiveness and solidarity of village society. Physical isolation and the rudimentary state of the market imposed a self-sufficiency whereby the typical village produced simply what it needed to feed and clothe its own members and to pay the land tax in kind. Any surplus was stored for future use in time of crop failure and famine. There was very little occasion to buy and sell.

The nature of the Tokugawa system transformed this pattern of farming; rural life began to change markedly, especially by the eighteenth century. As cities grew and communications improved, the peasant began to find a market to dispose of whatever surplus goods he produced. In addition to the great urban centers of Edo and Osaka, new castle towns were scattered across the countryside, and nearly every village was within reach of those growing population centers. Villages were thereby drawn into market networks that soon changed both their pattern of farming and their structure of social relations.

Commercial farming spread rapidly and widely during the Tokugawa Period. Villages began to grow crops that would fill the needs of the cities and towns; they began to specialize in the crops that their soil, climate, and market favored. Those necessities that they no longer produced could be purchased in the nearby market. Regional specialization in commercial crops therefore steadily increased: the Osaka area became famous for its mandarin oranges, cotton products, and fish fertilizers; central Honshu was known for its cultivation of mulberries and raising of silkworms; sugar cane was grown mainly in Kyushu; Shikoku produced paper, salt, and lumber. Small village enterprises such as sugar, salt, tea, oil, sericulture, and textile industries spread rapidly, as in fact did more substantial forms of rural enterprise, including the production of wine, soy sauce, ceramics, and iron. Peasants found in these rural industries sidelines to supplement their farm incomes.

With the commercialization of agriculture, the use of money spread. Buying and selling became a common aspect of village life. How commercial rural Japan had become by the end of the Tokugawa Period is suggested by the economic historian Sydney Crawcour. He estimates that "over half and probably nearer [to] two-thirds of output" in Japanese agriculture was marketed in one form or another. He cites a village shopkeeper in an economically advanced area of western Japan who as early as 1813 was selling "the following impressive list of commodities: ink, paper, writing brushes, *herasaki,* cauldrons, cutlery, needles, smoking pipes, tobacco, tobacco pouches, teapots, casserole dishes, rice-wine bottles, oil containers, vinegar, soy sauce, bean paste, salt, matting, noodles, kelp, hair oil, hair strings, hairpins, cotton cloth, socks, towels, bamboo trellis, carrying baskets, *zōri* [thongs], straw sandals, wooden clogs, tea, teacups, lucifers [matches], wicks, incense, fire pots, lanterns, oil, candles, rice wine, timber, hot water bottles, cakes, *sembei* [crackers], trays, funeral requisites, grain, *and other everyday necessities*"![2]

With the rising productivity in the countryside there went an increase in the average standard of living, but it was by no means evenly divided among the peasants. The farming class was every bit as stratified as the others. Most noticeable was the emergence of a class of wealthy peasants (*gōnō*), who clearly benefited the most from the commercialization of the agrarian economy. It was on their land that the greatest increases in productivity usually occurred, for they could afford better fertilizers and improved farm implements. They used their growing wealth to invest in the widely spreading rural industries—*sake* (rice wine) brewing, dyeing, silk and cotton weaving, and the like. Still another outlet for gōnō wealth was money lending, which permitted them to foreclose on mortgaged land in times of general economic distress and thereby to become large landholders.

Concentration of landownership and the spread of tenant farming was very noticeable in many of the more economically advanced sections of the country during the late Tokugawa Period. In many villages landless peasants constituted a significant group. The development of the market economy was bringing about new class relations in the village, as the cooperative nature of farming and the cohesiveness of the village declined. One result of this growing consciousness of the disparity of wealth in the villages was a sharp increase in the number of peasant uprisings in the last century of Tokugawa rule—a subject to which we shall turn in the next chapter.

Finally, we should not leave the topic of change in the countryside without noting one of the most intriguing aspects of the Tokugawa Period, that is, the leveling off in the rate of population increase after a sharp rise in the seventeenth century. The population of Japan is estimated at upwards of 18 million at the beginning of the Tokugawa Period. During the succeeding century, as a result of peace and the increase of arable land and agricultural productivity, population grew dramatically so that when the first national population survey was conducted in 1721 it revealed a population approaching 30 million.

Thereafter, for the remainder of the Tokugawa Period, the population leveled off. It used to be thought that population was held in check in Malthusian fashion by disease, famine, and other natural disasters and the consequent resort in desperation to infanticide and abortion. Recent research suggests an altogether different interpretation. Study of Tokugawa epidemics demonstrates a much lower incidence of epidemic diseases than in Europe and other parts of the world.[3] Cholera, typhoid, and bubonic plague were not problems, perhaps partly because of geographic isolation, partly because of the careful inspection of ships arriving from other parts of Asia, and partly because of customary sanitation measures. Although Japan suffered epidemics of measles and smallpox, their effects were no worse than in Europe. Japanese life expectancy of more than forty years in the late

Tokugawa Period was similar to that in Western Europe in the first half of the nineteenth century.[4]

The question then presents itself: If health and life expectancy were good, the economy and living standards improving, why did population level off in the second half of the Tokugawa Period? Recent studies suggest that the population stability was more the result of social controls designed to limit the size of families and the number of households within a village than it was of disaster and social demoralization. A village case study directed by Thomas Smith finds, for example, that infanticide was practiced by "the most respectable and stable part of the population" in order to achieve "overall family limitation; an equilibrium of some sort between family size and farm size; [and] an advantageous distribution of the sexes in children. . . ."[5] Susan Hanley elaborates the social practices that farm families took to optimize their size:

> The average number of children in the completed family from the end of the eighteenth century and well into the nineteenth was only three and a half children. This would have ensured a male heir for most but would have prevented numerous children who would have been a burden on the family and village when grown. Families used a number of means to regulate family size, of which birth control was only one. . . . Women married in their early to mid-twenties, which delayed and reduced the number of child-bearing years. It was also the custom for only one son in each household to marry. . . . Descriptions of abortion, abortionists, and the effects of this practice are abundant, and this form of birth control is known to have been widely practiced throughout Japan. Abortion was an undesirable practice but not a "sin." Infanticide was even condoned by the euphemism that it was a means of "returning" an infant at birth before it had become an individual and part of society. . . . The measures taken to lower to the minimum the number of nonproductive members in the household lead us to conclude that Japanese were seeking to create a population favorable to economic production.[6]

In short, such behavior bespeaks a surprising foresight and "rationality"—an attitudinal change that may well have conduced to Japan's subsequent industrialization. In fact, two scholars of this problem have concluded that "Tokugawa Japan as a whole was clearly not trapped in a low-level economic equilibrium with a high rate of population growth ready to sap whatever surplus the economy was able to generate. . . . In short, the pre-industrial population and economic development of Japan can be compared most readily with that of England. Japan, like England, experienced a rate of population increase well under one-half of 1 percent per annum, while output increased steadily at a higher rate."[7]

We may sum up our discussion of change in agrarian society during the Tokugawa Period by pointing out how recent scholarship has revised our view of the countryside. Traditional scholarship tended to stress the plight of the peasantry, its exploitation by the other classes, the oppressive rate of taxation, the increase of tenancy, and the corresponding concentration of landownership. The "stagnation" of population growth and the waves of peasant uprisings were seen as evidence of the farmers' hardship. In contrast, we now speak of a rising standard of living and of a land tax rate that was frequently not nearly as oppressive as was once thought, with the majority of farmers engaged in part-time jobs that added much to their income. The easing off in the rate of population growth is attributed less to famine and hardship than to deliberate measures that manifested an increased economic rationality on the part of the peasantry. All of this is not to say that there was not much backbreaking hardship. There was. Conditions varied from region to region—even from valley to valley. There was discontent in the countryside, some of it the result of specific policies of government and some of it of the new class relations in the village.

But if we limit ourselves here to economic developments—increased agricultural productivity, commercialization of the countryside, a relatively low rate of population increase—we have factors that help us explain Japan's rapid industrial development in modern times. Conditions in the villages were preparing the way. Although the political system was heading for trouble, society and the economy ought not to be thought of as declining; rather, we should think of them as growing so strikingly that they could scarcely be held within the bounds of the rigid system established at the outset of the Tokugawa Period.

Growth of the Merchant Class

We have already discussed some of the ways in which the new institutional structure of the Tokugawa system gave rise to a growing commercial economy. We should now consider the emergence of a sizable merchant class in the cities and the difficulties the Tokugawa system found in trying to accommodate it within its structure. This is a development of immense importance for understanding the tensions that were developing within the Tokugawa system by the eighteenth century.

Within the merchant class that grew up there was of course (just as in the other classes) a great deal of disparity. It was not a homogeneous group; rather it ranged from the Osaka financiers at the top, who held the purse strings of many of the daimyo, all the way down to the small shopkeepers, pawnbrokers, journeymen, and peddlers. In between these extremes were wholesalers and shippers who specialized in a variety of commodities and presided over the development of interregional trade. Within local areas there were retailers, brokers, and rural businessmen, some of whom worked in association with han governments to promote commercial development.

The Osaka financiers took advantage of the unique structure of the Tokugawa system to build great merchant houses. They based their strength, in the first place, on the rice-brokering business that was the backbone of Osaka's economy. The major daimyo of central and western Japan, needing cash principally for their alternate attendance requirements, marketed huge amounts of rice in Osaka, and they were dependent on the great merchants of the city to handle all aspects of the transactions. Those merchants began extending to the daimyo long-term loans at high rates of interest. They formed the Osaka banking system in 1670 and eventually dominated the credit system not only of the Osaka area but of all the major trading centers of Japan. Surprisingly sophisticated credit mechanisms and advanced methods of exchange bills developed in order to facilitate trade between these major centers.

Crawcour sums up the influence of these great financiers this way:

> Through their exchange and remittance business, they controlled the market in which the relative values of gold and silver—and thus in effect the rate of exchange between Edo and Osaka—were set, and acted as financial agents of the Shogunate. They thus collectively performed some of the functions of a central bank. As commercial and financial agents and major creditors of the various han, they had considerable influence on han economic policy and a practical monopoly of the main exports of the han. Through their handling of tax rice, which amounted to about three-quarters of the supply, they controlled the Osaka rice market and thus the wholesale rice market for the whole country.[8]

Because of the importance they had acquired to the functioning of the Tokugawa system, these financiers were often given quasi-samurai status, sometimes with stipends the equivalent of minor daimyo. Thus although official ideology was often opposed to the growth of the merchant class and commerce in general, in reality government (at all levels) was dependent on merchant groups for their special knowledge in conducting the financial affairs of the system. These groups were often licensed by authorities: given special monopolistic privileges in the expectation that they would stabilize prices, ensure adequate distribution, and make an annual fee payment.

Urban growth, the spread of a money economy, and the emergence of a vital merchant class were reflected in a vibrant new culture of the townspeople. This development is most closely associated with what is known as the Genroku Period: strictly speaking, only a fifteen-year period from 1688 to 1704, but sometimes designating a fifty-year period stretching roughly from 1680 to 1730, the most brilliant flowering of Japanese culture during the Tokugawa era.

The tenor of this culture was expressed by the term *ukiyo* (floating world), which was applied to certain facets of Genroku culture: for example, *ukiyo-zōshi* (stories of the floating world) or *ukiyo-e* (pictures of the floating world). Originally *ukiyo* was a Buddhist term referring to the sad impermanence of all earthly things, but during the Genroku Period it shed that religious connotation and came to suggest, rather, a life of pleasure that one accepts without thinking what might lie ahead. One writer in this period defined *ukiyo* as "living for the moment, gazing at the moon, snow, blossoms, and autumn leaves, enjoying wine, women, and song, and, in general, drifting with the current of life."[9] One might say that both the Buddhists and the townsmen of the Genroku Period agreed that life was fleeting; they simply disagreed as to what one should do about it.

Genroku culture was concentrated primarily in the pleasure quarters, the teahouses, the theaters, and even the bathhouses of Osaka, Kyoto, and Edo. The castle towns may have shared in Genroku culture, too, but they were certainly far behind. Despite the fact that official ideology put the trading classes at the bottom of the social scale, it was primarily they who were behind this cultural explosion, which included *kabuki,* the puppet theater, the wood-block print, and ukiyo literature.

Officials spent their time drawing up lofty Confucian exhortations or devising piecemeal laws in an attempt to control the ostentation, opulence, and extravagance of the trading class and the disruptive influence it was thought to be having on society. Kabuki is a case in point. For almost the entire Tokugawa Period (but especially during Genroku days) there was a running duel between the bakufu and kabuki, the bakufu trying to restrict it and the kabuki always responding with some ingenious evasion. Regarding kabuki as destructive of Confucian morality, the bakufu banned women from the stage in 1629, and in succeeding years issued regulations designed to segregate kabuki actors from the rest of society and to preserve an austerity of costumes and theater architecture thought to be appropriate for townspeople. Most important was the attempt to eliminate from plays subject matter that might have baneful political influence. Nonetheless some playwrights were able to get away with political satires. For example, one of the most famous playwrights, Chikamatsu Monzaemon (1653–1725), wrote a highly amusing satire of Tokugawa Tsunayoshi (1646–1709), the fifth shogun, who had an idiosyncratic attachment to dogs. Perhaps it was because he had been born in the zodiacal year of the dog. In any case Tsunayoshi was responsible for a stream of legislation protecting the canine family, which earned him the epithet "dog shogun": there were censuses of dogs, dog taxes, dog commissioners and physicians, public kennels, and much more. In a play written in 1714 Chikamatsu seized on Tsunayoshi and his pet projects as splendid objects of satire and by recasting these events in the earlier Kamakura Period was able to evade the censors.

This popular culture, its leading historian observes, marks "the first time commoners, the nonelite, became culturally important."[10] In part, it was made possible by the spread of literacy, the leisure for reading, and the rapid growth of a large publishing industry. Before the Tokugawa Period, printing was almost nonexistent except in Buddhist monasteries. Now it became a commercial enterprise, relying on woodblocks. At first the books were for serious readers: the Chinese classics, Buddhist works, and classical Japanese literature. Then publishers turned to practical guidebooks for a larger audience: flower arranging, garden design, clothing design, and travel accounts. By the mid-1600s publications written in simple language with few Chinese characters and relying mainly on the Japanese syllabary were published for a growing audience of urban commoners; stories and plays about everyday life in the cities became a popular art form. In more than twenty such books written during the Genroku Period, Ihara Saikaku, the son of an Osaka merchant, dazzled readers with stories on making love and making money. Saikaku was only the best known of many authors who wrote for the new audience in the cities. By the 1720s, Osaka had 24 publishers, Edo 47, and Kyoto 200. "While the shogun and daimyo continued their patronage of the higher culture and learning, the most original and lively developments," concludes Donald Shively, "took place among the populace of the cities."[11]

Notes

1. Thomas C. Smith, *Native Sources of Japanese Industrialization, 1750–1920* (Berkeley: University of California Press, 1988), 149.
2. E. Sydney Crawcour, "The Tokugawa Heritage," in *The State and Economic Enterprise in Japan,* ed. William W. Lockwood (Princeton, N.J.: Princeton University Press, 1965), 41.
3. Ann Bowman Janetta, *Epidemics and Mortality in Early Modern Japan* (Princeton, N.J.: Princeton University Press, 1987).
4. Susan B. Hanley and Kozo Yamamura, *Economic and Demographic Change in Pre-Industrial Japan, 1600–1868* (Princeton, N.J.: Princeton University Press, 1977), 317.
5. Thomas C. Smith, *Nakahara: Family Farming and Population in a Japanese Village, 1717–1830,* (Stanford, Calif.: Stanford University Press, 1977), 83.

6. John Whitney Hall, ed., *Early Modern Japan,* vol. 4 of *The Cambridge History of Japan,* ed. John Whitney Hall (Cambridge: Cambridge University Press, 1991), 699–700.
7. Susan B. Hanley and Kozo Yamamura, "Population Trends and Economic Growth in Pre-Industrial Japan," in *Population and Social Change,* ed. D. V. Glass and Roger Revelle (London: E. Arnold, 1972), 485–486.
8. E. Sydney Crawcour, "Changes in Japanese Commerce in the Tokugawa Period," in *Studies in the Institutional History of Early Modern Japan,* eds. John Whitney Hall and Marius B. Jansen (Princeton, N.J.: Princeton University Press, 1968), p. 196. Copyright © 1968 by Princeton University Press; Princeton Paperback, 1970. Reprinted by permission of Princeton University Press.
9. Howard Hibbett, *The Floating World in Japanese Fiction* (Oxford: Oxford University Press, 1959), p. 11.
10. Donald Shively, "Popular Culture," in *Early Modern Japan,* ed. Hall, 706.
11. Ibid.

Crisis in the Tokugawa System

The bakufu's difficulty in coping with the culture of the townsmen was indicative of the much larger problem that officials were having in dealing with the new social and economic conditions that the development of cities and commerce had created. It is useful to think of the Genroku Period as a kind of divide. On the one side, prior to it, the Tokugawa system was becoming established; its political, social, and economic institutions were being systematized. The samurai elite was adjusting to its new role as an administrative bureaucracy and to its new life in the castle towns. Population surged, city life sprang up, land under cultivation was greatly extended, and a new sedentary lifestyle took hold.

On the other side of the divide, the years after Genroku to which we must now turn our attention, faults were beginning to appear in the political system. "Since the Genroku period," lamented one scholar in the 1730s, ". . . the life of the country has deteriorated."[1] Contradictions emerged between the ideological premises that underlay the system and the reality of the way it was in fact operating. There is always a gap between the ideals of a social system and its actual behavior, but after Genroku the gap in Japan was too wide to be overlooked. Behind the facade of political stability, immense social and economic developments occurred that gradually transformed the system. In many different areas these developments created strains. Let us examine them rather arbitrarily under the headings of economic, social, and ideological problems.

Economic Problems

The fundamental problem creating strains within the Tokugawa political system was the transformation of its economic basis and consequent undermining of the premises upon which the system had been founded. The soaring expenditures of the bakufu and of the individual daimyo tended more and more to exceed their income, which was largely drawn from the land tax levied on the peasants. Expenditures of the lord grew continuously, partly because, with the urban growth, government became more complex. Then, too, it was sometimes less efficient. Laxity and corruption were not uncommon. Social functions associated with government became increasingly elaborate and expensive, and gift giving grew to immense proportions.

The alternate attendance system continued enormously expensive for the daimyo. By the latter part of the Tokugawa Period, the typical lord was devoting a substantial portion of his normal expenditures to costs connected with the system. In addition, not infrequently were emergency or extraordinary outlays required to rebuild mansions after fires, to entertain the shogun, or to cover the costs of marriages, funerals, and other ceremonies in Edo. The steady stream of sumptuary laws, which sought to restrict ostentation in food and dress, indicate that extravagance and conspicuous consumption were a way of life among the upper classes.

Government frequently was unable to generate the added revenues necessary to defray its soaring expenses. Some daimyo succeeded in developing additional sources of income, principally through development of new cash crops that were run as han monopolies, but for the most part they continued to be largely dependent on the land tax and on rice production, which accounted for a shrinking portion of the total economy. Daimyo were often at a disadvantage when they converted their rice income into money at Osaka. There, they were at the mercy of the astute merchant financiers and the vagaries of the rice market. It was possible, of course, that a good harvest, together with capable and honest administration, could increase the coffers of the shogun or the daimyo. In general, however, much more frequently revenues fell short because of bad luck or bad management, and expenditures rose because of extravagance, corruption, and the increased complexity of government.

A negative reason for the financial troubles of government was the overall failure to develop adequate methods for taxing the growing sectors of the economy. For example, the Tokugawa Period saw a great increase in agricultural productivity, which should have allowed the lord to increase the land tax. Yet research seems to indicate that land, from about 1700 on, ceased to be surveyed periodically and thus there was often no adequate accounting of increased productivity. Toward the end of the Tokugawa Period, therefore, in some areas taxes were based on assessments that were a century or more out of date. Why land surveys were neglected is difficult to say, but undoubtedly bureaucratic inertia and consideration of the massive administrative effort required to survey an entire domain were partly responsible.

Still another factor may have been fear of resistance from the peasants. One scholar who has made a careful study of this issue in the Kaga domain concludes, "To tax villages effectively daimyo needed a loyal, knowledgeable, and independent core of officials who had frequent contact with agriculture and the villages under their control. Yet samurai urbanization sacrificed precisely this intimacy and cost daimyo the ability to capitalize on improved crop yields."[2] Whatever the reasons, growing wealth in the agricultural sector was generally not taxed in any systematic way.

Nor was commerce, the most rapidly expanding part of the economy, taxed in a uniform, consistent manner. There were piecemeal attempts, but perhaps the lack of bookkeeping methods and of bureaucratic determination deterred government from more systematic means. Instead it relied, for example, on granting monopolistic privileges to merchant guilds in return for fees. Another type of commercial taxation, if it can properly be called such, was the exaction from wealthy merchants and farmers of forced "loans," which were generally not repaid. In the latter part of the period both the bakufu and the domains had frequent recourse to this method of raising revenues.

Social Problems

As a result of the increasing economic troubles in which government found itself, it was frequently unable to meet its most important financial commitment: the paying of warrior stipends. Often the lord solved his financial problems by passing them on to his retainers. By the end of the eighteenth century cutting warrior stipends, sometimes by as much as 50 percent, was common.

Such a solution may have temporarily eased the daimyo's economic problems, but it only added to increasing unrest in the society he had to govern. By the end of the Tokugawa Period, as a result of their diminished income, perhaps the majority of samurai lived in honorable but austere circumstances. Of course samurai income varied greatly between domains. For instance, a Tosa samurai traveling to Satsuma in late Tokugawa discovered that stipends considered low in his native Tosa would seem generous in Satsuma. It is clear, however, that nearly everywhere the number of "upper" samurai, living in comfortable circumstances, was small compared to the mass of samurai who lived in straitened circumstances. The well-being of the upper strata of the peasant and merchant class was often superior to that of the ordinary samurai. And this anomaly put a great strain on warrior loyalty; it was humiliating and contributed to deteriorating morale.

Like the daimyo and the bakufu, the samurai had to take steps to alleviate his financial difficulty. Many of his measures were makeshift and often they were degrading, sorely wounding warrior pride. Hard-pressed for money, some samurai adopted merchant boys into their family or married their children to the children of their merchant creditors. Another recourse was to pawn the family armor. Poorer samurai practiced infanticide to reduce their economic liabilities. A large number of the poorer samurai families eked out their inadequate stipends through cottage industries, such as the making of straw sandals. Occasionally, by the nineteenth century, some impoverished samurai simply abandoned their feudal duties, giving up their diminished stipends in return for a better living as commoners.

We ought not to think of the samurai as uniformly mired in poverty. Not only was there a great deal of differentiation within the class as a whole and considerable regional variation, it is also true that much of what is referred to as the increasing "poverty" of the samurai was relative. In the case of some members of the warrior class whose income remained stable, their discontent sprang from unfulfilled wants, rising expectations, and a feeling of being deprived of the fruits of a growing economy. In other words, for such warriors there was an element of psychological poverty involved: they felt themselves deprived because they were unable to buy commodities that members of other classes could afford.

We find a perfect example of growing prosperity among commoners in the upper levels of the farming class. The gōnō (wealthy peasants) were an anomalous group within the Tokugawa class structure. Officially, of course, they were peasants and lived in the village, but by the late Tokugawa Period they were set off from other commoners by their wealth and power in the countryside. Not only were they often village headmen and holders of much land, but they were also engaged in a variety of rural commercial enterprises, such as money lending, sake brewing, textile dyeing, or silk and cotton weaving. Their investments in land and rural industries enabled them to support a life-style quite in contrast to their official status. Through contributions to their daimyo's treasury many gained the right to wear swords, bear surnames, and send their sons to the domain academy—all privileges ordinarily reserved for the warrior. The social distance between this group and the samurai was thus rapidly narrowing, and the feelings of many aggrieved warriors at such signs of institutional disintegration and moral decay were summed up by one angry contemporary:

> Now the most lamentable abuse of the present day among the peasants is that those who have become wealthy forget their status and live luxuriously like city aristocrats. . . . They build [homes] with the most handsome and wonderful gates, porches, beams, alcoves, ornamental shelves, and libraries. . . . They themselves wear

fine clothes and imitate the ceremonial style of warriors on all such occasions as weddings, celebrations, and masses for the dead.[3]

Class relations were becoming diffuse and difficult to accommodate within the rigid class structure established at the outset of the Tokugawa Period. The spactacle of growing wealth within the commoner classes was doubtless evidence to warriors of institutional disintegration and of moral decay. Respect for rank and the traditional virtues of frugality, industry, and modesty seemed jeopardized. On the other hand, in the biographies of able and wealthy commoners at the end of the Tokugawa Period, plenty of resentment and frustration exists over the fact that the Tokugawa system set strict limits on their social advancement. One finds this particularly among the wealthy peasants.

Of course not all peasants were as fortunate as the gōnō. Like the other classes, there was great disparity of wealth: large numbers of the peasantry lived at the subsistence level, terribly at the mercy of the vicissitudes of the weather and the market. Famines on a nationwide scale occurred in the 1720s, the 1780s, and the 1830s as a result of unseasonable weather, and not coincidentally waves of peasant uprisings occurred during the 1780s and the 1830s. Such outbreaks were usually directed against the wealthy, the moneylenders, and local officials.

Few aspects of Tokugawa society have been as controversial as the interpretation of these peasant protests. They increased in number through the period: in the seventeenth century they averaged five a year; in the eighteenth century, twelve a year; and from 1800 to 1868, fifteen a year. Moreover, they became larger, more disorderly, and destructive. Many historians discern in these protests "deepening class conflict between lords and peasants";[4] but Stephen Vlastos, studying uprisings in northern Japan, found that "collective action took the form of property smashings and not political action against the ruling class." Conflict was within the peasant class as poor peasants turned their anger not against the samurai or the feudal political structures but against those closest at hand—the wealthy peasants and village leaders, who were also landlords, entrepreneurs, and moneylenders, whom they held responsible for their distress.[5]

These riots were the ultimate protest that peasants could make against unbearable conditions, and though they were often not political in intent they held political meaning, for this form of protest was a specter that any lord might fear in pondering the possibility of increasing the land tax. Nor were the uprisings simply blind outbursts. Often they had very specific goals, such as the remission of certain taxes, the removal of a particular official, or the correction of some local abuse.

The peasant disturbances of the 1830s culminated in a series of incidents that followed an abortive uprising in Osaka in 1837 led by Ōshio Heihachirō. Ōshio was a minor bakufu official who accused his superiors of callous disregard for the suffering of common people and plotted an uprising that he hoped would spark other attacks against the established order. Although fires raged for two days through the merchant section of the city, the rebellion was easily quelled by bakufu forces. News of the uprising, however, encouraged others in surrounding provinces.

Such indications of social strain and discontent have led many historians to write of the "decay of feudalism" and to stress in their descriptions the breakdown of the Tokugawa system. This is of course valid. But one should also stress growth—a society growing and changing so markedly that it could no longer be contained within the institutional bounds established by Tokugawa Ieyasu at the beginning of the period.

Ideological Problems

Social discontent within the samurai class was exacerbated by ideological problems that grew out of conflict between the theory and practice of the Tokugawa system. One such problem concerned the appointment of officials in the bakufu and han bureaucracies, which according to widely held principles should have been based on merit. In actual practice, however, after the early Tokugawa Period appointments were made mainly on the basis of social rank. With occasional exceptions the most important offices went to the higher-ranking samurai, and frustration over this situation among young, lower-ranking warriors became one of the greatest forces for change by the beginning of the nineteenth century. The historian Sir George Sansom, in fact, wrote that among all the causes of the anti-Tokugawa movement that led to the downfall of the bakufu, the most powerful was the ambition of young samurai. As the status system gradually hardened, official appointment came to be determined largely by hereditary succession and social rank. By the end of the Genroku Period, the vested interests were entrenched.

Among able, lively, lower-ranking young samurai grew a restless dissatisfaction with the rigidity of the system. They felt unjustly cut off from positions of power and respect; they favored more freedom of movement within the hierarchy; and they opposed hereditary restraints upon such mobility. Many writers who urged that the appointment and promotion of officials be based upon merit alone argued that because of environmental factors ability was to be found especially among lower warriors. They said that hardship and adversity made for intelligence and character, while the wealth and ease of upper-level warriors made for foolishness and corruption. Blaming the hereditary principle for the failures of government, they sometimes wrote thinly veiled attacks upon the daimyo, who, they implied, were pompous and weak. Despite the implications of these writings, they were not intended as a revolutionary attack on the system. The discontented young warriors were dissatisfied not so much with the system of social hierarchy itself as with their own position in it.

The educational system was partly responsible for the surfacing of this problem, for it tended to call attention to ability. With the spread of domain schools from the middle of the Tokugawa Period on, it became harder to conceal the wide discrepancies between talent demonstrated in the classroom and official appointment based upon hereditary rank.

Other aspects of Tokugawa ideology also manifested contradictions between theory and practice. Loyalty, for example, was the basic virtue upon which samurai training and discipline were organized, but the conditions upon which this key value was based had been utterly transformed during the course of the Tokugawa Period. A profound change in the nature of loyalty and in the relationship between vassal and lord had taken place. During the Warring States Period and the early years of Tokugawa rule, loyalty had two important characteristics.

1. *Loyalty was conditional.* It was based on a bilateral relationship between the lord and his vassal; the lord absolutely depended upon the loyalty of his samurai followers in order to maintain his position and his territory. Without it, his fief would quickly be lost to a neighboring lord. On the other hand, the vassals received in return for their allegiance a fief or a stipend. The relationship was, therefore, vital and mutually dependent, and it was conditional upon both sides fulfilling their functions. When a lord gave signs of weakness, it was not uncommon for vassals to desert him and join a neighboring lord who might better protect and reward them. There were many cases of treachery, of vassals overthrowing their lord. Loyalty was therefore a real, live value—to observe or renounce.

2. *Loyalty was also personal.* Because power was private, there was no higher authority (neither government nor law) that could enforce the relationship. "The lord," writes Craig, "had no court of appeal beyond his own strength should a vassal be disloyal."[6] Loyalty in the Warring States Period was often, Thomas Smith adds, "an intimate, intensely emotional relationship, based in no small part on the personal qualities of the lord, a relationship which existed between men who had fought side by side, grieved together at the loss of comrades, whose safety and families' safety depended on their keeping the faith."[7]

During the Tokugawa Period the lord-vassal relation underwent a silent but profound change.

1. *Loyalty became unconditional.* It was now based on a unilateral relationship; it lost its mutual dependency. With warfare ended, the lord no longer needed to worry about the loyalty of his vassals, for his position was guaranteed by the shogunate and it was virtually impossible for the vassals to leave or overthrow him. The loyalty of the vassal, in other words, was no longer conditional upon the lord's effectiveness as a leader, upon his ability to compensate and protect his retainers. The samurai, under the Tokugawa system, could do no other than give unquestioning obedience to his daimyo—even if his stipend were sharply reduced by his financially troubled lord (a measure no lord would have dared resort to in the Warring States Period).

2. *Loyalty became impersonal.* The relationship between lord and vassal became distant and formal, drained of much of its emotional content by the new circumstances. No longer their leader in war, the lord had less contact with his retainers. Owing to the alternate attendance system, many daimyo were born and raised in Edo and spent a great part of their mature life there. For long periods out of personal touch with conditions in the home fief, such a lord came to be looked on as an administrative head, sometimes little more than a titular leader.

Because their position was hereditary under the Tokugawa and no longer depended on their personal abilities, the lords often lacked qualities of leadership. The inability of government to deal with domestic and external problems called attention to this problem, and the daimyo came in for increasing criticism by the beginning of the nineteenth century. The daimyo, one contemporary writer observed scornfully, "were brought up by women, where no sound of the outside world penetrated and not even officials or retainers dared enter; therefore they knew nothing of men and affairs. Whatever nonsense they spoke was praised as wisdom, every action treated as a miracle of grace and dexterity. If they played chess or any other game, their companions contrived that they won, then threw up their hands, exclaiming 'My, how clever the lord is!'"[8] Although not typical, criticism of the daimyo as weak, foolish, self-indulgent, or incompetent was expressed with increased frequency as the crisis in the Tokugawa system deepened.

In these circumstances one can discern among warriors a longing for a more satisfying form of loyalty. For however much it was bereft of its former emotional significance, loyalty was still a primary value. Every samurai boy internalized it as he grew up. Yet it was scarcely fulfilling to give loyalty to one whose abilities and character were less than peerless or who appeared to be a distant unconcerned leader. In fact what seems to have occurred was that loyalty as a value remained strong but, as the lord became a more remote figure, it was directed more and more toward the han itself—a kind of "han nationalism," as Craig has called it. Or, to put it another way, loyalty was now given to the lord less because he was an admired individual leader than because he was a symbol of the han.

This transformation in the nature of loyalty helped to prepare the way for modern nationalism. Because loyalty was no longer closely tied to an individual but was rather directed toward the governmental unit with which warriors identified (i.e., their han), when Commodore Matthew C. Perry arrived and created the foreign crisis that threatened the nation, consciousness of belonging to Japan was heightened. Loyalty was rather quickly shifted from the han to the nation. Signs of growing national consciousness were, in fact, everywhere on the literary scene in the late Tokugawa Period. An awakened interest in the national tradition was apparent in the curriculum of many domain schools, which encouraged knowledge of Japan's past as a useful addition to Confucian studies.

Alternative Visions

The late Tokugawa Period was increasingly a world out of joint. It was pervaded by a sense of malaise, disarray, and failed expectations.[9] As the effectiveness of time-honored institutions eroded, their underlying concepts of authority and legitimacy lost the capacity to command unquestioning acceptance. As we have seen, institutions were undermined not simply by decay and decline. Life was becoming increasingly complex and diverse in ways that made the Tokugawa system less viable and satisfying. "The explosion of new forms of knowledge in late Tokugawa Japan was increasingly difficult to assimilate to the categories of the existing political system."[10] The sense of a unified and intact realm weakened, and one can discern a longing for a new basis of social solidarity and a restoration of order.

We may say that Japan experienced a cultural crisis in the last decades of Tokugawa rule that gave rise to alternative visions of order at all levels of society. New concepts of governance, new sources of moral values, and new religions appeared and offered solutions to the troubles of the time.

National learning or nativism (*kokugaku*) was one of the most important new visions to arise at this time. It began in the eighteenth century as a literary movement devoted to the study of Japan's ancient classics written prior to China's enormous cultural influence. Nativist scholars wanted to sort out what in Japanese culture was uniquely Japanese from what had been imported to understand better the distinctiveness of Japanese values and aesthetics. The key figure was Motoori Norinaga (1730–1801), a brilliant and complex thinker whom the literary historian Donald Keene regards as perhaps the greatest scholar Japan has produced. His most celebrated work was a study of the *Kojiki,* Japan's earliest historical work, which he considered

> an investigation into the Way of ancient Japan. The *Kojiki* was not only a sacred text, but contained the most reliable information on how the Japanese behaved before being infected with Chinese ideas. . . . The purely Japanese virtues—worship of the [Shintō] gods and of their descendant, the emperor—were contrasted with the superficial, meretricious reasoning of the Chinese and of Japanese infatuated with Chinese thought.[11]

Motoori rejected the secular rationalism of Confucian philosophy and sought a pristine Japanese spirit in ancient poetry and in purely Japanese prose works such as *The Tale of Genji.* He and other nativist scholars believed that the introduction of Confucianism into Japan had corrupted the pure and spontaneous spirituality the people had possessed when worshipping Japan's own Shintō deities. He encouraged greater understanding of Japan's cultural essence:

> I suggest that one first cleanse oneself of any defiled notions one may have acquired from reading Chinese texts, and then, holding fast to one's pristine Japanese heart, study our ancient texts well. If one does this, one will automatically learn about the Way that should be adopted and practiced. To know these things is to adopt and practice the Way of the Gods.[12]

Embedded in the literary studies of the nativist scholars was a religious dimension with profound political implications. Though still latent, these implications could be subversive of the Tokugawa system because nativism drew attention to the imperial institution and its mythical, divine origins and dismissed the secular Confucian rationalism that was an important part of the Tokugawa ideology. As one of Motoori's poems asserted:

> How vain it is
> For the men of China
> To discuss the reason of things
> When they know not the reason
> Of the miraculous.[13]

Nativism could provide the basis for a Japanese religion focused on the Emperor, who was descended from the greatest deity of antiquity, the sun goddess Amaterasu. It was left for Motoori's followers, especially Hirata Atsutane (1776–1843), to draw out the political implications of a national faith. Under their influence, it spread to the countryside where the religious dimension of nativist teachings had great appeal. Hirata's focus on the Shintō god of procreation was welcomed by the upper peasantry because it invested agrarian life with spiritual meaning. Moreover, the notion that they were subjects of the divine Emperor with an obligation to serve him gave them a new sense of the importance of their social standing.

Another new stream of thought that posed a challenge to the Tokugawa establishment was the Mito School. Like nativism it bespoke an increasing national consciousness in the late Tokugawa decades. In the coastal domain of Mito, north of Edo, a massive scholarly project devoted to the study of Japanese history, conducted for generations, called attention to the central timeless role of the imperial institution "as the embodiment, mystic or symbolic, of Japanese society and nationhood."[14] According to the Mito writers, all elements of the nation, each in its appropriate role in the hierarchy, were responsible for fulfilling their moral obligations to the Emperor. When disorder occurred in Chinese society, Confucian theory held that the Emperor had lost his Mandate of Heaven and could be removed. But in Japan the Emperor was divine, "one with Heaven," and therefore could never be overthrown. Instead, the Mito School stressed, it was the bakufu and the domains that must show reverence and uphold their mandate to rule by protecting the population from hardship. Just as nativism had given rise to a national faith, so the Mito School with its emphasis on the Emperor's divine nature gave government a religious basis and "signified the inseparability of worship, ceremony and governance."[15]

The nativist and Mito schools of thought implied clear challenges to the bakufu ideology and harbored potentially dangerous implications for the bakufu, especially if the bakufu was unable to gain control of the problems it faced. Even more striking evidence of the crisis of values, however, was the emergence of new religions with large followings among the common people of the cities and villages. The late Tokugawa Period proved to be one of the great seedtimes of Japanese popular religion. Historically, new religious cults tend to appear at times when unusual anxiety and economic hardship undermine long-accepted beliefs. Among the lower classes of the late Tokugawa Period numerous new sects sprang up with eclectic but basically Shintō teachings. The best known of these new religions was Tenrikyō (Teachings of Heavenly Truth), founded in 1838 by a peasant woman from a village near Nara. Like so many of the new sects, it promised salvation, peace, faith healing, and the comforting embrace of a new community of believers.

This new religious zeal, which represented a search for divine assistance and relief and for new forms of community, was not intended to have a political purpose. Nevertheless, as a leading authority on this phenomenon writes, "the new popular religions offered an ideal . . . that transcended the authority of the contemporary feudal system."[16] These became years of popular yearning for world renewal (*yonaoshi*) expressed not only in the new faiths but also in mass pilgrimages to religious sites such as the sun goddess's Grand Shrine at Ise in central Japan.

As these alternative visions of governance and values began to appear, the bakufu's problems clearly were not limited to social and economic issues but were also found in the erosion of the ideological foundations of Tokugawa rule. The Tokugawa class system and the justification of the hierarchy of bakufu, lords, and samurai to rule society had been based on faith in a natural order, based on cosmic principles derived from the teachings of the sages. But in light of the ineffectiveness of samurai government, a suspicion that the Tokugawa order, far from being sanctioned by changeless principles rooted in nature, might actually be an anachronism crept into the works of some of the most thoughtful and creative intellectuals of the late Tokugawa Period. It gave rise to what Tetsuo Najita calls "the moral crisis of the Tokugawa aristocracy."[17]

At the end of the eighteenth century a new stream of political thought concerned with the economic problems of government emerged. These writings implied that the survival of the Tokugawa system must depend on its effectiveness in solving the problems it faced and protecting the livelihood of the people. The writers, some of them from the merchant class, departed from abstract notions of ethics as the basis of governing and, instead, formulated new principles based on an economic view of politics. These political economists, as we may call them, discussed the failings of political leaders in dealing with matters of money, trade, and credit. "Economic knowledge, they asserted, was fundamental to politics, the art of 'ordering and saving the people'; for this reason, merchants and other commoners . . . ought to take part in the process of governance itself."[18] The revolutionary potential of such thoughts is obvious. As one of these political economists, Honda Toshiaki, wrote in 1798: "Whose fault is it that the people starve and good fields turn to waste? These evils cannot be blamed on laziness or disloyalty [in the people] but are owing to the crimes of the rulers. When I think of this I forget myself and breathe 'Heaven's punishment comes too slowly!'"[19]

Movements for Reform in Government

To deal with the mounting difficulties of government, reform movements were initiated within the shogunate and many of the domains. Generalizing about these movements is exceedingly difficult because the measures taken and the successes achieved varied greatly.

Generally, however, we may distinguish two main strands of reformist thinking. The first and dominant one was what we may call the *fundamentalist* approach, whose main purpose was to restore the fundamental or "purer" conditions of the early Tokugawa Period. Idealizing a purely agrarian economy, this approach sought in various ways to suppress or at least restrain the growing power of the merchant class. It stressed retrenchment in government and revival of the moral values of simplicity, austerity, and frugality. It was characterized by heavy reliance on sumptuary edicts, seeking to limit and curtail consumption. Only occasionally did this approach try to increase the income of government, and when it did it tended to be through a time-honored method, such as land reclamation. Some of the more extreme proponents of the fundamentalist school urged return of the samurai to the countryside, relocating them in the villages where they would be away from the corrupting influences of the towns. It was expected not only that the morale of the samurai would thereby be raised, but that the function of the castle town merchants would likewise be weakened.

The other approach to reform may be called the *realist* school because it accepted the growing commercialization of the economy and urged the authorities to adjust to it, not deny it. The realists agreed that the warrior class could not continue to stand aloof from and disdain financial matters. They urged a reorientation in Tokugawa thinking, a recognition that trade could be productive and that government could profit from the commercial segments of the economy. The realist school urged government to encourage the production of capital wealth and to use its political power to establish state enterprises and monopoly organizations. Some of its more extreme proponents urged abandonment of the seclusion policy and revival of foreign trade as a means of bringing wealth to Japan. The latter argument aroused bitter opposition, but the proposals for state-sponsored trade and industry were accepted to an increasing degree by the shogunate and many domain governments.

Some of the reform attempts by the bakufu and the han bureaucracies were a mixture of these two approaches, but most leaned toward fundamentalism and achieved only limited success. As Bolitho writes, "A wholehearted swing to innovation was rare. Much more usual was a blend, sometimes even a contradictory blend, of the novel with the traditional."[20] The bakufu had made several efforts at reform, but the wave of peasant uprisings in the 1830s and Ōshio's spectacular rebellion in Osaka in 1837, which set fires raging through the merchant quarters and brought bakufu troops to subdue the rebels, gave notice that the problems of government were far from solved.

The final effort of the shogunate to deal with these problems, prior to the intervention of the foreigners, came in the reforms of the early 1840s. The leading figure of the bakufu in this period was Mizuno

Tadakuni, who rose in 1841 to leadership in the Council of Elders, the shogunate's controlling administrative organ, and took charge of this last concerted reform program. His reforms leaned toward the fundamentalist approach, relying heavily on sumptuary legislation and, in addition, attempting to disband merchant associations and to stem the flow of immigrants into Edo from the countryside. Such traditionalistic reforms failed, for they treated the symptoms rather than the root causes of bakufu distress.

Japan's economy and society were far too changed and too dynamic to be pressed back into the mold of early Tokugawa institutions. The failure of Mizuno's reform program gave added support to the contention of realist reform thinkers that a comprehensive change in the political structure of the country was necessary, so that institutions might be adjusted to the changed conditions of the society and economy.

Notes

1. Quoted in Tetsuo Najita, "Political Economism in the Thought of Dazai Shundai (1680–1747)," *Journal of Asian Studies* 31 (August 1972), 836.
2. Philip C. Brown, "Practical Constraints on Early Tokugawa Land Taxation: Annual versus Fixed Assessments in Kaga Domain," *Journal of Japanese Studies* 14 (summer 1988), 400–401.
3. Quoted in Thomas C. Smith, *Political Change and Industrial Development in Japan: Government Enterprise, 1868–1880* (Stanford, Calif.: Stanford University Press, 1955), 17–18.
4. Herbert P. Bix, *Peasant Protest in Japan, 1590–1884* (New Haven, Conn.: Yale University Press, 1986), 221.
5. Stephen Vlastos, *Peasant Protests and Uprisings in Tokugawa Japan* (Berkeley: University of California Press, 1986), 159–167.
6. Albert M. Craig, *Chōshū in the Meiji Restoration* (Cambridge, Mass.: Harvard University Press, 1961), 145.
7. Thomas C. Smith, *Native Sources of Japanese Industrialization, 1750–1920* (Berkeley: University of California Press, 1988), 139.
8. Ibid., 169.
9. See James L. McClain, "Failed Expectations: Kaga Domain on the Eve of the Meiji Restoration," *Journal of Japanese Studies* 14 (summer 1988), 403–447.
10. Harry D. Harootunian, "Late Tokugawa Culture and Thought," in Marius B. Jansen, ed., *The Nineteenth Century*, vol. 5 of *The Cambridge History of Japan*, ed. John Whitney Hall (Cambridge: Cambridge University Press, 1989), 171.
11. Donald Keene, *World within Walls: Japanese Literature of the Pre-Modern Era* (Tokyo: Tuttle, 1978), 320–321.
12. Peter Nosco, *Remembering Paradise* (Cambridge, Mass.: Harvard University Press, 1990), 197.
13. Keene, *World within Walls*, 329.

14. Herschel Webb, quoted in J. Victor Koschmann, *The Mito Ideology: Discourse, Reform, and Insurrection in Late Tokugawa Japan, 1790–1864* (Berkeley: University of California Press, 1987), 36.
15. Harootunian, "Late Tokugawa Culture," in *The Nineteenth Century,* ed. Jansen, 191.
16. Yasumaru Yoshio, quoted in Harootunian, "Late Tokugawa Culture," in *The Nineteenth Century,* ed. Jansen, 217.
17. Tetsuo Najita, "Method and Analysis in the Conceptual Portrayal of Tokugawa Intellectual History," in *Japanese Thought in the Tokugawa Period, 1600–1868: Methods and Metaphors,* ed. Tetsuo Najita and Irwin Scheiner (Chicago: University of Chicago Press, 1978), 35.
18. Tetsuo Najita, *Visions of Virtue in Tokugawa Japan: The Kaitokudō, Merchant Academy of Osaka* (Chicago: University of Chicago Press, 1987), 284.
19. Smith, *Native Sources,* 172.
20. Harold Bolitho, "The Tempō Crisis," in *The Nineteenth Century,* ed. Jansen, 135.

The Meiji Restoration

At this point, while the bakufu and many domains were still struggling with their unresolved problems, the foreign crisis developed and very suddenly brought matters to a head. We may think of it as a catalyst, speeding up the reaction to pressing domestic problems that otherwise might have been allowed to continue unresolved for some time longer.

The foreign crisis quickly galvanized the forces of change. The remarkable responsiveness of Japanese society to the Western challenge is thus, in part, to be understood as resulting from the gradual buildup of social and economic problems during the preceding century. Had Japan not been characterized at this time by institutional incapacity, widespread social unrest, and an anxious groping by political leaders for new reform measures, the Japanese response would doubtless have been more ponderous and reluctant.

Tokugawa Foreign Relations

Let us begin by considering the background of the foreign crisis. One of the key control measures instituted by the founders of the Tokugawa system was the strict management of foreign relations. The most striking part of this effort was the restriction of contacts with the outside world. In the early 1800s the term *sakoku,* meaning closed country, began to be used to describe the policy of national isolation. In actuality, Tokugawa Japan was not so totally isolated as is sometimes thought.

Historians are increasingly inclined to believe that the primary intent of the seclusion edicts between 1633 and 1639 was to enhance the legitimacy of the shogunate by resolutely bringing foreign relations under its control. The eradication of Christianity and the restrictions on travel abroad were indicative not so much of isolationist sentiment as of the bakufu's determination to establish its authority both internally and externally. Because Japan's relations with the Western world were drastically restricted, Western historians may have overemphasized the degree of Japanese seclusion during the Tokugawa Period. "The bakufu," writes Ronald Toby, "never intended entirely to isolate Japan from foreign intercourse."[1] Politically, culturally, and commercially, Japan's foreign relations with Asia continued to thrive. "As a result," Marius Jansen observes, "sakoku seems more symbol than fact."[2] Although only 700 or so Dutch ships entered the port of Nagasaki over the next two centuries, private trade with Chinese merchants was far greater. Between 1635 and 1852 more than 5,500 Chinese ships came to Nagasaki. Commerce with Korea through the island domain of Tsushima grew to significant proportions, and in recognition of its importance Korea dispatched twelve official embassies to Japan during the Tokugawa Period. Trade with the Ryukyus, which brought goods from China and Southeast Asia, was acknowledged by more than twenty embassies to the Tokugawa Bakufu. Through the visits of Korean and Ryukyuan emissaries, imported books, and reports prepared by Dutch and Chinese ship captains, the shogunate established channels to gain news of the outside world. One of Japan's leading cultural historians recently sized up the "seclusion" policies as

> the embodiment of Tokugawa political wisdom. Seclusion eliminated the factor of instability in foreign relations and let the shogunate focus its energies on perfecting the administrative setup. At the same time, the country wasn't really walled off. You might say it was surrounded at most by a bamboo blind or a silk curtain that let the breeze in and allowed the administration to maintain a balance between internal and external pressures in both the economic and cultural spheres. The shogunate could bring in the things it needed and keep out what it didn't. It could take in all the information it needed and keep out what it didn't. It could take in all the information it found useful without letting out any information it didn't want to. In this way it ensured the nation's security, both externally and internally. It was brilliant. . . . For all the talk of seclusion, Japan was probably receiving more information from other countries than any other non-Western country of the time.[3]

Obtaining knowledge of the outside world was largely the work of a small number of Japanese known as "Dutch scholars," who were familiar with Western technology and science. As early as 1720, the seclusion edicts had been eased to the extent of allowing Western books to circulate in Japan as long as they did not expound Christian doctrine. This decision was made by Tokugawa Yoshimune, a shogun who had a serious interest in the Western calendar as well as curiosity about astronomy, watchmaking, geography, and other topics he learned about from the agents of the Dutch trading station who visited Edo. By the mid-eighteenth century some translation work was beginning and "Dutch studies" gained importance as the efficacy of Western medicine began to be demonstrated. By the eve of Commodore Perry's arrival, as a result of the small but growing number of Dutch scholars, the Japanese had a considerable store of knowledge of the West and of its technology. They had access to translations of Western treatises on astronomy, chemistry, geography, mathematics, physics, and (as attention turned to problems of defense) on ballistics, metallurgy, and military tactics. Many scholars have argued that, at that time, knowledge of Western science was already more widespread in Japan than in any other Asian country.

It was only in the early nineteenth century, when Dutch supremacy in the Far East had ended and other Western powers began aggressive challenges to the bakufu's system of foreign affairs, that the seclusion policy assumed a more negative, inflexible, and xenophobic form. National isolation became more a reality as the bakufu took new steps to close the country by announcing that Westerners would be expelled by force. In its Expulsion Edict of 1825, the bakufu declared that Western barbarians "have become steadily more unruly, and, moreover, seem to be propagating their wicked religion among our people. . . . Henceforth whenever a foreign ship is sighted approaching any point on our coast, all persons on hand should fire on and drive it off."[4]

Although this edict was moderated somewhat in 1842 to permit foreign ships to receive supplies before being forced to leave, the policy of national isolation had now become the inviolable law of the land. In the face of new, aggressive challenges from the West, the bakufu expected to uphold this policy by force if necessary.

The Coming of the Foreign Crisis

In contrast to domestic problems, which had been developing since the Genroku Period, the foreign intervention occurred abruptly, with a suddenness and intensity surely unexpected by most politically conscious Japanese. There had been forewarnings—occasional omens—as early as the 1790s, but they were infrequent and easily forgotten in the press of more immediate concerns.

Russia had posed the initial problems. Its envoys and traders began appearing on the islands north of Hokkaido in the 1790s, seeking to open trade relations with Japan. In every case they were rebuffed, and after 1813 there was no further contact for several decades. In the meantime, however, the British, having extended their power into India and Malaysia, had begun to build up a China trade and to probe Japanese coastal waters. A series of incidents ensued, beginning in 1808 when a British frigate sailed into Nagasaki harbor demanding supplies of food and water. It was not, however, until word was received of the Opium War (1839–1842) in China, which ended in British acquisition of Hong Kong and the forced opening of five ports to British trade and residence, that concern spread in Japan that a serious challenge to the policy of restricting foreign contacts was imminent. To the Japanese who thought about it, expanding British power in the Far East represented a distinct threat. The Dutch, in fact, acting through their trading station representatives in Nagasaki, warned the bakufu in 1844 of the situation and urged that the country be opened voluntarily before Western nations undertook to force Japan to this decision.

As it transpired, while Britain was preoccupied with its new involvement in China, the United States took the lead in forcefully testing the bakufu's policies. The opening of Chinese treaty ports presaged a new era of national rivalry among the Western powers in the Far East with America too acquiring trading interests on the China coast. Taken with the settlement of the disputed claims to the Oregon Territory in 1846 and the acquisition of California in 1848, these interests gave the American government cause for much greater attention to Pacific affairs. In 1852 President Millard Fillmore approved the mission that would be headed by Commodore Perry to try to establish relations with the Japanese government. The Perry mission originated in the desire to protect shipwrecked American sailors and to acquire coaling stations and the right for ships to take on provisions. But deeper than those reasons lay the hope for trade and the conviction that America had a destiny to expand its interests in the Pacific.

Although apprised by the Dutch of the mission well in advance, the bakufu was nonetheless uncertain how to deal with it. When Perry arrived with his squadron of four ships and anchored off the coast on July 8, 1853, political opinion in Edo was confused and divided. Almost all of those who thought about the problem were agreed on the need for strengthening defenses to meet the threat of foreign attack. On other questions of foreign policy, thought was sharply divided between the *kaikoku* (open country) school and the *jōi* (expel the barbarian) school.

The kaikoku school was closely associated with and drew its strength from "Dutch learning" (*rangaku*), the work of a small number of Japanese scholars who had been compiling knowledge of the West. Keenly aware of the West's more advanced technology and of Japan's military weakness, the Dutch scholars argued pragmatically that Japan needed Western weapons and techniques to defend itself; therefore it must avoid war with a Western power, at least until it had a chance to strengthen itself—even if that meant giving in to foreign demands for the opening of ports.

Those who favored opening the country were generally of what we have called the realist school of reform thought, regarding foreign trade as an opportunity for bakufu profit and therefore as contributing directly to the solution of the financial problems of government. Of course a good deal of variation was found among those who advocated an open country, but most of them saw it primarily as a matter of national defense. They saw an open country not necessarily as good in itself but rather as a means to create a strong and independent Japan.

One of the leaders of this kind of argument was Sakuma Shōzan (1811–1864), a samurai-scholar who exercised considerable influence, partly through his followers and partly through his lord, who was a bakufu councillor. As a young man he studied Western gunnery, and then, turning to other aspects of Dutch studies, became convinced of the critical importance of such technology to his country's defense. In particular, his thinking was influential for its insistence on the application of pragmatic ideas rather than abstract moral principles. Thus he referred again and again to his belief that "Eastern ethics and Western science" were both proper in their separate spheres. Confucian morals remained valid as a criterion for personal behavior, but it was necessary for political leaders to look beyond Confucian scholarship for answers to the practical problems of governance. Impressed by the example of Peter the Great, he proposed the appointment of "men of talent in military strategy, planning, and administration" to carry out a program of national strengthening by establishing relations with foreign countries, obtaining the advantages of foreign technology, and building up defense through a new political structure.

Sakuma was assassinated in 1864. His views had been violently opposed by jōi samurai, who passionately believed that opening the country would bring political and cultural disaster. To them China's defeat in the Opium War was attributable less to Western military techniques than to the contamination of Chinese society by Western customs and religion. Jōi thinking was often pervaded by an intense xenophobia and by a national consciousness and zealous commitment to the imperial institution as the mystic embodiment of the Japanese nation we saw in the last chapter in the writings of the nativist and Mito scholars.

Aizawa Seishisai of the Mito School, whose *New Theses* (*Shinron*) inspired the jōi samurai, wrote in 1825, for example, that Western countries represented less a military than an ideological threat. They were able to cultivate a spiritual unity and allegiance in their people through their state cult of Christianity. By indoctrinating their peoples with a state religion, Western rulers achieved mass loyalty both in their own peoples and in those they colonized. In this way they were able to enlist the common people into large armies and mobilize their energies in pursuit of state goals:

> The Western barbarians . . . all believe in the same religion, Christianity, which they use to annex territories. Wherever they go, they destroy native houses of worship, deceive the local peoples, and seize those lands. These barbarians will settle for nothing less than subjugating the rulers of all nations and conscripting all peoples into their ranks. . . . Should the wily barbarians someday be tempted to take advantage of this situation and entice our stupid commoners to adopt beliefs and customs that reek of barbarism how could we stop them?[5]

To counter the ideological threat the bakufu should have the Emperor propagate a Japanese state religion to cultivate national unity and mass loyalty. Aizawa called this spiritual unity *kokutai* or "what is essential to make a people into a nation." Lacking this popular allegiance Japan was in jeopardy. "Should the barbarians win over our people's hearts and minds, they will have captured the realm without a skirmish."[6] In retrospect we can see that Aizawa was asserting the need for nationalism—what in Japan later was called the "emperor system"—in order to integrate the common people into the struggles of the nation.

A similar defense of jōi was offered by Confucianists, who thought that Western religion would undermine the ethical basis of Japanese society and who believed that Western trade, bringing greater wealth to merchants, would in turn be destructive of morals. They did not accept Sakuma Shōzan's pragmatic advocacy of preserving traditional ethical values while adopting the new technology. "To say that we can accept Western science although we must reject Western moral teaching as evil and wrong," wrote the conservative Ōhashi Totsuan, "is like telling people that although the mainstream of a river is poisoned yet they can safely drink from the sidestreams."[7] In a sense, he and like-minded Confucianists were right. The threat was cultural, for it would be impossible (as was subsequently demonstrated) to preserve traditional values unchanged once Western science was accepted.

In their moral conservatism the jōi advocates appeared to have much in common with the fundamentalist school of domestic reform. They saw positive benefit in armed resistance to the Westerners, for they expected hostilities to revive samurai morale and to restore habits of discipline and frugality. Furthermore, they regarded foreign trade as harmful, bringing a loss of specie and further disruption of the economy. Nevertheless, the jōi samurai were symptomatic of the alternative visions of order discussed in the last chapter. They seemed to be conservative because of their opposition to Westerners, but in reality they could be a revolutionary force. Many of them proved open to change if it would provide a solution to the crisis in Tokugawa society, a new basis of social solidarity, and a restoration of order.

The Treaties

Commodore Perry presented his demands for treaty relations in the summer of 1853 and then withdrew, warning that he would return the following spring for an answer. Abe Masahirō, the head of the bakufu's Council of Elders and the effective head of government owing to the incompetence of the shogun, temporized. Faced with sharp divisions of opinion, aware that antiforeign feeling was strong but believing that Western demands could not long be resisted, he sought to gain consensus by requesting all the daimyo to express their opinions regarding American demands. This unprecedented step amounted to a confession of the bakufu's weakness, nor did the daimyo's responses produce the basis for concerted action vis-à-vis the foreign powers. "Abe's policy of government by consensus," writes Bolitho, "was a disastrous mistake. In a sense it is understandable that Abe should have been receptive to the ideas of others. After all, he seems to have had very few of his own." When a translation of Millard Fillmore's letter was shown to the daimyo for their views it elicited a bewildering variety of responses:

> Of those replies remaining to us, two favored accepting the American demands; two more favored accepting them for a while; three favored allowing the United States to trade, subject to certain other restrictions; one suggested allowing trade for a short time, while preparing to attack; three advocating treating the foreigners politely for a longer time, and then, once an adequate defense had been prepared, expelling them; four supported prolonged negotiations, preparing an adequate defense the while, and then refusing; eleven urged fighting on Perry's return; three were undecided. Clearly it was impossible to derive a mandate from this response. . . . By his policy of consultation, Abe managed to do the Tokugawa Bakufu a great deal of harm. At its best, the process was time-wasting, helping to defer decisions that should have been taken quickly. At its worst, it invited a degree of interference in Bakufu policy-making that was paralyzing in its effect.[8]

Within bakufu circles, during the winter of 1853–1854, policy was debated. The most powerful of the house (fudai) lords, Ii Naosuke, expressed what soon became the dominant view in the bakufu when he advocated a positive, kaikoku response, adding: "When one is besieged in a castle, to raise the drawbridge is to imprison oneself and

Commodore Perry arrives to meet with the Japanese. *National Archives*

make it impossible to hold out indefinitely."[9] He therefore urged a period of trade that would allow Japan to acquire the knowledge necessary to defend her independence.

When Perry returned, this time with a flotilla of eight ships, the bakufu acceded to his demands. A treaty was signed on March 31, 1854 (the so-called Kanagawa Treaty of Friendship), which provided that two ports, Shimoda and Hakodate, would be opened to American ships and limited trade, and that an American consular agent was to be permitted to reside in Shimoda. Prior to the signing of the treaty there was a ceremony at which the Americans presented several tokens of their civilization as gifts, including a model railroad, a telegraph set, farm tools, and a hundred gallons of whiskey. The Japanese, for their part, put on a demonstration of *sumō* wrestling, and the Americans then responded with a minstrel show. Afterwards Perry, who had something of the self-confident and pompous air of another American military figure who arrived in Japan almost a century later, concluded that "Japan had been opened to the nations of the West" and that "the Japanese are, undoubtedly, like the Chinese, a very imitative, adaptive, and compliant people and in these characteristics may be discovered a promise of the comparatively easy introduction of foreign customs and habits, if not of the nobler principles and better life of a higher civilization."[10]

Shortly after the signing of the Kanagawa Treaty, the bakufu concluded similar treaties with Britain, Russia, and Holland. The shogunate took solace from having forestalled any large-scale opening to trade, but this comfort proved short-lived for, unsatisfied with anything less than full commercial treaties, the Western powers in succeeding years put increased pressure on the shogunate to grant still further concessions. Again, it was an American, Townsend Harris, who played the leading role. Harris came to Shimoda in 1856 as the first American consul. He set about at once to persuade the authorities that further opening to trade was inevitable and that it would be far better to conclude a reasonable agreement with his country than to await the forceful demands of other powers. As evidence, he pointed to the outbreak of the Anglo-French War in 1856 and to the likelihood that the British fleet assembled for the war against China would next be used to extract a commercial treaty from the Japanese. Harris's tact and persistence paid off. Hotta Masayoshi, who had succeeded Abe Masahirō as the senior member of the bakufu's Council of Elders, was convinced of the irresistibility of foreign demands as well as the positive benefit of foreign intercourse for the building of Japanese defenses. "Our policy," he concluded, "should be to stake everything on the present opportunity, to conclude friendly alliances, to send ships to foreign countries everywhere and conduct trade, to copy the foreigners where they are at their best and so repair our own shortcomings, to foster our national strength and complete our armaments, and so gradually subject the foreigners to our influence until in the end all the countries of the world know the blessings of perfect tranquillity and our hegemony is acknowledged throughout the globe."[11]

On July 29, 1858, the Harris Treaty was signed. It became the model for similar treaties signed in the following weeks with Britain, France, Holland, and Russia. They provided essentially three things: (1) Edo, Kobe, Nagasaki, Niigata, and Yokohama were opened to foreign trade; (2) Japanese tariffs were placed under international control and import duties were fixed at low levels; and (3) a system of extraterritoriality was established, which provided that foreign residents would be subject to their own consular courts rather than to Japanese law.

These unequal treaties imposed for the first time in Japan's history extensive restrictions on its national sovereignty, and, while they did not require the cession of any territory (such as the powers required elsewhere in Asia), they placed Japan in a semicolonial status. In the long run the treaties became a symbol of the national impotence that was exposed by renewed contact with the West, and recovery of national independence and international respect became an overriding goal, which the Japanese pursued with extraordinary tenacity. In the short run the treaties ignited political conflict that destroyed bakufu authority and led, a decade later, to the establishment of a new government.

Declining Fortunes of the Bakufu

By breaking with the 250-year tradition of the Tokugawa government and referring Perry's demands to all the lords for their frank opinion, the shogunate unwittingly encouraged open debate and criticism of all its policies. In this situation it became increasingly difficult to stop the unraveling of bakufu authority. In 1858 Hotta Masayoshi, the effective head of government, sought the approval of the imperial court to the draft of the Harris Treaty—tantamount to still further confession of weakness. He hoped thereby to defuse what he knew would be bitter opposition to the treaty, but he also revealed the declining authority of the bakufu, and, when the court refused, this was clear for all to see. Rebuffed by the newly emboldened Emperor and nobles, Hotta was forced to resign.

Under his replacement, Ii Naosuke, the strongest of the fudai lords, there was a brief resurgence of bakufu strength. Ii took forceful steps to assert his authority. Disregarding the attitude of the imperial court, he ordered the signing of the Harris Treaty and afterward compelled the court to give its consent. Then he ordered into retirement or house arrest all the daimyo who had opposed his policies. These strong-arm methods, however, further inflamed the bitterness that many fanatical samurai felt toward the bakufu for having conceded so much to the barbarians. On a snowy day in March 1860, as his procession was entering the gate of the shogun's castle, Ii was assassinated.

It was a decisive event. Ii's successors proved less able and less forceful than he; the full tide of antibakufu sentiment, which had been gathering since 1854, now swept over them. They were unable to control the flow of events that carried the bakufu toward its demise. After the assassination, opponents of the shogunate and its policies looked to the imperial court as a counterweight. The daimyo of Satsuma proposed a "union of court and bakufu" to improve the position of the court. The shogunate accepted the proposal, hoping to use the court's prestige to shore up its own, but to gain court backing it was forced to make several damaging concessions. The bakufu was compelled to appoint to high positions in the shogunate reform-minded officials who were to implement the "union." Under the influence of these officials, the bakufu approved a relaxation of its control measures, permitting family hostages to leave Edo and diminishing the alternate attendance requirement to a mere 100 days every 3 years. Symbolically, the most important concession was the agreement of the shogun that he would travel to Kyoto to consult with the court on national policies, thereby rendering himself to some extent accountable to the Emperor. When Tokugawa Iemochi made the trip in the spring of 1863, even his extraordinary procession of 3,000 retainers could not conceal the momentous fact that it was the first time since the seventeenth century that a shogun had felt compelled to visit Kyoto.

In the aftermath of these concessions, the bakufu found it difficult to exercise its will over the most powerful daimyo. The domain of Chōshū tried to carry out an antiforeigner policy by firing on foreign vessels passing through the Shimonoseki Strait, adjacent to the domain. When, under pressure from the powers, the bakufu sent an emissary to Chōshū ordering that it desist, extremist samurai in the domain killed him as he fled after delivering the message. Shortly thereafter forces from Chōshū marched on Kyoto and attempted to stage a coup and establish its influence in the imperial court.

The attempt failed, but the shogunate decided to organize a punitive expedition to punish Chōshū's overt disobedience and its breaking of the Tokugawa peace. A force of 150,000 samurai, drawn from the chief domains, was assembled on the borders of Chōshū in late 1864, but the participation of many of the domains was half-hearted and the bakufu therefore could not plan a sustained campaign. Instead, through the mediation of Saigō Takamori of Satsuma, a lenient settlement was agreed upon, requiring a formal apology and the suicide of three senior officials held to be responsible for the attempted coup in Kyoto.

Despite the qualified character of its success, the bakufu took heart from this assertion of its leadership. It tried to achieve total restoration of its authority by reimposing the alternate attendance system, by sending troops to Kyoto to establish control over the court, and by acquiring French technical assistance in building up its military strength. The specter of a bakufu attempt to reestablish its former supremacy alienated many lords and brought the two most powerful domains, Chōshū and Satsuma, together in a secret alliance to work for the restoration of imperial rule. The alliance became operative in 1866 when the shogunate, confronted with renewed defiance from Chōshū, organized a second punitive expedition. This time several of the major domains, including Satsuma, refused to participate; Chōshū, using modern weapons and buoyed by superior morale, roundly defeated the bakufu forces, who sued for peace and withdrew.

Samurai Activists

In the last chapter we discussed the deep discontent among able lower-ranking warriors, who felt unjustly cut off from higher office by the rigidities of the hereditary system. This latent discontent came to the surface in many of the prominent domains after Perry's arrival, for the treaties raised fierce emotions and opened up political issues to much wider discussion. Moreover, they created a sense of crisis in which the argument for promoting men of talent took on new force, and the effectiveness of the traditional ruling segment of the samurai was more insistently called into question.

Not only were the new activists of lower rank, they were young—representatives of a generation that was to provide Japan with new leadership in the aftermath of the Meiji Restoration. Because of their temperament, their involvement in plots and conspiracies, and their resort to violence and assassination, many were known as *shishi* (men of spirit). They were a wenching, impulsive, devil-may-care type of young man, passionately devoted to the imperial cause, which they called the highest loyalty of all. "The shishi had no care for the morrow. He was brave, casual, carefree, took himself very seriously where 'first things' were concerned, and was utterly indifferent where they were not. Irresponsible in many matters, he was also a roisterer, given to wine and women."[12] Flouting conventional standards of morality and feudal discipline, the shishi were symptomatic of a search for a more satisfying loyalty and for a new political and social order.

Lacking a clear revolutionary program, they reacted to Perry's coming with a burst of emotion that was initially directed at the barbarian. Only after the bakufu acquiesced in the Harris Treaty did they vent their fury on the shogunate and others of the ruling elite, whom they held personally responsible for the plight of Japan. Ii Naosuke and many other officials were assassinated by shishi angered at their failure to expel the foreigner.

Yoshida Shoin (1830–1859) is one of the best remembered of these activists for the influence he had on Chōshū samurai. He studied under Sakuma Shōzan in Edo, became convinced of the need for Western learning for the defense of Japan, and attempted to leave Japan with Perry's squadron to continue his studies in America. He was apprehended by bakufu officials and returned to Chōshū, where he opened a school and gathered about him a group of shishi passionately committed to the imperial institution and to national defense. Among his group of students were future leaders of modern Japan, including Yamagata Aritomo and Itō Hirobumi. The signing of the Harris Treaty of 1858 aroused them, as it did shishi all over the country, to violent action. The fury that had previously been directed at the barbarians was now turned on the bakufu. In many domains young samurai of all ranks became involved in politics, and fanatical activity by shishi sought the removal of "evil" officials who stood in the way of radical opposition to the foreigners.

The shishi, however, were soon given convincing demonstrations of the irresistibility of Western military power, which served to calm

their fanaticism and redirect their energies along more thoughtful paths of action. In Chōshū the attacks in 1864 by the combined fleets of Great Britain, France, Holland, and the United States, precipitated by the domain's attempt to close the Shimonoseki Strait to foreign shipping, convinced many samurai activists of the futility of opposing Western demands for commercial rights.

Word of such demonstrations of Western military strength traveled, and by 1865 it had combined with increased knowledge of the outside world in general to create a widespread acceptance among activists and officials alike that military reform was essential, and that in order to buy expensive ships and weapons foreign trade was imperative. What was more, to build such weapons a knowledge of science and technology was required. By this time, many military reformers were also ready to acknowledge the organizational needs of industry and finance, and some were beginning to speculate about the reorganization. It was the combined action of Chōshū and Satsuma that brought the latter phase to fruition.

Chōshū-Satsuma Alliance

As we have seen, these two outer domains, which had been vanquished in the battles that established the Tokugawa hegemony, emerged rapidly in the years after Perry's arrival to play the leading roles in the overthrow of the shogunate and the establishment of a new government. A number of reasons impelled them to take the lead. As outer domains excluded from the central government and generally distrusted by the shogunate, they had a tradition of hostility toward the Tokugawa. Craig tells us of some of the ways this anti-Tokugawa bias was kept alive in Chōshū:

> One ceremony embodying this animus was held annually on the first day of the new year. Early in the morning when the first cock crowed, the Elders and Direct Inspectors would go to the daimyo and ask, "Has the time come to begin the subjugation of the Bakufu?" The daimyo would then reply, "It is still too early; the time is not yet come." While obviously secret, this ceremony was considered one of the most important rituals of the han. Another comparable custom in a more domestic setting has also been recorded. Mothers in Chōshū would have their boys sleep with their feet to the east, a form of insult to the Bakufu, and tell them "never to forget the defeat at Sekigahara even in their dreams." In the case of Satsuma, every year on the fourteenth day of the ninth month the castle town samurai would don their armor and go to Myōenji, a temple near Kagoshima, to meditate on the battle of Sekigahara.[13]

Of more immediate importance than those formless thoughts of revenge was the fact that both domains were among the very largest in terms of productive capacity and both had an unusually large number of samurai. They were therefore extremely strong domains, and their strength was enhanced by financial solvency. Chōshū for nearly a century had regularly saved a portion of its income and had invested it in profitable enterprises, thus accumulating capital that could be used in time of emergency. Satsuma owed its solvency to a highly profitable state-operated sugar monopoly. These resources contributed to high morale in the samurai class and enabled Chōshū and Satsuma during the 1860s to buy rifles, cannons, and ships. Without the 7,000 rifles that it purchased from the West, Chōshū probably would have been defeated in the second bakufu punitive expedition. Still another advantage that favored the two outer domains was the fact that commercial development had not progressed so far there as in many areas more centrally located, and as a consequence class unrest had been less erosive of morale than in places close to the major urban centers.

For these reasons, as bakufu authority began to crumble, Chōshū and Satsuma emerged as the leading domains in the struggle to resolve the national crisis. At first they were rivals, each proposing its own solution to the crisis. Satsuma, as we have seen, became identified with the proposal of a "union of court and bakufu"; in 1862 it was able to win important concessions from the bakufu in the appointment of reformist officials, the moderation of the alternate attendance requirement, and the agreement for the shogun to travel to Kyoto to consult on national policy. Chōshū, on the other hand, put forth a rival and more extreme proposal for solution of the national crisis, favoring a more resolutely proimperial court stand and demanding the expulsion of the foreigners.

By the end of 1864 it became apparent to both domains that neither plan alone was satisfactory. After the shelling of its forts by the combined foreign fleet, Chōshū's leadership had to acknowledge the futility of expelling the barbarians. Satsuma, for its part, was dismayed by the bakufu attempts to assert its traditional supremacy in 1864–1865 by reinstating the alternate attendance system, dispatching troops to Kyoto to establish control of the court, and gaining French technical assistance to build up its own power. In this situation, the antagonism between Chōshū and Satsuma was gradually overcome by their mutual interest in preventing a reassertion of Tokugawa supremacy.

In Chōshū, after the first bakufu punitive expedition, a civil war occurred that brought to power a new han government determined to press the struggle against the shogunate. The new government owed its triumph to mixed rifle units of samurai and commoners, some of which were commanded by former followers of Yoshida Shoin. When in August 1866 the bakufu sought to topple this new government and organized its second punitive expedition against Chōshū, it faced an army that was better disciplined and armed. Moreover, Satsuma this time refused to participate in the expedition, for the two domains had earlier that year concluded a secret alliance pledging mutual support. Chōshū's easy victory over bakufu forces obviated the need for overt aid from Satsuma. A year later, however, the two domains openly joined forces to administer the coup de grace to the demoralized shogunate. Acting in collusion with friendly elements in the imperial court, they seized the palace on January 3, 1868, and had the boy Emperor, Mutsuhito (1852–1912; later known as the Meiji Emperor), proclaim the end of the Tokugawa regime and the restoration of imperial rule. In the ensuing weeks, Chōshū and Satsuma troops, now calling themselves imperial forces, engaged the bakufu army and, though outnumbered, quickly put it to flight. After two and a half centuries the Tokugawa Shogunate had come to an astonishingly sudden end.

The Significance of the Meiji Restoration

Much controversy has surrounded the Meiji Restoration, and the problems of interpreting its meaning have sharply divided historians. Should it be called a "revolution"? Was it motivated primarily by class interests or by ideology? What was the extent of Western influence? What was the relation between long-range socioeconomic change in the Tokugawa Period and the reforms that came after 1868? What role, if any, did the populace play in these events?

If we were to look at the events up to 1868 and no farther, then it is possible to see only a coup d'état—the displacement of one feudal group by another. Satsuma and Chōshū vanquished the Tokugawa, much as the reverse had occurred over two and a half centuries earlier. Thus Albert Craig concludes that "the Meiji Restoration was not a revolution, not a change in the name of new values—such as *liberté, égalité,* and *fraternité* in the French Revolution. Rather, it was what is far more common in history, a change carried out in the name of old values. It was a change brought about by men intent on fulfilling the goals of their inherited tradition. It was a change brought about unwittingly by men who before 1868 had no conception of its eventual social ramifications."[14] Studying the Tokugawa downfall from the perspective of Chōshū's motivation in joining Satsuma, Craig was impressed by the weakness of class consciousness, the strength of the vertical ties of samurai loyalty to the han, and the passive attachment of commoners to local political units. The morale of samurai in Chōshū was high. They were motivated to oppose the bakufu not by economic grievances but rather by their long-standing enmity toward the clan that had done in their ancestors centuries before. Craig concludes that "dissatisfactions . . . were not the sole or even the chief internal factor determining the course of the Restoration. On the contrary . . . the Restoration stemmed more from the strength of the values and institutions of the old society than from their weaknesses."[15]

The strength of traditional institutions and values helps explain the Restoration but not the revolution that ensued after 1868. Why did the Chōshū and Satsuma forces, if they were intent on preserving their traditional values and institutions, not build another bakufu? Why did they proceed to destroy the old order? Here most writers emphasize the nationalism of the new ruling elite, their determination to make whatever changes were required to restore national sovereignty. The motivations that initially inspired their campaign to destroy the Tokugawa gave way to recognition that traditional institutions were not equal to the tasks of national defense. In this sense, William Beasley concluded that the Restoration is best considered a "nationalist revolution, perhaps thereby giving recognition to the nature of the emotions that above all brought it about."[16]

Patriotism was certainly a prime motivation for the revolutionary changes that the new leaders embarked upon, but does this emotional reaction to the foreign crisis tell the whole story? If old values were strong in the outlying domains of Chōshū and Satsuma, as Craig contends, they were nonetheless weakened in many parts of the heartland, where the economic basis of the system had been transformed, where the problems of government were unsolved and morale sorely tried. The fact that the bakufu structure fell as easily as it did and was not replaced by another feudal military government owed much to the debilitation and frustration that long-term social and economic change had wrought. The intense emotional reaction of the shishi to the bakufu's capitulation to foreign demands, and the dissatisfactions among peasants, inarticulate or backward-looking as they may have been, nonetheless were symptomatic of a disposition for radical change from the traditional social order. Beasley believes that the Restoration lacked "the avowed social purpose that gives the 'great' revolutions of history a certain common character," but other historians are not so sure.[17]

The old society was no longer seen as a source of strength by significant numbers of all classes. Many writers now argue that in addition to a patriotic desire to respond to the foreign crisis, the Restoration was motivated by radical dissatisfaction with the domestic social order. Najita objects to interpretations of the Restoration as simply a political process, with limited revolutionary inspiration, whereby "a small group of ambitious samurai . . . restored the archaic king to enhance their narrow political interests."[18] So narrow a focus obscures the breadth of revolutionary discontent that set the stage for the

Restoration. He and other historians believe that the role of ideas and social movements has been slighted.

Until recent years the role of new ideas and revolutionary thinking in laying the basis for the Restoration has been underrated. It was often said that the leaders of the Restoration lacked a clear blueprint for the future, a clearly articulated set of goals they wanted to achieve. Many historians are giving attention to a rising tide of radical thinking that began in the eighteenth century when, in the face of the commercialization of the economy, the official orthodoxy clearly was no longer an adequate description of reality. Although most Tokugawa thinkers were conservative and fell into the category of fundamentalist reformers, urging a rollback of the changes that had occurred, some thinkers were clearly of what we have called the realist school, who saw systemic change as both inevitable and desirable. They called for revolutionary changes of policy that foreshadowed the Meiji reforms. To take just one example, the political economist Honda Toshiaki, writing about 1800, advocated radical structural changes to solve the crisis at hand. He urged an agenda of change that foreshadowed the policies of national wealth and power that the Meiji government subsequently implemented. In place of a feudal structure, Honda wanted a highly centralized government that could control the economy, establish universal education, adopt Western science, construct a merchant marine, conduct foreign trade, and provide a strong national defense.

A recent school of historical writing rejects a narrow political focus and argues that such a limited view overlooks the social foundations of revolutionary change. These historians stress the role of the populace or the "crowd" in setting the stage for the Restoration. They depict a restless and volatile society, rife with discontent and disorder, its stability undermined not just by the coming of foreigners but by the ineffectiveness of government. The resulting anomie took many forms, not necessarily political or coherent, but nonetheless reflective of a widely felt sense of dislocation and disarray, particularly in central Japan, in those areas most affected by social and economic change. George Wilson points to a diversity of expressions of popular anxiety in which hundreds of thousands of people participated at the end of the Tokugawa Period: new religions, millenarian movements, mass pilgrimages to sacred places, urban riots and reveling, and peasant uprisings. The malaise that pervaded the populace "emboldened unhappy elements within the samurai elite," Wilson writes. "The samurai elite and the popular movements were simultaneously groping for a new and stable order in Japan."[19] There was a breakdown of public order. "Commoners became disobedient, rude, and abusive of officials, and were less and less deterred by threats of dire punishment."[20] A vacuum in society cried out for strong and purposeful leadership.

The new government set about restoring order after 1868, suppressing many of the signs of disarray and malaise, consolidating power, and creating a national ethic that would answer the popular need for surety and direction.

We are left with a complex view of causation. At its heart, the Restoration was a political change carried out by a party within the old samurai elite and coming from the traditional feudal enemies of the Tokugawa. As their symbol, the anti-Tokugawa forces restored the Emperor, the traditional source of political legitimacy, to the center of government. They did not seek to interfere with landholding patterns, but rather confirmed the wealthy peasants in their dominant position in the countryside. To this extent, the Restoration was conservative. But it was precipitated by profound social and economic change and pervasive discontent among all classes of Japanese that undermined the legitimacy of the Tokugawa system. To a growing number of reform thinkers, Tokugawa institutions no longer seemed adequate to cope with the new social and economic conditions. The role of the foreign crisis was to bring into sharp focus the impotence of the old system and to prompt revolutionary action to create a new order.

An important key to understanding Japan's rapid response to the challenge of the West in the years after 1868 (in contrast to the slow response of other countries in Asia) is the fact that discontent with the old order was widespread and felt in every social class. The country was ready for change. In other words, saying simply that the new leaders were impelled by nationalism or the desire to make Japan the military equal of Western nations is not sufficient. In other Asian countries there was also plenty of patriotic feeling and understanding of Western technological superiority. What was distinctive about the Japanese case, as Thomas Smith observes, was "the conviction that the traditional social order was not itself a source of strength."[21] Had Perry come to a country that was more stable, a country that was more content with its institutions, the response would have been very different.

Notes

1. Ronald P. Toby, *State and Diplomacy in Early Modern Japan: Asia in the Development of the Tokugawa Bakufu* (Stanford, Calif.: Stanford University Press, 1991), 8.
2. Marius B. Jansen, *China in the Tokugawa World* (Cambridge, Mass.: Harvard University Press, 1992), 3.
3. These are the observations of Haga Tōru. See Yamazaki Masakazu and Haga Tōru, "Reexamining the Era of National Seclusion," *Japan Echo* 19 (winter 1992), 73–75.
4. Bob Tadashi Wakabayashi, *Anti-Foreignism and Western Learning in Early Mod-*

ern Japan: The New Theses of 1825 (Cambridge, Mass.: Harvard University Press, 1986), 60.

5. Ibid., 168–169.
6. Ibid., 124.
7. Carmen Blacker, "Ōhashi Totsuan: A Study in Anti-Western Thought," in *Transactions of the Asiatic Society of Japan,* series 3, vol. 7 (Yokohama: Asiatic Society of Japan, 1959), 165.
8. Harold Bolitho, "Abe Masahirō and the New Japan," in *The Bakufu in Japanese History,* ed. Jeffrey P. Mass and William B. Hauser (Stanford, Calif.: Stanford University Press, 1985), 182.
9. William G. Beasley, *Select Documents on Japanese Foreign Policy, 1853–1868* (London: Oxford University Press, 1955), 117.
10. William G. Beasley, *The Meiji Restoration* (Stanford, Calif.: Stanford University Press, 1972), 96.
11. Ibid., 117.
12. Marius B. Jansen, *Sakamoto Ryōma and the Meiji Restoration* (Princeton, N.J.: Princeton University Press, 1961), 98.
13. Albert M. Craig, *Chōshū in the Meiji Restoration* (Cambridge, Mass.: Harvard University Press, 1961), 20–21.
14. Ibid., 360.
15. Ibid., 353.
16. Beasley, *Meiji Restoration,* 424.
17. Ibid., 423.
18. Najita Tetsuo, "Conceptual Consciousness in the Meiji Ishin," in *Meiji Ishin: Restoration and Revolution,* ed. Nagai Michio and Miguel Urrutia (Tokyo: United Nations University, 1985), 87.
19. George M. Wilson, *Patriots and Redeemers in Japan: Motives in the Meiji Restoration* (Chicago: University of Chicago Press, 1992), 80.
20. James W. White, "State Growth and Popular Protest in Tokugawa Japan," *Journal of Japanese Studies* 14 (winter 1988), 24.
21. Thomas C. Smith, *Native Sources of Japanese Industrialization, 1750–1920* (Berkeley: University of California Press, 1988), 152–153.

Revolution in Japan's Worldview

The term Meiji Restoration is applied not only to the events leading up to the overthrow of the Tokugawa Shogunate, but also to the whole cluster of reforms that followed. For more than two decades, from 1868 down to 1890, a series of reforms was promulgated that established constitutional government and put Japan on the road to industrialization. As they groped for alternatives to the old order, Japan's new leaders drew heavily for inspiration on the ideas and institutions of Western societies. Later we shall consider those institutional reforms and the beginning of Japanese industrialization, but we need first to discuss why Japan proved so open to new ideas and hence so responsive to the Western challenge.

One of the most extraordinary features of modern Japanese history is that sudden change in its view of the world. The Japanese as a people demonstrated extraordinary "intellectual mobility"—an unusual flexibility of thought, which allowed the predominant opinion of its leaders to shift very rapidly from xenophobia to xenophilia, from hatred of Western barbarians to adulation of Western culture. Some Japanese underwent a gradual metamorphosis in their worldview; many others seemed to have undergone swift emotional conversions. Accounting for the rapidity with which attitudes were reversed is often difficult. Certainly the iconoclastic writings of political economists in the late Tokugawa Period prepared the way. Nevertheless, the new leaders of the government that came to power in 1868 had no clear idea of the extent of the reforms they wished to undertake, nor of the kinds of institutional changes they wished to make. But they did declare, in the Imperial Charter Oath, which they had the boy Emperor issue in 1868, that "knowledge shall be sought for all over the world, and thereby the foundations of imperial rule shall be strengthened" and that "all absurd customs of olden times shall be abandoned and all actions shall be based on international usage." These phrases signified a new openness to the outside world, and for the next two decades there followed a period of extraordinary borrowing, a period often described as one of intoxication with Western things and Western ideas. Where other Asian countries remained committed to their traditional knowledge and institutions, Japan undertook sweeping changes. A leading survey of modern world history concludes that this "Westernization of Japan" during the Meiji Period (1868–1912) "still stands as the most remarkable transformation ever undergone by any people in so short a time."[1]

In order to understand this sudden shift in attitude, it is well to remember that many Japanese "Westernizers" were in a manner anti-Western. For them, Westernization was a means to an anti-Western end: by adopting the techniques and institutions of Western society they hoped to eliminate all manifestations of Western power, especially the unequal treaties, from their country. The jōi goal of expelling the foreigners, in other words, remained unchanged. (Although when we come to the 1880s and the craze for Western things reaches a peak—and we find Japanese leaders wearing top hats, studying ballroom dancing, going to masked balls with foreign women, and living in Western-style houses—we may begin to wonder just how anti-Western Westernization really was!) Essentially, the observation is valid that national security remained the object even during the twenty-five years after 1868, when Japanese leadership looked to Western countries for models of all kinds of institutional reforms.

The table[2] on page 79 shows where Japan turned in the first Meiji years for specific models of new organizations. Later, as we shall see, in creating constitutional and bureaucratic organizations the Meiji leaders turned especially to German models. In addition to these specific models for organizations, Meiji leaders also adopted general Western models of such organizations as the newspaper, factory, incorporated enterprise, railway, and stock exchange.

Another frequent observation about the sudden reversal of attitudes is that Japan had a tradition of borrowing—of adopting and assimilating foreign culture to its own ends. In contrast to the ethnic self-sufficiency of the Chinese, Japan as an island country was keenly aware of the value of cultural assimilation in its history.

It is important to bear in mind as well the timing of the Western challenge. Momentum for change had been gathering for many decades. Had discontent not been so widespread, it stands to reason that the disposition to set aside many aspects of tradition would have been correspondingly less. But there was no great struggle to preserve the old order; it fell quite easily. The failure of the Tokugawa shogunate to deal not only with its manifold domestic problems but with the foreign threat, which materialized in the first infringements of national sovereignty in Japan's history, prepared the way for change. The fact

Source	Organization	Year Initiated
Britain	Navy	1869
	Telegraph system	1869
	Postal system	1872
	Postal savings system	1875
France	Army	1869
	Primary school system	1872
	Tokyo *Keishi-chō* (police)	1874
	Judicial system	1872
	Kempeitai (military police)	1881
United States	Primary school system[a]	1879
	National bank system	1872
	Sapporo Agricultural College	1879
Germany	Army[a]	1878
Belgium	Bank of Japan	1882

[a]Reorganization on a new model.

that the Western challenge coincided in Japan with domestic political revolution was exceedingly important: for those coming to power in such circumstances are free to make radical reforms in a way that people long entrenched are not.

Moreover, the nature of the new political leadership was of critical importance. The Meiji leaders were young: their average age in 1868 was slightly older than thirty. They came out of the old samurai elite. As such they proved keenly perceptive of Western military strength and its basis in scientific and technological achievement. They were, therefore, more disposed to accept whatever changes seemed necessary to increase Japanese strength than was true, for example, of the scholar-gentry in China. The goal of national strength justified, in turn, myriad social and economic changes.

As a feudal elite they had not owed their position to the possession of a traditional body of knowledge, as did the Confucian literati in China. Hence, they felt much less threatened by Western learning. Nor were they bound to the past, in a social sense, so strongly as were many traditional elites. Their ties to the land had been broken in the seventeenth century when they had moved from the countryside to the new castle towns. Their power was rooted in bureaucratic positions rather than in landholding. Hall stresses that they

> did not constitute an entrenched land-based gentry as in China, able to back up their interests in the face of modern change. Without an economic base, the resentment they felt toward the reforms

> which deprived them of their feudal privileges was soon dissipated. Instead, they were forced to ride with the times, to join the new government or to seek security in the new economic opportunities which were offered them. . . . In other words, they were a leaven for change rather than an obstacle.[3]

Because they were free of the fear that most aristocracies have of losing land and property, the samurai proved remarkably receptive to new ideas and institutions. "Few ruling classes," writes Thomas Smith, "have been so free of economic bias against change."[4]

Fukuzawa and the New Westernism

No one wrote more persuasively or with greater influence on behalf of the new disposition toward wholesale borrowing from Western culture than Fukuzawa Yukichi (1835–1901). Japan's submission to the challenge of the Perry mission and to the subsequent demands for the forced opening of the ports was initially regarded as a political failure, for which the Tokugawa were blamed. As the magnitude of Western military superiority came to be understood, however, the failure was more often seen as a cultural one, requiring sweeping, fundamental reforms. Fukuzawa was the leading proponent of this line of thought.

Born into a family of lower samurai from the province of Buzen in northern Kyushu, Fukuzawa as a young man evidently chafed under the restrictions of the feudal hierarchy. In his autobiography he wrote,

> the thing that made me most unhappy in Nakatsu [the domain in which he grew up] was the restriction of rank and position. Not only on official occasions, but in private intercourse, and even among children, the distinctions between high and low were clearly defined. Children of lower samurai families like ours were obliged to use a respectful manner of address in speaking to the children of high samurai families, while these children invariably used an arrogant form of address to us.

And Fukazawa went on, with typical modesty, "in school I was the best student and no children made light of me there. But once out of the school room, those children would give themselves airs as superiors to me; yet I was sure I was no inferior, not even in physical power. In all this, I could not free myself from discontent though I was still a child."[5]

His chance to leave Nakatsu came in 1854 when he was nineteen years old. It was the year after Perry's arrival, and Fukuzawa was sent to Nagasaki and then to Ogata's school in Osaka for the so-called Dutch studies. Four years later he was sent to Edo by the han officials and ordered to establish a school for Dutch studies that other young samurai from his han could attend—the school that later grew into

The first Japanese embassy to the United States at the Navy Yard, Washington, D.C., 1860.
National Archives

Keiō University. He soon learned English and in 1860 gained passage on a ship to San Francisco, which was part of the official mission going to the United States for ratification of the Harris Treaty.

While in San Francisco it was not so much the technological achievements that impressed Fukuzawa, for his years of Dutch study had acquainted him with the scientific principles involved:

> Our hosts in San Francisco were very considerate in showing us examples of modern industry. There was as yet no railway laid to the city, nor was there any electric light in use. But the telegraph system and also Galvani's electroplating were already in use. Then we were taken to a sugar refinery and had the principle of the operation explained to us quite minutely. I am sure that our hosts thought they were showing us something entirely new, naturally looking for our surprise at each new device of modern engineering. But on the contrary, there was really nothing new, at least to me. . . . I had been studying nothing else but such scientific principles ever since I had entered Ogata's school.[6]

What fascinated him far more were social practices and institutions, such as relations between the sexes, family customs, life insurance, the postal and banking systems, hospitals, and lunatic asylums. On this and succeeding trips (to Europe in 1862 and to America again in 1867) he took copious notes on his observations. Fukuzawa first gained fame in 1866 with publication of his book *Seiyō jijō (Conditions in the West),* one of the most important books published in Japan in modern times. It was immensely popular because it described the kinds of everyday social institutions in Western countries that the Japanese were most curious about. In short order he published a number of sequels and became an established authority on the West.

Fukuzawa took no active part in the Restoration. But when he realized that the new Meiji government was receptive to reform proposals, the whole tenor of his writings changed. Instead of merely recording information about Western society, he began vigorously urging the adoption of Western values and institutions and the fundamental transformation of Japanese culture. In his later books he went beyond the proposals of Sakuma Shōzan and others who had advocated adoption of Western science while preserving traditional values and social practices. Fukuzawa argued that one could not cling to Confucian ethics and acquire an understanding of Western science, because the former carried with it an attitude toward nature and society that was irreconcilable with scientific habits of thought. The essence of modern civilization, he contended, was found in the cultivation of individual qualities of independence, initiative, and self-reliance. Because he believed that the feudal system and Confucian values stunted those qualities, he made all-out attacks on traditional Japanese culture.

In one of his most important treatises, *Gakumon no susume (An Encouragement of Learning),* he began with words that became famous, "Heaven did not create men above men, nor set men below men," and thus succinctly summarized the revolt against inflexible hereditary status that had been brewing throughout the latter half of the Tokugawa Period. He went on to explain that a young man's position in society should be determined by his grasp of utilitarian knowledge. He therefore, throughout his writings, attacked Confucianism, traditional education, and authoritarian government. As an educator, newspaper editor, and advisor to politicians, he exercised immense influence over the generation of Japanese that opened the country and rebuilt its institutions.

Women, Family, and the Limits of Reform

The extent to which Fukuzawa carried his radical critique of the old society is illustrated by his views on women and the family. In *Bummei-ron no gairyaku (An Outline of Civilization),* he located the fundamental flaw of Japanese culture in its basic institution—the family. By inculcating values of absolute power on the one hand and unquestioning deference on the other, the Japanese family suppressed the spirit of independence that had formed Western civilization. Fukuzawa and other early Meiji reformers blamed the family for the absence of values on which modern scientific civilization depended. They said that it provided the foundation for authoritarian government.

The reformers frequently expressed hope of replacing the extended hierarchical family groups with independent nuclear households consisting of only parents and children and marked by the elevation of women to a new status. Fukuzawa's best-known essay in this regard was a critique of the seventeenth-century Confucian tract *The Great Learning for Women,* which had been used in the Tokugawa Period to instruct samurai wives and daughters in their roles and behavior. The tract instructed them that the "great lifelong duty of a woman is obedience"; and that the "five infirmities" (indocility, discontent, slander, jealousy, and silliness) found in "seven or eight of every ten women" arise from and exacerbate "the inferiority of women to men."[7] A woman should cure these maladies through introspection, self-reproach, and by learning to look to her husband "as though he were heaven itself." In his essay "A New Great Learning for Women" (1899), Fukuzawa advocated modern education for women and the right to inherit property. Fukuzawa's fellow reformer, Mori Arinori, who had served as Japan's first envoy to America (1870–1872), wrote in "Essay on Wives" that marriages should have greater equality; and when he subsequently married he insisted that the union be governed by a Western-style contract—Fukuzawa was a witness—to demonstrate the equality of the partnership.

These reform efforts, however, had limits: the reformers found practicing what they preached difficult. Mori subsequently dissolved his marriage, explaining that his wife had become "peculiar and flighty" as a result of the new relationship and that "to attempt a marriage like that with an uneducated Japanese woman was my mistake."[8] Fukuzawa's own daughters later related that their father raised them in the strictest orthodoxy: they were not given a modern education and their views were not consulted in the choice of their marriage partners. Evidently in those reforms that dealt with the most fundamental institutions of life, especially the changes in their own families, the reformers were hard-pressed to live up to their ideals. In such things Fukuzawa was less than wholehearted and once confessed, regarding some of his reform proposals, "A wine merchant is not always a drinker, a cake dealer does not always go in search of sweets. You should not make hasty judgment of the dealer's taste for what he sells in his shop." Fukuzawa may have believed, rationally, that for the good of the nation Japan needed to change its social values, but emotionally he remained tied to the old ways. As one

Fukuzawa Yukichi in 1887. *Kyodo News Service of Japan*

prominent scholar concluded, "Lurking deep in [Fukuzawa's] heart and blood was the old samurai spirit."[9]

Agents of Cultural Revolution

To understand the responsiveness of Japanese society and the rapidity with which changes that led to industrialization and constitutional government were instituted, it is important to emphasize that the revolution was carried out from above, by a party from the traditional elite. At the time of the Meiji Restoration, as we have seen, social malaise was expressed in many ways, including new religions, millenarian movements, and popular revelry in the cities of central Japan, but there was no great immediate social upheaval. No knockdown drag-out struggle erupted between the old ruling class and a rising bourgeoisie, challenging samurai authority and demanding political rights. "There was no democratic revolution in Japan," Thomas Smith writes, "because none was necessary: the aristocracy itself was revolutionary."[10] The young samurai who came to power in 1868 carried out sweeping reforms that included doing away with the privileges of their own class.

Of great significance in determining the outlook of the new government were the impressions formed by an official mission to the United States and Europe from 1871 to 1873. Comprising more than 100 members, many of whom had never before been abroad, the mission was headed by Prince Iwakura Tomomi, the most prestigious member of the new ruling group, and it included the key leaders Ōkubo Toshimichi, Kido Kōin, and Itō Hirobumi. The mission's ostensible purpose was to make preliminary soundings for revision of the unequal treaties but more fundamentally, Iwakura said, the mission was "to discover the great principles which are to be our guide in the future."[11] The journey lasted nearly two years and permitted a thorough examination of the world's most advanced nations. The group's members wanted to discover the sources of Western power and wealth so that a plan for strengthening the Japanese state could be worked out. They began with visits to nine cities in the United States, followed by sojourns in England and Scotland, France, Belgium, the Netherlands, Germany, Russia, Denmark, Sweden, Italy, Austria, and Switzerland. In the course of the trip, Ōkubo Toshimichi wrote to a colleague at home that they were leaving no stone unturned: "Courts, prisons, schools, trading firms, factories and shipyards, iron foundries, sugar refineries, paper plants, wool and cotton spinning and weaving, silver, cutlery, and glass plants, coal and salt mines, . . . —there is nowhere we haven't gone."[12]

The final report of the Iwakura mission was a massive 2,000-page, five-volume chronicle of the mission's observations and the conclusions of its leaders. The most striking aspect of the report is its pervasive optimism. One might suppose that the visitors would have been overwhelmed by Western civilization and the task of trying to match its achievements. Instead one finds a bold self-confidence that what the West had accomplished was of recent origin and that Japan through careful planning and hard work could catch up:

> Most of the countries in Europe shine with the light of civilization and abound in wealth and power. Their trade is prosperous, their technology is superior, and they greatly enjoy the pleasures and comforts of life. When one observes such conditions, one is apt to think that these countries have always been like this, but this is not the case—the wealth and prosperity one sees now in Europe dates

> to an appreciable degree from the period after 1800. It has taken scarcely forty years to produce such conditions. . . . How different the Europe of today is from the Europe of forty years ago can be imagined easily. There were no trains running on the land; there were no steamships operating on the water. There was no transmission of news by telegraph. . . . Those who read this record should reflect upon the lesson to be drawn for Japan. . . ."[13]

The conversion of Ōkubo Toshimichi, one of the strongest men in the new government, illustrates the enthusiasm that many of the Meiji leaders acquired for full-scale reform. What he saw in the West deeply influenced his thinking; England especially impressed him. He recorded his awe at "the excellence of the English transportation network with its railways and canals reaching into remote areas and with its well-kept carriage roads and bridges." Industrial enterprises in city after city affected him: the textile mills of Manchester, the shipbuilding yards of Liverpool, the Armstrong gun factory of Newcastle, and iron and steel works of Sheffield. Ōkubo confided to his traveling companions that before leaving Japan he had felt his ambitions were realized: centralizing power in the imperial government had been a great achievement. Now, however, he saw that many tasks remained, that Japan did not begin to compare with "the more progressive powers in the world."[14]

So he returned to Japan with new ambitions and threw himself into further reforms, inspired by the Western example, with a zeal that was especially apparent in his personal life. He began to adopt many of the trappings of Western civilization. With great fastidiousness, for example, he wore European dress, and was the first to appear at court with a Western-style haircut. He built a pretentious Western-style house, appointed with Western furniture, and boasted to his friends that "even foreigners to whom I have shown the house have praised it so I am quite pleased."[15] Daily he rode to the government offices in a fine two-horse English carriage. But more important, he began to push national reforms beyond the limits of what he had earlier seen as his goals. Centralization of power in a new imperial government was not sufficient; Japan would have to carry out sweeping reforms of its whole society if it were to become the equal of the Western powers.

The government hastened the adoption of the new technology and new institutions by hiring more than 3,000 foreign advisors over the course of the Meiji Period. They included engineers, technicians, field workers, military consultants, teachers, and financial and legal advisors. In all they contributed the equivalent of 10,000 years of service. Most of this work was during the first fifteen years of the Meiji Period. Then, once the Japanese had fully exploited the Westerners' expertise and learned the new ways, they replaced the foreign advisors with Japanese. At the same time, in "the first great student migration of modern times," more than 11,000 passports were issued for overseas study between 1868 and 1902. In excess of one-half went to the United States, but the government-sponsored students increasingly were sent to Germany once it became the preferred model in organizing Japan's governmental, legal, and military organizations.[16]

In addition to the industrial and military power that adoption of Western technology promised, another important motivation for Japanese cultural borrowing was the drive for national equality and respect. Ōkuma Shigenobu, one of the prominent Meiji leaders, later wrote that "to attain an equal footing with the other powers . . . has been the impulse underlying all the national changes that have taken place."[17] From 1868 to 1894 the prime goal of Japanese foreign policy was revision of the unequal treaties, so as to stand on equal footing with Western countries and escape the semicolonial status to which extraterritoriality and tariff control had relegated Japan. Leaders of the government concluded from discussions with Western diplomatic representatives that revision of the treaties depended not only on the development of national power but on legal and administrative reforms that would make Japan a "civilized" country capable of proper treatment of foreign nationals. The government moved quickly to plan such reforms. Committees appointed to compile penal and civil codes took French law as a model and engaged the French jurist Gustave Emile Boissonade to advise them in compiling laws. A German legal expert, Hermann Roesler, was entrusted with drafting a commercial code. As we shall see, the desire to impress Westerners with Japan's civilized progress was also a constant stimulus to the establishment of constitutional government.

The zeal for treaty revision elicited many bureaucratic efforts to reform Japanese customs. Government policy sought to modify traditional morality to avoid the criticism and disapproval of foreigners. Ordinances forbidding public nakedness and mixed bathing in public bathhouses explained that, although "this is the general custom and is not so despised among ourselves, in foreign countries this is looked on with great contempt. You should, therefore, consider it a great shame."[18]

Efforts to win foreigners' approval also included methods of artful persuasion. In 1883 the Rokumeikan, a gaudy Victorian hall, was opened in Tokyo so that government officials could entertain foreign residents with cards, billiards, Western music, and lavish balls. Itō Hirobumi, the Prime Minister, gave a spectacular costume ball for foreign residents, in which he appeared as a Venetian nobleman and Inoue Kaoru, the foreign minister, as a strolling musician. It is clear from such episodes that the government leaders were pressing a Westernization policy not only as a means of strengthening the nation, but also as a part of the treaty revision effort.

A primary agent of the cultural revolution in the early Meiji Period was the new educational system. Education took on the burden of imparting a knowledge and understanding of Western culture and thereby preparing the young for occupations in an industrial society. The classical curriculum, which had already been modified in the late Tokugawa Period, was now almost wholly replaced by the study of Western languages, by scientific and technical training, and by a variety of disciplines whose content was adopted from Western education.

Japanese statesmen and intellectuals in the early Meiji Period often looked back with contempt and distaste at the school system of the Tokugawa Period. Western-style and Tokugawa-style education appeared in sharp contrast in their minds. Fukuzawa was undoubtedly the most articulate advocate of the new learning, which he regarded as practical, scientific, and useful; and he was the most bitter critic of the traditional Confucian-oriented learning in Tokugawa Japan, which he regarded as stagnant, useless, and unprogressive. In a typical passage he wrote:

> The only purpose of education is to show that Man was created by Heaven to gain the knowledge required for the satisfaction of his needs for food, shelter, and clothing, and for living harmoniously with his fellows. To be able to read difficult old books or to compose poetry is all very nice and pleasant but it is not really worth the praise given to great scholars of Chinese and Japanese in the past.
>
> How many Chinese scholars have been good at managing their domestic affairs? How many clever men have been good at poetry? No wonder that a wise parent, a shopkeeper, or a farmer is alarmed when his son displays a taste for study! . . . What is really wanted is learning that is close to the needs of man's daily life.
>
> A man who can recite the chronicles but does not know the price of food, a man who has penetrated deeply into the classics and history but cannot carry out a simple business transaction—such people as these are nothing but rice-consuming dictionaries, of no use to their country but only a hindrance to its economy. Managing your household is learning, understanding the trend of the times is learning, but why should reading old books be called learning?[19]

This passage reflects the contempt that Fukuzawa and his contemporaries in the 1870s felt for traditional education, with its emphasis on single-minded study of the Confucian classics. Today, however, with the advantage of perspective, we can look back and see many valuable contributions that the Tokugawa educational system made to the efforts by Fukuzawa and others to strengthen their country and transform it into a great industrial power.

In the first place, the Japanese during the Tokugawa Period had a vast educational network. The decades leading up to the Restoration saw a growing popular desire for self-improvement; society offered opportunities to apply improved skills, and the result was a surge of educational aspiration. By 1868 more than 11,000 schools of all kinds operated throughout Japan, ranging from the bakufu and domain schools for samurai to private academies and local schools (*terakoya*) for the commoners. The following table suggests the popular enthusiasm for schooling in the years before and immediately after the Restoration.

Development of Types of Schools by Date of Establishment[20]

Year	Private Academies	Local Schools	Domain Schools
Before 1750	19	47	40
1751–1788	38	194	48
1789–1829	207	1,286	78
1830–1867	796	8,675	56
1868–1872	182	1,035	48
Total	1,242	11,237	270

Private academies, such as Ogata's school for Dutch studies in Osaka, which Fukuzawa attended, were generally in the homes of established scholars who could draw students from all classes and all parts of the country. The numerous local schools, run by public-spirited citizens without official support, offered rudimentary training in reading, writing, and arithmetic to merchants, farmers, and town dwellers.

At the end of the Tokugawa Period almost all the children of the samurai class attended some kind of school for some period of time, and by the 1860s about 40 percent of male children and 15 percent of female children attended school. Herbert Passin estimates that attendance in the immediate pre–Meiji Period was about 1,300,000 children, and he points out that this figure corresponds almost exactly with school attendance in 1873, the first year of the modern school system. "Japanese were prepared for a modern school system because by the end of the Tokugawa Period millions of families had assimilated the routines it required into their mode of life. . . . In other words, the Japanese population was ready for the formal routines and disciplines of modern education because it had already had a long experience of learning in a setting of formal routines and disciplines."[21] The point is that the sheer presence of education as a widespread part of the environment, regardless of its content, is important.

Additionally, a much more apparent advantage that Tokugawa education bequeathed the Meiji Japanese was a high literacy rate.

Passin estimates that by the end of the Tokugawa Period 40 percent of males were literate. Richard Rubinger, a careful student of the Tokugawa education system, cautions that these estimates are rough and problematic.[22] In any case, Japanese literacy rates in 1868 do appear to compare very favorably with contemporary European countries. It made the Japanese a potentially highly skilled population, and as Dore stresses, it helped implant the idea of progress and the notion of self-improvement. Education was sometimes a means of advancement in Tokugawa society, and it therefore created an emphasis on "achievement" and "ambition." By the end of the Tokugawa Period a desire to excel pervaded the schools. Dore provides an amusing example from a memoir describing how a boy and three of his dormitory friends in the 1850s engaged in a prolonged reading competition in a domain school: "We really went all out that month. If one of us got a page ahead the others would turn pale. We hardly took time to chew our food properly, and we drank as little water as possible in order that the others should not get ahead in the time wasted going to the lavatory—so keen were we to get a line or two ahead of the others."[23] The drive to excel, already far developed in late Tokugawa times, was surely in part responsible for the explosion of individual energies that characterized the Japanese of the Meiji Period and their desire to rise in the social hierarchy. A precept taught commoners in a local school makes clear how the ethic of achievement, reinforced by the threat of shame, was inculcated in children: "Illiteracy is a form of blindness. It brings shame on your teacher, shame on your parents, and shame on yourself. . . . Determine to succeed, study with all your might, never forgetting the shame of failure."[24] It is also worth mentioning, as Dore does, that the high literacy rate derived from Tokugawa education made the Japanese people more accessible to new ideas and new techniques, and it facilitated development of national consciousness. Both of these factors were important ingredients of the reforms Fukuzawa sought.

Finally, another aspect of the Tokugawa legacy that Fukuzawa and his contemporaries tended to forget was the fact that many of the things they advocated had already been developing in late Tokugawa times. Practical subjects, for example, had been given increasing attention despite a certain resistance by conservative Confucianists. Among the common people vocational education was widespread, and the shogunate and some of the important domains had already made major efforts in the development of technical training. The recognition of ability and special training, which was such an important underlying element of the ideology of early Meiji education, had already started in the 1840s. The heritage of Tokugawa education, therefore, was not so burdensome as Fukuzawa seemed to believe. In fact, an extensive modern educational system could not have been so readily established without it.

In 1871 the Ministry of Education was established, and the following year the Fundamental Code of Education was promulgated, emphasizing in its preamble that education should be universal and utilitarian. It set the ambitious goal that "there shall, in the future, be no community with an illiterate family, or a family with an illiterate person." It made four years of education compulsory for every child. Although that goal was not immediately realized, by the turn of the century more than 90 percent of the children of statutory school age were in school.

The content of the new education was almost entirely drawn from the West. Dr. David Murray of Rutgers University was brought to Japan in 1873 as an advisor to the Ministry of Education. He and other American advisors were instrumental in the adoption of classroom readers that were almost direct translations of American textbooks, in the acceptance of coeducational common schools as the basic unit of the school system, and in the formation of teachers' colleges and vocational (particularly agricultural) schools. After the ban on Christianity was lifted in 1873, missionaries played a prominent role in the founding of new educational institutions, many of which later became colleges and universities. Principally by this vehicle, Christianity exercised a strong influence on the better-educated Japanese.

The new schools became agents of cultural and therefore social revolution. Success no longer depended on traditional skills acquired in the family; rather it depended on mastery of some aspect of the new learning, such as mechanical engineering, French law, double-entry bookkeeping, or English conversation. These were skills learned in the new schools—which were open to everyone. In this sense, "all classes of Japanese," in Thomas Smith's valuable phrase, "were born cultural equals" in the Meiji Period.[25] The adoption of industrial technology created a great number of new educational groups, and professions opened up in industry, finance, journalism, education, and bureaucracy.

Education became the prime mechanism for social advancement. "Getting on" in the world, rising above one's father's station, became the consuming ambition of the "youth of Meiji." Japanese society thus became much more mobile. Young men longed to leave the countryside, go to the cities, and enter new occupations. Many youth from humble origins rose meteorlike to the heights of leadership in this freer society. That Samuel Smiles's *Self Help* was one of the most popular of the translated works in the Meiji Period was testimony to the emphasis upon getting ahead through hard work and ambition.

For a whole generation of youth in the 1870s and 1880s innovation and foreignness became vogue. As Dore writes: "Wearing a stovepipe hat, eating beef, forming a joint-stock company, using soap instead of friction, running committees by formal rules, planting new strains of wheat, consuming tobacco wrapped in paper rather than in a pipe, reading the Bible, adopting double-entry bookkeeping, sitting on chairs, were all parts of the new, Western, and, in the cant-phrase of the time, 'civilized and enlightened' way of life."[26] Many Japanese came to identify with patterns of Western civilization, believing them representative of universal patterns of development to which all progressive nations must conform. As Japan advanced it must inevitably become more like Western societies. Progress, in this view, required discarding traditional Asian institutions, customs, and patterns of social behavior. There was a general revulsion from an Asian identity. Fukuzawa wrote in 1885 that Japan should "escape from Asia":

> Today China and Korea are no help at all to our country. On the contrary, because our three countries are adjacent we are sometimes regarded as the same in the eyes of civilized Western peoples. Appraisals of China and Korea are applied to our country . . . and indirectly this greatly impedes our foreign policy. It is really a great misfortune for our country. It follows that in making our present plans we have not time to await the development of neighboring countries and join them in reviving Asia. Rather, we should escape from them and join the company of Western civilized nations.[27]

This kind of alienation from Japan's own cultural heritage provided a powerful impetus to institutional reform in the generation after the restoration.

The Challenge of the Japanese Enlightenment[28]

Let us sum up the dominant themes of influence exercised by Western culture during the period of civilization and enlightenment (*bummei kaika*) that held sway in the first two decades of the Meiji Period. The full sweep of European enlightenment and nineteenth-century liberal thought was introduced into Japan in a very short space of time. Western liberal civilization challenged Japan's traditional beliefs, its traditional social organization, and its traditional system of government with such ceaseless persistence as to throw nearly every area of life into a state of turmoil.

The first major theme of the Japanese enlightenment was that advocates of Western values were dominated by a negative view of Japan's traditional institutions and the learning that underlay them. Fukuzawa wrote of this sweeping rejection of his heritage: "If we compare the knowledge of the Japanese and Westerners in letters, in techniques, in commerce, or in industry, from the smallest to the largest matter . . . there is not one thing in which we excel. . . . In Japan's present condition there is nothing in which we may take pride vis-à-vis the West. All that Japan has to be proud of . . . is its scenery."[29]

Second, despite this thorough rejection of Japanese civilization, the enlightenment advocates held almost limitless hope for the future. As with the enlightenment in Europe, an optimistic belief held sway that human effort could master the sociopolitical environment, just as science had made it possible to master the physical environment. Japan's optimism carried over into a fierce determination to exert whatever effort was required to catch up with the West. In 1874 one of Japan's leading reformers wrote, "How will we catch up with and overtake the Western powers if we allow Sunday to be a holiday for our people?"[30]

A third dominant theme of the Japanese enlightenment stressed the cultural example of the West. Because universal laws of nature governed human behavior, Japan could, if it developed in accord with these laws, progress in the same way that Western nations had. Progress, in other words, was unilinear; it was determined by universal forces of historic development rather than by the particular trends of national history. Civilization in the West had progressed further along this universal path of development and therefore it could be looked to as an example. Civilized development meant not only that people would use the same machines; they would also think and behave in similar ways, eat the same kinds of food, wear the same kinds of clothing, live in houses of similar architecture, and enjoy the same kinds of art. A Japanese cultural identity had no place here.

A fourth dominant theme was a wholehearted commitment to science, technology, and utilitarian knowledge. The classical curriculum in the schools must be replaced by a practical learning useful for daily life. Fukuzawa's well-known condemnation of Tokugawa scholars as "rice-consuming dictionaries" concluded that "managing your household is learning, business is learning, seeking the trend of the times is learning."

Fifth, the enlightenment promulgated a new view of humanity with revolutionary implications for society and the state. It was necessary to foster a new set of values on which a more open, constitutional, and enlightened government could be founded. The Japanese enlightenment was by no means democratic in the twentieth-century sense of advocating universal suffrage or economic equality, but it did oppose old forms of social stratification and government by a closed elite. It favored an open and mobile society in which economic rewards would be commensurate with individual talent and effort. The enlightenment writers generally argued for a parliamentary government that would function through rational deliberation and enlightened legislation with responsible ministries and an impartial, law-abiding administration. They espoused free trade ideals and put their faith in an emerging internationalism. Fukuzawa saw little future for a narrow nationalism: "A country is a gathering of people. Japan is a gathering of Japanese and England is a gathering of Englishmen. Japanese and Englishmen alike are members of a common humanity; they must respect each others' rights."[31]

These enlightenment themes drew their support from the discrediting of the old society by social and economic change and by its incapacity to deal with the foreign crisis. But the extreme adulation of the Western cultural model could not sustain itself once the vogue had passed; it was too destructive of Japanese pride. Moreover, many of the new social values introduced during the enlightenment decades of the 1870s and 1880s ran counter to deeply ingrained mores of the Japanese people and, above all, were incompatible with the institutions of the countryside where the vast majority of the populace had its roots. Finally, the Meiji leaders saw that the values of the enlightenment could not coexist with the formation of the strong national consciousness required to unite the hearts and loyalties of all the people in the struggle to industrialize.

Notes

1. R. R. Palmer and Joel Colton, *A History of the Modern World,* 8th ed. (New York: Knopf, 1995), 582.
2. D. Eleanor Westney, *Imitation and Innovation: The Transfer of Western Organizational Patterns to Meiji Japan* (Cambridge, Mass.: Harvard University Press, 1987), 13.
3. John Whitney Hall and Marius B. Jansen, eds., *Studies in the Institutional History of Early Modern Japan* (Princeton, N.J.: Princeton University Press, 1968), 187.
4. Thomas C. Smith, *Native Sources of Japanese Industrialization, 1750–1920* (Berkeley: University of California Press, 1988), 142.
5. *The Autobiography of Yukichi Fukuzawa* (New York: Schocken, 1972), 18.
6. Ibid., 115.
7. Quoted in Jennifer Robertson, "The Shingaku Woman," in *Recreating Japanese Women, 1600–1945,* ed. Gail Lee Bernstein (Berkeley: University of California Press, 1991), 92.
8. Michio Nagai, "Mori Arinori," *Japan Quarterly* 11 (1964), 98–105.
9. Maruyama Masao, "Fukuzawa, Uchimura, and Okakura: Meiji Intellectuals and Westernization," *The Developing Economies* 4 (December 1966), 601.
10. Smith, *Native Sources,* 134.
11. Quoted in Marlene J. Mayo, "Rationality in the Meiji Restoration," in *Modern Japanese Leadership: Transition and Change,* ed. Bernard S. Silberman and Harry D. Harootunian (Tucson: University of Arizona Press, 1966), 356.
12. Quoted in Marius B. Jansen, "Modernization and Foreign Policy in Meiji

Japan," in *Political Development in Modern Japan,* ed. Robert E. Ward (Princeton, N.J.: Princeton University Press, 1968), 153.

13. Mayo, "Rationality in the Meiji Restoration," 357–358.
14. See Sidney Devere Brown, "Ōkubo Toshimichi: His Political and Economic Policies in Early Meiji Japan," *Journal of Asian Studies* 21 (February 1962), 189–190.
15. Ibid., 191.
16. Marius B. Jansen, *Japan and Its World: Two Centuries of Change* (Princeton, N.J.: Princeton University Press, 1980), 64–65.
17. Quoted in Joseph Pittau, *Political Thought in Early Meiji Japan* (Cambridge, Mass.: Harvard University Press, 1967), 39.
18. Quoted in Ronald P. Dore, *City Life in Japan,* (Berkeley: University of California Press, 1958), 159–160.
19. Quoted in G. B. Sansom, *The Western World and Japan* (New York: Knopf, 1950), 454.
20. This table is adapted from Richard Rubinger, *Private Academies of Tokugawa Japan* (Princeton, N.J.: Princeton University Press, 1982), 5.
21. Herbert Passin, *Society and Education in Japan* (New York: Columbia University Press, 1965), 54–55.
22. Marius B. Jansen and Gilbert Rozman, eds., *Japan in Transition from Tokugawa to Meiji* (Princeton, N.J.: Princeton University Press, 1986), 211.
23. Ronald P. Dore, *Education in Tokugawa Japan* (Berkeley: University of California Press, 1965), 211.
24. Ibid., 323.
25. Smith, *Native Sources,* 147.
26. Ronald P. Dore, "Latin America and Japan Compared," in *Continuity and Change in Latin America,* ed. John J. Johnson (Stanford, Calif.: Stanford University Press, 1964), 239.
27. Quoted in Kenneth B. Pyle, *The New Generation in Meiji Japan: Problems of Cultural Identity, 1885–1895* (Stanford, Calif.: Stanford University Press, 1969), 149.
28. This section draws on my chapter, "Meiji Conservatism," in Marius B. Jansen, ed., *The Nineteenth Century,* vol. 5 of *The Cambridge History of Japan,* ed. John Whitney Hall (Cambridge: Cambridge University Press, 1989).
29. Albert M. Craig, "Fukuzawa Yukichi: The Philosophical Foundations of Meiji Nationalism," in *Political Development,* ed. Ward, 120–121.
30. See William R. Braisted, trans., *Meiroku Zasshi: Journal of the Japanese Enlightenment* (Cambridge, Mass.: Harvard University Press, 1976), 406–407.
31. Craig, "Fukuzawa Yukichi," 118.

Beginnings of Industrialization

Much of the interest in Japan in the recent past has arisen from the fact that it was the first non-Western society successfully to carry out an industrial revolution, that this was achieved with rapidity, and that the nation's economy in the postwar period recovered and advanced in an extraordinary fashion. The fact that Japan was able to achieve industrialization with a dearth of natural resources and with relatively little financial assistance from outside has further heightened the interest in its industrialization.

In this chapter we shall be concerned with the transition phase of the Japanese economy, the critical years from 1868 to 1885 when Japan mobilized its material and human resources and laid the foundations for modern economic growth. The great unsettled issue in the study of this period is that of determining the prime force behind the drive to industrialize. The part that government played in initiating the industrialization of Japanese society has been the subject of much discussion and controversy. There has been a tendency to credit the state with a larger role than it actually played in the process. We shall see in the course of this chapter that private enterprise—the activities of individual Japanese—played no less critical a role than the state. What the government *did* do was provide the setting for industrialization, destroy old institutions that had proved obstacles to an industrial policy, and create in their place new ones that would facilitate industrialization. It created the "infrastructure" of communication and financial institutions that was essential to the efforts of private entrepreneurs.

Initially, the most important contribution of the state was that the new Meiji leaders set economic growth and achievement of industrial strength as national goals. This decision was not something that emerged suddenly in 1868 but was, rather, the outcome of a long development that we have briefly traced in the rise of the realist school of thought in the late Tokugawa Period. Adherents of the realist school, as we have seen, believed that government must itself adopt a policy of encouraging industry and commerce as a means of solving its own economic problems and of increasing its own strength. That policy gained support in many of the han toward the end of the Tokugawa Period, and the new leaders of the national government after 1868 effectively implemented it.

The Catch-Up Vision

In addition to learning a great deal more about the sources of Western industrial and military power, the Meiji leaders who went abroad with the Iwakura Mission strongly reconfirmed their views of the predatory nature of international politics. Above all, they came back impressed with the need for national self-reliance. Both Ōkubo and Itō subsequently recalled the advice that German Chancellor Otto Bismarck had given them. The Iron Chancellor cautioned them to prepare Japan for the intense competition among nation-states. The official narrative of the Iwakura Mission records that Bismarck counseled them that "although people say that so-called international law safeguards the rights of all countries, the fact is that when large countries pursue their advantage they talk about international law when it suits them, and they use force when it does not . . . small countries try and try to get a favorable decision only to fail sadly; it happens time after time that they can hardly maintain themselves and have to endure insult and aggravation even though they do their best to maintain their sovereignty." Bismarck concluded that everything he had learned convinced him that a nation-state could preserve its independence only through policies of strength and the cultivation of patriotism among the people.[1]

Bismarck's words reinforced what the Meiji leaders had already decided: Japan must rely only on itself. The world Japan entered was one of struggle not just for survival but for superiority over other states. Two years before the departure of the mission, Iwakura had written in a memorandum on foreign affairs, "Although we have no choice in having intercourse with the countries beyond the seas, in the final analysis those countries are our enemies. Why are they our enemies? Day by day those countries develop their arts and their technology with a view to growing in wealth and power. Every country tries to become another country's superior. Country A directs its efforts at country B, country B at country C—they are all the same. That is why I say, all countries beyond the seas are our enemies."[2] The members of the mission returned from the West further convinced of the imperative for Japan to become self-sufficient in its economy and in its military strength; for that purpose a sharply focused but long-range view of Japan's national interest must be the foundation of comprehensive plans for Japan's development.

It was a remarkable feat for the mission to have taken more than half of the Meiji leadership abroad for nearly two years. For the period of their absence they had installed a caretaker government led by Saigō Takamori, Itagaki Taisuke, and Ōkuma Shigenobu. By written agreement this caretaker group was to hold any new policies in abeyance until the return of the Iwakura Mission. They understood that once the mission returned with conclusions about what was necessary to achieve treaty revision, new policies would then be formulated to guide Japan's future course.

Prior to the departure of the mission, much of the work of political consolidation of the new administrative state structure had been set. The central government had been strengthened, the autonomy of the old feudal domains largely overcome, and a monolithic bureaucracy established. Moreover, the leaders wholeheartedly agreed that unification of the tax system and the military had to be addressed, that samurai privilege had to be terminated, and that an education policy must be fixed in the service of the state.

Sufficient prior agreement allowed the caretaker government to promulgate a new education law in 1872 and a national conscription law in 1873. But the caretaker government went beyond this and, influenced especially by the forceful Satsuma warrior Saigō Takamori, was on the verge of a major foreign policy decision that would have sanctioned a punitive expedition against Korea for its rejection of diplomatic ties with the new Meiji government. This matter of a Korean expedition brought to a head the issue of priorities for the new government.

In debates after the Iwakura Mission returned, Ōkubo Toshimichi emerged as the most powerful of the oligarchs. In fact, the period from 1873 until his assassination by samurai dissidents in 1878 has been termed a period of "Ōkubo despotism." The stolid and determined Ōkubo had made up his mind in the course of the Iwakura Mission that *fukoku-kyōhei* (enriching the country, strengthening the military), the general objective of the Meiji Restoration, was more than a slogan. Fukoku-kyōhei must entail the formulation of far-reaching policies to transform Japanese society in an all-out effort to catch up with the West. Embarking on a Korean invasion at this juncture, he wrote, might open the way to British intervention in Japanese affairs that would further the dependency relationship of the domestic economy. "We in Japan must give careful thought to this, taking steps quickly to stimulate domestic production and increase our exports, so as to repair our weakness by attaining national wealth and strength."[3]

Ōkubo and his colleagues returning from the mission carried the day, and the Korean expedition was cancelled. The decision was characteristic of the circumspection and prudence, the shrewd perception of international conditions, and the foresight that characterized the

Meiji leadership. In dismissing short-term considerations of national pride, Ōkubo was exhibiting a long-range perspective that distinguished Japanese political leadership throughout the catch-up effort. Despite the Korean slight, he set his sights on the long-range future: "Shameful though it be, a thing may have to be endured; just though it be, it may not always be pursued."[4] In opposing the Korean venture, Ōkubo was certainly not resisting armament, but he was favoring the building of an industrial foundation upon which military strength could be built.

If fukoku-kyōhei was to succeed, Ōkubo now knew, the Meiji government must formulate a clear set of policies and take the lead: "Our people are particularly lacking in daring: to encourage them to overcome this weakness and to study industry and overcome its difficulties is a responsibility the government must assume."[5] Ōkubo's task in the 1870s was to focus the leadership's thinking on Japan's international position and the policies of domestic reform that must be instituted to begin the centurylong pursuit of "catch-up." Ōkubo has been called "the Colbert of Japan," after Louis XIV's minister of finance, who fostered the role of the state in manufacturing and commerce, for no one else in the Meiji government articulated the mercantilist vision with such persistence and influence as Ōkubo. He was unimpressed by the free trade theories of Fukuzawa and other enlightenment thinkers. Ōkubo dismissed such theories, believing that the state must take the lead in promoting industry. "These [state-run] industries are absolutely necessary," he argued, "even though they go against the laws of political economy." Japan was "something different" (*ibutsu*) and needed "different laws" to develop.[6]

Itō Hirobumi also counseled his countrymen against following English economic theory. He wrote: "Now from the lips of Englishmen comes the argument of free trade, and they plot how to introduce it in our country. Since they are really thinking of their own gain, there is great danger to our country from their arguments. Japan should follow the example of the United States and establish a protective tariff to ensure the prosperity of domestic manufactures. When the tariff has outlived its usefulness, then Japan should imitate England and permit free trade."[7] The lengthy memo on "the encouragement of industry" (*shokusan kōgyō*) that Ōkubo wrote in 1874 showed that he understood that the British had pursued protectionist policies until British industry was strong enough to outdistance other economies. Japan needed a clear strategy to pursue the development of its economy, and Ōkubo and other Meiji leaders found German economic thinking more relevant than that of other countries. Germany, as Thorstein Veblen argued in his classic work, *Imperial Germany and the Industrial Revolution*, was the first nation to pursue a systematic industrial policy and the scientific development of its economy. The German historical school of economics was particularly influential. It had arisen in the nineteenth century to challenge the laissez-faire liberalism of Adam Smith. Because it favored the intervention of the state to ensure that the interests of the nation-state were served, the German historical school resonated with the realist thinking that the Meiji oligarchy had imbibed in the late Tokugawa era.

The catch-up vision that suffused the motivation ofŌkubo and the other Meiji leaders became over time a national consensus, a goal repeatedly held up as one toward which all Japanese must aspire. Takahashi Korekiyo, who later became finance minister and prime minister, exhorted his students in an 1889 farewell address at Tokyo Agricultural College: "Gentlemen, it is your duty to advance the status of Japan, bring her to a position of equality with the civilized powers and then carry on to build a foundation from which we shall surpass them all."[8] Moreover, the imperative of self-reliance, in spite of the craze for Western things, was widely accepted. Trade was a means of vanquishing the foreigners. "The only real difference [between us and the jōi swordsman of yesteryear]," said a Mitsubishi official, "is that we fight them by means of economics and trade." The founding statement of the Maruzen Company expressed the same patriotic fervor:

> The foreigners did not come to our country out of friendship; their real reason for being here is to trade. . . . Their main object is solely to seek profits through trade. When we sit idly by and allow them to monopolize our foreign trade, we are betraying our duty as Japanese. If we once allow them to take over our foreign trade, if we are aided by them, if we rely on them, if we borrow money from them, if we are employed in their companies, if we invite them into our companies, if we respect and admire them, if we run around at their orders, if we fall into that kind of condition, there could not possibly be a greater disaster to our country. A country in that situation is not a country.[9]

The Beginnings of an Industrial Policy

With this vision in mind,Ōkubo and his colleagues began to formulate what ultimately became an industrial policy of the modern Japanese government. It took shape step by step with many influences, including Tokugawa realist thinking, but we can begin to see in the 1870s and 1880s the early outlines of its principal characteristics. Its first element was the active leadership of the state in the economy. When Ōkubo returned from the Iwakura Mission, he became head of the Ministry of Industry which had been established in 1870 to encourage the development of industries, especially "mining, iron-making, railroad and telegraph," which were deemed essential to the production of the "necessities of a military nation" such as "warships, guns, ammunitions and all other arms that a nation cannot do without even a single day." In short, the ministry's founding statement clearly articulated the interconnectedness of the industrial and military goals—that is, of fukoku-kyōhei.

A second principal characteristic of the government's industrial policy as it began to take shape was import substitution. The commercial treaties imposed by the Western powers in 1866 had placed Japanese tariffs under international control and at such a low level that the domestic economy was thrown open for import of Western manufactured productions. As a result, between 1867 and 1880 Japan ran trade deficits in all but two years. The government took the lead in promoting industries that would compete with the imports. The most important product in the import-substitution policy was cotton goods—textiles, threads, yarns—which were imported in large quantities in the early Meiji years because of their superiority over domestic handicrafts.

Third, Japan would successively adopt as rapidly as possible the elements of Western technology that would increase its production of technologically sophisticated products. Beginning with cotton textiles, private industry with government support acted decisively in the 1880s to import the most advanced English technology. Government support came in the form of financing but probably more important in the form of a favorable institutional environment (for example, commercial codes, the banking system, cartels) for the importation of new technology. As a result, over the next several decades, Japan evolved from being an importer of cotton textiles, to being an exporter, to being a successful world competitor with England. In other key industries such as shipbuilding and steel production the Meiji government supported private industry's adoption of the most efficient technology through preferential loans, low taxes, and massive subsidies.

A fourth characteristic of the industrial policy the Meiji leaders were formulating was the development of exports, initially handicrafts, tea, and raw silk, but moving steadily into more value-added products. This strategy of *bōeki rikkoku,* or building an economy through international trade, made Japan capable of producing products increasingly competitive in price and quality in international markets.

A fifth principal characteristic was a determination to avoid relying on foreign loans. This decision was the result partly of the leadership's desire to avoid dependence on the Western powers and partly of the fact that Japan was not considered a good risk. The Meiji government took over the debts of the bakufu and of several large domains and it incurred a debt of its own to defray the costs associated with establishing the Bureau of Currencies. Nevertheless, all debts to foreigners were paid back by 1875. Thereafter, only two loans were floated prior to the end of the nineteenth century, both were in the London capital market and both were government bond issues.

Attributing a settled industrial policy to the early Meiji leaders is premature. They were still groping and experimenting, but as they took steps to deal with Japan's economic predicament and to plan for the future, they gradually formulated policies that fixed Japan's course for years to come. Let us now turn to the problems the leadership faced.

The State of the Economy in 1868

On the surface, Japan in 1868 appeared to have a relatively backward economy. It was still heavily agricultural with approximately 80 percent of the gainfully occupied population engaged in farming. The American educator W. E. Griffis recorded in 1876 that he was amazed at "the utter poverty of the people, the contemptible houses, and the tumble-down look of the city as compared with the trim dwellings of an American town."[10] (He was speaking of the town of Fukui, where he spent much of his time.) This, however, was no ordinary backward economy. In chapters 2 and 4 we discussed a great deal of evidence that pointed to economic change and development in the Tokugawa Period. As we saw, agriculture in many parts of the country was drawn into a well-developed system of national markets that encouraged specialization and stimulated productivity. Moreover, a goodly number of farm families were engaged in part-time nonagricultural occupations. A variety of cottage industries developed, such as brewing, ceramics, paper, food processing, mining, metals, and woodworking. As a consequence, many kinds of commercial and handicraft skills were widespread among Japanese farm families. The growth of the cottage industries reflected the rise and spread of attitudes conducive to economic change and development. In other words, probably the greatest resource that the Japanese economy had as it began its period of growth was a well-educated, economically motivated, and highly disciplined population. The growth of traditional manufactures during the late Tokugawa Period had tutored this population in specific skills, attitudes, and commercial practices, which made it highly responsive to further economic development.

While Griffis may have found the town of Fukui poor in comparison with the American towns with which he was familiar, other Westerners who had traveled more widely in Asia were impressed by the general well-being of the population, by the variety and abundance of goods sold in the towns and cities, and by the amount of traveling and shipping they saw. Townsend Harris, America's first diplomatic representative in Japan, wrote of the people of Kawasaki: "They are all fat, well-clad, and happy looking, but there is an equal absence of any appearance of wealth or of poverty." And of the population of Edo he observed, "The people all appeared clean, well-clad, and well-fed; indeed I have never seen a case of squalid misery since I have been in Japan."[11] The English diplomat Sir Rutherford Alcock wrote in 1859: "The evidence of plenty, or sufficiency at least, everywhere meets the eye; cottages and farm-houses are rarely seen out of repair—in pleasant contrast to China where everything is going to decay. . . . The men and women . . . are well and comfortably clad—even the children. . . . There is no sign of starvation or penury in the midst of the population—if little room for the indulgence of luxury or the display of wealth." In another location he recorded: "The impression is irresistibly borne in upon the mind, that Europe could not show a happier or better-fed peasantry."[12]

The economic historian Crawcour sums up his impressions of the economy in the 1860s as "reasonably, but not outstandingly productive for a traditional economy."[13] It was its potential and its responsiveness to economic stimuli that made the economy unusual. When exposed to the stimulus of foreign technology and foreign markets, the accelerated growth of the traditional economy made Japan's industrialization possible. During the Meiji Period the growth of agricultural output and of the production of traditional industries provided the capital accumulation that could be transferred to the modern sector of the economy by means of the land tax. This growth provided the exports which in turn gave the needed foreign exchange for buying raw materials abroad. Moreover, it satisfied the growing demands of the rising population. Therefore, traditional skills, resources, and their products provided the crucial building blocks for the foundation of a modern industrial society.

The Role of Government

Whether, in the absence of the stimuli of foreign markets and foreign technology, the commercial and agricultural development that was taking place in Tokugawa Japan would have led directly into modern industrial growth is a highly problematic and speculative question that need not concern us here. The steam engine did not have to be invented a second time. Industrial capitalism and modern techniques of production did not have to be invented in Japan. Instead, what was needed in the Japanese situation in the mid-nineteenth century was strong leadership, whether from the public or from the private sector, to mobilize Japan's domestic resources and to import the new technology.

In several important ways the government played a critical role in laying the foundations for industrialization. In the first place, it unified the administration of the country. This entailed a removal of restrictions that had impeded travel and commerce among different parts of the country during the Tokugawa Period. The old system of passports and barriers that had controlled traffic along the major highway was repealed, and citizens were now free to travel and choose their own place of residence. The new leaders strengthened the central government—for example, by abolishing the domains and creating a national army. In keeping with this unifying spirit, the government lifted existing feudal constraints on the internal market. The economic straightjacket into which the bakufu had put the economy was loosened, as a multitude of restrictions controlling commodity prices, the passage of commodities from one domain to another, and the operation of the market were removed. In addition, most barriers to foreign trade were withdrawn. The export of rice, wheat, copper, and raw silk, once prohibited, was now allowed.

Second, the new government also carried out a reform of the class structure. On the face of it, this was one of the most astonishing aspects of the Meiji Restoration. The party of samurai that came to power in 1868 proceeded to abolish the legal underpinnings that had made their class a privileged elite. The daimyo were handled without great difficulty. As we have seen, many of them had become merely titular leaders by the late Tokugawa Period, ineffective men whose actual power had long since declined. Moreover, many of the domains were in serious financial straits and the position of the daimyo was therefore one of considerable difficulty. Initially many of the daimyo were made governors of the newly established prefectures, and this helped ease any resistance. More important, they were given government bonds, and later titles, in the new nobility, which allowed them to continue to live with considerable means and prestige.

The new government likewise moved quickly to deal with the problem of samurai stipends and privileges. When the domains were abolished, it inherited the burden of paying samurai stipends, though it paid them at reduced rates. Nonetheless, between 1872 and 1876 stipends constituted anywhere from 25 percent to 100 percent of ordinary revenue, and it was clear that the new government, faced with competing demands for expensive Western-style reforms, especially in military and educational matters, could not continue indefinitely to support a hereditary elite. Accordingly in 1876 the government commuted samurai stipends into interest-bearing bonds that would mature in twenty years, thus limiting and in the meantime substantially reducing the government's fiscal obligations. Meanwhile, the trappings of the old samurai elite were likewise cut off. Everyone was made equal before the law. Everyone was to have the right to a family name. Positions in the bureaucracy were thrown open to all classes. Former members of the samurai class were permitted to enter any trade they wished. The practice of sword bearing, the samurai's badge of social prestige, was ended.

Third, beyond administrative unification of the country and reform of the class structure, the most important institutional reform that the government carried out at this time to prepare the way for economic growth was the land tax reform. This was critical because agriculture continued for many decades to be the chief source of national revenue. To effect all of the reforms necessary for modern economic growth, government had to have substantial income and, for much of the Meiji Period, the land tax was the primary source. It was therefore vital that the determination and collection of this tax be modernized. During the Tokugawa Period the land tax had been collected nearly everywhere in *kind,* as a *fixed percentage of the annual harvest.* Not only was that method unwieldy, but also, because the tax was based on the amount of the annual harvest and was affected by changes in the market price of rice, planning government expenditures was impossible.

Between 1870 and 1873 a series of reforms was instituted. First, land tax payments in kind were replaced by a uniform money payment, making this revenue independent of the price of rice. Second, the sale and disposal of land was made legal, thus giving formal recognition to a practice that had for a long time existed in one form or another. The landowners were made responsible for payment of the land tax and land titles were issued to them. Third, to do away with the annual fluctuation in tax revenue geared to the state of harvest, the new tax was assessed according to the value of the land. The net effect of the reforms, therefore, was to establish a standard tax that would be paid regularly in cash, thus providing the government with a known amount of revenue.

In addition, without raising their average tax burden, the reform encouraged farmers to increase their capital investment (better implements, seed selection, and fertilizers, and increased drainage and irrigation), thereby contributing to a steadily increasing agricultural productivity during the Meiji Period. Because Japan was still predominantly rural and agrarian with the farm sector accounting for 70 percent of employment, half the gross domestic product, and three-quarters of all tax revenue, the land tax reform was a major achievement. It entailed assessing the value of more than 85 million parcels of land and issuing in excess of 109 million certificates of land ownership. Because the reform replaced the inequitable Tokugawa land tax system and did not raise taxes, "the Meiji government was able to put a quick end to the disturbances and uprisings resulting from it." In sum, because it succeeded in solidifying the social foundations of the new government and in stabilizing its principal source of income, the land tax reform is regarded by some scholars as "the single most important reform of the Meiji Restoration."[14]

The administrative unification of the country, the reform of the class system, and the institution of the new land tax notwithstanding, government also played a critical role in providing prerequisites to economic growth by creating an infrastructure of communications, public utilities, and financial services. Moving very resolutely and effectively in these fields, the government by 1880 had succeeded in linking nearly all of the major cities by telegraph. Railway construction, which was, of course, more costly and technically difficult, proceeded less rapidly. A rail line was built from Tokyo to Yokohama in 1872; Kobe and Osaka were linked two years later; and in 1877 the latter line was extended to Kyoto. During those early years of railway construction the Japanese gained necessary technical know-how in construction, operation, and management of the railroads. As time went by, railway building accelerated. By the turn of the century, nearly 5,000 miles of railroad had been laid.

Also absolutely essential to future economic development were the reforms that the new government carried out in the field of currency and banking. The Tokugawa economy had been characterized by a chaotic variety of coin and paper money. One of the first achievements of the Meiji government was, therefore, the adoption of a new, standardized currency. In 1872 a modern banking system was begun

An early railroad scene near Yokohama harbor. The artist, Hiroshige (believed to be the third in his family), probably executed this print to commemorate the 1872 opening of Japan's first railway line, between Tokyo and Yokohama. *From the collection of Mr. and Mrs. Jack N. Greenman, Forth Worth, Texas*

with the issuance of the National Bank Act. It led ultimately to the establishment of more than 150 banks, which depended heavily upon capital supplied by samurai commutation bonds. By the 1890s Japan had achieved a modern banking system with a nationally integrated structure of interest rates. Though the complexities and problems of establishing a modern banking system were by no means easily resolved, we may note here that, as with schooling, an accumulation of sophisticated techniques during the Tokugawa Period greatly facilitated the development of modern institutions. Even before 1868 many merchants were familiar with deposits, advances, bill discounting, and exchange transactions.

Of critical importance too, was the government's role in establishing an elastic and stable currency. In the late 1870s the economy was characterized by a galloping inflation that threatened to wreck the government's efforts to create conditions for modern economic growth. At this critical juncture the government was fortunate in having an extremely shrewd and astute finance minister. Matsukata Masayoshi was appointed to that office in 1881. For the next four years he pursued a financial policy of tight money and austerity, which produced "the most severe deflation of modern Japanese economic history." Matsukata, writes Henry Rosovsky,

> combined firmness and wisdom with a strong belief in financial orthodoxy, and succeeded by 1885 in regaining control of the economic situation. He cleared the decks, and made it possible for modern economic growth to begin. . . . For five years he stayed on the same road, and by then the original government targets—adequate revenues, sound currency, modern banking—were safely and permanently achieved. The Matsukata deflation was strong medicine, but in our view it had life-saving qualities. . . . Thus, by about 1885–1886 the main targets of the government, first set in 1868, were in hand; a central bank was functioning, currency, purged of inconvertible paper, had become "respectable," and revenues were consistent with expenditures. It took government nineteen years to accomplish this; from that time the economy was free to move progressively.[15]

The Role of Private Capital

We may discern two schools of thought regarding the prime force behind the drive to industrialize. Oversimplifying somewhat, we may term one the "growth-from-above" school and the other, which rose in reaction to the first, we may call the "growth-from-below" school.

The growth-from-above school holds that measures instituted by the government and by a closely associated small group of industrialists provided the major impetus. This point of view draws inspiration from comparative economic history, which tends to expect that in the early stages of economic growth strong government leadership is required. Alexander Gerschenkron argued from the examples of Germany and Russia that "the more backward the economy, the more the reliance on the state rather than on private enterprise." Adherents of the growth-from-above school stress the importance of the establishment of national banks, the government's role in importing technicians, sending students abroad, and investing in the industrial sector. In particular, they point to the role of official entrepreneurship in the establishment of model factories. Construction of modern cotton mills and the purchase of British spinning machinery by the government in the early Meiji Period set an example for private enterprise, by overcoming the initial ignorance of machine technology and factory organization. Then, once private inertia was overcome, these "model plants" were sold to private industry at low prices and on easy terms. Thomas Smith writes that without government help "private capital would have been no more successful in developing machine cotton spinning in the decade after 1880 than it had been in the decade before; in short, in this field as in all others except silk reeling, the government was responsible for overcoming the initial difficulties of industrialization."[16]

To explain the motivation behind the drive to industrialize, many adherents of the growth-from-above school emphasize the patriotism and samurai spirit of the Meiji leaders and of the entrepreneurs who were closely associated with them. They argue that the traditional merchant class of the Tokugawa Period was largely lacking in the qualities of opportunism, inventiveness, and risk-taking that ordinarily characterize modern entrepreneurship. Instead, they find motivation arising out of the nationalistic or community-centered spirit of the old samurai class. As a result of their training, the samurai, in this view, possessed a selfless dedication to the nation that moved them to work for a wealthy, powerful country able to ward off Western imperialism. As one writer puts it, "in the case of Japan, the feudalistic samurai or their sons shouldered the leadership role of the Meiji entrepreneurs. Unlike any other nation, the development of capitalism was guided by bureaucrats who were samurai and by business leaders who were also of samurai origin. . . . Thus, the Meiji entrepreneurs were strongly motivated by the semi-feudal spirit of *shikon shōsai* (the soul of the samurai with business acumen)."[17] Why did Japan alone among non-Western countries make a rapid transition to industrial society? These scholars found the answer by pointing to the unique cultural tradition of its leadership. The spirit of bushidō—the warrior's code—inspired elements of the samurai class to selfless devotion to their nation, led others to invest their commutation bonds in the new

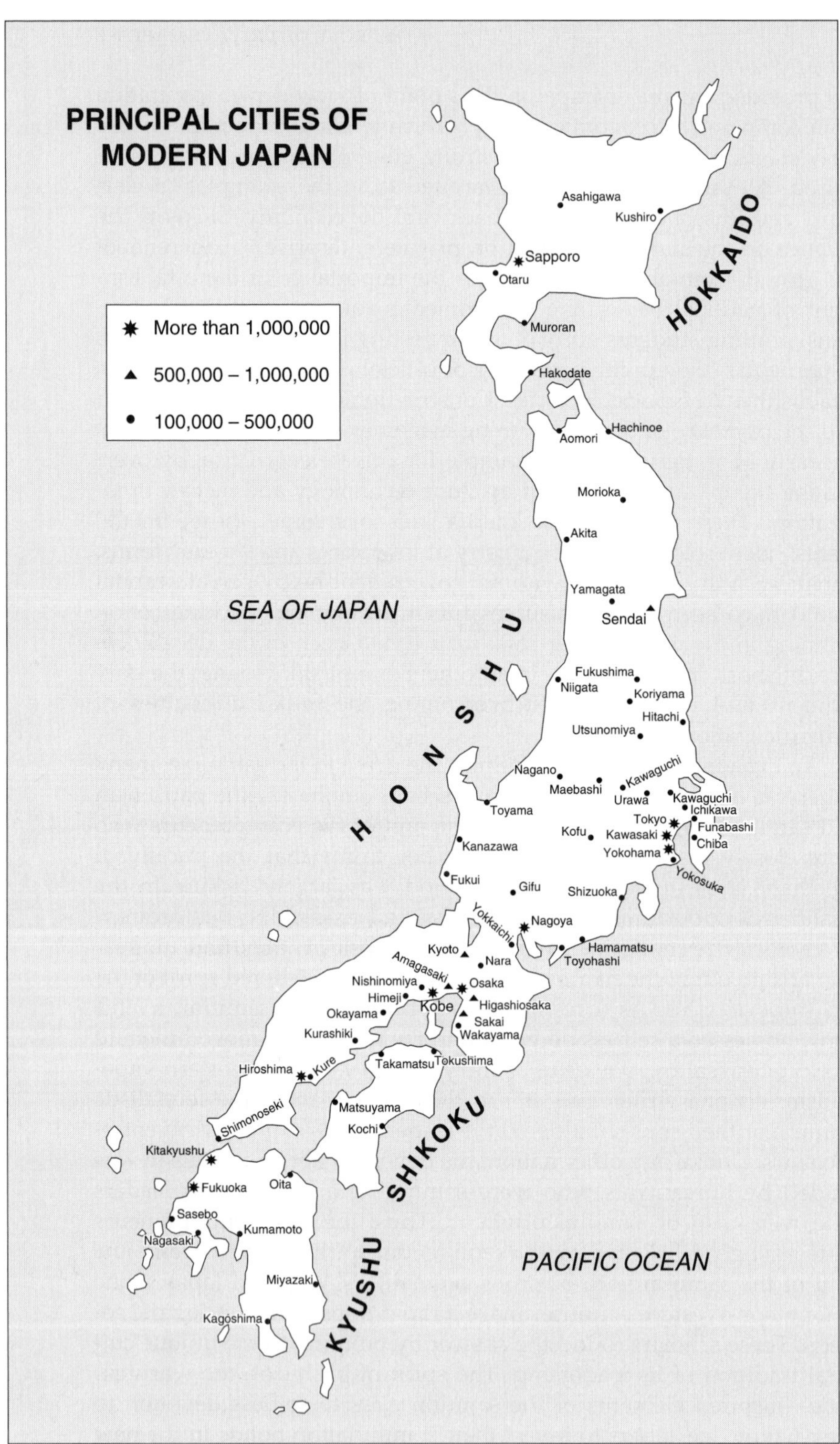
PRINCIPAL CITIES OF MODERN JAPAN
More than 1,000,000
500,000 – 1,000,000
100,000 – 500,000
HOKKAIDO
HONSHU
SHIKOKU
KYUSHU
SEA OF JAPAN
PACIFIC OCEAN
Asahigawa
Kushiro
Sapporo
Otaru
Muroran
Hakodate
Aomori
Hachinoe
Morioka
Akita
Yamagata
Sendai
Fukushima
Niigata
Koriyama
Hitachi
Utsunomiya
Nagano
Maebashi
Kawaguchi
Urawa
Kawaguchi
Ichikawa
Toyama
Tokyo
Funabashi
Kofu
Kawasaki
Chiba
Kanazawa
Yokohama
Yokosuka
Fukui
Gifu
Shizuoka
Yokkaichi
Nagoya
Kyoto
Hamamatsu
Toyohashi
Nara
Amagasaki
Osaka
Nishinomiya
Himeji
Kobe
Higashiosaka
Okayama
Sakai
Kurashiki
Wakayama
Takamatsu
Tokushima
Hiroshima
Kure
Matsuyama
Shimonoseki
Kochi
Kitakyushu
Fukuoka
Oita
Sasebo
Nagasaki
Kumamoto
Miyazaki
Kagoshima

national banks, and so fueled Japan's industrialization. In other words, the growth-from-above scholars stress a unique motivation behind Japanese industrialization—an "irrational, non-capitalist, dynamic and romantic approach of the pioneering entrepreneurs."[18]

On the other hand, the growth-from-below school argues that the traditional interpretation "overemphasizes the contribution of government and large-scale enterprise to increases in output, and that proper emphasis should also be placed on the contribution of the myriad of smaller rural and urban entrepreneurs who used more labor-intensive methods of production that embodied relatively simple improvements in technology, who acted in response to opportunities for profit, and who were relatively independent of the government."[19] These critics point out that the model factories were losing money when the government sold them off in the early 1880s and that afterward, in the hands of private managers, they earned substantial profits. The conclusion drawn, therefore, is that private enterprise was not incapable of successfully developing modern industries.

Likewise these adherents downgrade the significance of the contribution of samurai to the beginning of banking. They point out that the commutation of samurai bonds was essentially passive participation—in other words, the samurai lacked alternatives for investment. Instead, these critics are impressed with the contributions of members of the old *heimin* (commoner) class. "While the participation of samurai in new banks was passive," writes Kozo Yamamura, "the heimin class participated actively in the majority of new banks by supplying the necessary cash (20 percent of the initial capital) and the entrepreneurial energy in the form of directors and initiators in obtaining charters."[20]

As a consequence of their emphasis upon the role of the commoner class, adherents of the growth-from-below school emphasize the profit motive rather than the peculiar patriotism of the samurai class. Studies of Meiji entrepreneurs par excellence such as Iwasaki Yatarō or Yasuda Zenjirō, both founders of leading industrial combines, show them to be on many occasions cold, ruthless, competitive profit-maximizers—very much in the tradition of Andrew Carnegie, Cornelius Vanderbilt, and John Rockefeller.

Many of the Meiji entrepreneurs emerged from the gōnō, the wealthy peasant class in the villages. The experience of their families had done much to prepare them for this new capitalistic undertaking. In the first place, they sprang from a tradition of leadership acquired in the villages, where many of their fathers had served as village headmen. Second, they had accumulated capital through investment in rural enterprises. Third, the experience in undertaking rural enterprises gave them qualities of initiative, self-reliance, and risk-taking that the traditional city merchants in the Tokugawa Period had long since lost. Fourth, the gōnō were rendered both ambitious and frustrated by their position in the Tokugawa class structure. During the late Tokugawa Period, as we have seen, they had been able to share in the attributes of the samurai class—occasionally buying the right to wear swords, send their sons to fief schools, and take surnames. Yet they were not treated like bona fide samurai, and this experience frustrated them. They were therefore anxious to rise in the world, to do better than their fathers. Fifth, as a group the wealthy peasantry had always placed a high value on education and hard work. The interest in education, coupled with the wherewithal to acquire it, contributed powerfully to the emergence of young landlords' sons in the business elite.

An excellent example of this phenomenon is Shibusawa Eiichi, who rose from peasant origins to become the founder of several of Japan's impressive modern companies. His father was a village headman and rural entrepreneur who had invested widely in village industries such as indigo. Like many wealthy farmers' sons, Shibusawa received a samurai education. Through the good offices of a friend, he entered the services of the Tokugawa family and in this capacity accompanied a Tokugawa prince to France in 1867. When he returned a year later, having the extensive knowledge of the West that he did, he was able to enter the new Ministry of Finance in a prominent position. He resigned from the ministry in 1872 in order to enter banking and shortly became president of the First National Bank. His mastery of the field of banking led him ultimately into connections with more than 500 diverse industrial enterprises in many different capacities, such as president, director, or major shareholder. One of Shibusawa's impressive early entrepreneurial achievements was in the field of cotton spinning. He imported the latest technology and in 1880 directed the construction of the Osaka spinning mill, which, owing to its up-to-date technology and efficient organization, proved extremely profitable. It became a model for the development of other successful textile ventures in Japan.

However the debate between these two schools is ultimately resolved, we may conclude that the government played an important role in creating the environment within which growth could take place. Establishing a unified national administration, mobilizing human resources, and skillfully using fiscal policy were essential contributions of the state. Moreover, through what is now called "administrative guidance" (that is, through guarantees, subsidies, and preferential access to bank funds), the government used its influence to encourage economic growth. On the other hand, a new breed of entrepreneurs was clearly emerging in the private sector, and their ambition, inventiveness, and opportunism contributed immensely to the expansion of commerce and industry in this period. As Crawcour concludes, "Before World War I, growth-from-above and growth-from-below proceeded together."[21]

Notes

1. Marius B. Jansen, "Modernization and Foreign Policy in Meiji Japan," in *Political Development in Modern Japan*, ed. Robert E. Ward (Princeton, N.J.: Princeton University Press, 1968), 158.
2. Ibid., 158–159.
3. William G. Beasley, *The Meiji Restoration* (Stanford, Calif.: Stanford University Press, 1972), 377.
4. Ibid., 378.
5. Thomas C. Smith, *Political Change and Industrial Development in Japan: Government Enterprise, 1868–1880* (Stanford, Calif.: Stanford University Press, 1955), 40–41.
6. Albert M. Craig, "Kido Kōin and Ōkubo Toshimichi: A Psychohistorical Analysis," in *Personality in Japanese History*, ed. Albert M. Craig and Donald H. Shively (Berkeley: University of California Press, 1970), 296.
7. Japan, of course, did not have tariff autonomy at this time. Marlene J. Mayo, "Rationality in the Meiji Restoration," in *Modern Japanese Leadership: Transition and Change*, ed. Bernard S. Silberman and Harry D. Harootunian (Tucson: University of Arizona Press, 1966), 344.
8. Quoted by E. Sydney Crawcour, "Industrialization and Technological Change," in Peter Duus, ed., *The Twentieth Century*, vol. 6 of *The Cambridge History of Japan*, ed. John Whitney Hall (Cambridge: Cambridge University Press, 1988), 389.
9. Quoted in Arthur Tiedemann, "Japan's Economic Foreign Policies, 1868–1893," in *Japan's Foreign Policy, 1868–1941: A Research Guide*, ed. James W. Morley (New York: Columbia University Press, 1974), 130.
10. Quoted in E. Sydney Crawcour, "The Tokugawa Heritage," in *The State and Economic Enterprise in Japan*, ed. William W. Lockwood (Princeton, N.J.: Princeton University Press, 1965), 27.
11. Ibid., 26–27.
12. Ibid., 26.
13. Ibid., 44.
14. Kozo Yamamura, "The Meiji Land Tax Reform and Its Effects," in *Japan in Transition*, ed. Jansen and Rozman, 382–397.
15. Henry Rosovsky, "Japan's Transition to Modern Economic Growth, 1868–1885," in *Industrialization in Two Systems: Essays in Honor of Alexander Gerschenkron*, ed. Henry Rosovsky (New York: Wiley, 1966), 135.
16. Smith, *Political Change*, 63.
17. Tsuchiya Takao, quoted in Kozo Yamamura, *A Study of Samurai Income and Entrepreneurship* (Cambridge, Mass.: Cambridge University Press, 1974), 214.
18. Johannes Hirschmeier, *The Origins of Entrepreneurship in Meiji Japan* (Cambridge, Mass.: Cambridge University Press, 1964), 289.
19. Hugh Patrick, "Japan: 1868–1914," in *Banking in the Early Stages of Industrialization*, ed. Rondo Cameron (New York: Oxford University Press, 1967), 241.
20. Kozo Yamamura, "A Re-examination of Entrepreneurship in Meiji Japan (1868–1912)," *Economic History Review* (spring 1968), 156.
21. Crawcour, "Industrialization and Technological Change," in Duus, ed., *The Twentieth Century*, 390.

Building the Nation-State

The task of building a modern nation-state engaged the Meiji leaders for the entire period of their hold on government, from 1868 through the turn of the century. The feudal organization of the country into more than 200 semiautonomous fiefs had to be replaced by a new political structure that would centralize government and provide a unifying national spirit to galvanize the energies of the Japanese people for the tasks of building an industrial society.

Ordinarily, description of the process of nation building tends to concentrate on the formation of constitutional government, but in actuality the task was larger than simply establishing the Meiji Constitution. The fundamental task of the Meiji leaders was to mobilize the masses and integrate them into a new political system that would capture their loyalties and win their hearts. It involved a variety of techniques for mass mobilization and, above all, it required an effective ideology. Japanese scholars often refer to this process as the building of the emperor system.

Initial Problems

In contrast to the historic development of constitutional government in many Western nations, the Japanese experience was not one of a rising bourgeoisie bent upon achieving political rights. Rather, constitutional government was instituted "from above," the creation of a politically astute elite that had as its goal national power and equality with Western nations.

Within the loose alliance of oligarchs who controlled the regime in its early years, there was only limited consensus as to what kind of political structure should best be established in Japan. The oligarchy, which was composed chiefly of samurai from Satsuma and Chōshū (but included one or two from Tosa and Hizen, as well), had been united by their leadership of the anti-Tokugawa campaign but had achieved no more than broad agreement on the shape that political reforms should take. It took two decades of trial and error and struggle among them before the details of the new system of government were worked out. One step upon which all could agree was the need for administrative unification of the country. There was a notable consensus that until feudal divisions were done away with, essential reforms of the military, of education, and of the economy would be impossible. Accordingly, the Meiji leaders, as we have seen, moved quickly to establish a highly centralized political structure. In 1869 the daimyo were induced to accept the title of imperial governor of the land they had held in fiefs. This was prelude to abolition of the domains and their reorganization as prefectures governed by appointees of the central government. The relative ease with which this centralization was achieved is comprehensible if we recall how weak most of the daimyo had become by late Tokugawa days, and how beset most domains were by fiscal troubles.

This unification, in turn, made possible the conscription law of 1873, which called for the replacement of the separate samurai armies of the many domains with a single national army based upon universal conscription. All able-bodied males, regardless of their social background, were liable for three years of active military service. The conscription law represented a decisive break with the past, which was required by the goal of building national strength.

Many of the oligarchs had come to the view that a hereditary elite was no longer consonant with national unity and efficiency of government. Itagaki Taisuke from Tosa, himself from a well-to-do middle samurai family, pointed out in 1871 how essential to national strength was the mobilization of the loyalties of all the people: "In order to make it possible for our country to confront the world and succeed in the task of achieving national prosperity, the whole of the people must be made to cherish sentiments of patriotism, and institutions must be established under which people are all treated as equals." To bring the ablest men into government, he said, it was necessary to do away with the old class divisions. "We should seek above all to spread widely among the people the responsibility for the civil and military functions hitherto performed by the samurai . . . so that each may develop his own knowledge and abilities . . . and have the chance to fulfill his natural aspirations."[1] Itagaki was not only summarizing the arguments developed during the Tokugawa Period for the promotion of talent, he was as well laying down one of the basic propositions of modern leadership.

After centuries of existence as a hereditary elite, the samurai had by 1876 lost all their exclusive privileges: superior education, possession of bureaucratic office, stipends, and sword bearing. The new government could not afford to continue supporting a hereditary elite, and it needed to cast a wider net for talent in administration. Inevitably, as the new government pressed ahead with its reforms, it engendered growing hostility among many groups of the dispossessed. The administrative unification of the country and the reforms that the government had carried out to put it on a solid basis were severely tested by several major samurai uprisings that occurred in the mid-1870s. Significantly, they all occurred in the southwest where the new Meiji leadership had emerged. The reason for this was that the uprisings were led by disaffected oligarchs—members of the original Meiji government who had withdrawn from it because of disagreements over policy, particularly disagreement over the extent of political reforms.

The government survived those challenges to its authority. But the final and by far the greatest of the samurai uprisings, the Satsuma Rebellion of 1877, required the full application of the new government's resources. The rebellion was led by Saigō Takamori, who left government service in 1873 over the Korean controversy. At issue in this controversy was whether to invade Korea, which had affronted Japanese sensibilities by rebuffing the overtures of the new Meiji government for diplomatic recognition. The controversy led to a fundamental division. A number of the oligarchs, including Saigō and Itagaki Taisuke, favored an invasion of Korea as a means of asserting Japan's national dignity and of giving vent to samurai frustration and energy. After protracted controversy their views were overridden by Ōkubo Toshimichi, Iwakura Tomomi, and others who had recently returned from Europe convinced of the primacy of domestic reforms. Ōkubo argued that war would divert resources badly needed to stimulate industry. He concluded that Japan must pursue a prudent foreign policy, seeking first to revise the unequal treaties, before undertaking bold overseas commitments. His arguments carried the day and set the basic course of government policy for the next two decades. Saigō therefore resigned from the government and returned to Satsuma in high dudgeon.

If opposition to the new government was to succeed it could have no more magnetic leadership than Saigō gave it. He was, in the words of Craig, "the most potent personality in Japanese history."[2] He combined a burly physique (his collar size was 19-1/2 inches), charisma, and personal dynamism with a devotion to classic samurai values of stern integrity and disdain for physical danger. Although Ōkubo, his boyhood comrade from Satsuma, adopted Western ways, Saigō still dressed in simple clothes. He supported the policy of fukoku-kyōhei as necessary to strengthen Japan, but he was "opposed to the excessively rapid changes in Japanese society and was particularly disturbed by the shabby treatment of the warrior class. Suspicious of the new bureaucratic-capitalist structure and of the values it represented, he wanted power to remain in the hands of responsible, patriotic, benevolent warrior-administrators who would rule the country under the Emperor."[3] When the Korean expedition was overruled, he retired to Satsuma, where inevitably he attracted thousands of followers. He became the leader of a company of 40,000 disaffected samurai who eventually rebelled in January 1877. By September the government's new national army, superior in numbers and weaponry, had quelled the uprising, and Saigō took his own life on the battlefield. In later years, Saigō was apotheosized as a great national hero, the epitome of the classic samurai who clung to his ideals with single-minded sincerity rather than make the compromises required for worldly success.

The Satsuma Rebellion was the last real challenge to the new Meiji order. There were other short-lived uprisings, such as the Chichibu Revolt in 1884 brought on by acute economic distress among medium and small farmers, but they lacked the means to mobilize effective opposition. The government's policies ensured that the propertied and educated had a substantial material stake in the emerging order. As Stephen Vlastos writes,

> the wealthy farmers, landlords, entrepreneurs, and the commercial and educated classes benefited enormously from the progressive reforms of Meiji—especially reforms that brought citizen equality, meritocracy, protection of private property, and promotion of capitalist economic growth. . . . However, the classes marginalized by the Meiji reforms, groups that were losing social power as a result of modernization, faced an entirely different situation. The traditional warrior and small-scale subsistence farmer did not fit into the new order, and the government sacrificed their social needs quite ruthlessly to speed national integration and capital accumulation.[4]

The Movement for Constitutional Reform

Although such militant opposition was suppressed, the government still faced the challenge of other disaffected oligarchs, whose opposition took the form of the first political parties in Japan. Itagaki was the leader of the early party movement, known as the *Jiyū minken undō* (the People's Rights Movement), forming in 1874 the *Aikoku-kōtō* (the Public Party of Patriots). As we have seen, Itagaki had earlier argued that abolition of Tokugawa class restrictions was necessary in order to unify the people and to mobilize their energies for national goals. As a party leader, he now used very similar reasoning in arguing for creation of a national assembly, namely, that it would provide a means of marshaling the popular will in support of the policies of the state. He and his associates, initially from Tosa, resented the tight grip on power that the Satsuma-Chōshū group was acquiring. The constitutional order must be established, he asserted, to ensure that the will of the people was expressed through a representative form of government. For the next decade, Itagaki and his party, which was subsequently reorganized as the *Jiyūtō* (Liberal Party), invoked Western liberal ideas to attack the oligarchy and to demand the formation of an elective national assembly.

There has been considerable debate among scholars regarding the importance of the People's Rights Movement. Was it strong enough to compel the Meiji oligarchs to loosen their grip on power, to share control of the government with the people, to institute parliamentary institutions, and to begin the road to democratic government in modern Japan? There is no question that the Meiji government was compelled to take into account the demands of the opposition groups. Nonetheless, it would be wrong to think that the Meiji leaders were opposed to constitutional government or that they were forced to establish it contrary to their disposition. In fact, their interest in establishing a constitution and a national assembly antedated the People's Rights Movement. From the time of the Restoration there had been among the leadership a keen interest in the idea of both a constitution and a national assembly. The Imperial Charter Oath, issued in April 1868, which set forth in broad strokes the outline that the Meiji leaders had for their future course, declared in its first article that "assemblies shall be widely convoked and all affairs of state shall be determined by public discussion." This article represented a general commitment to broaden the basis of government and to rectify the Tokugawa failure to consult widely about the formation of national policy. Precisely how this broader basis of government was to be achieved remained to be gradually hammered out through debate within the oligarchy.

Western political systems engaged the keen interest of the Meiji leaders and were carefully studied in the first years of the Meiji Period. Actually, the first students sent abroad by the bakufu in the 1860s, Nishi Amane and Tsuda Mamichi, had published their studies of the theories of parliamentary government, separation of powers, and the constitutionalism that prevailed in Western society. Likewise, Fukuzawa Yukichi's *Seiyō jijō* was influential in its explanation of the workings and theoretical basis of parliamentary politics in the West. Interest in Western constitutionalism was further heightened by the Iwakura Mission.

Constitutional government was regarded as an essential aspect of the treaty revision effort. Establishing a constitution would, it was thought, lend credence to the assertion that Japan was a civilized country with up-to-date political practices, perfectly capable of meeting the accepted standards of the nineteenth century. But more than that, a constitution and a national assembly were seen as a way of mobilizing Japanese loyalties and evoking popular identification with the new government. In other words, the institutions would in themselves be a source of national strength; they would interpret issues to the people, serving to transmit the wishes and goals of the central government. Furthermore, the assembly would serve as a safety valve for social discontent, allowing the ventilation of grievances through the participation of popular representatives in the central government.

Japan's new leaders, committed to the immense task of building an industrial society in the course of their generation, had to find ways of overcoming the disruption of vested interest, the social dislocation, and the psychological strain that this task entailed. They found in Western society no dearth of examples of popular discontent and even rebellion that had obstructed the goals of political leadership. They were therefore intent upon finding ways of spurring on the populace, of achieving national unity, and of preventing harsh antagonisms that would make impossible—or at least much more difficult—the task of building an industrial society.

The "Opinion on Constitutional Government," which Yamagata Aritomo, one of the leading oligarchs, wrote in 1879, illustrates the reasons why they favored constitutional government and a national assembly. While regarding political parties and other forms of opposition to the government as wrong and immoral, Yamagata believed that, in order to overcome divisions within society, popular estrangement from government, and economic discontent, it was necessary that the governed have the right to participate in national administration. "If we gradually establish a popular assembly and firmly establish a constitution, the things I have enumerated above—popular enmity towards the government, failure to follow government orders, and suspicion of the government, these three evils—will be cured in the future."[5] Yamagata, in other words, was setting forth what became the basic rationale among bureaucrats throughout the modern period for popular participation in government: the governed should be brought into the governing process not as a natural, innate right but rather as a means of achieving national unity.

Itō Hirobumi, who had emerged as one of the leading oligarchs by 1880, reflected a common view that ran through the thinking of most oligarchs about constitutional government when he wrote that "today conditions in Japan are closely related to the world situation. They are not merely the affairs of a nation or a province. The European concepts of revolution, which were carried out for the first time in France about 100 years ago, have gradually spread to the various nations. By combining and complementing each other, they have become a general trend. Sooner or later, every nation will undergo changes as a result."[6] There was a sense of inevitability about the establishment of Western forms of government. This feeling was a manifestation of the belief that Western civilization represented a universal path of progress. Just as those countries provided a pattern for economic and social development, so, it was thought, they provided a pattern for political development as well.

At issue among the oligarchs was the nature of the future constitutional setup and the speed with which it should be established. A critical turning point was reached in the so-called Crisis of 1881. The issue was raised by Ōkuma Shigenobu, an oligarch from Hizen, who favored the immediate establishment of a British-style system with a cabinet responsible to an elected legislature. Ōkuma's proposal was rejected, and in a power struggle with the Satsuma-Chōshū group, he and his following in the Ministry of Finance were forced from the government, but at the same time the remaining oligarchs came to a decision and publicly promised to promulgate a constitution and establish a national assembly by 1890.

Itō Hirobumi took charge of drafting the constitution. In 1882 he departed for Europe on an imperial mission to study the constitutional systems there and to collect material for the formulation of the Meiji

Itō Hirobumi with his family. *Library of Congress*

Constitution. Although he observed practices in several countries, he was most impressed by the Prussian Constitution and its operation because of the evident similarities between the Prussian experience and Japan's own. In point of fact, it had already been decided prior to Itō's mission that Japan should adopt a Prussian-style constitution. So for that reason Itō, according to plan, spent the greater part of his journey in Berlin, where he heard lectures by the legal scholar Rudolph von Gneist over a period of many months. From there he moved on to Vienna, where he sought the advice of Lorenz von Stein, who reinforced the conservative views regarding parliamentary government that he had received in Berlin. "By studying under two famous German teachers, Gneist and Stein," he wrote to a fellow oligarch in Japan, "I have been able to get a general understanding of the structure of the state. Later I shall discuss with you how we can achieve the great objective of establishing Imperial authority. Indeed the tendency in our country today is to erroneously believe in the works of British, French, and American liberals and radicals as if they were Golden Rules, and thereby lead virtually to the overthrow of the state. In having found principles and means of combatting this trend, I believe I have rendered an important service to my country, and I feel inwardly that I can die a happy man."[7] The mission returned from Germany in late 1883, and thereafter Itō began work in earnest, drafting the constitution with the help of several advisors, including Hermann Roesler, a German legal consultant to the Japanese government.

The Meiji Constitution

The Meiji Constitution was promulgated on February 11, 1889. Although scholars since World War II have found fault with it and stressed its authoritarian aspects, the constitution nonetheless represented a great forward step for Japan in the establishment of representative institutions. It was greeted at the time with near unanimous acclaim.

The Emperor was the central symbol of the new political structure, and the constitution was presented to the nation as a "gift" from him to his people. The Emperor was to exercise all executive authority, the individual ministers being directly responsible to him, and he had supreme command of the army and navy. In addition, he had the right to suspend temporarily the Diet (the bicameral legislature), to dissolve its Lower House, and to issue ordinances when the Diet was not in session. Only he could initiate amendments to the constitution. The Emperor was "sacred and inviolable" as the descendant of a dynasty "which has reigned in an unbroken line of descent for ages past." Sovereignty, in short, resided in him.

Separate legislation provided that the Lower House of the legislature was to be elected by all males paying taxes of 15 yen or more (approximately 5 percent of the total male population). The Upper House, composed of members of the new peerage and imperial appointees, was to serve as a check on the Lower House. The constitution gave the Lower House the right to pass on all permanent laws and in addition the power of the purse strings; however, the government was given a loophole by which it could extricate itself from Lower House control over the budget. This loophole provided that were the budget for a particular year to go unapproved by the Lower House, then the budget of the previous year would automatically go into effect.

Basically, the constitution embodied the concept of popular political participation that had always been in the minds of the oligarchs: the national assembly as a means of achieving national unity. It was not a democratic concept, as was clearly indicated by the fact that the Emperor alone appointed ministers of the state, who were responsible to him and not to the legislature. The oligarchs spoke of the cabinet (which was not even mentioned in the constitution) as "transcendental," that is, as a body whose concerns and interests "transcended" the narrow, selfish political concerns of all groups in the state.

Establishment of a Modern Bureaucracy

"The key to understanding Japanese political life," an astute historian wrote in 1940, "is given to whoever appreciates fully the historical role and actual position of the bureaucracy."[8] Accustomed to the primary importance of political parties in the Anglo-American tradition and the subordinate role of bureaucracies, most Western historians of modern Japan have focused their attention on the development of political parties under the Meiji Constitution. Only recently have we come to see that the role of the bureaucracy in the political system is one of the key themes of modern Japanese history. What are the origins of the modern bureaucracy?

For the first decades after the Restoration, positions in government were held by men chosen by the Meiji leaders and their subordinates. Most were former samurai. Because samurai had monopolized government positions in the Tokugawa Period, they were able to depend on influential friends in government. Their appointments were the result of favoritism and personal contacts, and there were no formal criteria for advancement in government service.

Once the Meiji political system was established, however, the oligarchs turned their attention to creation of a permanent civil service. Yamagata, in particular, was determined to insulate government office holders from party influence. He wanted bureaucrats to be an elite corps of administrators, servants of the Emperor above and beyond politics. Knowing that party members would be seeking appointments to positions in government, Yamagata devised plans for a demanding civil service examination to be required of all officeholders below the rank of cabinet minister. An examination system for government office had existed in traditional China, but Japan had depended on hereditary rank as the determinant of government position in the Tokugawa Period. Between 1887 and 1899 a series of regulations created the modern civil service; and an examination system was introduced requiring extensive knowledge of jurisprudence and various types of law including constitutional, administrative, commercial, and civil. Years of university study would be required to pass the examination, training that party members would rarely possess. An 1899 ordinance instigated by Yamagata removed vice-ministers, bureau chiefs, and prefectural governors from political appointment. They had to come up through the ranks of the civil service. By 1900 free appointment of officials outside the civil service was limited to cabinet ministers, ambassadors, and confidential secretaries. Determined to limit the potential influence of the party men, Yamagata sought to ensure also that the parties would not intrude into the military bureaucracy. By ordinances issued in 1900 only generals and lieutenant-generals, admirals, and vice-admirals on active duty could serve as army or navy minister. By seeking to prevent civilian control of the military, these ordinances helped to strengthen the independence of the army and navy.

As a result of Yamagata's efforts, the bureaucracy grew into a powerful elite with fierce pride in its traditions of service to the emperor and the nation. The esprit de corps was strengthened by arduous training. The failure rate on the civil service examination was close to 90 percent. Those who succeeded justifiably felt a special sense of achievement and looked forward to working their way up the hierarchy, potentially to section chief (*kachō*), bureau chief (*buchō*), or vice-minister (*jikan*). At the highest levels, bureaucrats were overwhelmingly graduates of Tokyo Imperial University. At the end of the Meiji Period in 1912, all seven cabinet vice-ministers and twenty-eight of thirty-six bureau chiefs were Tokyo Imperial University graduates. Between 1900 and 1945, 115 of the 135 prefectural governors were graduates of Tokyo Imperial University; 10 were from Kyoto Imperial University.

We shall have many occasions to see how great was the influence of the bureaucracy in the political system as it developed in modern Japan. Suffice it to say, at this point, that 91 percent of all laws enacted by the Diet under the Meiji Constitution from 1890 to 1947 were written by bureaucrats.

From the 1890s on, the civil bureaucracy grew into a powerful and pervasive presence in Japanese life. From 29,000 in 1890 it grew to a total of 1,300,000 employees by 1928, when it was four times the combined strength of the army and navy. Low-ranking bureaucrats had a profound influence on the life of ordinary Japanese. Robert Spaulding writes that

> the police, for example, had operational responsibility for a bewildering variety of government programs and policies in addition to public safety, traffic control, and criminal investigation and apprehension. They enforced economic controls, discouraged unionism, inspected factories, censored publications, licensed commercial enterprises, arranged for public welfare aid, supervised druggists and public baths, controlled public gatherings, managed flood control and fire prevention, maintained surveillance of people suspected of dangerous thoughts, and did countless other things.[9]

The New Nationalism

For the quarter of a century preceding 1890 Japan had passed through a time of unprecedented ferment, a time of experimentation and groping, as it sought to reorient its institutions to the realities of the international order into which it was so suddenly thrust. Building an industrial society had required supplanting much of the old order with techniques and institutions borrowed from the West. As the bureaucracy and the military, as commerce, industry, and education fell under the sway of Western example, there developed among the educated segment of society an intense ambivalence about traditional Japanese and the new Western cultures.

Such ambivalence, we have come to recognize, has been a characteristic problem of intellectuals in most late-developing societies, which must of necessity borrow new technologies and institutions from the advanced industrial countries. Under such circumstances, intellectuals are often strongly attracted to the progressive, scientific, and liberal aspects of Western civilization and simultaneously alienated from institutions and values of their own culture that suddenly appear outmoded. Yet, at the same time, building an industrial society is motivated by strong nationalist sentiments and therefore requires a strong urge for pride in one's own civilization. Nationalist sentiments and cultural pride were all the more intense in the heyday of imperialism, and admiration for Western culture the more perplexing because it was Western nations that offered the challenge to national sovereignty.

Many Japanese intellectuals argued that government policy in establishing Western institutions had gone too far, that it was demeaning to adopt, wholesale, the values and practices of Western civilization. As the articulate editor of a leading newspaper, *Nihon,* put it:

> If a nation wishes to stand among the great powers and preserve its national independence, it must strive always to foster nationalism. . . . Consider for a moment: if we were to sweep away thoughts of one's own country, its rights, glory and welfare—which are the products of nationalism—what grounds would be left for love of country? If a nation lacks patriotism how can it hope to exist? Patriotism has its origin in the distinction between "we" and "they" which grows out of nationalism, and nationalism is the basic element in preserving and developing a unique culture. If the culture of one country is so influenced by another that it completely loses its own unique character, that country will surely lose its independent footing.[10]

On the other hand, many in the intellectual elite saw the institutions of the West as representative of the road to national progress and regarded Western values and institutions as of universal applicability. They tended to view cultural nationalism as reactionary. Wrote one editor, "We study physics, psychology, economics, and the other sciences not because the West discovered them, but because they are the universal truth. We seek to establish constitutional government in our country not because it is a Western form of government, but because it conforms with man's own nature. We pursue the use of railways, steamships, and all other conveniences not because they are used in the West, but because they are useful to all people."[11] The upshot of this "debate" in intellectual circles was a deep sense of uncertainty and restlessness. One young writer summed up the feeling when he said, "What *is* today's Japan? The old Japan has already collapsed, but the new Japan has not yet risen. What religion do we believe in? What moral and political principles do we favor? It is as if we were wandering in confusion through a deep fog, unable to find our way. Nothing is worse than doubt or blind acceptance."[12]

Government leaders recognized the problem, but they looked at it in a different way. They were concerned not so much about cultural pride per se, but rather about problems of maintaining order and reestablishing stability and unity in political life. They needed to mobilize mass support for the goals they had set for the nation. To provide the ideological glue that would hold the new political structure together, the Meiji leaders set about building an imperial ideology that would at once legitimize their rule and function as a binding and integrative force, enabling the Japanese people to act in concert and to deal effectively with their domestic and international problems. Itō put it this way:

> What is the cornerstone of our country? This is the problem we have to solve. If there is no cornerstone, politics will fall into the hands of the uncontrollable masses; and then the government will

> become powerless. . . . In Japan [unlike Europe] religion does not play such an important role and cannot become the foundation of constitutional government. Though Buddhism once flourished and was the bond of union between all classes, high and low, today its influence has declined. Though Shintoism is based on the traditions of our ancestors, as a religion it is not powerful enough to become the center of the country. Thus in our country the one institution which can become the cornerstone of our constitution is the Imperial House. For this reason, the first principle of our constitution is the respect for the sovereign rights of the Emperor. . . . Because the Imperial sovereignty is the cornerstone of our constitution, our system is not based on the European ideas of separation of powers or on the principle enforced in some European countries of joint rule of the king and the people.[13]

To build support for the modern state they were creating, the Meiji leaders resorted to the traditional language of loyalty and obligation and drew on a mythical past to yield a distinctive national ideology. They needed to focus popular sentiment on the imperial institution. We may think that the Japanese people in all eras instinctively revered the Emperor as the primary symbol of their history. But this was not necessarily the case. A German doctor, Erwin Baelz, who came to Japan in 1876 to serve as the Emperor's physician, lamented the popular indifference. Baelz wrote in his diary on November 3, 1880, "The Emperor's birthday. It distresses me to see how little interest the populace take in their ruler. Only when the police insists on it are houses decorated with flags. In default of this house-owners do the minimum." National veneration of the imperial institution had to be promoted. A new image of the emperor, it was felt, had to be created.

Leadership plays a critical role in the promotion and making of nationalism. Recently several scholars have drawn attention to what they call "the invention of tradition." They distinguish between the persistence of practices from the past that may be called "customs" and the establishment of practices that claim to be remnants from the past but that are actually artificially created, conceived, and instigated by elites. The latter may be called "invented tradition." The invention of tradition is a key element of modern nationalism and is not unique to Japan. To promote nationalism the elites manipulate and rework ideas, institutions, and cultural symbols from the past to forge a nationalist ideology that will serve present purposes yet still resonate with basic values and sentiments on which the social system rests. In the coming pages we shall see how Japanese leaders manipulated tradition to create a new national ideology. It took many forms, but they were all related: family state ideology, the institutionalization of State Shintō, the ideology of industrial harmony, and the ideal image of Japanese womanhood.

In 1890, just as the new legislature opened, the government issued a document of vital importance, the so-called Imperial Rescript on Education, which set forth the cardinal principles of this ideology. It exhorted the people to "be filial to your parents, affectionate to your brothers and sisters; as husbands and wives be harmonious; as friends, true; bear yourselves in modesty and moderation . . . always respect the constitution and observe the laws; should emergency arise, offer yourselves courageously to the State; and thus guard and maintain the prosperity of Our Imperial Throne coeval with heaven and earth."

In those Confucian terms the leaders set forth the concept of the family state, of the Emperor as the father of the nation and the subjects as his children. The Rescript, which became a part of daily school ceremonies, thereby equated political obligations with filial piety and sought to imbue the Emperor and his government with the sanctity and legitimacy that would suppress political opposition and dissent. As one scholar observes, "the Emperor became a substitute for the charismatic leader so prominent in the modernization of most nonwestern societies of a later period, a substitute that was more permanent, more deeply rooted in the culture, and more invulnerable to attack."[14]

At the same time as it issued the Imperial Rescript on Education, the government began the conscious use of mass education to inculcate the new ideology. Textbooks, formerly only loosely controlled, became standardized and uniform—subject to the control of the increasingly powerful Ministry of Education. Schools, which in the early Meiji Period had done so much to introduce Western concepts, now became a prime force in building nationalism, which was essential if the modern state was to evoke the self-sacrifice of millions of Japanese. Passages such as the following, in a school textbook of 1910, became common: "It is only natural for children to love and respect their parents, and the great loyalty-filial piety principle springs from this natural feeling. . . . Our country is based on the family system. The whole country is one great family, and the Imperial House is the Head Family. It is with the feeling of filial love and respect for parents that we Japanese people express our reverence toward the Throne of unbroken imperial line."[15]

In addition to the new national conscript army and the increasingly tight control of educational policy, another agency of centralization was the organization of local government, established largely as the handiwork of Yamagata. The purpose of the Town and Village Code of 1888 was to amalgamate more than 76,000 Tokugawa hamlets into some 15,000 administrative towns and villages, thereby enabling the central government to extend its influence into local communities, which had heretofore possessed a considerable degree of autonomy. By shifting loyalties from the hamlet, traditionally the object of identification for its inhabitants, to the new administrative towns and villages, Yamagata expected that material and spiritual resources might be efficiently mobilized for national purposes.

The nationalist purposes of the Meiji state were further served by the reorganization and centralization of local religious practices. The government took important steps to establish what we call in retrospect State Shintō. We can find no better example of the government's manipulation of tradition to serve its own purposes. As Helen Hardacre writes, "Shintō, as adopted by the modern Japanese state, was largely an invented tradition."[16] To strengthen the new administrative towns and villages as centers of national loyalty, the government in 1906 ordered the merger of all the Shintō shrines and establishing in their place one central shrine in each administrative village. Before the merger order, Japan had more than 190,000 shrines, the great mass of them small and devoted to the concerns of local inhabitants—healthy children, good crops, and prosperous communities. Communal spirits or deities (*kami*) were worshipped according to simple rituals to elicit their protective powers. These local observances were the product of popular practices since prehistoric times. At the national level since earliest times the Japanese imperial line had based its claims to sovereignty on Shintō myths that proclaimed the imperial family's descent from the sun goddess Amaterasu. The political authority of the imperial court was sanctioned by this indigenous religion. The Meiji government, therefore, could elaborate and reshape the deeply rooted traditions of the imperial cult in a modern setting. The central bureaucracy sought to remold local folk religion everywhere into a powerful source of nationalism. "The study of Shintō's relations with the state provides many examples of the invention of tradition to unite disparate elements into a modern nation."[17] Shrine liturgy was standardized to stress devotion to the Emperor rather than local concerns. Shintō priests were placed under the disciplinary rules of regular civil government officials. In the years immediately following the shrine merger order, the number of local shrines throughout the nation dropped dramatically. At the same time, new ones were founded to serve nationalist ends. The best example is the Yasukuni Shrine established in Tokyo in the early Meiji Period, which commemorated all those who died on the loyalist side in the Meiji Restoration and in Japan's modern wars. "The significance of enshrining the soul of a human being in Yasukuni is that the rite of enshrining is an apotheosis symbolically changing the soul's status to that of a national deity."[18] Hardacre adds that "Yasukuni shrine, of all the invented traditions of State Shintō, most profoundly colored the character of popular religious life."[19]

By the early years of the twentieth century, the government was thereby succeeding in politically mobilizing the leaders of local society. Village headmen, elementary school principals, Shintō priests, prominent landlords, and other local activists were imbued with the national ideology and charged with responsibility for achieving Japan's imperial destiny. They became interpreters of the national mission to the masses. As such, they played a key role in the national community that the Meiji leadership was disciplining for the forced march to industry and empire.

Ideology soon took on a life of its own. One tendency in historical writing has been to see imperial ideology as nothing but a top-down process, as a creation instilled by Meiji leaders and bureaucrats in an obedient and deceived citizenry. For invented tradition to be successful, however, it must resonate with the values on which the social system rests. As Robert Smith writes, "outright falsification of the past will fail, but an adroit combination and reordering of some of its elements that remain faithful to existing predispositions will be of great benefit to those who wish to persuade the people of the legitimacy of their goals."[20] Clearly statesmen did take the lead in the process of inculcating the ideology. However, precisely because reverence for the Emperor, the values of the family, and suspicion of foreigners and their religion and intentions struck a strong and responsive chord, people outside the government became some of the most fervent purveyors of this nationalist ideology. As Carol Gluck writes, "the strongest views—the hard line—often came from outside the government, from the *minkan,* as it was called, from 'among the people.'"[21] When the leading Japanese Christian of the day, Uchimura Kanzō, declined to bow before the Imperial Rescript on Education in a ceremony honoring its presentation, it was journalists, scholars, and townspeople who berated him. When a Presbyterian minister, Tamura Naoomi, criticized the indigenous family system, it was the media and fellow Japanese Christians who denounced him for a lack of patriotism. When a professor at Tokyo Imperial University, Kume Kunitake, wrote an objective historical essay describing Shintō as the "survival of a primitive form of worship," it was Shintōists and nativist scholars who hounded him out of his job. The pressure to conform to the national orthodoxy, Marius Jansen points out, came not so much from the government as from "forces within Japanese society. Colleagues, neighbors, publicists, relatives—these were the people who hounded the Kumes, the reformers, and the liberals."[22]

In sum, just as important as government indoctrination in explaining the sway that nationalist ideology held was the remarkable receptivity to this effort by people outside the government. Self-appointed ideologues proclaimed national solidarity, harmony between ruler and people, loyalty, filial piety, and colonial expansion as inherent in the national character. They stressed that all spiritual authority resided in the Japanese state, and they denounced Christianity and Western liberalism as incompatible with the national polity. We can view the popular reception of a national ideology that reasserted familiar ideals as a reaction to the sense of uprootedness, emotional stress, and dislocation produced by rapid social change.

Notes

1. William G. Beasley, *The Meiji Restoration* (Stanford, Calif.: Stanford University Press, 1972), 384–385.
2. Albert M. Craig and Donald H. Shively, eds., *Personality in Japanese History* (Berkeley: University of California Press, 1970), 274.
3. Ivan Morris, *The Nobility of Failure: Tragic Heroes in the History of Japan* (New York: Holt, Rinehart, and Winston, 1975), 248.
4. Marius B. Jansen, ed., *The Nineteenth Century,* vol. 5 of *The Cambridge History of Japan,* ed. John Whitney Hall (Cambridge: Cambridge University Press, 1989), 426–427.
5. Quoted in George M. Beckmann, *The Making of the Meiji Constitution* (Lawrence, Kan.: University of Kansas Press, 1957), 130.
6. Ibid., 132.
7. Quoted in Nobutake Ike, *The Beginnings of Political Democracy in Japan* (Baltimore: Johns Hopkins University Press, 1950), 175–176.
8. E. H. Norman, *Japan's Emergence as a Modern State* (New York: Institute of Pacific Relations, 1940), 206.
9. Robert M. Spaulding, Jr., "The Bureaucracy as a Political Force, 1920–45," in *Dilemmas of Growth in Prewar Japan,* ed. James William Morley (Princeton, N.J.: Princeton University Press, 1971), 36–37.
10. Quoted in Kenneth B. Pyle, *The New Generation in Meiji Japan: Problems of Cultural Identity, 1885–1895* (Stanford, Calif.: Stanford University Press, 1969), 75.
11. Quoted ibid., 90.
12. Quoted ibid., 7.
13. Quoted in Joseph Pittau, *Political Thought in Early Meiji Japan* (Cambridge, Mass.: Harvard University Press, 1967), 177–178.
14. Robert A. Scalapino, "Ideology and Modernization: The Japanese Case," in *Ideology and Discontent,* ed. David E. Apter (New York: Free Press of Glencoe, 1964), 103.
15. Quoted in Wilbur M. Fridell, "Government Ethics Textbooks in Late Meiji Japan," *Journal of Asian Studies* 29 (August 1970), 831.
16. Helen Hardacre, *Shintō and the State, 1868–1988* (Princeton, N.J.: Princeton University Press, 1989), 3.
17. Ibid., 4.
18. Ibid., 90.
19. Ibid., 8.
20. See *Cultural and Social Dynamics,* vol. 3 of *The Political Economy of Japan,* ed. Shumpei Kumon and Henry Rosovsky (Stanford, Calif.: Stanford University Press, 1992), 28.
21. Carol Gluck, *Japan's Modern Myths: Ideology in the Late Meiji Period* (Princeton, N.J.: Princeton University Press, 1985), 9–10.
22. Marius B. Jansen, ed., *Changing Japanese Attitudes toward Modernization* (Princeton, N.J.: Princeton University Press, 1965), 80–81.

Imperialism and the New Industrial Society

The 1890s marked a watershed for Japan. The mood and the concerns of the nation underwent dramatic change. During the generation after 1868, Japan had been preoccupied with domestic reforms, intent on reordering its society and government. By 1890, however, the new political order was established and a new sense of discipline and purpose was evident in the nation's life.

Most important in bringing about the transformation of mood and concerns was the Japanese entrance into international affairs in an unprecedented way. Since the Restoration the prevailing policy had been to concentrate the energy and resources of the nation on domestic reforms and to avoid involvement in overseas entanglements. The primary goal of foreign policy had been to achieve a successful revision of the unequal treaties to escape from semicolonial status, and that goal required concentration on domestic reforms. The policy bore fruit when, in mid-1894, the Western powers agreed to sign treaties providing for the end of extraterritoriality. Little more than two weeks after revision of the unequal treaties was achieved, Japan declared war on China and embarked upon its first great foreign adventure in three centuries.

The Sino-Japanese War of 1894–1895 was of immense importance in the history of international relations because it revealed the full extent of China's weakness and set off an intense competition among the imperial powers for control of the resources and markets of East Asia. Japan was inevitably swept into this maelstrom and obliged to subordinate all its other concerns to the protection and extension of its interests. During the period from 1895 to 1915, which we shall concentrate on in this chapter, Japan emerged as one of the world's great powers, and the rise of its imperialism influenced nearly every aspect of the new industrial society that was taking shape in this period.

Japanese Imperialism

The circumstances and motivations of Japanese imperialism during its first phase from 1894 to 1914 have been the subject of historic controversy. There is no simple explanation. Many factors were responsible for the strong imperialist drive that emerged in Japan at the turn of the century.

One important factor was the nationalist desire for equality with the Western powers. Together with constitutional government, industrialization, and a modern military, a colonial empire was a mark of status in the civilized world. The Meiji ambition to make Japan "a first-class country" (*ittō-koku*) helped to inspire expansionism. Thus it is not altogether surprising to find that even "liberals" such as Fukuzawa who greatly admired Western standards of civilization (*bummei*) had no qualms about supporting imperialism. In an unguarded moment he exclaimed in 1882, "We are Japanese and we shall someday raise the national power of Japan so that not only shall we control the natives of China and India as the English do today, but we shall also possess in our hands the power to rebuke the English and to rule Asia ourselves."[1] In its more benevolent form, this nationalist drive was justified as fulfilling Japan's mission to be the leader of Asia. The journalist Tokutomi Sohō declared in 1895 that Japan's destiny was to "extend the blessings of political organization throughout the rest of East Asia and the South Pacific, just as the Romans had once done for Europe and the Mediterranean."[2]

Another factor was the economic motivation of maintaining access to the raw materials and markets of East Asia, which might be denied Japan if neighboring countries fell under the domination of one or another of the Western powers. A fundamental objective of the oligarchs was to build a modern economy as the basis of national power, and this meant establishing a strong export market for the products of its light industry. Asia and the Pacific, which lacked indigenous modern industry, were seen as the most promising market for Japanese textiles, cement, canned goods, and other products. As Peter Duus writes, "the Meiji leaders feared that unless Japan was more active abroad economically as well as politically, opportunities for trade and investment available to Japan in the region would slip into the hands of competitors. It was important that Japanese rather than Russians or Frenchmen build railroads in Korea, that Japanese as well as Englishmen established cotton mills in Shanghai, that Japanese rather than Americans control the textiles market in Manchuria, or that Japanese rather than Chinese carry foreign goods to Taiwan."[3] There can be no question that imperialism at the turn of the century was motivated by the drive to acquire economic advantages and interests in the region.

The most important factor in the imperialist drive, however, was strategic. The prevailing political instability of East Asia outside of Japan created both problems and opportunities. In Korea and China old impotent governments were being undermined by revolutionary movements at the end of the nineteenth century. The impending collapse of these weak governments caused consternation in Japan because they might be replaced by Western control with consequent jeopardy to Japan's security. Japan's more rapid development together with the institutional backwardness of other countries in East Asia created a situation in which Japan could almost inevitably expect to dominate its neighbors. As a consequence, to the extent that one can separate strategic and economic objectives, it was the need for security that was the primary motive for imperialist expansion. In fact, as Mark Peattie writes,

> No colonial empire of modern times was as clearly shaped by strategic considerations. . . . Many of the overseas possessions of Western Europe had been acquired in response to the activities of traders, adventurers, missionaries, or soldiers acting far beyond the limits of European interest or authority. In contrast, Japan's colonial territories (with the possible exception of Taiwan) were, in each instance, obtained as the result of a deliberate decision by responsible authorities in the central government to use force in securing territory that would contribute to Japan's immediate strategic interests.[4]

The empire grew by a kind of inexorable strategic logic that was implied by Yamagata who, addressing the Diet as prime minister at its opening session in 1890, explained his security strategy: "The independence and security of the nation depend first upon the protection of the line of sovereignty (*shukensen*) and then the line of advantage (*riekisen*). . . . If we wish to maintain the nation's independence among the powers of the world at the present time, it is not enough to guard only the line of sovereignty; we must also defend the line of advantage . . . and within the limits of the nation's resources gradually strive for that position."[5] In other words, Japan's security depended not only on protecting the actual territorial limits of the nation but also on establishing Japan's dominant influence in areas beyond. In 1890 Yamagata had Korea in mind as the neighboring area that fell within the "line of advantage." Subsequently, when Japanese control of Korea was achieved, the line of advantage extended into southern Manchuria where, to ensure the security of Korea, Japan must also establish its dominant influence. Such strategic thinking was not unique to Japanese leadership but it was unusually influential, partly because the Japanese Empire, unlike the far-flung European and American empires, was in close proximity to the home islands.

It should not surprise us that Yamagata thought in such strategic terms. He was a military man from his young days, becoming known as "the father of the modern Japanese army" for his attention to its development. He commanded forces that suppressed the Satsuma Rebellion, but it was his appointment later in life, after he had already been prime minister, to command the First Army at the outset of the Sino-Japanese War in 1894 that he recalled as "the happiest moment of my life." As a young man his ambition had been to become a master

Yamagata Aritomo. *Bettmann Archive*

spearsman. Late in life he still practiced on a great fig tree outside his bedroom. The tree eventually died from his thrusts.[6]

In the final analysis, strategic concerns and security objectives motivated the Meiji leaders in their creation of the Japanese Empire. Economic interests, while important, were secondary to the political objectives of expansion.

By the end of the 1880s, as the Meiji political order was nearing completion, Japan's leaders were giving serious attention to the play of forces in the international environment. Yamagata and the heads of the military services had come to the conclusion that East Asia was likely to be the scene of fierce competition among the imperial nations. The vacuum of power on the continent invited it. Russia's decision to build the Trans-Siberian Railway confirmed their fears, for the new line would likely require a warm water terminus in Korea or South Manchuria. It became a cardinal principle of Japanese foreign policy that the security of the Japanese islands depended on preventing Korea from falling under the control of a third country. As the Prussian advisor to the Meiji army put it, the Korean peninsula was "a dagger thrust at the heart of Japan."[7] The General Staff, moreover, concluded that the "independence" of Korea could only be secured by control of neighboring Port Arthur and the Liaotung Peninsula. With those strategic objectives in mind, the government steadily built up the nation's military and naval power.

By 1894 intrigue and chaotic politics in Korea had created tense relations between China and Japan, each seeking to assert influence over the course of Korean politics. The Japanese foreign minister at this time wrote in a personal memoir, "I sensed that the wisest course to follow now was to precipitate a clash between ourselves and the Chinese" for whom he had only contempt. China was a "bigoted and ignorant colossus of conservatism" whose people "have never known how to observe the good faith that is indispensable in diplomacy," and it was mired in "centuries old stupor" while the "imbecile Korean government . . . simply did not know how to comport itself during times of war or peace as an independent state" and showed "the deeply suspicious animosity and unscrupulous recourse to treachery which are characteristic of the Korean people."[8]

War broke out on August 1 and the superior planning and readiness of the Japanese military were quickly apparent. The war lasted only eight months. The uninterrupted successes of the Japanese army, the total destruction of the Chinese fleet, and the surrender of Weihaiwei persuaded China of the futility of further struggle. The Treaty of Shimonoseki, signed April 17, 1895, ceded the Pescadores, Formosa, and the Liaotung Peninsula to Japan, recognized Korean independence, and obliged China to pay a large indemnity, to open additional ports, and to negotiate a commercial treaty.

It was an immensely popular war and greatly stimulated growth of the nationalist sentiment that the government had been seeking to promote through many of its new institutions. Victory brought the pride that had been wanting during the preceding decades of cultural borrowing from the West. As Tokutomi Sohō wrote in the midst of the war: "Now we are no longer ashamed to stand before the world as Japanese.... Before, we did not know ourselves, and the world did not yet know us. But now that we have tested our strength, we know ourselves and we are known by the world. Moreover, we *know* we are known by the world!"[9] Fukuzawa Yukichi expressed a common sentiment when he pointed out that triumph in the war had been a vindication of the Meiji reforms. "One can scarcely enumerate," he wrote in 1895, "all of our civilized undertakings since the Restoration—the abolition of feudalism, the lowering of class barriers, revision of our laws, reform of the military, promotion of education, railroads, electricity, postal service, printing, and on and on. Yet among all these enterprises, the one thing none of us western scholars ever expected thirty or forty years ago was the establishment of Japan's imperial prestige in a great war.... When I think of our marvelous fortune I feel as though in a dream and can only weep tears of joy."[10]

This new self-confidence, however, was almost at once deflated. On April 23, 1895, Germany, Russia, and France demanded that the Japanese government renounce possession of the Liaotung Peninsula "in the interests of the peace in the Far East." The incident was profoundly humiliating. The German minister to Tokyo read the demands of the three powers to Hayashi Tadasu, the Japanese vice-minister of foreign affairs, in a garbled and blunt text written in Japanese. Hayashi could scarcely understand the German's confusing pronunciation, but one phrase came through clearly: "Japan cannot defeat the united strength of Russia, France, and Germany."

Too weak to oppose the three powers, Japan was compelled to retrocede the Peninsula. This event, known as the Triple Intervention, made a profound impression upon the nation, underlining its diplomatic isolation and increasing its sense of insecurity. Tokutomi Sohō, who became Japan's leading nationalist editor, was traveling about southern Manchuria, savoring Japan's new territory, when he heard that it had to be given up. "Vexed beyond tears" and disdaining to remain on the lost territory, he returned at once to Japan. But before embarking from Port Arthur, he scooped a handful of earth into a handkerchief, and he returned to Japan with this "souvenir of what has been, for a time, Japanese territory." For years he kept it on his desk in his newspaper office as a reminder to himself of the importance of national power.[11]

The government set to work with a vengeance to expand military preparedness. Government leaders resolved that the nation should bear whatever burden was required to redress this bitter outcome. Hayashi, who had experienced firsthand the humiliation of the Triple Intervention, wrote with bitter determination in June 1895 what Japan's strategy must be:

> We must continue to study and make use of Western methods; for among civilized nations applied science constitutes the most important part of their military preparations. If new warships are considered necessary we must, at any cost, build them; if the organization of our army is inadequate we must start rectifying it from now; if need be, our entire military system must be changed.
>
> We must build shipyards for the repair of our vessels. We must build steelworks to provide us with guns and munitions. Our railway network must be enlarged to enable us to carry out a speedy mobilization of our troops. Our merchant fleet must be expanded to enable us to transport our armies overseas. . . . At present Japan must keep calm and sit tight, so as to lull suspicions nurtured against her; during this time the foundations of her national power must be consolidated; and we must watch and wait for the opportunity in the Orient that will surely come one day. When this day arrives Japan will decide her own fate; and she will be able not only to put into their place the powers who seek to meddle in her affairs; she will even be able, should this be necessary, to meddle in their affairs.[12]

With fierce determination the nation set about preparing for conflict with Russia, whose interests lay athwart Japanese ambitions on the continent.

Taxes were progressively raised as military expenditures more than tripled in the decade from 1893 to 1903. Yamagata wrote to a friend in 1895 that the situation in East Asia would grow worse and that Japan must be prepared for war in ten years with the Russians, who soon seized the southern part of the Liaotung Peninsula for themselves. Both the army and navy undertook long-term programs to build up their strength.

Meanwhile, to allow time for military preparation, Japanese diplomacy sought and achieved a modus vivendi with Russia. The agreement reached between the two countries in effect accepted a balance of their respective interests in Manchuria and Korea. Japan's economic interests on the Korean peninsula were growing rapidly at the turn of the century. It was trading cotton products in return for foodstuffs and, above all, promoting an ambitious program of railway construction.

But the most impressive achievement of Japanese diplomacy was the signing on July 30, 1902, of the Anglo-Japanese Alliance. For Japan the alliance not only overcame its previous diplomatic isolation, but

Admiral Tōgō Heihachirō, naval hero of the Russo-Japanese War. *National Archives*

also provided the first military pact on equal terms between a Western and a non-Western nation, thereby representing a great symbol of Japan's newfound respect among the imperial powers. The treaty, which promised British assistance if Japan became embroiled in conflict with more than one power, strengthened Japan's hand in its rivalry with Russia.

When renewed negotiations between the two countries over their interests in Korea and Manchuria broke down in February 1904, Japan went to war, beginning with a surprise attack on the Russian fleet at Port Arthur. The Japanese army, in a succession of battles in Manchuria, defeated but could not wholly dispatch the Russians. To crush the Russian armies would have required more resources than the Japanese possessed. Both the oligarchy and the army General Staff were therefore prepared to negotiate an end to the war. The Tsar, however, hoped to turn the tide by sending the Baltic fleet around the world to overwhelm the Japanese navy. The Battle of the Japan Sea in May 1905, in which Admiral Tōgō Heihachirō's forces routed the Russian fleet, drew world attention. President Theodore Roosevelt wrote to a Japanese friend of Tōgō's triumph:

> This is the greatest phenomenon the world has ever seen. Even the Battle of Trafalgar could not match this. I could not believe it myself, when the first report reached me. As the second and third reports came, however, I grew so excited that I myself became almost like a Japanese, and I could not attend to official duties. I spent the whole day talking with visitors about the Battle of the Japan Sea, for I believed that this naval battle decided the fate of the Japanese Empire.[13]

Roosevelt was subsequently persuaded by the Japanese to mediate between the two belligerents.

The war required an unprecedented mobilization of the nation's resources. The government mobilized one-fifth of the male working population for some form of war service and sent 1 million men to the front. Casualties mounted to more than 100,000 and the financial cost was immense. Its cost was ten times that of the Sino-Japanese War and stretched the economy to the limit. To sustain so heroic an effort, the war was justified as a great popular undertaking. Nothing in the nation's history had so heightened political awareness as this war. When the peace treaty was signed at Portsmouth, New Hampshire, in 1905, riots in many Japanese cities expressed the disappointment of the Japanese populace at the terms of the treaty and revealed their heightened political consciousness. Though the people had been led to expect much more from the treaty negotiations, Japan nonetheless emerged from the war with acquisition of the southern half of Sakhalin, the recognition of its paramount interests in Korea, the lease of the Liaotung Peninsula, and railway rights in southern Manchuria.

Historians usually describe the Russo-Japanese War as an event that brought Japan great power status and won her worldwide acclaim. It is true that the war does represent a landmark in modern world history: throughout Asia, leaders of subjected peoples drew inspiration from the Japanese example, believing that they too could import Western science and industry, rid themselves of white control, preserve their national character, and themselves oversee the process

SIBERIA
SAKHALIN
Trans-Siberian Railroad
Khabarovsk
Amur R.
Manchouli
Chinese Eastern Railroad
Ussuri R.
Sungari R.
MANCHURIA
OUTER MONGOLIA
Harbin
Vladivostok
Changchun
South Manchurian Railroad
Mukden
Shaho
Liaoyang
Yalu R.
KOREA
SEA OF JAPAN
Peking
Shanhaikuan
Chinchou
Liaotung Peninsula
Tientsin
Dairen
Port Arthur
P'yongyang
Seoul
Weihaiwei
Inchon
JAPAN
Tokyo
Yellow R.
Shantung Peninsula
Tsingtao
EAST CHINA SEA
Pusan
Shimonoseki
PACIFIC OCEAN
CHINA
NORTHEAST ASIA c. 1904
FORMOSA
PESCADORES

of industrialization. Jawaharlal Nehru, for example, recorded in his autobiography that the Japanese victory was a memorable event in his early life; he described it as "a great pick-me-up for Asia," which kindled his nationalism and his determination to "fight for India."[14] Similarly, Sun Yat-sen, recalling the profound impression made on Chinese revolutionaries, said that "we regarded that Russian defeat by Japan as the defeat of the West by the East."[15]

The attraction that many Asian leaders felt to Japan, however, did not survive the decade following the Russo-Japanese War. During this period Japan made very clear its expansionist intentions. Following the Portsmouth Treaty, Japan established a protectorate over Korea, and Itō Hirobumi was sent to Seoul to serve as resident-general. He hoped to carry out a benevolent modernization of Korea, which would gain the support of the Korean people as well as serve Japan's national purposes, but he underrated a nascent Korean nationalism. From the beginning of the protectorate, Korean resentment and resistance presented problems. Ultimately Itō himself paid with his life, assassinated by a Korean patriot in the railway station at Harbin in 1909, and the following year Tokyo annexed Korea into the Japanese Empire.

What is striking about this period is that, in spite of the fact that Japan seemed to have fulfilled the Meiji dream by revising the unequal treaties, joining the ranks of the great powers, and acquiring impressive overseas possessions, it was nonetheless beset by a keen sense of insecurity and vulnerability, a sense of the fragility of its position. The resources of the nation had been stretched taut during the war with Russia, and now there could be no relaxation even though hostilities had ended. The strategic requirements of Japan's empire were quite formidable. It included both insular possessions, which required a strengthened fleet, and continental territory, which required a strengthened army. From 1905 to 1914 soaring government expenditures for industrial capital formation and for military and colonial enterprises brought about extensive foreign borrowing, international payments problems, and a mounting tax burden on the citizenry. The political leadership faced an acute economic crisis.

The fearful demands that industrialization and imperialism were placing on Japanese society created a pervasive sense of uneasiness. The Meiji novelist Natsume Sōseki, despairing of the pace at which his country was driving itself, prophesied "nervous collapse" and admonished his countrymen not to be deluded into thinking of Japan as capable of competition on an equal footing with the great powers.

The famous poem, "Do Not Offer Your Life," which Yosano Akiko addressed to her brother who was drafted in 1904 at the height of the conflict bespoke a longing for a return to the private concerns of the family and home:

Dearest brother,
I weep for you.
Do not offer your life.
Did your mother and father,
Whose love for you, last born,
Surpassed all others,
Teach you to wield the sword?
To kill?
Did they rear you these twenty-four years,
Saying:
'Kill and die'?

You,
Who shall inherit the name of our father—
A master proud of his ancient name
In the commerce of this town of Sakai—
Do not offer your life.
Whether Port Arthur falls or not
Is no matter.
Do you not know
That this is nothing
To the house of a merchant?
Nothing?

Do not offer your life.
The Emperor himself does not go
To battle.
The Imperial Heart is deep;
How could he ever wish
That men shed their blood,
That men die like beasts,
That man's glory be in death?

Dearest brother,
Do not offer your life
In battle.
Mother, whom father left behind
This past autumn,
Suffered when
In the midst of her grief
Her son was called away.
Even under this Imperial reign,
When it is heard
That the home is safe and secure,
Mother's hair has grown whiter.

Do you forget
Your forlorn young wife
Weeping,
Hidden in the shadows of the shop curtains?
Or do you think of her?
Consider a young woman's heart when
After less than ten months
Her husband is taken away!
Alas, who else
Than you alone
Is she to rely on
In this world?
Do not offer your life![16]

The Christian novelist Tokutomi Roka (whose brother Tokutomi Sohō was a leading proponent of imperialism) was oppressed by a foreboding of disaster. He urged his country in 1906 to turn away from reliance on military power: "Awake, Japan, our beloved fatherland! Open your eyes and see your true self! Japan, repent!"[17] Other writers favored a shift to a less assertive international position, a "little Japanism," that would abstain from continental expansion and imbroglios with the powers and would lay stress instead on improving living standards at home by developing industry and trade.

But their voices were a minority opinion. The majority strongly favored improvement of Japan's continental position. Japanese imperialism was driven by continuing preoccupation with strategic advantage and a peculiar combination of nationalist pride and insecurity. In a 1907 document enunciating "the aims of imperial national defense," the military listed Japan's hypothetical enemies as Russia, the United States, Germany, and France in that order and recommended arms expansion to greater than twice the level achieved at the end of the Russo-Japanese War. There was to be no respite, no turning back.

The bureaucracy was already hard at work organizing material and spiritual support for the mounting costs of government, trying to evoke the effort and self-sacrifice required for industry, empire, and status as a world leader. Bureaucrats in their public appearances explained that the burden the people must bear would not be lighter even though the war with Russia was over. A civil servant in Yamaguchi prefecture, for example, gave a speech several times in 1906 to local officials. Japan, he said, as a result of victory in the war, had joined the ranks of the world's first-class nations and had to expand its military and diplomatic establishments abroad as befitted its new status. It needed to invest great sums in industrial growth and education so that its people might develop the resources required to support the Japanese Empire. The people had an obligation to contribute to the achievement of Japan's destiny by paying higher taxes. Although the military war was over, Japan was now engaged in economic warfare, which in some ways would be more trying than actual combat. He spoke of the coming "peaceful war" in which every country would be Japan's enemy. If Japan's strength was to increase, the country must inevitably come into economic conflict with other countries. National unity would be imperative. Young men, old men, children, even women, he concluded, would be in the battles and must obey orders as in any war.[18]

This pursuit of empire and of status as a great power colored all other aspects of Japan's national development. Most particularly, it affected the way in which the new industrial society took shape. A successful imperialist policy required a unified nation at home, with every part of society subordinated to the whole, with the state taking precedence over the individual citizen and over social groups. Leaders in business and government recognized that the new society as it came into being would disturb vested interests, create psychological strain, and cause social dislocation. If the drive for industry and empire was to be sustained, national loyalties would have to be continuously reinforced and every effort made to overcome the forces of disintegration.

The Problems of Industrial Society Come to Japan

Because of the timing of its industrialization, Japan experienced the social problems attendant upon that process in a much different context than did the "early developing" industrial nations of the West. As a "late developer," Japan had the opportunity to profit from observing the problems that the first industrializers had encountered and to try to avoid them. Marx wrote in the preface to *Das Kapital* that "the industrially more developed country presents to the less developed country a picture of the latter's future." What Marx, however, did not acknowledge was the possibility that the less-developed country could, through the use of political initiatives, change the course of its industrialization and thereby avoid or mitigate the kinds of problems that the pioneers had experienced. Veblen wrote in 1915 that Japan had a special "opportunity," by which he meant that by industrializing while feudal values were still strong Japan could avoid much of the social cost that had plagued other nations. Personal ties, vertical relations of loyalty and obedience, would permit a much smoother industrialization than if economic individualism took hold.

The Japanese leaders themselves, years before Veblen's essay, had shown that they were aware of the opportunity they had to benefit from the Western example, to try to plan a calmer and less searing transition.

We find among Japanese bureaucrats and intellectuals a striking sensitivity to the lessons of Western history. We should learn, said one prominent official in 1896, from the "sad and pitiful" history of British industrialization. And, he added "it is the advantage of the backward country that it can reflect on the history of the advanced countries and avoid their mistakes."[19] The economist Kawakami Hajime urged in 1905 that Japan maintain a balance between its agrarian society and the new manufacturing sector, arguing that Japan could not survive the destruction of its agriculture:

> Unfortunately, as the pioneer of the industrial revolution, England overlooked this great truth and that was probably inevitable in the trend of the time. But fortunately we have the history of England's failure and there is no need to repeat that history. Are there not opportunities for countries that lag behind in their culture? . . . The history of the failures of the advanced countries is the best textbook for the follower countries. I hope that our statesmen and intellectuals learn something from this textbook.[20]

For statesmen it was Japan's international position that gave urgency to averting the class antagonisms to which industrial civilization in the West had given rise. This was uppermost in the mind of one of the leading oligarchs, Ōkuma Shigenobu, when he wrote in 1910 that Japan was in an extremely advantageous position to secure the cooperation of capital and labor: "By studying the mistaken system that has brought Europe such bitter experience in the last several decades, businessmen, politicians, and officials in Japan can diminish these abuses." Relying on the force of laws and family customs, they would "prevent a fearful clash" and plan "the conciliation of capitalists and laborers."[21]

Thus, as Japan was making the transition to industrial society, its leaders were already thinking of the social problems likely to accompany the process. Their concern was made keener by the fact that European socialism was making its influence felt on radical intellectuals in Japan by the turn of the century. Following the Sino-Japanese War, a small but dedicated group of intellectuals and skilled workers tried to organize craft unions. The government, however, responded by passing the Peace Preservation Law of 1900, whose Article 17 outlawed strikes and other primary activities of labor unions.

As a result of the hostility of government, labor leaders after 1900 increasingly turned to politics. They became convinced that the regime would have to be changed, either peacefully or by force. In 1901 they organized the Social Democratic Party, which, although it did not have a long history—the Home Ministry closed it down hours after it was established—did attract attention to the new socialist movement and elicit the concern of government leaders. Denied the opportunity to organize effective trade unions or a political party, the young socialists turned to methods of "education." In 1903 they established a newspaper, the *Heimin Shimbun*, which took strong and provocative positions against militarism, capitalism, and imperialism. In its pages was published the first complete translation of the *Communist Manifesto.* The newspaper opposed the war with Russia and for its pains was eventually forced out of business, while its editors were continually subject to police pressure. Frustrated in all their efforts, some of the socialists turned to anarchism and terror. Ultimately a number of them were implicated in a plot to assassinate the Meiji Emperor, and the government took the opportunity to move with severity to stamp out the anarchist movement. In the notorious High Treason Case of 1911, twelve radicals were hanged, three days after sentence had been passed.

As concern with social problems took root in Japanese intellectual and bureaucratic consciousness, the almost naive faith in the perfectibility of human society, which had characterized the early Meiji years, began to fade. Industrialization and imperialism put fearful demands upon society, and confidence in the future gave way to ambivalence. Every plus had its minus. The new technology was creative but also destructive; it offered new opportunities and prospects but at a high cost in human suffering and dislocation. As a result of the growing concern over the social problems that industrialization was likely to create, Japanese business and government leaders took the initiative in trying to prevent class hostilities, especially the alienation of the working class.

Origins of Japanese Labor-Management Relations

Studies of the Japanese factory system have called attention to several peculiar characteristics of industrial relations in present-day Japan, which have gained widespread attention owing to Japan's rapid economic growth. Many of these characteristics took shape during the period we are discussing, when the new industrial society was forming. It has been pointed out, first of all, that the large Japanese firm today has a low labor turnover—most employees enter a firm at the beginning of their working life and remain there until retirement. There is an understanding that the worker will not leave that company for industrial employment elsewhere, and, at the same time, the company will not discharge him, barring the most extreme circumstances. A second notable characteristic is the strong tendency of workers to identify with the fortunes of the company for which they work, to feel a deep sense of loyalty, and to organize unions according to their place of employment rather than by craft among many companies. Enterprise-based unions, indeed, are quite common. Third, wages are determined more by seniority than by function or ability. In contrast to, say, an American firm—where wages are often related to the individual's contribution to efficient and maximal production—in the Japanese factory, economic rewards are most often determined by age and length of service. This characteristic naturally reinforces the low rate of labor turnover because a worker is clearly penalized for changing jobs and conversely is strongly rewarded for stability. Fourth, Japanese firms provide notably high levels of welfare services for their employees. These include better sick pay provisions, retirement pensions, and a variety of other benefits, including housing, education loans for workers' children, medical services, transport subsidies, and a variety of organized sports and social facilities.

These distinctive practices of Japanese labor relations were the result of a long evolutionary process beginning at the turn of the century—as Andrew Gordon writes, "a dialectic process involving the interaction of workers, managers, and bureaucrats, all taking initiatives at some point and responding to events at others."[22] Some aspects of modern labor relations were influenced by the past. For example, the common Japanese practice of organizing unions at the place of employment rather than by craft had its "roots in the past. With no tradition of effective guild networks as a model they organized by workshop and factory with hardly a second thought."[23]

Japanese cultural values stressing loyalty and the extension of quasi-kinship relations to groups beyond the family also played a part in the evolution of the system. Managers and bureaucrats often invoked "Japan's beautiful customs" of obedience, loyalty, and harmony to conciliate labor. Workers, however, responded that management must demonstrate the benevolence expected of superiors in hierarchical relations. Japanese workers were not as docile and diligent as is sometimes thought. They were not passive bystanders as the employment system emerged. Rather they demanded better treatment, respect, and improved status. They were motivated less by new, Western concepts of workers' "rights" or class struggle than by a desire to be treated with benevolence by their employers in a way that would justify worker loyalty. Workers believed that the employment relationship was similar to relationships between lord and vassal, master and servant, parent and child, requiring benevolence on one side and loyalty and obedience on the other. Independent of a modern labor union movement, which was still only in its infancy in the first decades of the century, industrial workers were coming together, forming workshop struggle groups, and negotiating with management. They appealed to a status ideology common in Tokugawa peasant uprisings. Thomas Smith sees worker protests as "deeply rooted in the history of the struggles of villages and towns for hierarchical justice from regional lords during the Tokugawa period." The measures adopted—welfare services, greater security of employment, bonuses, and other aspects of the Japanese employment system—were "largely those that workers had for years been demanding as improvements of status and 'treatment.' They were adopted by management piecemeal, reluctantly, with a considerable time lag."[24]

Managers responded to these demands because of several immediate factors. One was the continuing problem that employers had of preventing labor turnover—retaining skilled workers once they had been trained at a time when the supply was limited. Because of the newness of the skills involved, the enterprises devoted great attention to the training of their workers. Once trained, such workers were at a premium, and great attention had to be given to preventing their leaving for other work. At the turn of the century, when the shortage of skilled labor was severe, the turnover rates ran between 50 percent and 100 percent per year. Workers would simply abandon one employer for another, seeking higher wages, better working conditions, and a different experience. As a result, to encourage long terms of service the new industrial employers began to extend to skilled male workers a variety of incentives, such as retirement and sick leave benefits and regular salary increases heavily based on seniority.

Another factor encouraging development of the Japanese employment system was the growing awareness of the problems that industrialization had engendered in Western society. Labor strife, class divisions, worker alienation, social unrest, and the growth of radical ideologies were seen in Japan as inevitable products of industrialization unless leadership took steps to prevent them. The fact that labor organizations, strikes, and socialist groups were beginning to appear in Japan at the turn of the century reinforced this pattern of thought.

Because of the problem of labor turnover and because of the keen sensitivity to the Western experience with the social problems of industrialization, the larger firms, like Mitsubishi and Mitsui, took the lead in improving working conditions—such schemes as sick pay and retirement benefits, the establishment of the principle of "lifelong employment," salary increases according to seniority, and the development of profit-sharing bonus schemes—as a way to enhance the loyalty of employees. Large textile firms, with their reliance on the labor of young peasant girls, began to emphasize "familylike relationships" and the establishment of welfare programs. For example, Mutō Sanji, president of the Kanebo Cotton Textile Company in the early twentieth century, was a leader in developing a managerial ideology that emphasized paternal concern for employees and tried thereby to win their loyalty and affection. His welfare measures, Dore writes, included

> a crèche [nursery] for working mothers, a workshop environment improvement fund with a claim to a percentage share of profits, much improved bathing and recreational facilities in the dormitories, an improved company housing scheme for married employees, subsidized consumer co-operatives for those living in company houses, a suggestions scheme, a complaint box grievance procedure . . . , a company news sheet . . . , a kindergarten to absorb the noisy children of night workers . . . and sick pay, pension and welfare fund . . . covering, for example, funeral expenses for members of the workers' family, paid by equal contributions from the worker and the firm.[25]

The government also became involved in measures that contributed to the development of the Japanese employment system. Leaders in the bureaucracy early in this century paid special attention to the practices instituted in Western countries to deal with the problems of industrial labor, and consequently they played an influential role in establishing welfare programs in Japan in hopes of forestalling labor unrest. As a result of government pressure, the first factory act was passed in 1911. It provided minimum standards for employment in manufacturing establishments with fifteen or more workers. The impetus for this early legislation, it is important to note, came not from the laboring class or from pressure groups, but rather from bureaucrats in the Home Ministry, who had paid special attention to the development of factory legislation in Europe. The bureaucrat most responsible for this law boasted that it had been passed not as a result of an angry labor movement but out of a benevolent concern of the state to maintain in the course of industrialization Japan's "beautiful customs" of harmony among all its citizens:

> In the future, our capitalists . . . will be steeped in the generous spirit of kindness and benevolence, guided by thoughts of fairness and strength. The factory will become one big family: the factory chief as the eldest brother and the foreman as the next oldest. The factory owner himself will act as parent. Strikes will become unthinkable, and we can look forward to the increased productivity of capital—the basis for advances in the nation's wealth and power.[26]

More important, the government also played an active role in trying to accommodate such differences as did arise between labor and management. In 1919, following an alarming number of strikes and much civil disorder, the government established the Conciliation Society, which promoted workers' councils and consultative committees as a means of co-opting the union movement and of channeling worker grievances. But perhaps the most important contribution of government was its propagation of the collectivist ethic throughout the nation. This ethic stressed vertical relations of loyalty and obedience, with a spirit of cooperation and self-sacrifice in all social groups. It generally set forth the concept of the "family nation," depicting Japan as distinct from the Western countries, where social unrest and class hostilities were described as endemic. In sum, as Dean Kinzley writes, the government in its approach to the problems of industrial relations was once again relying heavily on the "invention of a tradition."[27]

The Role of Women in Industrialization

In addition to this pattern of labor-management relations that began to take shape in the new heavy industrial sector, Japanese industrialization had other distinctive features. It is important to emphasize that, in contrast with Europe, the leading sector of modern industry in Japan was not heavy industry but textiles. The fact that light industry played the leading role until the 1930s demonstrates the importance of Tokugawa economic growth as a precondition to modern success. "The growth of the modern textile industry was made possible by the specific skills, attitudes, roles, capital accumulations, and commercial practices brought into being mainly during the period of 'premodern growth.' Without these preconditions, the stimulus of foreign technology and foreign markets would not have resulted in the rapid expansion of the textile industry under private auspices after 1880."[28]

The textile industry successfully assimilated modern techniques and then dominated the manufacturing sector until the 1930s. "It was also," as Gary Saxonhouse observes, "the harbinger of what has now become a familiar Japanese developmental pattern: import substitution followed by worldwide export success." In 1890 Japan was still a net importer of cotton yarn but by the 1920s Japan dominated the world market for cotton textiles. By 1937, 37 percent of all cotton fabrics in international trade were made in Japan.[29]

Not only the dominance of light industry in Japan's early industrialization needs to be underlined here, but also the support that this offers for the school of interpretation that stresses the contribution "from below"; that is, the role of private capital and entrepreneurship. Saxonhouse stresses the great technological sophistication achieved in the textile industry that contained "many relatively small-scale mills which were, for the most part, fostered neither by the great *zaibatsu* nor by the Japanese government."

The most distinctive feature of Japan's early industrialization was the critical role played by women in the labor force. In the decades leading up to World War I, 60 percent of the industrial labor force and more than 80 percent of the workers in the textile industry were female. Moreover, they were typically young, unmarried women from impoverished farm families who stayed at work about two years. They formed, writes Gail Lee Bernstein, "the backbone of Japan's Industrial Revolution."[30] Until recently, economic historians, frequently extolling the "amazing success" of Japanese industrialization, have paid scant attention to the experience of women factory workers that Sharon Sievers contends "matched, if it did not surpass, the worst conditions of both Europe and the United States."[31]

The work of women as reelers in cotton- and silk-producing regions of the Tokugawa Period was common and their treatment was relatively benign. Frequently this work entailed short-term migration, living away from home to reel and earn money to supplement the family income. Returning, they would teach reeling techniques to other women. The work was hard but not despised and the supervision was fairly compassionate.

By the 1880s, with the introduction of mechanization and the need to compete in the international marketplace, longer hours and harsher working conditions spread through the textile industry. The filiatures were located in rural areas where the wage structure was low, the raw materials were nearby, and experienced female reelers were available. Girls were recruited from the poorest farm families, those in most need of supplemental income, and the starting age was as young as ten. They worked every day from twelve to fifteen hours in oppressive and unhealthful conditions. Many contracted tuberculosis and pleurisy. They lived in prisonlike dormitories, as many as fifty to a room, sharing bedding, with the doors kept locked after working hours, ostensibly to protect them but actually to try to limit the high runaway rate. Nearly half the girls ran away in the first months, and only one in ten stayed for three years. Company songs taught them that they were reeling for the nation, that employers were their second parents. But they had their own songs:

> Factory work is prison work,
> All it lacks are iron chains.
>
> More than a caged bird, more than a prison,
> Dormitory life is hateful.[32]

Manipulative recruiters designed a wage-payment system that made the cost of quitting enormously high. Contracts were signed with the girls' parents who received an advance that had to be repaid in full if the contract were not fulfilled. Girls were thus caught between obligations to family and the severity of supervisors overseeing their work.

As Bernstein points out, the textile industry was intimately linked with the industrial revolution, women's work, and agriculture. Women's earnings helped pay rents to the landlords who in turn invested in the textile mills. As the industry developed, Japan succeeded in capturing substantial shares of the international market. By 1909, for example, Japan had become the world's chief exporter of raw silk; and by the 1920s, 90 percent of the raw silk exported from Japan was sold in the United States.

Agrarian Society

Agriculture played a critical part in making possible the emergence of an industrial society in Japan. By producing export products and substitutes for imports, it helped provide the foreign exchange that was necessary to buy machinery and raw materials from abroad. The growing productivity of agriculture in the Meiji Period likewise provided a needed supply of staples to feed, relatively inexpensively, the growing population in the cities. Moreover, agriculture contributed through the land tax a substantial part of the government income that built the infrastructure for industrialization and also a portion of the capital that developed industries. Because of the agricultural expansion, the transition to industrial society took place without a drastic lowering of the living standards in the countryside, which, had it occurred, would doubtless have been a threat to political stability.

Nonetheless, by the turn of the century the burden that agrarian society was bearing in the process of industrialization was becoming apparent and causing increasing concern in the Japanese bureaucracy. We discussed earlier how the gōnō had acquired increasing amounts of land in the villages during the later years of the Tokugawa Period. The Meiji Restoration led to the confirmation of the landlords' position by giving to them title deeds to the property they had acquired. At the beginning of the Meiji Period approximately 30 percent of the cultivated land was tenanted. The increase in tenancy was aggravated by the land tax reforms of the 1870s, which, by requiring peasants to pay a fixed annual tax in money, worked hardship for the poor landowners, who frequently lost their lands by foreclosure. This was particularly true in the period of the Matsukata deflation (1881–1885). As Crawcour writes, "between 1884 and 1886, in the aftermath of the Matsukata deflation, foreclosures—many for the nonpayment of taxes—transferred almost one-eighth of the country's cultivated land into the hands of creditors. By the end of the century, landlords, who had not been a particularly influential group at the beginning of the Meiji era, annually collected rents equivalent to almost a quarter of Japan's rice crop."[33] Tenant-farmed land increased not only through foreclosures, but also because landlords developed new lands that were cultivated by tenant farmers. The tenancy rate soared and by the turn of the century nearly 45 percent of cultivated land was tenanted.

Leaders of the bureaucracy sensed growing unrest in the villages as the gap between classes grew. Moreover, the increasing tax burden on the citizenry made the government particularly sensitive to the problem of villages. It must be remembered that at the turn of the century 80 percent of the population still lived in communities whose population was less than 10,000. The government was, therefore, keenly concerned with preserving the cohesiveness of local society.

Indeed, without the material and spiritual support of towns and villages, the mounting cost of government could not have been borne. Requirements of armament, new colonial possessions, and industrial expansion caused central government expenditures to triple in the decade prior to the Russo-Japanese War, reaching 289 million yen in 1903; they more than doubled in the course of the war, and then remained at just less than 600 million yen down to 1913, by which time nearly half of the national budget was devoted to the army and navy, military pensions, and war debt service. Because the cost of the Russo-Japanese War was more than six times the ordinary revenues for 1903, extensive recourse was had to borrowing—particularly abroad. Taxes were raised, and lower- and middle-income classes bore an increasing share of the burden. There was some increase in the land tax, but the sharpest rise was in various excise taxes on such consumer commodities as textiles, kerosene, sugar, and salt. Indirect taxes rose from 96 million yen in 1903 to 152 million yen in 1905 and to 231 million yen in 1908. Responsibility for public works and education was increasingly delegated to local government, causing local taxes to grow alarmingly and bringing their total to more than 40 percent of national tax revenue after the turn of the century.

To strengthen the cohesiveness of local society and thereby provide a stronger basis for Japanese imperialism and industrialization, the central government in the decade following the Russo-Japanese War went to great lengths to shore up the administrative towns and villages that had been created through mergers ordered by the Town and Village Code of 1888. The government sought to strengthen them by encouraging the development of plans for improvement of landlord-tenant relations, by developing new crops and industries, and by reclaiming land. In addition, the effort was being made to revitalize local Shintō shrines and to focus their ceremonies on national loyalties revolving about the imperial throne. Campaigns to reward "model villages" and "model headmen" were sponsored, and, most important of all, the government sought to organize local groups nationally. Youth groups, for example, which had been organized within individual villages during the Tokugawa Period, were now organized into a nationwide hierarchy (with a membership of 3 million by 1913), and great emphasis was placed at all levels of the organization upon national loyalties and devotion to the imperial cause. Local military

Japanese schoolboys in 1905 study language textbooks. *Library of Congress*

associations were formed in nearly every village and again were organized into a hierarchy under the supervision of the army. They were instrumental in building respect for the army and its values. These associations, established in virtually every local community, numbered in excess of 11,000 in 1910. Likewise of great importance was a campaign by the central government to encourage the formation of agricultural cooperatives. A law regulating the conditions under which farmers could form credit, consumer, marketing, and producers' cooperatives was enacted in 1900. By 1913 the government reported the existence of more than 10,000 cooperatives with a membership in excess of 1,160,000.

In this way, the central government reached down into local village society, to mobilize loyalties and to extend them to the national level. Of great importance, of course, in this effort was the rapid growth of school attendance. By 1900, 95 percent of the children of compulsory school age were attending primary schools. Here they were subject, as we have seen, to increasingly intense indoctrination in the new national ideology.

The emerging industrial society was thus shaped in nearly every way by political and military ambitions that Japan's leaders formulated for the nation. Landlord-tenant relations, moral instruction in the schools, allocation of economic resources, employer-employee relations—everything was to be subordinated to national greatness, to

Japan's status as a first-rate power. The twentieth century, as the popular journalist Kayahara Kazan wrote during the Russo-Japanese War, "is not a time for individual heroes to vie with one another for fame. It is the time for national expansion and growth. This nationalism which has turned imperialism is now playing an unprecedented role in the drama of world history. Japan stands in the middle of this whirlwind, this ocean current of imperialism." Individual Japanese must devote themselves to the tasks of the nation, for Japan, he continued, "is destined to create an East Asian economic empire." This was "the ideal of a great people."[34]

Notes

1. Quoted in Kenneth B. Pyle, *The Japanese Question: Power and Purpose in a New Era* (Washington, D.C.: American Enterprise Institute, 1992), 18.
2. Quoted in Kenneth B. Pyle, *The New Generation in Meiji Japan: Problems of Cultural Identity, 1885–1895* (Stanford, Calif.: Stanford University Press, 1969), 181.
3. Peter Duus, "Economic Dimensions of Meiji Imperialism: The Case of Korea, 1895–1910," in *The Japanese Colonial Empire, 1895–1945*, ed. Ramon H. Myers and Mark R. Peattie (Princeton, N.J.: Princeton University Press, 1984), 133.
4. Peter Duus, ed., *The Twentieth Century*, vol. 6 of *The Cambridge History of Japan*, ed. John Whitney Hall (Cambridge: Cambridge University Press, 1988), 218.
5. Quoted in Roger F. Hackett, *Yamagata Aritomo in the Rise of Modern Japan, 1838–1922* (Cambridge, Mass.: Harvard University Press, 1971), 138.
6. Albert M. Craig and Donald H. Shively, eds., *Personality in Japanese History* (Berkeley: University of California Press, 1970), 265.
7. Myers and Peattie, eds., *The Japanese Colonial Empire*, 15.
8. See Mutsu Munemitsu, *Kenkenroku: A Diplomatic Record of the Sino-Japanese War, 1894–95*, ed. and trans. Gordon Mark Berger (Tokyo: University of Tokyo Press, 1982), passim.
9. Tokutomi Sohō, quoted in Pyle, *New Generation*, 175.
10. Quoted in Kenneth B. Pyle, "Japan Faces Her Future," *Journal of Japanese Studies* 1 (spring 1975), 347.
11. Pyle, *New Generation*, 180.
12. Quoted in Richard Storry, *Japan and the Decline of the West in Asia, 1894–1943* (London: Macmillan, 1979), 30.
13. Quoted in Shumpei Okamoto, *The Japanese Oligarchy and the Russo-Japanese War* (New York: Columbia University Press, 1970), 119.
14. Quoted in Kenneth B. Pyle, "The Technology of Japanese Nationalism: The Local Improvement Movement, 1900–1918," *Journal of Asian Studies* 33 (November 1973), 51.
15. Marius B. Jansen, *The Japanese and Sun Yat-sen* (Cambridge, Mass.: Harvard University Press, 1954), 211.
16. © OUP 1963. Reprinted from *Thought and Behaviour in Modern Japanese Politics* by Masao Maruyama, edited by Ivan Morris by permission of Oxford University Press, 154–156.

17. Quoted in Pyle, "Technology of Japanese Nationalism," 51.
18. Ibid., 57.
19. Quoted in Ronald P. Dore, "The Modernizer as a Special Case: Japanese Factory Legislation, 1882–1911," *Comparative Studies in Society and History* 11 (1969), 439.
20. Quoted in Kenneth B. Pyle, "Advantages of Followership: German Economics and Japanese Bureaucrats, 1890–1925," *Journal of Japanese Studies* 1 (autumn 1974), 129–130.
21. Quoted ibid., 130.
22. Andrew Gordon, *The Evolution of Labor Relations in Japan: Heavy Industry, 1853–1955* (Cambridge, Mass.: Harvard University Press, 1985), 5–6.
23. Ibid., 417.
24. Thomas C. Smith, *Native Sources of Japanese Industrialization, 1750–1920* (Berkeley: University of California Press, 1988), 236–270.
25. Ronald P. Dore, *British Factory–Japanese Factory* (Berkeley: University of California Press, 1973), 395.
26. Quoted in Sheldon Garon, *The State and Labor in Modern Japan* (Berkeley: University of California Press, 1987), 30.
27. W. Dean Kinzley, *Industrial Harmony in Modern Japan: The Invention of a Tradition* (New York: Routledge, 1991).
28. Smith, *Native Sources*, 44.
29. Gary R. Saxonhouse, "Country Girls and Communication among Competitors in the Japanese Cotton-Spinning Industry," in *Japanese Industrialization and Its Social Consequences*, ed. Hugh Patrick (Berkeley: University of California Press, 1976), 97.
30. Gail Lee Bernstein, "Women in the Silk-Reeling Industry in Nineteenth-Century Japan," in *Japan and the World: Essays on Japanese History and Politics in Honor of Ishida Takeshi*, ed. Gail Lee Bernstein and Haruhiro Fukui (Basingstoke: Macmillan, 1988), 74.
31. Sharon L. Sievers, *Flowers in Salt: The Beginnings of Feminist Consciousness in Modern Japan* (Stanford, Calif.: Stanford University Press, 1983), 57.
32. E. Patricia Tsurumi, *Factory Girls: Women in the Thread Mills of Meiji Japan* (Princeton, N.J.: Princeton University Press, 1990), 98.
33. E. Sydney Crawcour, "Industrialization and Technological Change," in *The Twentieth Century*, ed. Duus, 408–409.
34. Quoted in Akira Iriye, *Pacific Estrangement: Japanese and American Expansion, 1897–1911* (Cambridge, Mass.: Harvard University Press, 1972), 97.

Crisis of Political Community

The Meiji Period, one of the most remarkable epochs of modern world history, came to a close in 1912 with the death of the Emperor whose reign had witnessed Japan's emergence as the leading power in Asia. His passing was mourned by literati as well as by the masses, in a striking display of emotion that showed how deeply the new nationalism had touched the Japanese people. "A dense mass of humanity again thronged the great open spaces outside the Palace walls last night," wrote the correspondent for the London *Times*, "continually moving up to the Emperor's gate, there to kneel in prayer a few minutes and then pass on once more. The crowd was drawn from all classes, and all preserved the highest degree of orderliness and silence save for the crunching of the gravel under wooden sandals and the low continuous murmur of prayers. . . . One who looked over the sea of bowed heads outside the Palace wall could not desire better proof of the vitality of that worship of the Ruler. . . ."[1] Feelings were further heightened on the day of the funeral, September 13, when General Nogi Maresuke, the military hero of the Russo-Japanese War, and his wife committed ritual suicide in the manner of the classic samurai who loyally followed his lord even in death. The most significant novelists of the time, Natsume Sōseki and Mori Ōgai, found that the emotional experience of these events changed the course of their writing. They were drawn away from preoccupation with the Western world back to their own cultural traditions for the thematic material in their subsequent novels.

The new Emperor Yoshihito, who gave the name Taishō to the years of his reign (1912–1926), was a weak and uncertain figure. It was a poorly kept secret that the Taishō Emperor's illnesses frequently involved mental aberrations. On one occasion while reading a ceremonial message to the Diet he rolled up the scroll and began peering, as through a telescope, at the startled legislators. Such behavior seems not to have diminished reverence for the imperial institution, yet it was perhaps symbolic of the nation's passage into a time of trouble.

This was not to say that the early years of the new Emperor's reign did not bring substantial new national achievements. The outbreak of World War I in Europe in the summer of 1914 provided extraordinary opportunities to advance the twin objectives of empire and industry, which the nation had pursued through the Meiji era. The preoccupation of the European powers allowed Japan to seize German holdings in Shantung and German islands in the South Pacific: the Carolines, Marianas, Marshalls, Palau, and Yap. More important, conflict among the great industrial nations meant that new markets and new demands for Japanese goods brought sudden economic expansion and prosperity. Exports nearly tripled during the war years, reflecting an unprecedented boom in industrial production.

But the period after World War I witnessed a succession of crises in Japanese society, and the problem of maintaining a stable political community sorely tried Japanese leadership. During the preceding fifty years the Japanese masses had slowly been awakened to political experience. By the first decades of the twentieth century it was becoming clear that they could no longer be kept out of political life. Industrialization and universal education contributed to this end; by the turn of the century there was a large number of newspapers and magazines designed for a mass audience. The increasing involvement of the populace in the issues of the day caused the leadership growing concern.

One result of this activation was that the political parties began to call for a broadened suffrage—ultimately, universal male suffrage. Many of the Meiji leaders desperately feared this demand, believing that it would threaten the existing social order. Yamagata had warned his colleagues that universal suffrage would be tantamount to a socialist revolution. His fears were fed by evidence that industrialization was engendering new tensions and divisions in society: the labor movement grew more militant, landlord-tenant disputes multiplied, and radical groups proliferated. Those antagonisms were greatly intensified by the economic expansion during World War I and by the influence of socialist ideas from abroad. The basic question posed by events in the 1920s was whether the political system formed in the early Meiji Period had the resilience and the flexibility to absorb the newly awakening groups into its processes, and to accommodate satisfactorily the tensions and antagonisms of a burgeoning industrial society.

Evolution of the Political System

There is no question that the Meiji political institutions had the capacity to change, at least up to a point, for in the decades after the establishment of the new governmental structure in 1890 the system evolved in largely unexpected directions. The Meiji Constitution envisaged a political community directed by a small elite at the head of an extensive bureaucracy. In theory, this elite would consult public opinion as it was expressed in the Diet, but the elite would be fundamentally neutral, standing above the groups and factions represented in the legislature and acting in the interests of the whole nation. Although the Japanese state never lost its elitist character, the conditions of the several decades after 1890 created a much more complex and often unwieldy group that controlled the fortunes of the state.

The most noteworthy change in the political system was the growth in the power and influence of the parties. None of the oligarchs in 1890 accepted the idea of party cabinets. Instead they spoke of "transcendental cabinets"—comprising members of the oligarchy whose interest and loyalty supposedly transcended narrow party and factional interests and loyalties. Itō seems to have felt that party cabinets were possible some time in the distant future, when the parties had become truly national bodies; others, such as Yamagata, saw nothing of the kind. Yamagata confided to the Emperor in 1899: "My interpretation of the constitution differs from that of Itō and Ōkuma. I am absolutely opposed to a party cabinet. My only hope is that Imperial authority will be extended and Imperial prestige will not decline."[2]

But all the oligarchs were wrong in their expectation that the parties could be circumscribed. There were several reasons why, almost from the beginning of the new Meiji constitutional order, the parties were able to develop new power. In the first place, while the elected House of Representatives lacked any legal control over the prime minister and his cabinet, it did have the negative power to withhold support from legislation proposed by the cabinet. More important was the veto power that the House exercised over the budget. Although the framers of the constitution had provided that, should the House prove recalcitrant, the previous year's budget would automatically come into force, in a time of rapidly mounting government expenditure, particularly at the turn of the century, this provision was little help. The Diet could greatly damage the plans of a cabinet by its refusal to sanction a proposed budget.

Although the cabinet had extensive powers to dissolve the Diet, it was forced to deal carefully with the parties and not to resort too often to arbitrary dissolution, else constitutional government would simply break down. The nation had invested its pride in making the new system work. Even after treaty revision had succeeded, the oligarchs were still anxious to demonstrate to the West—and to themselves as well—that they were equal to the challenge. As late as 1899, Itō remarked that, "If there is one mistake in the progress and direction of constitutional government, there will be those who question the suitability of constitutional government for the Orient. This is what concerns me."[3] In short, it was a national goal that constitutional government should be made to work in Japan.

The lack of unity and the ambivalence among the oligarchs with regard to the workings of the new system provided opportunities for expansion of party power. Although Yamagata was in many respects dead set against concessions to the parties, Itō was willing to seek accommodation with them—particularly with the more moderate forces within the Diet. Moreover, the parties had already by the 1890s gained some measure of public support, which also provided stimulus for the oligarchy to meet some of their demands.

The parties went through a number of distinct phases in their gradual rise to a share in power. The first phase, from the opening of the Diet in 1890 to the beginning of the Sino-Japanese War in 1894, was characterized by implacable hostilities between the oligarchy and the parties. The latter posed repeated obstacles to the passage of government budgets, and the oligarchy responded by frequently dissolving the Diet. During the second phase, from 1895 to 1900, tentative short-lived alliances were struck between the cabinet and elements in the House. This was a time of rapid expansion of armaments, and the oligarchs were willing to make limited concessions to the parties in order to gain the passage of budgets. Those alliances, however, tended to break down once the oligarchs had won their way.

Nevertheless the realization was taking hold among the top members of the oligarchy that they had no recourse but to put such coalitions on a firm and stable basis. A third phase, therefore, of determined mutual accommodation between the two groups ensued from 1900 to 1918. This phase was inaugurated by Itō's decision to join a parliamentary party. In 1900 he accepted the presidency of the *Seiyūkai* (Friends of Constitutional Government Party). In 1913, another oligarch and protégé of Yamagata, Katsura Tarō, followed suit by forming his own party. It was during this phase that parties acquired the form and organization characteristic of Japanese conservative parties ever since. Having found party support indispensable to their power, the oligarchs now brought many of their followers in the bureaucracy into the parties they headed. Not only did the parties become "bureaucratized," but the reverse process was also taking place. Government agencies gradually came to be interpenetrated by party men.

In the working out of this process of accommodation between party and bureaucracy, no one was more important than Hara Kei (Takashi), perhaps the most astute politician in modern Japanese history. Hara, who had served in the bureaucracy but left it to pursue a distinguished career in journalism and business, helped Itō form the Seiyūkai and soon became the mastermind behind its emergent power. By making concessions to the Yamagata faction, which dominated the government in the early 1900s, Hara gained access to key appointments within the bureaucracy. The most important concession he could offer was Seiyūkai support for the budget of the government, which was particularly hard-pressed financially at the time of the Russo-Japanese War. In return, he had himself appointed to the office of home minister, a position that brought with it control of the entire network of local government, including power to appoint prefectural governors and to allocate government funds for public works. Hara used these powers to build Seiyūkai support at the local level. To potential followers he could offer local office and the pork barrel. He built up the strength of Seiyūkai supporters in the provinces by channeling resources to build dams, schools, and railroads in their areas. In the face of this growing power, other parties in the Diet were forced to coalesce out of self-defense, forming an anti-Seiyūkai coalition in 1913 called the *Dōshikai,* renamed the *Kenseikai* in 1916 and the *Minseitō* in 1927. In this development we may find the origins of two-party politics.

The stage was now set for a fourth phase in the development of the parties, which began in 1918 with the naming of Hara as prime minister. During this phase, which lasted until 1932, the parties attained a position of quasi supremacy in the political system. That is to say, it became common during this period to give the prime ministership to the head of one of the parties. It was, of course, not constitutionally necessary (from 1922 to 1924 there were in fact three nonparty cabinets), but rather represented the acknowledgment by the elder statesmen (*genrō*), who advised the Emperor in the selection of the prime minister, that the balance of power in the political system had shifted in favor of the party elites. Their rise to power did not involve the parties' making a fundamental change in the political structure; instead, they succeeded in the shrewd infiltration and conciliation of the institutional forces established by the Meiji Constitution—the oligarchy, the bureaucracy, and the military. Because they were compelled by the constitutional order to turn inward for power, particularly to the bureaucracy, the parties did not become mass-based organizations. They built up their strength at the local level with men of influence who could be rewarded with office and with governmental benevolences. Nonetheless, this fourth phase seemed to optimistic observers to augur a trend toward the ascendancy of parliamentary politics and a growing influence of the common man over his government. Such observers therefore called this phase the era of Taishō democracy.

The Elitist Nature of the Taishō Political System

For a brief period in the 1920s it appeared that the trends of the time, quite contrary to the intentions of the Meiji oligarchs, favored the emergence of a democratic political system. Two-party politics, responsible party cabinets, extension of civic rights to larger numbers of citizens, and the rise of democratic political philosophies were important developments. But they should not be mistaken for the entire system. The optimists who proclaimed the emergence of Taishō democracy were focusing their attention on a new but limited aspect of the political system in the post–World War I period. The system was dominated by a complex interplay of elites of whom the party leaders were only one part. For a brief time the party leaders were able to coordinate and accommodate the different elites, and to that extent the political system in the Taishō Period might be regarded as becoming an elitist democracy. In the end, however, hopes for democratic politics proved evanescent and no breakthrough to a new political structure was achieved.

There was, as Taichirō Mitani writes, a built-in ambiguity in the constitutional structure: "The Meiji constitution, in somewhat ambivalent fashion, emphasized the emperor as the supreme constitutional monarch and granted him imperial sovereignty, yet at the same time it rejected the idea of direct imperial rule."[4] The Emperor, "sacred and inviolable," as the Constitution said, was above and beyond politics. The various organs of state were independently responsible to an Emperor who was in practice politically aloof. The result was to create an extraordinary division of powers. The Ministers of State were individually responsible to the Emperor, thus weakening the prime minister, because the Meiji Constitution neither mentioned a cabinet nor provided for the concept of collective responsibility. The army, the bureaucracy, the judiciary were all separately responsible to the Emperor. To manage this plurality of power centers, some kind of extraconstitutional means had to be found to coordinate them. The Meiji oligarchs could make the constitution work because their factional ties cut across the various organs of state. Having created the system themselves they naturally had a pervasive web of personal ties through which they could maintain a coherent and stable system.

By the Taishō Period, however, government had grown in size and complexity, the founding fathers had passed from the scene, and elite factions were becoming more discrete and competitive. Let us consider the fragmentation of power and the different elite interests.

In addition to the newly emergent party elites in the Lower House, there were the members of the Upper House, the House of Peers. As the constitution provided, they were "composed of members of the Imperial Family, of Nobles, and of Deputies who have been appointed by the Emperor." Intended as a conservative force, it had powers almost equal to those of the Lower House and therefore could exercise a virtual veto over legislation forwarded to it. Its ability to block legislation was a powerful check on the Lower House.

Another conservative group consisted of various advisors to the

Emperor. They were consulted in many issues of state but most important in the choice of prime minister, which the constitution gave to the Emperor. The genrō, an extralegal group of Meiji leaders, was the key consultative group. It had formed in the 1890s, but after the death of Yamagata in 1922 and Matsukata in 1924, only Saionji Kimmochi remained as "the last of the genrō." He together with a group of former prime ministers performed this critical advisory function. Other influential advisors close to the Emperor included the Imperial Household Minister and the members of the Privy Council.

Bureaucratic leaders were also powerful. Proud and prestigious, they styled themselves servants of the Emperor, disdainful of private interests and devoted to the nation's well-being. Their expertise and technical competence at drafting legislation and administering the laws was based on their meritocratic selection and durability. On balance they were conservative, but they could also be reformist when the national interest seemed to require it.

Another powerful elite was the military. Owing to Japan's growing imperial commitments and the complexity of strategic planning and organization, the army and navy emerged as strong political forces. The constitution placed them directly under the Emperor with direct access to him and not responsible to the cabinet. They jealously guarded their independence, or "the right of autonomous command" as they called it. This autonomy gave them a powerful role in foreign policy, and the military maintained its own overseas representatives independent of the Foreign Ministry. The army and navy elites exerted great leverage over the formation and the life of cabinets through ordinances that limited those eligible to serve as Minister of War or Minister of Navy to certain high-ranking military officers, as we have seen. A threat to resign gave them sway over policy-making.

The final group was the business elite, comprising leaders of the great business combines, the zaibatsu, whose power had grown rapidly as a result of the recent industrial growth. They had cultivated close ties with the government in order to receive subsidies, preferential treatment, and legislative favors; and as political campaigns became more expensive, political leaders looked to them for contributions.

It was an unwieldy political system. Moreover, the elites who led this plurality of power centers were not themselves monolithic. Factions existed within each of them. In the bureaucracy, for example, turf battles and intramural struggles over jurisdictional issues arose among the various ministries. The army had a Chōshū faction and an anti-Chōshū faction. And so on.

For a time in the 1920s, the conservative political parties succeeded in mediating among the elites, thereby dominating the political system. They managed to orchestrate the different power centers in the system by controlling the budget and permanent legislation. They created alliances in the Upper House to neutralize its power. They recruited former bureaucrats into positions of party leadership and collaborated with the key groups in the Home Ministry and the Justice Ministry to win them over. The army, needing party support for its budget request, struck alliances and, as a consequence, bonds between the military leadership and the parties grew closer. In 1925 an army general, Tanaka Giichi, became president of the Seiyūkai. In such fashion, the parties interpenetrated the various power centers at a time when the influence of the Meiji leaders as advisors to the Emperor was waning.

The party leaders, for a brief time, thus became the spider at the center of a web of elite groups. They became the core body able to coordinate the fragmented constitutional structure. The supposedly popular parties had actually turned inward to the various centers of elite power created by the Meiji Constitution in order to establish their control. In this sense we may term the structure of Taishō democracy an elitist democracy. All democracies were more or less elitist in this period, but Japan's was more so.

The intellectuals who were the theorists of Taishō democracy in fact conceived of it in this elitist way. They did not advocate popular sovereignty, government by the people. That would be unconstitutional because the Meiji Constitution placed sovereignty with the Emperor. They favored government for the people. They were ambivalent toward the masses. On the one hand, the goal of government should be the welfare of the people. On the other hand, the people were not yet ready for full political participation: the people had to be prepared through "political education" and a "transformation of their knowledge and morality." The most famous of the Taishō democratic theorists, Yoshino Sakuzō, was a professor at Tokyo Imperial University. His term for democracy was *mimponshugi,* which literally translated means "the principles of people centeredness," and it carried the connotation of government on behalf of the people. Intellectual liberals such as Yoshino "expected the representative process to produce a moral elite (or a meritocratic elite) not unlike themselves."[5]

Turmoil in Society

The term *Taishō democracy* is used in two senses. It is used, as we have just seen, to refer to the emergence of party cabinets and the possibility of revising the political structure. But it is also used in a broader social sense to denote the awakening of the masses to politics and the appearance of liberal and sometimes radical movements for reform.

The political parties gained their dominance at one of the most difficult periods in Japanese history. This was not auspicious. The parties, battling each other and seeking to maintain their position vis-à-vis the other elites, scarcely had the time or the objectivity required to resolve the multiple crises that wracked society in the post–World War I era.

The economic impact of the war had created a far more complex society than the one the oligarchs had sought to manage at the beginning of the twentieth century. Then, as we have seen, the bureaucracy had been hopeful that, by acting early before industrialism created the severe problems of Western societies, Japan could avoid similar unrest and conflict. Such sanguine views were quickly dashed in the postwar period. Social unrest, militant labor, and radical ideologies were all present for everyone to see. One could no longer speak of "prevention" and "acting early." The choice was now either to enact immediate social reforms to alleviate unrest, or else to resort to intensified national mobilization and suppression. The elites, gripped by a sense of crisis and fearful of social disintegration, usually chose the latter alternative.

The postwar period began with the Rice Riots in August 1918, when demonstrations swept the country in protest over a sharp increase in the price of rice. Riots involving more than 1 million people were reported in forty-two of forty-seven prefectures. The Rice Riots were the largest popular demonstration in Japanese history prior to the Anti-Security Treaty demonstrations in 1960. Troops were called out in twenty-six prefectures to quell the attacks on rice dealers and profiteers. The elites were fearful and alarmed by the activization of the masses and the appearance of incendiary thought. Yamagata wrote to the conservative journalist Tokutomi Sohō expressing his fear of chaos; and Tokutomi responded: "The rise in prices and the importation of anarchism fan each other and will give rise to social revolution. . . . You cannot imagine how much the thinking and ideals of the young today are confused. . . . Please destroy this letter."[6] Further evidence of the volatile nature of the people when aroused by social and economic issues came in the sudden rise in 1919 of labor disputes, numbering 497—ten times the number five years earlier. The number of labor unions mushroomed, and among the most important ones there was a trend toward radical thought and militant proposals. By 1920 the wartime boom was spent, a sharp recession had set in, and the nation began a decade of recurrent economic upheavals.

This unrest spread to the countryside, ordinarily regarded as the foundation of a stable order. Yokoi Tokiyoshi, a leading spokesman for conservative rural values, had written in 1913 that in the face of rising radicalism in the city "we can only depend upon the peasants. The city will forever be a factory of revolution, while the country will always be the protector of the social order." Yet in the postwar period tenancy disputes became more numerous than industrial labor disputes, escalating from 256 in 1918 to more than 2,700 by 1926. Nearly one-half of the arable land was worked by tenants, and, particularly in areas where the number of absentee landlords was increasing most rapidly, the high rate of rents stirred resentment. In some areas tenant unions organized and multiplied with startling rapidity. From 173 tenant unions in 1917 the movement grew to 4,582 unions a decade later with a membership of 365,322. These unions engaged in collective bargaining with landlords, presenting demands for improving the lot of the tenants. What was the significance of the striking rise of these tenant unions?

Few issues in modern Japanese history are debated with greater intensity than the significance of changes in rural society in the interwar period. Not only among historians in Japan, but also among Western scholars we find a wide range of disagreement. Barrington Moore, for example, sees the incomplete nature of the Meiji Restoration—that is, the lack of land reform—and the commercialization of agriculture as impoverishing the tenant farmers who worked nearly one-half the arable land. The resulting radicalism of this class, in this view, was repressed by the landlords and the government and channeled into support for fascism and militarism in the 1930s. In sharp contrast, the historian Richard Smethurst sees industrialization creating a substantially improved standard of living for the typical farmer, including the tenant, and his emergence in the Taishō Period as "not merely a pawn to be buffeted by an unjust market system . . . [but as] a positive actor, an 'economic animal,' a small entrepreneur, if you will, who increasingly made every effort to maximize profits by using new techniques to produce more and better cash crops. . . . Commercial agriculture and other parts of Japan's modernization process allowed the cultivator to take greater and greater control of his own destiny."[7] Tenant unions, rather than being centers of radical protest, were pragmatic means to pursue a better living.

However we interpret the militancy of tenant farmers, as victims of exploitation or as profit-maximizers, their membership in unions underscores our fundamental theme about the Taishō Period—that the growing activization of the masses posed a challenge for the elitist political structure. The countryside was changing. In the Tokugawa Period, only certain members of the wealthy peasant class were literate. By the 1920s schools and literacy, magazines and newspapers, military service and mobility raised the sights of most small farmers and tenants, loosened their reliance on the local elite, and changed their attitudes. "Poverty was no longer their fate," writes one authority on the period, "but the product of circumstances that they had the power to change."[8]

What in particular heightened the crisis atmosphere then was the extraordinary influx of radical thought. The Russian Revolution, the popularity of Wilsonian democracy, the growing alienation of intellectuals from the social order in Japan, and the unrest in society that we have just mentioned, all led to a striking diversity of ideologies that could not but be worrisome to government leaders. Their nervous concern was demonstrated, for example, by the hounding of a young Tokyo Imperial University professor, Morito Tatsuo, for publishing a rather innocuous article on the Russian anarchist Peter Kropotkin's social views. In 1922 the Japanese Communist Party was established and became at once the subject of unremitting police repression. On the campuses liberal democracy and socialism were popular. The parties were not unaffected by those trends, and particularly among the opposition members, support for universal manhood suffrage grew. Hara Kei blocked such a proposal in 1920, confiding in his diary that enactment would have brought on revolution.

It is of course possible to exaggerate the extent of social unrest. For example, despite the signs of turmoil among industrial laborers, almost 60 percent of the industrial workforce was composed of women, primarily young peasant girls who, prior to marriage, would work on short-term agreements in the textile industry. Occasionally these women participated in or even led strikes in the textile mills, but their usual way of protesting conditions was to run away. Because they were short-term and highly vulnerable workers, they lacked incentive to struggle for long-term improvement of factory conditions. At the high point of the prewar labor movement in the 1930s, fewer than 6 percent of unionized workers were women. Male industrial workers also were not easily drawn into radical labor movements. In fact, a sizable number of the male workers were fresh from the village and still imbued with traditional values of loyalty and obedience. In the countryside, despite the new unrest, it was still true that the great majority of tenants were not members of the tenant unions and were not involved in disputes. Even among the intellectual class, only a small minority favored radical change of the existing order.

Nonetheless, the ruling elites were fearful. Left-wing activities seemed incendiary, and there was no telling how high the flames of unrest might be fanned. Moreover, was not the revolution in Russia the product of only a small group of people? The situation was rendered even more critical by the great Kanto earthquake, which struck Tokyo, Yokohama, and the remainder of the Kanto Plain moments before noon on September 1, 1923. The intense shock brought the collapse of tens of thousands of buildings and the death of thousands, and far greater destruction was wrought by the fires that began everywhere in the aftermath of the quake. By the time the flames burned out, more than 130,000 people were dead, billions of dollars of damage had been done, and more than one-half of Tokyo and most of

Yokohama were laid waste. In the ensuing chaos and confusion, rumors spread that Koreans resident in Japan were committing acts of sabotage. Vigilante terrorism resulted in the slaying of thousands of Koreans. Matsuo Takayoshi, the most careful student of this pogrom, sets the figure at somewhere between 2,500 and 6,000 Koreans murdered. Police were involved in the slaughter, as they also rounded up scores of radicals. In one police station nine alleged Communists were shot to death; in another, Ōsugi Sakae, the leading anarchist, and his wife and nephew were strangled in their jail cell by a police captain. The paroxysm of violence left little room to doubt the volatility of the new mass society. As political leaders set about laying plans for reconstruction of the capital region, their apprehension over the social unrest was noticeably heightened. As a kind of aftershock from the earthquake, in December the Prince Regent Hirohito was shot at by a young radical angered by the antileftist violence after the earthquake. The cabinet that had taken office only the day after the quake immediately resigned.

Among the elite there was a division of opinion as to whether their proper, safest response to this unrest ought to be some kind of progressive adjustment of social and political institutions that would accommodate the new forces or whether, on the contrary, it was necessary to depend on a tightening authoritarianism that would control not only political behavior but also thought. The issue of universal male suffrage illustrated this division. When it surfaced in the first decade of the century, conservatives such as Yamagata opposed it as destructive of the social order. Other leaders, however, saw it as a "safety valve" for unrest and believed that if the masses continued to be excluded from participation they would end up alienated and revolutionary. After World War I the opposition Kenseikai Party took that position and used it against Hara, who opposed extending suffrage, fearing that it might weaken Seiyūkai power. Popular support for universal manhood suffrage continued to build, and many conservatives came to favor it, arguing that it would broaden political support for the state and contribute to national integration. Shortly after the earthquake, the Seiyūkai decided to back universal male suffrage. It became law in 1925. At one stroke, the size of the electorate was made four times larger, numbering in excess of 12 million.

In spite of their backing the suffrage bill, the conservative elites did not regard the prospects of a mass political community with equanimity. Rather they felt the need for further measures to limit the range of political debate and for intensified efforts to mobilize the populace to instill deeper commitment to national loyalties. Makino Nobuaki, an influential elder statesman, for example, said that universal suffrage would lead to social disintegration if it were interpreted as supporting egalitarian ideals. It was necessary, he concluded, to organize a league of all the semigovernmental organizations, such as the youth groups, military associations, and women's auxiliaries to cooperate with the shrines, temples, and schools in emphasizing national spirit and traditional values of respect for hierarchy and social harmony.

More important, the same session of the Diet that passed the new suffrage bill also approved by a vote of 246 to 18 the Peace Preservation Law of 1925, which greatly narrowed the range of permissible political debate by outlawing groups that sought to alter the form of government or to abolish the system of private ownership. In the ensuing years the police used this law to round up members of the Communist Party, their alleged sympathizers, and others of left-wing persuasion. Such pressure contributed to the weakness of the new leftist parties that were attempted after 1925, but those parties suffered as well from internal squabbling and from a certain intellectual orientation that divorced them from the mass support they sought.

The crisis atmosphere deepened in the latter half of the 1920s as the economy slid toward the depression. Government planners had been beset by recurrent economic crises, none of which were settled in a satisfactory long-term manner, with the result that chronic instability and a general malaise plagued the economy throughout the 1920s, exacerbating tensions and unrest in society. Policymakers had failed to restore equilibrium after the unprecedented surge of growth and inflation during the war. "The basic problem," writes Hugh Patrick, "was that prices in Japan had risen more than they had abroad; once the war ended, Japan was not able to compete sufficiently in international markets, despite the war-induced growth and diversification of her industry."[9] At the highest level there was a costly indecisiveness in dealing with this problem with the result that growth lagged.

The small shopworker and farmer particularly encountered hard times. Agriculture stagnated and farm prices declined, because of both the import of cheap rice from Korea and Taiwan and the declining world market for Japanese agricultural goods, particularly silk. The recurring crises and government ineptness proved, however, but a prelude to the disaster that befell the industrialized world, including Japan, in 1929. The onset of the world depression brought collapse of the export market. Most damaging was the collapse of the international market for silk, Japan's principal export commodity and a product upon which most farm families depended for part of their income. By 1930 two-thirds of the net income produced in agriculture was spent on rents, taxes, and farm debt. Policymakers continued to flounder, compounding the effects of the depression by returning Japan to the gold standard at the end of 1929. Real farm income fell precipitously, with a calamitous effect on the standard of living in the villages. By the end of the 1920s social unrest in both cities and countryside had created a pervasive political malaise.

Women's Groups and the State

The attempts of the state to preserve a stable political community in the midst of the disruptions of rapid industrialization is a key theme of the Taishō Period. The government continuously reinforced the ideology of the family state and assimilated groups activated by rapid economic and social change. Since early in the Meiji Period it had been a firm principle that the governed should be brought into the governing process, not as a natural, innate right but rather as a means of achieving national unity. We have seen the techniques that the government used to integrate farmers, youth, veterans, and other groups into loyal service to the state. We have also seen how the government undertook reforms that would forestall the alienation of groups. The reforms designed to protect factory laborers and to extend male suffrage were based not on theories of innate rights but rather on the state's need to maintain the cohesiveness of society.

In some ways the most surprising reform initiative by the government was its 1931 proposal to give women voting and officeholding rights at the local level, in cities, towns, and villages. The proposal was surprising because for decades the government had sought to keep women away from all political matters and engaged solely in domestic responsibilities. In laws issued in the Meiji Period it was explicitly stated that only males could vote or serve in government positions. On the eve of the opening of the Diet in 1890, legislation prohibited women from joining political groups or even attending meetings where political issues were discussed. Again, in the Police Law of 1900, Article 5 forbade women and minors from attending political meetings.

The ideal of femininity in the ideology of the Meiji state is summed up in the slogan "good wife, wise mother" (*ryōsai kembo*), which was widely promoted by government leaders. Women were exhorted to contribute to the nation through efficient management of the household, responsible upbringing of children, frugality, and hard work. This ideology was a Japanese version of contemporary Western ideals of female domesticity. In contrast to the Tokugawa definition of a woman's dutiful role in samurai tracts where the woman was admonished to obey her husband and parents-in-law, the Meiji woman now had a part to play in nation building. More than duties, she now had a mission.

Female education therefore had a clear focus on training for domestic roles, or what we might call home economics, in order to serve the nation. As one of the Meiji Period's elite male educators wrote in 1909:

> Our female education, then, is based on the assumption that women marry, and that its object is to fit girls to become "good wives and wise mothers." The question naturally arises what con-

stitutes a good wife and wise mother, and the answer requires a knowledge of the position of the wife and mother in the household and the standing of women in society and her status in the State. . . . [The] man goes outside to work to earn his living, to fulfill his duties to the State; it is the wife's part to help him, for the common interests of the house, and as her share of duty to the State, by sympathy and encouragement, by relieving him of anxieties at home, managing household affairs, looking after the household economy, and, above all, tending the old people and bringing up the children in a fit and proper manner.[10]

In the Taishō Period the role of women in society and in politics was reopened partly as a result of the spread of women's education, the emergence of women's organizations, and the rise of a small but noteworthy women's movement. By 1920 virtually all girls acquired the compulsory coeducation of six years. More than 150,000 were attending the higher girls' schools (secondary-level institutions). Beyond that, for the select few, there were women's schools such as Tsuda College founded in 1900 by Tsuda Umeko, who had earlier studied at Bryn Mawr College in the United States. An emergent class of professional women in teaching, nursing, clerical positions, white-collar work, and other professions was evident in the post–World War I period.

Observing this emergence of middle-class working women, journalism responded with discussions of new roles for "the new woman." In 1911 Hiratsuka Raichō, a graduate of Tsuda, founded the magazine *Seitō (Bluestocking)*, initially intended to be a literary magazine for women. As Hiratsuka wrote, however, she soon discovered she could not avoid politics: "That our literary activities would put us in direct opposition to the ideology of 'good wife, wise mother' was not totally unexpected. What we did not expect was to have to stand and fight immediately all of the traditions of feudalism in the society."[11] In the opening issue of *Seitō*, Yosano Akiko in a poem entitled "The Day the Mountains Move" declared that: "All the sleeping women/Are now awake and moving."[12] The journal quickly became a forum for the advocacy of new social and political roles for women. In the 1920s feminists turned their energies toward political activism through new women's organizations that demanded gender equality and political rights. The movement drew encouragement from the contemporary extension of the franchise to women in Western countries.

In light of the forces that were giving women a more conspicuous social role, the political elite changed its mind about excluding women from the political world and concluded that integrating women in the political community would strengthen the Japanese state. Official

Poet and feminist writer Yosano Akiko. *Kyodo News Service of Japan*

gender ideology therefore began to change in the 1920s. Diet members asserted that women must be taught to be "members of the State" and "a woman cannot be a good wife and wise mother without a knowledge of politics." In 1922 the Diet revised Article 5 of the Police Law and permitted women to attend and sponsor political-discussion meetings, though they still could not belong to political parties. This step also triggered the determination of the bureaucracy to mobilize women for other, more traditional purposes of the state: to encourage their support of saving and frugality, family discipline, and patriotic training of children. The Home Ministry formed women's organizations at all levels of society, just as it had done earlier for youth, veterans, and other groups.

At the end of the 1920s bureaucrats and party leaders agreed that women should have the suffrage in local elections. They crafted legislation that would grant adult women the "civic rights" to vote and hold office in local governments. Home Ministry bureaucrats believed, as one put it, that women's participation in local government was logical because "cities, towns, and villages are to a certain degree extensions of the household when it comes to, say, schools, sewers, or public toilets." The Home Minister's views were expressed more carefully. "Women think conservatively," he said. "Thus it will be enormously beneficial for women to take part in local government to maintain the order of State and Society by blocking radical change."[13] Lest there be any mistaken notion that the proposal was based on gender equality, the ministry inserted a provision in the government's legislation requiring a successful woman candidate to obtain her husband's consent before taking office. In 1931 the bill passed the Lower House but was overwhelmingly defeated in the highly conservative House of Peers by a vote of 184 to 62. Suffrage for women became a dead issue until 1945.

Despite the failure of suffrage as a means of integrating women into the political sphere, considerable evidence indicates that mobilization of women for purposes of the state was in a measure successful, not simply as a strategy of assimilating the women's movement but also because there was in actuality a pattern of cooperation between middle-class women's groups and the state. Many of the middle-class women's organizations chose to work with bureaucrats and their officially sponsored groups. As one historian contends, "to many women's leaders the road to power and influence lay in assuming public roles, often in alliance with the state."[14] They joined with bureaucrats to encourage other women to take the lead in public causes that appeared to lie within the special domain of women. Middle-class women leaders gained visibility in the political world through campaigns to increase household savings, improve welfare and health measures for mothers and children, and other civic-minded causes. Later, in the militarist 1930s, even liberal feminists began to collaborate with the state as women's groups grew to play a prominent role in wartime mobilization, dealing with problems of factory women, families of deceased servicemen, and conservation of scarce materials.

Vulnerability of the Political Parties

We have seen how the political parties steadily gained unexpected power within the Meiji constitutional system in the first decades of the century. They had achieved this position not by championing popular causes or by seeking reform of the political system, as some of the diehards in the parties would have liked, but instead by accommodating to the needs of the bureaucracy, by trading party support of government programs for positions in the bureaucracy, and by regional development projects that built up party support at the local level. This process of mutual accommodation opened the corridors to political power, and not a few writers in the 1920s saw Japan traversing the path toward political democracy that Western industrial nations had followed earlier. On closer look, this rise to power—that hardheaded realists such as Hara had achieved—was bought at some considerable cost to the integrity and independence of the parties. Yet, to be fair, one may well conclude that, given the institutional structure within which the parties found themselves, there was no practical alternative to the course that they followed.

What characteristics had the established parties acquired by the 1920s? In the first place, they were not organizations with which the masses were affiliated or in which people could readily identify their own interests and aspirations. Rather, the parties were highly elitist groups, membership in which required payment of dues, sponsorship, and the like. At the local level, therefore, their power was not in grassroots organization but rather in ties with district bosses, local officeholders, and families of influence whose loyalty and effectiveness in delivering the vote could be amply rewarded.

We should emphasize as well that the record of the parties' in enacting reform legislation, in times that cried out for remedial measures, was unimpressive. The two major parties were broadly similar in their conservative orientation. They both supported imperial sovereignty, empire, and the capitalist foundation of society. They also both favored some degree of popular participation in the political process, not from a belief in popular rights but because it would serve to ensure social cohesion, maintain the system, and thereby strengthen the nation. Beyond this broad similarity, however, the two parties were clearly different in the means that they advocated to achieve these ends. The Seiyūkai, in power from 1918 to 1922 and 1927 to 1929, was the more conservative. As we have seen, Hara built the Seiyūkai's power by accommodating the bureaucratic, military, and business elites. At the local level the party was dependent on landlord support. The Seiyūkai's instincts were therefore decidedly conservative, and it resisted many reform proposals. In 1925 it elected Tanaka Giichi, an army general, as its president, and the party took an increasingly hard line in foreign policy as well as in domestic. The rival party, the Kenseikai (renamed the Minseitō in 1927), which was in power from 1924 to 1927 and 1929 to 1931, was somewhat more liberal in both domestic and foreign policy. It drew support from liberal elements in the bureaucracy and the business community, and its power base was more urban. It offered an agenda of moderate reforms designed to accommodate some of the newly activated social forces. It won passage of a Tenancy Conciliation Law in 1924 to help mediate disputes and passage of universal male suffrage the following year. The Minseitō proposed further reform legislation that eventually came before the Diet for decision in 1930 and 1931. There were bills to establish rights of labor unions, to recognize the right of tenants to negotiate reductions in years of poor harvest, to lower the male voting age to twenty, and as we saw, to permit women to participate in local government. As Sheldon Garon writes, "these controversial bills would have faced formidable opposition under the best of circumstances from employers, landlords, the Seiyūkai, and conservatives in the House of Peers and the Privy Council."[15] In the course of their deliberations, these bills all had to be watered down to satisfy the vested interests. The Minseitō succeeded in shepherding these bills through the Lower House, but they were defeated in the House of Peers in 1931. Thereafter even this mild reform agenda was overwhelmed by the events of the Manchurian crisis, the depression, and rightist attacks on the parties.

The parties by their nature were heavily committed to satisfying the major interest groups—particularly the landlord and business classes. From the beginning, landlords had exercised great power in party headquarters, for they had the funds and local influence that party strength was built on in the provinces. The most notable phenomenon in the 1920s was the apparent degree of influence that the new business combines, the zaibatsu, acquired. Influence by industrialists within the government and the political parties was not new; it extended back to the early Meiji Period when, as we have seen, government played an important role in initiating industrialization and established close ties with the new captains of industry. What was new was the enormous concentration of capital that took place during and after World War I. Nothing exemplified the dual structure of the economy better than these giant combines, highly modern and efficient, towering above the rest of economic society, which was still largely organized in small shops and farms. Zaibatsu such as Mitsui and Mitsubishi encompassed a great variety of enterprises, including extractive industries, manufacturing companies, transportation networks, and banking and trading firms. The industrialists were a politically alert group, profoundly interested in many government issues, such as taxes and subsidies, patent and labor laws. They tried to control legislation by influence peddling—gift giving, entertainment, intermarriage with the other elites, and the like—and by financial support to the political parties. Bribery and other forms of corruption were widely charged against the parties in the 1920s. It is doubtful that Japanese political parties were any more corrupt than parties in the other industrial states, but the important point was their vulnerability at a time when quasi-Confucian suspicions of commerce were still alive and quasi-Confucian moral standards were still expected of the political community.

This brings us to a final and perhaps the most important characteristic of the parties, namely, their ultimate failure to justify or to legitimize themselves within the realm of Japanese values. The prevailing nationalist ideology stressed social harmony, selfless dedication to the state and society, loyalty and obedience to superiors. We have seen how government had taken that collectivist ethic, which had its roots deep in the cultural history of the Japanese people, and built it into an effective ideology to help overcome the strains of industrialism. It was inculcated in primary education textbooks and a variety of quasi-bureaucratic organizations—the youth groups, the military associations, and so on. This ideology resonated with the values of society. In the village this ethic had never died out, but was still the way of life. Cooperation, deference to authority, conformity with the needs of the community, subordination of individual interests to the consensus, maintenance of harmonious relations with fellow villagers—these values remained of transcendent importance. As our discussion of the dual economy has shown, agrarian society had been *relatively* little changed by industrialization. In the 1930s more than one-half the labor force was still employed in agriculture. Moreover, even in the cities the influence of the village could hardly be forgotten, for "three quarters of the politically participant adults in 1930 were born in villages."[16] The government, therefore, had a broad base of collectivist values upon which to build an ideology that likened the state to a harmonious family with the Emperor as the father figure.

In the face of such powerfully rooted ethical assumptions, parliamentary politics was always suspect. The hurly-burly in the Diet of competing interests, majority rule, influence peddling, partisanship, and open conflict ran sharply against the grain of that collectivist ethic. It was one thing to accept the turmoil and tensions of party rule in "normal" times, but economic instability and social unrest mounted in the late 1920s. Finally, there came as well a crisis in Japan's foreign relations. The result was a crisis in the political community that party supremacy could not survive. One moderate military leader, Ugaki Kazushige, wrote in his diary in June 1931, "Two-party politics can be a meaningful way to generate good policy for a wealthy, advanced nation. But a weak, poorly endowed late developer needs to seek the welfare of the people not only at home but in development abroad. This requires national unity, and two-party conflict is not welcome."[17]

The Meiji constitutional system had been predicated on organic unity and on the perseverance of shared values, that is, the consensus among the bureaucrats, the military, and the Diet members. Prior to 1918 that system had worked tolerably well under the tutelage of the oligarchs, but by the mid-1920s they had disappeared from the political scene and centrifugal forces had weakened the pattern of leadership and decision-making that had guided the Meiji state. For a brief time the parties picked up the task of coordinating the various elites, but the parties' grip on power was always tenuous and, in a state dedicated to imperial sovereignty, they were terribly vulnerable. In the midst of severe social and economic problems, the political community was characterized by drift and a loss of mastery. What was more, the activation of the masses had added a disturbing new element to politics. Following the institution of universal manhood suffrage, the labor and socialist movements turned to the organization of proletarian parties, which, although they gained only 2 percent of the membership in the House in the 1928 elections, nonetheless were a source of concern in the midst of unrest and circulation of radical thought. This sense of drift and loss of mastery in the political community, in conjunction with a major crisis in foreign relations, set the stage for the demise of party supremacy and the rise of militarism.

Notes

1. Quoted in Jun Etō, "Natsume Sōseki: A Japanese Meiji Intellectual," *American Scholar* 34, no. 4 (autumn 1965), 616.
2. Quoted in Roger F. Hackett, *Yamagata Aritomo in the Rise of Modern Japan, 1838–1922* (Cambridge, Mass.: Harvard University Press, 1971), 199.
3. Quoted in George Akita, *Foundations of Constitutional Government in Modern Japan, 1868–1900* (Cambridge, Mass.: Harvard University Press, 1967), 84.
4. Taichiro Mitani, "The Establishment of Party Cabinets, 1898–1932," in Peter Duus, ed., *The Twentieth Century,* vol. 6 of *The Cambridge History of Japan,* ed. John Whitney Hall (Cambridge: Cambridge University Press, 1988), 60.
5. Peter Duus and Irwin Scheiner, "Socialism, Liberalism, and Marxism, 1901–1931," in *The Twentieth Century,* ed. Duus, 678–679.
6. Quoted in Michael Lewis, *Rioters and Citizens: Mass Protest in Imperial Japan* (Berkeley: University of California Press, 1990), 82.
7. Richard Smethurst, *Agricultural Development and Tenancy Disputes in Japan, 1870–1940* (Princeton, N.J.: Princeton University Press, 1986), 228–229.
8. Ann Waswo, "The Transformation of Rural Society, 1900–1950," in *The Twentieth Century,* ed. Duus, 578.
9. Hugh T. Patrick, "The Economic Muddle of the 1920s," in *Dilemmas of Growth in Prewar Japan,* ed. James William Morley (Princeton, N.J.: Princeton University Press, 1971), 225–226.
10. Quoted in Robert J. Smith, "Gender Inequality in Contemporary Japan," *Journal of Japanese Studies* 13 (winter 1987), 8.
11. Sharon L. Sievers, *Flowers in Salt: Beginnings of Feminist Consciousness in Modern Japan* (Stanford, Calif.: Stanford University Press, 1983), 164–165.
12. Laurel Rasplica Rodd, "Yosano Akiko and the Taishō Debate over the 'New Woman,'" in *Recreating Japanese Women, 1600–1945,* ed. Gail Lee Bernstein (Berkeley: University of California Press, 1991), 180.
13. Sheldon Garon, "Women's Groups and the Japanese State: Contending Approaches to Political Integration, 1890–1945," *Journal of Japanese Studies* 19 (winter 1993), 32–33.

14. Ibid., 28.
15. Sheldon Garon, *The State and Labor in Modern Japan* (Berkeley: University of California Press, 1987), 178.
16. Ronald P. Dore and Tsutomu Ouchi, "Rural Origins of Japanese Fascism," in *Dilemmas of Growth*, ed. Morley, 209.
17. Quoted in Andrew Gordon, *Labor and Imperial Democracy in Prewar Japan* (Berkeley: University of California Press, 1991), 268.

The Road to the Pacific War

Few countries in modern history have been as subject to forces of the international environment as Japan. The reasons might be endlessly debated. Some observers might attribute the fact to geography and to geopolitical factors that have made East Asia so tumultuous an area of the globe. Most would emphasize economic factors that have made the Japanese economy particularly vulnerable to changes in the international market. Others might point to cultural factors that have rendered the Japanese peculiarly receptive to foreign influences and trends. Still others would emphasize historical contingencies and the particular timing of Japan's emergence from isolation, which came with the arrival of Western power and imperialism in the Pacific.

Whatever the causes, Japan has been ceaselessly buffeted by outside forces and its modern history uniquely shaped by them. During most of this time the nation moved cautiously, ever sensitive to such currents of power politics and cultural development. The leaders of Japan sought to use those currents, to capitalize on those trends by moving with them, with circumspection seeking to turn them to its advantage, and in this prudent fashion to achieve its national ambitions.

From the time of the Restoration down to the 1930s, Japan was motivated by a sense of insecurity, both physical and cultural, and by ambition for national power, respect, and equality. Those motives, intertwined and often inseparable, made up the peculiar nationalism that impelled its historic advance. Japanese diplomacy was remarkable for the way in which it sought to pursue those national ambitions by accommodating to the international system, as the leaders understood it. Thus, for example, during the first twenty-five years of the Meiji Period, revision of the unequal treaties was pursued by determinedly adopting European legal institutions and usages. With rare, isolated exceptions, that pattern of approach continued to guide Japanese diplomats. Only in the militarist era of the 1930s, to which we now turn, did Japan appear to abandon that circumspection, to assert willfully its own way in international affairs and attempt to establish its own destiny in defiance of the forces rising up against it.

The Ending of the Imperialist System

World War I was to transform the international system in East Asia, much as it would transform the context of Japanese domestic politics. On the eve of the war, a stable order apparently prevailed among the imperial powers, after two decades of struggle. Finding itself isolated and outmaneuvered in the Triple Intervention of 1895, Japan had worked its way into the power structure by using skillful diplomacy, backed on occasion by military force. The Anglo-Japanese Alliance of 1902 established a pattern of cooperation with Britain and contributed to the development of an understanding with the United States. In a series of agreements, the latter acknowledged Japan's position in Northeast Asia, in 1905 acquiescing to the Japanese protectorate of Korea. At the same time, Russia and Japan had by war delimited their spheres of interest, with the former now relegated to protecting its remaining hold on northern Manchuria. The "system" was in rough equilibrium by this time, with the interests of each power more or less acknowledged: the United States in the Philippines, France in Indochina, Britain in the Yangtze Valley and in South China, Germany in the Shantung Peninsula, and Russia and Japan in Northeast Asia.

World War I upset this balance, and eventually the East Asian power structure collapsed. The outbreak of war in Europe in the summer of 1914 and the preoccupation of the European powers allowed Japan, under the guise of the Anglo-Japanese Alliance, to seize German holdings in Shantung and German-held islands in the South Pacific: the Carolines, Marianas, Marshalls, Palau, and Yap. Hard on the heels of those swift maneuvers came the delivery in January 1915 of Japan's Twenty-One Demands on China. This was an incident fraught with importance for the future of international relations in East Asia: first, because it was interpreted as a unilateral departure from the system of understanding developed among the powers in the preceding two decades; and second, because it marked a growing Japanese-American estrangement and the emergence of the United States' role as protector of the new Chinese Republic.

The Twenty-One Demands sought Chinese recognition of the transference of German rights in Shantung to Japan; the employment of Japanese nationals as political, financial, and military advisors in China; Chinese purchase of arms from Japan; and permission for Japan to construct railways connecting the Yangtze Valley with the South China coast. The demands elicited a sharp reaction in England and even more so in the United States, where President Woodrow Wilson reached the conclusion that the American people must be "champions of the sovereign rights of China." What was more, there was dissension within the Japanese government, particularly among the elder statesmen or genrō, who had not been included in the planning of the demands and who opposed the kind of diplomacy that needlessly riled the powers and damaged the Japanese image in China. Yamagata was especially disturbed, having warned a year earlier that "if we fail to dissipate China's suspicion of us, [it] will rapidly turn against us and turn more and more to America."[1] The Japanese government subsequently modified the demands, but the episode augured ill for Sino-Japanese relations and prefigured the problems that beset Japanese-American relations in the 1930s. For the nascent Chinese nationalist movement, the Twenty-One Demands stood as a symbol of Japan's predatory designs and, as Yamagata had feared, nationalism took on an increasing anti-Japanese tone in the aftermath.

It is of course possible to date the origins of the Japanese-American estrangement a decade earlier, in the tensions that developed after the Russo-Japanese War. In part the estrangement grew from racial friction raised by immigration to the West Coast. In 1905 the California legislature had unanimously passed a resolution calling on the government to limit immigration, characterizing Japanese immigrants as "immoral, intemperate, quarrelsome men bound to labor for a pittance." The following year the San Francisco School Board established an Oriental Public School for Japanese, Korean, and Chinese children. A "gentlemen's agreement" was worked out to resolve the crisis, whereby the school board rescinded its order and the Japanese government took it upon itself to prevent the issuance of visas to laborers bound for the mainland United States. But the incidents were frequently interpreted in the Japanese press as fresh evidence that Japan was still not accepted on an equal footing with the Western powers. The animosities aroused by those events also called attention to the potential conflict of interests of the two countries in the Pacific. The military in both countries, as a consequence, began to pay more attention to the relative strength of each other's armaments and to the possibility of a military encounter.

The clash of interests was, however, more sharply drawn by the Twenty-One Demands, for subsequent to their presentation the United States made clear its intention of maintaining an Open Door for American trade and investment in China and its growing opposition to Japan's continental aspirations. Wilson's "new diplomacy" proclaimed self-determination and the sovereign rights of every people, and from the time of the demands he made increasingly plain his opposition to international power rivalries at China's expense.

The issues raised by the immigration problem and by the Twenty-One Demands reappeared at the Paris Peace Conference in 1919.

Wilson was deeply embarrassed over his failure to support the Japanese request that a racial equality clause be inserted in the League of Nations Covenant, which would state "that the principle of equality of nations and the just treatment of their nationals . . . [shall be] a fundamental basis of future international relations in the new world organization." The Anglo-American powers, fearful of its implications as to immigration, abstained from voting on the proposal, which was equivalent to voting against it. For the Japanese delegation, which included a number of future prime ministers and foreign ministers (Konoe Fumimaro, Matsuoka Yōsuke, Shigemitsu Mamoru, and Yoshida Shigeru), it was interpreted as another painful reminder that they were still not accepted by the Western world.

Though the principles of the "new diplomacy" were primarily intended for Europe, Wilson wanted to apply them to Asia as well and spare China further buffeting. He told his European counterparts at the Paris conference that "there was nothing on which the public opinion of the United States of America was firmer than on this question that China should not be oppressed by Japan."[2] The balance of power among the imperialists in East Asia would have to be replaced by a new order, in which all would refrain from military and political expansion. The test of Wilson's determination came over the settlement of the Shantung issue. Should Japan be allowed to keep the former German concession? Wilson finally acquiesced, believing that Japan would otherwise refuse to join the League, and recognition of Japanese interests in Shantung was written into the Treaty of Versailles.

Nonetheless, a new phase of East Asian international relations was opening, only in part because of America's shift in policy toward Japan's aspirations on the continent. Japan was confronted as well with increasing diplomatic coolness from another direction. Her special position in Korea and Manchuria had been protected under the imperialist system by agreements with Russia since 1905. But after 1917 the Soviet Union repudiated those agreements, owing to both ideological reasons growing out of Leninist doctrine on imperialism and strategic reasons that included closer Sino-Soviet relations. Perhaps even more ominous for the future, Japan now faced a rising tide of Asian nationalism in the form of anti-Japanese student demonstrations, which broke out on March 1, 1919, in Korea and on May 4, 1919, in Peking.

The Washington Treaty System

Hara and other perceptive Japanese leaders were acutely aware of such "new world trends" and came to feel that it was inevitable that Japan move in accord with them. They signaled their willingness to trim down Japan's continental aspirations, accept the disappearance of the former structure of imperialist diplomacy, and participate in a redefinition of mutual relations among the powers. A conference for this purpose was convened in Washington, D.C., at American initiative, in the autumn of 1921. American insistence led to the replacement of the expiring Anglo-Japanese Alliance by the innocuous Four-Power Treaty, in which Britain, Japan, America, and France agreed to confer should the rights or possessions of any of the four in the Pacific be threatened. A Nine-Power Treaty laid down the principles that were to guide the new order in East Asia: condemning spheres of influence in China, pledging equal opportunity for commerce and industry, and promising to respect the "sovereignty, the independence, and the territorial and administrative integrity of China." The conference sought to forestall a runaway naval arms race and to provide mutual security in the Five-Power Naval Limitation Treaty, which restricted competition in battleships and aircraft carriers by setting a ratio of 5:5:3 for Britain, the United States, and Japan, respectively. The Japanese delegation believed this ratio of capital ships was sufficient to guarantee Japanese dominance in the western Pacific.

Japanese acceptance of the new framework of international relations was exemplified by the attitudes of Shidehara Kijurō, who was ambassador to Washington at the time of the Washington Conference and who was to serve as foreign minister (1924–1927 and 1929–1931). He shared the American vision of a liberal capitalist world order characterized by peace, political harmony, and economic interdependence. Cooperation with the United States was, after all, good business; the United States was Japan's largest supplier of capital and best trading customer, purchasing 40 percent of Japan's exports in the 1920s. Shidehara therefore advocated a posture of internationalism and peaceful development of Japan's overseas trade. Japan's policy, he held, should be to seek economic advancement in China and promotion of its own interests within the framework of international agreement. This willingness to abstain from aggressive pursuit of its political interests in China was, of course, pleasing to American policymakers. Franklin Roosevelt, who had earlier been among the sharp critics of Japan in the U.S. Navy, wrote in 1923 that the two nations "have not a single valid reason, and won't have as far as we can look ahead, for fighting each other."[3]

Yet there were many flaws marring the vision that Shidehara and the American policymakers shared. One appeared glaringly, the year after Roosevelt's statement, when Congress passed the Japanese Exclusion Act of 1924. Secretary of State Charles E. Hughes was "greatly depressed" by it and wrote that Congress "has undone the work of the Washington Conference and implanted the seeds of an antagonism which are sure to bear fruit in the future."[4] It made no difference that the Japanese themselves had been guilty of violent racism months earlier, in the massacre of thousands of Koreans after the earthquake; the Japanese media saw the new legislation as a national affront, and many writers interpreted it as further evidence of American perfidy.

Perhaps a more fundamental flaw in the new international vision was the failure of the high hopes held for economic expansionism. Partly, as we have seen, owing to the mistakes and indecisiveness of Japanese economic policymakers, foreign trade did not perform up to expectation. There were many obstacles. The United States followed a strongly protectionist course, and Britain was making preferential tariff agreements within its empire that were detrimental to Japanese exports. In China, too, the nationalist movement demanded tariff autonomy and increasingly opposed Japanese economic interests. When to all these obstacles was added the onset of the Great Depression, the discontent and restlessness with Shidehara's internationalist diplomacy mounted. "It is a good thing to talk about economic foreign policy," said Matsuoka Yōsuke with sarcasm in the Diet in January 1931, "but we must have more than a slogan. Where are the fruits? We must be shown the benefit of this approach."[5] Matsuoka, who was to become foreign minister in 1940, believed that Shidehara's vision was bankrupt and that Japan must, by force if necessary, create its own economic bloc.

Throughout the 1920s a strong undercurrent of opposition arose in Japan to Shidehara's cooperation with the new order established by the Washington Conference. Beginning with the Versailles Peace Conference, many Japanese had regarded Wilsonian principles with suspicion. Konoe Fumimaro, who became Japan's most important political leader in the 1930s, denounced the League of Nations and the Washington Treaty System as high-sounding principles to mask Anglo-American self-interest. Britain and the United States, he consistently argued, were trying to contain Japan's legitimate aspirations on the continent. "We must overcome the principles of peace based on the maintenance of the status quo," Konoe wrote, "and work out new principles of international peace from our own perspective." Konoe and a growing number of other "revisionists" said that the Washington Treaty System must be revised to ensure an equitable distribution of land and natural resources among the world's great powers. Japan as a late developer was being denied its just place by the Anglo-American powers, who were trying to preserve the status quo, pitting the "have nations" against the "have-not nations." Late-developing countries such as Japan, said Konoe, were condemned "to remain forever subordinate to the advanced nations" and, unless something was done to allow Japan "equal access to the markets and natural resources of the colonial areas," Japan would be forced to "destroy the status quo for the sake of self-preservation."[6]

The most ominous threat to the Shidehara diplomacy was the challenge that the rising tide of nationalism in China represented for Japan's interests there. Shidehara worked with considerable skill to try to remove obstacles to the expansion of Japanese trade and investments in China, but history was hardly on his side. As China struggled painfully for institutional change and national unification, the question was insistently put to Japanese foreign policymakers: would Chinese nationalism cost Japan its special position in China? The *Kuomintang,* the Nationalist Party in China, embarked on its campaign of national unification, accompanied by radical antiforeign outbursts and by slogans demanding an end to the unequal treaties that the powers (including Japan) had forced China to sign. Beyond the problem of Japan's economic advancement was the still thornier question of Manchuria. If the Kuomintang campaign succeeded, could Japan preserve its treaty rights and interests in Manchuria? As this question was raised, Shidehara's "soft" policy of internationalism and support for the Washington Treaty System began to rouse bitter resentment at home.

The Joining of Domestic and Foreign Crisis

In the years from 1928 to 1932 the ferment of political community at home was brought to crisis point by the onset of the Great Depression and by the rising opposition to the framework of foreign relations established by the Washington Conference. Resentment against the government's China policy was intense among leaders of the Kwantung Army, the unit of the Japanese army assigned to protect Japanese interests in Manchuria. They feared that without strong measures an opportunity to secure the Manchurian holdings would be lost. In 1928 as the Kuomintang troops moved closer to Peking and successful extension of nationalist authority throughout North China, extremist elements in the Kwantung Army arranged the bombing of the train carrying Chang Tso-lin, the Manchurian warlord. Their expectation that this act would create disorder and give a pretext for expanded control of Manchuria failed to materialize, but the inability of Tokyo to punish the extremist elements in the army revealed not only the weakness of party government but also the potential for future insubordination.

Increasing tensions with China coincided with mounting discontent and unrest at home, as conservatives in and out of the government believed that Japan was besieged by radical thought. Following the general elections of 1928, the first in which the so-called proletarian parties participated, the nervous government on March 15, 1928, carried out a mass roundup of leftists. After sacking their headquarters, the government invoked the Peace Preservation Law of 1925 to disband the Labor Farmer Party, the All-Japan Proletarian Youth Federation, and the Council of Japanese Labor Unions, which had fallen under the domination of the Communist Party. A year later the police arrested more than 1,000 additional leftists in another lightning roundup.

The sense of crisis in society was further heightened by the collapse of the economy and the hardship it brought. From 1929 to 1931 exports fell by 50 percent, with disastrous effect on both city workers and farmers. In the cities unemployment rose and in the countryside, as the bottom fell out of commodity prices—especially silk and rice—real income was reduced by about one-third from its 1925 levels. The government responded, as it had customarily to economic crises, by initiating another vigorous campaign of nationalist mobilization, on the one hand attacking leftist ideology as an un-Japanese importation from abroad and on the other hand exhorting still more intense loyalty to Japanese values and to the imperial symbol. In the past such campaigns had helped to dilute class consciousness and to undermine leftist social movements, but in this case the program contributed to an extremist patriotic movement, led by right-wing groups that proved difficult for even the government to control. Nervous bureaucrats, heretofore concerned with control of leftist groups, now found the secretive ultranationalist groups a bigger threat to social stability. It is a key to the events that followed to understand that decades of indoctrination, intended to overcome the social problems of industrialization by unifying the nation around traditional values of loyalty and solidarity, had created a populace highly receptive to the appeal of the most extreme nationalist slogans. In this time of social and economic crisis, when left-wing organizations were subject to intense scrutiny, radical right-wing groups came to exercise influence on restive elements in the army and in the civilian population.

Such an atmosphere made the party governments, which as we have seen had failed to develop a sense of legitimacy in the Japanese value system, particularly vulnerable to charges of failure and corruption. Above all, it made the maintenance of Shidehara's diplomacy, with its emphasis on internationalism and cooperation with the Anglo-American powers, increasingly difficult. The London Naval Conference of 1930, which was intended to extend the Washington Treaty System, was particularly ill timed in the light of domestic developments in Japan. The prevailing 5:5:3 formula for capital ships was applied by the conference to heavy cruisers; and, in effect, a 10:10:7 formula for light cruisers was established for Britain, the United States, and Japan. Admirals in all three countries opposed the London treaty, but in the volatile atmosphere existing in Japan the opposition was explosive. Prime Minister Hamaguchi Osachi was charged with having compromised Japan's national security and with having trammeled the independent judgment of the naval command for the sake of a spurious friendship with the Anglo-American powers. On November 14, 1930, presaging an era of what a *New York Times* correspondent called "government by assassination," a young ultranationalist stepped from a crowd of well-wishers in Tokyo Station and shot the prime minister as he was preparing to board a train.

In the tense months that followed, Shidehara's hopes of establishing a new order in East Asia through cooperation with the United States and England were dashed by the determination in the Kwantung Army to resolve the Manchurian issue. It is surely true that the Anglo-American powers had not done enough to encourage and aid the hopeful effort of Shidehara, and by 1931 the opportunities for avoiding a collision between Japanese and Chinese nationalism were nearly gone. As one authority writes, "a strong government in Japan might have restrained army action in Manchuria and postponed a showdown with China on the basis of some compromise settlement on the issue of Japanese treaty rights. But the government in Tokyo was too weak and too unwilling to risk its existence by a strong stand." The government was subjected to increasing pressure from rival politicians and from the press to assert Japan's supremacy, and, on the Chinese side, Chiang Kai-shek was under pressure to adopt an inflexible attitude toward Japan. By the summer of 1931 "nothing short of the miraculous could prevent a clash in Manchuria."[7]

With the tacit consent of members of the General Staff, field grade officers of the Kwantung Army provoked an incident in Manchuria on the night of September 18, 1931. A small explosion on the tracks of the Japanese railway just north of Mukden was taken as sufficient pretext for mobilizing the Kwantung Army, attacking Chinese troops in the area, and expanding Japanese control. It was a critical moment for party government in Japan, although the response was in many ways foreordained by the nature and character the parties had formed as they rose to power. It was a moment when strong leadership and an appeal to traditions of responsible civilian government might have been effective, but the parties were accustomed to circumspection, compromise, and negotiation with the other elites. The Minseitō government of Wakatsuki Reijirō, who had succeeded Hamaguchi, temporized and attempted tactfully to limit the sphere of army action in Manchuria. But tact was ineffectual.

The weakness of the government, the diffuseness of decision-making power, the general confusion and uncertainty attending both domestic and foreign turmoil—all created an opportunity for resolute action by the Kwantung Army. It pushed ahead to conquer all of Manchuria and establish a Japanese puppet state, Manchukuo. Wakatsuki resigned and was replaced by a Seiyūkai cabinet headed by Inukai Tsuyoshi. It was the last party government in prewar Japan.

The efforts of the aging Inukai to restore order were ill-starred. His own party's Diet members voted to withdraw from the League of Nations, should that body censure Japan's action in Manchuria. Ultranationalism as a popular phenomenon now gained strength. Fanatic groups, committed to cleansing the body politic by replacing the political and economic elites and carrying out a "restoration," assassinated the former finance minister in February 1932, then the chief director of the Mitsui zaibatsu in March, and finally Inukai himself on May 15.

Going It Alone

After decades of sowing the winds of nationalism among the Japanese people, the elites were now reaping the whirlwind. They had used education, the media, and a variety of grassroots organizations to mobilize nationalist sentiment among the populace for the hard struggles required to support industrialism and imperialism, and now the government was caught in a trap of its own making. Popular nationalism became a runaway force, extremely difficult to control—especially where government was so weak and so cumbersome. This nationalism was particularly unruly among leaders of society at the local level—the elementary school principal, the Shintō priest in the village, the mayor and headman of the community, the head of the local chapter of the military association, and the like. That stratum of lower middle-class leadership, which had climbed only halfway up the ladder of success, was the group toward which government mobilization efforts had been particularly directed. Such local leaders had been exhorted to interpret Japan's mission to the masses, and charged with responsibility for fulfilling Japan's destiny. As "true believers" in the collectivist ethic, they were the most impatient with the cosmopolitanism of the business elite and the squabbles and corruption of party politicians. Ultranationalist groups seeking radical solutions to the nation's problems could count on their support.

Nationalism gripped every part of Japanese society. Even the Communists—in overwhelming numbers—underwent swift conversions in prison in the early 1930s, renouncing their earlier theories and in many cases joining enthusiastically in the rhetoric of nationalism. Leaders of the ultranationalist groups set the tone of Japanese politics in the ensuing several years. Following Inukai's assassination, the one remaining genrō, Saionji Kimmochi, turned to moderate elements in the military to lead in the formation of cabinets, hoping that they could succeed where party politicians had failed in controlling the extremist elements in the army. For the next four years, from 1932 through 1936, the country was governed by cabinets twice headed by admirals. It was no easy matter to maintain moderate policies in the face of mounting ultranationalist sympathies, which were fueled by a growing sense of isolation as the seizure of Manchuria drew international condemnation. When the League of Nations voted 42 to 1 to condemn Japan as an aggressor, the Japanese delegation walked out of the hall and out of the League.

The Manchurian Incident thus proved a turning point—a point at which Japan abandoned the general policy of cooperation with the powers, which had for the most part controlled its international behavior since 1868, and chose to pursue its own destiny in East Asia, to trust its own strength to protect and advance its interests. The leadership now spoke of an "Asian Monroe Doctrine," declaring Japan's responsibility for maintaining peace in Asia. In thus choosing to abandon its customary circumspection, and to withdraw from the Washington Treaty System, Japan set formidable requirements for the nation's defense. To maintain the strategic posture demanded by its "Monroe Doctrine" and by the commitment to Manchukuo, Japan now needed military power sufficient for three major tasks: to defeat the Soviet army, whose strength on the borders of Manchuria had been vastly augmented; to guarantee the security of the home islands against the U.S. fleet; and to compel the Chinese government to accept Japan's position in Manchuria and northern China.

These three strategic objectives required a military capability that Japan was never able to achieve. The Meiji oligarchs would have been appalled at the incautious way in which policy commitments were made that exceeded the nation's capacities. How was it that Japan's leaders in the early 1930s embarked on so perilous a course? In part, the answer lies in the fragmented nature of decision-making in the Japanese government, which at that time lacked a strong, central controlling leadership able to exercise its will over all factions of the administration, and able to coordinate and develop prudent and balanced policy goals. In part, too, it lies in the combination of ambition for Asian leadership and frustration with the Washington Treaty System and with events in China. Moreover, leaders in the early 1930s were making policy in an atmosphere often dominated by the ultranationalist sentiment that, although they may not have sympathized with it, subtly affected and conditioned their thinking.

Initially the reorientation of national policy seemed to be a success. In spite of the League's condemnation, Manchuria was now secure to be developed and integrated into the Japanese industrial machine. Moreover, in the years after the Manchurian takeover, Japanese economic policy scored phenomenal success in achieving rapid recovery from the depression. Patrick calls it "one of the most successful combinations of fiscal, monetary, and foreign exchange rate policies, in an adverse international environment, that the world has ever seen."[8] To a considerable extent it was a matter of good luck. In the aftermath of Manchuria, the government was required by the new international conditions to begin a rapid buildup of its industrial and military plant. Over the next two years the government increased expenditures by 26 percent, under a great deal of pressure not to raise taxes. Therefore the increased government spending was deficit financed, and as a result greatly enlarged private demand and consequently stimulated the economy. Most of the increase in government spending during the 1930s was, of course, for military purposes, but all sectors of the economy benefited. Japan gave up the gold standard in December 1931, and this proved a boon for Japanese exports. Overall, the growth rate of the real net domestic product during the 1930s was more than double that of the previous decade. Economic growth however did not, as it sometimes does, moderate policy. If anything, it seemed to confirm the new course.

In the five years after the seizure of Manchuria violence and ultranationalist sentiment continued very much a part of the domestic political scene. Rival cliques vied for ascendancy in the army, resorting to assassination of one of the top generals in 1935, and culminating the next year in an all-out insurrection. On February 26, 1936, fourteen hundred soldiers from the First Division in Tokyo, led by young officers plotting a radical reconstruction of the government, rebelled. They seized control of the Diet and the main army and government offices and murdered the finance minister, the lord keeper of the privy seal, and the inspector general of military education. The prime minister, the last of the genrō, Saionji, and other leaders narrowly escaped. With the Emperor's backing, the rival faction subdued the young officers' insurrection and disposed of its leaders. Discipline was reestablished, but the range of political debate was still further narrowed and ultranationalist sentiment heightened.

The Question of Japanese "Fascism"

Having withdrawn from the League of Nations and the Washington Treaty System, Japan drew closer to the European fascist powers to overcome its international isolation. Konoe and other Japanese leaders had long identified Japan's plight as a "have-not" country with Germany and Italy: they too were latecomers to industrialization who felt denied access to needed land and natural resources by the prevailing international order. In 1936 Japan concluded the Anti-Comintern Pact, which provided for cooperation with Germany and a defensive alliance against the Soviet Union. Four years later, in 1940, the Tripartite Pact was signed with Italy and Germany, which committed Japan to a military alliance that would confront the United States and Britain.

Because of this alliance and because the political principles that

Japanese leaders espoused in the 1930s were similar to those of Germany and Italy, it became common from this time to label the Japanese political system as "fascist." In its expansionist foreign policies and militant nationalist ideologies, which demanded fundamental revision of the international status quo, Japan's program bore many similarities to those of Hitler and Mussolini. In all three countries, leaders responded to crisis, as Andrew Gordon writes, "by repudiating parliamentary rule and turning to shrill nationalism, anti-communism, and antidemocratic, yet capitalist, programs to restructure the economy and polity and mobilize for total war."[9]

Yet, in important ways, the Japanese experience was different. The 1930s produced no Japanese mass leader, no Hitler or Mussolini haranguing the people. There was only the awed reverence for the Emperor, who remained a distant symbol of national identity. No vanguard party or mass movement succeeded in overthrowing the Meiji Constitution and establishing a new political order. It is true that many right-wing organizations advocated a new political order. By the mid-1930s more than fifty rightist journals with a total circulation approaching 100,000 proposed various blueprints for radical change. Although they expressed the tensions that domestic and foreign crisis had wrought in society, the rightist movements did not succeed in overthrowing the existing order. They influenced the climate of opinion, but the uprisings by young right-wing terrorists and junior officers in 1932 and 1936 both failed.

The long-established military and bureaucratic elites remained in control. Therefore, Japan's leading postwar political scientist, Maruyama Masao, called the new policies "fascism from above," because it was the bureaucratic elites who directed Japan's precipitous response to the multiple crises. To other observers, the Japanese case differed so significantly from European fascism that the term becomes misleading when applied to Japan. Two Stanford scholars, for example, Peter Duus and Daniel Okimoto, conclude that "The leaders of the 1930s . . . were 'the brightest and the best,' not the posturers, street fighters, and misfits who took power in fascist Europe. With occasional exceptions like Konoe Fumimaro, most were bureaucrats not so very different from the leaders who had dominated in the 1920s. They were graduates of Teidai [Tokyo Imperial University], the National Military Academy, or the National Naval Academy—products of the meritocratic process of elite recruitment."[10] Although Duus and Okimoto dismiss fascism as a useful concept of analysis, Gordon finds sufficient commonality among Italian fascism, German Nazism, and Japanese militarism to retain the term.

However one may resolve this controversy, it is essential to be clear about what did happen in Japan—a shift in power from the parties to other elites. Following the 1932 assassination of Prime Minister

The Emperor reviewing army troops in 1937. *UPI/Bettmann Newsphotos*

Inukai, the last of the party prime ministers until after the war, the power of the parties sharply declined. This loss of influence, however, did not mean that the military simply took over the apparatus of the state. On the contrary, the institutionalized pluralism of the Meiji state continued. That is, the structure of multiple elite power that we analyzed in our discussion of the Taishō political system remained, but the parties were no longer able to play the critical role of coordinating the elites. What occurred in the 1930s was a shift in the relative power among the elites. The military and the bureaucratic elites gained increased power, but they never succeeded in consolidating their power into a monolithic or totalitarian system comparable to the regimes in Germany and Italy. Despite many efforts in the 1930s by reformists inside and outside the government to restructure the constitutional system and overcome the pluralistic distribution of power inherent in the Meiji state, the existing political system survived fundamentally intact. Therefore, as Gordon Berger writes, "the apparently sharp break in political development between the 1920s and 1930s was less apparent than many have insisted." Even after the country went to war with the Anglo-American powers in 1941, "pluralistic elite politics persisted."[11]

As the influence of the political parties receded, the military and bureaucracy gained the upper hand in political struggles. They had the technical expertise and nationalist agenda to fit the times. They had complementary strategies to deal with the national crisis. Among the military, a school of strategic thinking known as "total war planning" became dominant. In the bureaucracy, a group of so-called reform bureaucrats, preoccupied with strategies for surviving the Great Depression, proposed plans for a state industrial policy and a managed economy. The merging of these military and bureaucratic schools of thought was a key development in domestic politics.

Total war planning was a product of new strategic thinking in the aftermath of World War I. Army strategists concluded that future warfare in the twentieth century would require the mobilization of the full resources of the nation-state. It would require a self-sufficient industrial base that would not be vulnerable to economic pressure from other countries. This concern with economic security led military planners in the 1920s to the pursuit of autarky and to the control of resource-rich territories such as Manchuria. Moreover, it was their conviction that Japan must have a comprehensive plan for mobilization of the domestic economy. If Japan hoped to maintain its great-power status, it must have a self-reliant industrial base and must be able to mobilize all its human and material resources for protracted conflict. In 1927 the Seiyūkai cabinet, headed by army General Tanaka Giichi, established a central mobilization agency, the Cabinet Resources Bureau, to create comprehensive plans for all of Japan's economic activity. Military planners succeeded in getting legislation to enhance the efficient production of strategic industries. The first example of such a law with military implications was the Petroleum Industry Law in 1934.

The joining of the domestic and foreign crises, that is the great depression and the Manchurian Incident, brought total war planners in the military into common cause with civilian bureaucrats who wanted increased state intervention in the economy to bring an end to the great depression. These so-called reform bureaucrats appeared in many of the ministries at this time. They were not new; they had long favored social reforms that would strengthen national cohesiveness. Many of them had worked with parties, particularly with the Minseitō, to try to achieve social reforms in the 1920s. Frustrated by the failures of those efforts and faced with the growing domestic and foreign crisis, they looked for stronger political allies and strengthened government control of the society and economy. They found these allies among the military men who had come to believe that Japan needed an industrial policy.

Within the newly established Ministry of Commerce and Industry, economic bureaucrats formulated strategies for reorganizing industry to achieve economies of scale, adopt new technologies, and so increase the productivity of the labor force. German theories of achieving greater efficiency through "industrial rationalization" were influential. These theories entailed limiting competition through government-sponsored trusts and cartels. In 1931, the reform bureaucrats succeeded in gaining Diet approval of the Important Industries Control Law, which legalized cartels among Japanese enterprises and gave government the authority to oversee production levels, prices, and marketing. As a result, more than a score of cartels were established in key industries to limit competition and restore profitability.

Total war planners and reform bureaucrats both saw the need for strict control of the economy and for centralization of political power to achieve policy integration. The state must manage resource allocation. Coal, iron, and steel, the sinews of military-industrial power, must have priority, while civilian goods should be limited to a minimum. Working together the military and civilian bureaucrats secured Diet approval of a series of laws designed to help individual strategic industries with government financing, tax benefits, and protective measures designed to curtail foreign and domestic competition. First came the Petroleum Industry Law in 1934. In 1936, the Automobile Manufacturing Law gave the government licensing authority. Toyota and Nissan were licensed; Ford and General Motors were not and had to close their operations. Similar laws in the next three years were passed for steel, machine tools, aircraft, shipbuilding, and many other industries. The laws gave government the authority to exercise some administrative guidance, but they left private ownership and a large measure of private management intact.

In the face of mounting foreign tension in the late 1930s and influenced by fascist thinking in Germany, the military planners and reform bureaucrats sought still tighter state controls over the economy and society. As one young economic planner (who later played a key role in postwar Japan's rapid economic growth) wrote in 1937: "It is no longer possible to realize this goal [of a managed economy] by simply depending on entrepreneurs' initiative. Nowadays, the state has to exercise its power and directly assume its leadership in economic activities. In a semiwar situation, an economy led by the state has to be coercive."[12] It was necessary to establish "state capitalism" and shift the economy from "profit orientation" to "production orientation."

In 1937 the military and civilian bureaucrats succeeded in establishing the Cabinet Planning Board to serve as a kind of "economic general staff" to bring together skilled technocrats who would devise comprehensive controls by the state. The following year the bureaucrats overrode conservative resistance from the party and business elites and won passage of a national mobilization bill to establish widespread controls over production, profits, finance, foreign trade, and transportation. Two years later, the so-called New Economic Structure provided for still greater government control of industry. At the same time, feeling a need to achieve greater consensus among the elites and to ensure Lower House support for government programs and citizen identification with the goals and policies of the state, the military and bureaucratic planners set out to create a new political party that would embrace all existing groups in the Diet. On October 12, 1940, all political parties were dissolved and replaced by the Imperial Rule Assistance Association. Intended as a mass political party that would be the nucleus of a new political structure, it never fulfilled this function because local leaders and conservatives in the old-line ministries resisted a surrender of their power to the new organization.

On paper, Japan appeared to be in the grip of a totalitarian political-economic structure, inspired in many respects by fascist institutions in Europe. The reality, however, was different. Zaibatsu and business leaders often resisted government controls that were in any case implemented in helter-skelter fashion. As Mark Peattie writes, "The myriad of controls, under which Japan fought first the China War and then the Pacific War, provided no overall coordination, but rather left the prosecution of these conflicts scattered among various and competing agencies. At the same time, Japan's economy, subjected to conflicting pressures from business and military leadership, remained partly free and partly controlled. Such a system could hardly be called totalitarian and in any event was ultimately disastrous for Japan's war effort."[13] How closely, then, did the Japanese system approach the totalitarian experience in Europe? One of the most careful scholars of this issue concludes that "severe schisms within bureaucratic and military leadership groups prevented any individual or faction from achieving a dictatorship or degree of political control analogous to that of contemporaneous wartime regimes in Germany, Italy, and the Soviet Union. Conservative forces in parliament, business, the bureaucracy, the right wing, and traditional local elites in the countryside blunted the reformists' attempts to reorganize the state, enhance their own power, and establish a monolithic system of governmental controls over all political and economic activities."[14]

The Coming of the Pacific War

In the summer of 1937 Japan blundered into war with China. It was not a war that the army General Staff wanted. The truth is that even the most able of the total war planners were acutely aware that it would require considerably more time to develop and integrate an effective industrial structure before Japan would be prepared for all-out war. To them it was critical to avoid hostilities and concentrate on a fully coordinated effort to develop Japan's economy. But having chosen to abandon the principles of the Washington Treaty System, and operating in an atmosphere dominated by ultranationalist goals and a growing willingness to resort to military solutions, the government was ill-prepared to restrain itself. In June 1937 Konoe Fumimaro was chosen by Saionji to become prime minister. Prince Konoe was a widely respected figure from an old noble family, who might, it was thought, succeed in uniting the country and restraining the military. He spoke of achieving "social justice" in domestic affairs, but he proved a weak and ineffectual leader. It was during his first tenure as prime minister (June 1937–January 1939) that the nation stumbled into full-scale war with China and during his second tenure (July 1940–October 1941) that fateful steps were taken toward Pearl Harbor.

Since 1931 the general consensus held that if new conflict came, it would most likely be with the Soviet Union. A prime goal of the General Staff, therefore, was to concentrate on the economic development of Manchukuo and its integration into the industrial complex of Japan so as to increase the strength of the military establishment. Conflict with the nationalist government in China was, therefore, to be avoided as a hindrance to the implementation of the plans designed to prepare for war with Russia. The General Staff in the spring of 1937 had, in fact, ordered Japanese commanders of military forces in north China to avoid incidents that might disrupt the status quo. When a minor skirmish broke out on July 7, 1937, between Chinese and Japanese troops stationed in the Marco Polo Bridge area, just outside of Peking, the Japanese army sought to achieve a quick local settlement. But the incident could not be so easily contained; instead it swiftly escalated

Schoolgirls in celebration at the Imperial Palace after the fall of Nanking in December 1937.
National Archives

into full-scale hostilities. Chiang Kai-shek, the nationalist leader, under immense pressure to resist Japanese encroachment, was doubtless determined not to allow any new pretext such as the Manchurian Incident of 1931 to serve the Japanese expansionist cause. He therefore responded to the Marco Polo Bridge Incident by dispatching four divisions to north China. Konoe responded with an ill-advised sword-rattling statement, which only served to confirm Chiang in his suspicions, and hopes of attaining a local settlement evaporated.

It is not easy, even in retrospect, to see how conflict between China and Japan could have been avoided. History sometimes brings nations into logjams from which they are extricated only by force. Chinese nationalism could no longer tolerate the status quo with Japan. Yet Japanese of all persuasions looked at Japan's position in China as sanctioned by economic need and by their destiny to create "a new order in Asia" that would expel Western influence and establish a structure based upon Asian concepts of justice and humanity. Chiang's government was regarded as an obstruction that had to be overcome on the way to this "new order," and so in 1938 Konoe called for an all-out campaign to "annihilate" the nationalist regime. The expectation was that Chinese resistance would be short-lived: a "fundamental resolution of Sino-Japanese relations" could be achieved by compelling the

Prime Minister Konoe leaving his residence for a conference with the Emperor, 1937. *UPI/Bettmann*

nationalists to accept Japanese leadership in creating an Asian community of nations, free of Anglo-American capitalism and Soviet Communism. It was a fateful decision. It tragically underrated the difficulties involved, not least the strength of Chinese nationalism; it justified tighter controls at home and brought vastly heightened tensions with the United States. Atrocities committed against Chinese citizens, especially the pillaging and the rape and massacre of many tens of thousands at Nanking in early 1938, left a lasting outrage against the invaders. But Japanese leadership pushed ahead with supreme nerve justifying their goals with Pan-Asian slogans and, ultimately, with the vision of a Greater East Asia Coprosperity Sphere from which all vestiges of Western imperialism would be erased.

The dilemma that Japanese diplomacy had struggled with ever since the Manchurian Incident now became still more difficult, for as the China conflict expanded, the nation was the less prepared to deal with the Soviet army on the Manchurian border and the American fleet in the Pacific. A succession of border skirmishes with the Red Army revealed the vulnerability of the Kwantung Army; at the same time the U.S. Navy was now embarked on a resolute program of building additional strength in the Pacific. By the spring of 1940 the Japanese navy General Staff had concluded that America's crash program would result in its gaining naval hegemony in the Pacific by 1942, and that Japan must have access to the oil of the Dutch East Indies in order to cope with American power. Konoe's impulsive and unstable foreign minister, Matsuoka Yōsuke, set out to resolve the impasse by a swift demarche. In the autumn of 1940 he signed the Tripartite Pact with Germany and Italy, in which the signatories pledged to aid one another if attacked by a power not currently involved in the European war or the fighting in China. Matsuoka thereby hoped to isolate the United States and dissuade it from conflict with Japan, thus opening the way for Japan to seize the European colonies in Southeast Asia, grasp the resources it needed for self-sufficiency, and cut off Chinese supply lines. Furthermore, to free his northern flank he signed a neutrality pact with the Soviet Union in April 1941; and when Hitler attacked Russia in June the Manchukuo-Soviet border seemed wholly secure. Within weeks Japanese troops entered Indochina.

American reaction to the Tripartite Pact was, to Matsuoka, unexpectedly strong. President Franklin D. Roosevelt forbade any further shipment of scrap iron to Japan, and after the entry into Indochina he embargoed oil. Negotiations between Secretary of State Cordell Hull and Ambassador Nomura Kichisaburō foundered in a morass of confusion and ineptness. It is doubtful that negotiations had much opportunity for success in any case at this juncture—given the positions taken by the two sides. Hull's insistence on Japanese withdrawal from China was seen as nullifying a decade of foreign policy and reducing Japan to a second-class power.

Rather than turn back, Japanese leaders were prepared to take risks. "Nothing ventured, nothing gained," Matsuoka concluded. "We should take decisive action."[15] And the new prime minister, General Tōjō Hideki, was quoted as saying, "Sometimes people have to shut

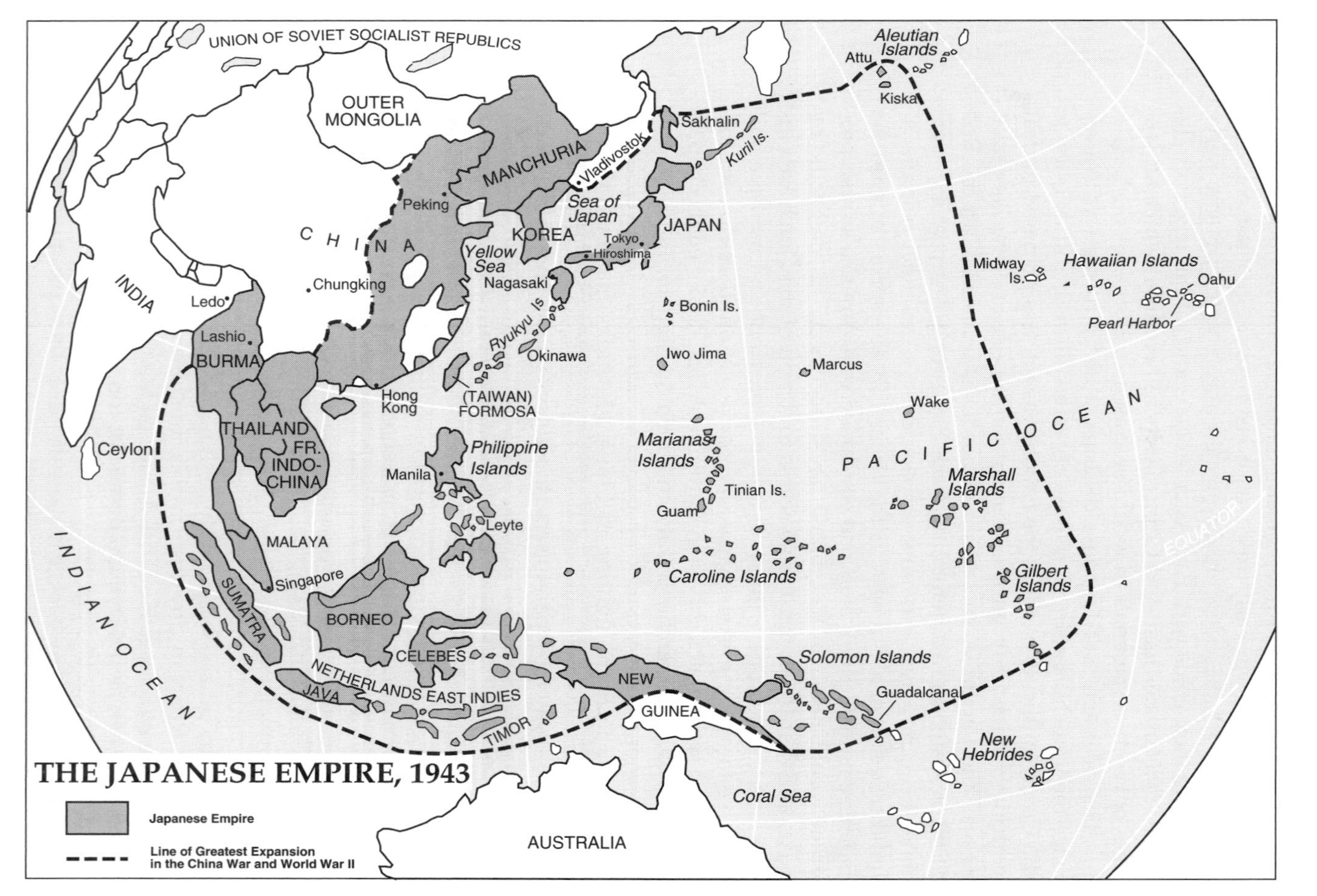
THE JAPANESE EMPIRE, 1943
Japanese Empire
Line of Greatest Expansion in the China War and World War II
UNION OF SOVIET SOCIALIST REPUBLICS
OUTER MONGOLIA
MANCHURIA
Vladivostok
Sakhalin
Kuril Is.
Aleutian Islands
Attu
Kiska
Peking
CHINA
Chungking
INDIA
Ledo
Lashio
BURMA
KOREA
Sea of Japan
JAPAN
Tokyo
Hiroshima
Nagasaki
Yellow Sea
Ryukyu Is
Okinawa
Bonin Is.
Iwo Jima
Marcus
Midway Is.
Hawaiian Islands
Oahu
Pearl Harbor
Hong Kong
(TAIWAN) FORMOSA
THAILAND
FR. INDO-CHINA
Ceylon
Philippine Islands
Manila
Leyte
Marianas Islands
Tinian Is.
Guam
Wake
PACIFIC OCEAN
Marshall Islands
Gilbert Islands
EQUATOR
Caroline Islands
MALAYA
Singapore
SUMATRA
BORNEO
CELEBES
NETHERLANDS EAST INDIES
JAVA
TIMOR
NEW GUINEA
Solomon Islands
Guadalcanal
New Hebrides
Coral Sea
AUSTRALIA
INDIAN OCEAN

their eyes and take the plunge."[16] The navy General Staff in particular pressed for war, arguing that oil reserves were limited and American naval strength increasing. Ultimately its reasoning was accepted, and the president of the Privy Council explained to the Emperor a month before Pearl Harbor, "It is impossible from the standpoint of our domestic political situation and of our self-preservation, to accept all of the American demands. . . . If we miss the present opportunity to go to war, we will have to submit to American dictation. Therefore, I recognize that it is inevitable that we must decide to start a war against the United States. I will put my trust in what I have been told: namely, that things will go well in the early part of the war; and that although we will experience increasing difficulties as the war progresses, there is some prospect of success."[17]

The approach of war was accompanied by a crescendo of nationalist sentiment that had as its main theme a determination to establish not only Japan's strategic autonomy in East Asia but also its cultural autonomy and independence from the West and its own sphere of influence in which Japanese culture would predominate. This preoccupation with Japan's unique cultural identity had been a central theme in modern Japanese nationalism since the 1890s. Partly to compensate for the massive borrowing from the West that industrialization entailed, nationalism asserted Japanese moral superiority. The war brought to a culmination these themes of cultural self-determination. In a study of attitudes in the Pacific War, John Dower found Japanese thinking characterized by an "intense self-preoccupation" that emphasized Japanese virtue and purity.[18] Nationalists characterized Anglo-American values of individualism, liberalism, and capitalism as motivated by materialism and egocentrism. In contrast, Japanese society had its foundations in spiritual commitments of selfless loyalty to the welfare of the entire community. As a result, society attained a natural harmony and solidarity in which everyone found their proper place. This moral order had divine origins in the unique imperial line, and the Japanese consequently had a mission to extend its blessings to other peoples. Japan's purpose in the war was to create a "new world order" that would "enable all nations and races to assume their proper place in the world, and all peoples to be at peace in their own sphere." As the "leading race" of Asia, Japan should create a Coprosperity Sphere in which there would be a division of labor with each people performing economic functions for which their inherent capabilities prepared them. Nationalist writings often contained themes of Pan-Asianism and liberation of Asians from Western imperialism. A report produced by Japanese bureaucrats, however, privately described the goal of the new order as creation of "an economic structure which would ensure the permanent subordination of all other peoples and nations of Asia to Japan."[19] Cultural policies throughout the

Coprosperity sphere stressed "Japanization," reverence for the Emperor, observance of Japanese customs and holidays, and use of Japanese as the common language.

Japan paid a terrible price for the bold gamble of its leaders in 1941. Abandoning the cautious realism that had traditionally characterized Japanese diplomacy, the nation entered into a conflict that cost it the lives of nearly 3 million Japanese, its entire overseas empire, and the destruction of one-quarter of its machines, equipment, buildings, and houses. Generations were left physically and psychologically scarred by the trauma.

The outcome was heavy with historic irony. War sentiment in Japan had been impelled by an ultranationalist ideology that sought to preserve the traditional values of the Japanese political order, that vehemently opposed the expansion of Bolshevik influence in Asia, and that wanted to establish the Japanese Empire. Instead, war brought a social-democratic revolution at home, the rise of Communism in China, and—for the first time in Japan's history—occupation by an enemy force.

Notes

1. Quoted in Marius B. Jansen, *Japan and China: From War to Peace, 1894–1972* (New York: Rand McNally, 1975), 202.
2. Quoted in Charles E. Neu, *The Troubled Encounter: The United States and Japan* (New York: Wiley, 1975), 99.
3. Quoted ibid., 117.
4. Quoted ibid., 124.
5. Quoted in Akira Iriye, "The Failure of Economic Expansionism," in *Japan in Crisis,* ed. Bernard S. Silberman and Harry D. Harootunian (Princeton, N.J.: Princeton University Press, 1974), 265.
6. Quoted in Akira Iriye, *The Origins of the Second World War in Asia and the Pacific* (London and New York: Longman, 1987), 38–39; and Yoshitake Oka, *Konoe Fumimaro: A Political Biography,* trans. Shumpei Okamoto and Patricia Murray (Tokyo: University of Tokyo Press, 1983), 10–13.
7. Akira Iriye, *After Imperialism: The Search for a New Order in the Far East, 1931–1933* (Cambridge, Mass.: Harvard University Press, 1965), 295–296.
8. Hugh T. Patrick, "The Economic Muddle of the 1920s," in *Dilemmas of Growth in Prewar Japan,* ed. James William Morley (Princeton, N.J.: Princeton University Press, 1971), 256.
9. Andrew Gordon, *Labor and Imperial Democracy in Prewar Japan* (Berkeley: University of California Press, 1991), 335.
10. Peter Duus and Daniel I. Okimoto, "Fascism and the History of Prewar Japan: The Failure of a Concept," *Journal of Asian Studies* 39 (November 1979), 70.
11. Gordon M. Berger, "Politics and Mobilization in Japan, 1931–1945," in Peter Duus, ed., *The Twentieth Century,* vol. 6 of *The Cambridge History of Japan,* ed. John Whitney Hall (Cambridge: Cambridge University Press, 1988), 105, 146.

12. Bai Gao, "Arisawa Hiromi and His Theory for a Managed Economy," *Journal of Japanese Studies* 20 (winter 1994), 125.
13. Mark Peattie, *Ishiwara Kanji and Japan's Confrontation with the West* (Princeton, N.J.: Princeton University Press, 1975), 219.
14. Berger, "Politics and Mobilization," in *The Twentieth Century*, ed. Duus, 105.
15. Quoted in Jansen, *Japan and China*, 404.
16. Maruyama Masao, *Thought and Behavior in Modern Japanese Politics*, ed. Ivan Morris (Oxford: Oxford University Press, 1969), 85.
17. Quoted in Jansen, *Japan and China*, 405.
18. John W. Dower, *War Without Mercy: Race and Power in the Pacific War* (New York: Pantheon, 1986), 205.
19. Ibid., 288–290.

12

Japan's American Revolution

In the weeks and months after Pearl Harbor the Japanese Empire was aggrandized by success after success. The British naval base at Singapore was seized in February 1942, and the following month the entire Dutch East Indies was in Japanese hands; by April Japanese forces controlled a major part of the Philippines and by May they had penetrated far into the northern reaches of Burma, where they could cut off the supplies flowing into China.

At home a new feeling of destiny was in the air. After years of inconclusive fighting in China, there was a broadly expressed sense of joy and relief that total war had been declared. A distinguished novelist and critic, Itō Sei, wrote that on first hearing of the declaration of war, "I felt as if in one stroke I had become a new man, from the depths of my being." He went on:

> This war is an absolute act. It is not merely an extension of politics or the reverse side of politics. It is a struggle which the [Japanese] people had some day to fight in order to convince themselves from the bottom of their hearts that they are the most excellent people on the face of the globe. We are the "yellow race" our enemies talk about. We are fighting to determine the superiority or inferiority of the discriminated-against peoples. Our struggle is not the same as Germany's. . . . [1]

But as the president of the Privy Council had forecast to the Emperor on the eve of Pearl Harbor, Japan experienced growing difficulties as the war continued. By mid-1942, following the battles of the Coral Sea and Midway, Japanese forces were on the defensive. In most of the countries that the Japanese entered, the ideology of Pan-Asianism and of the Greater East Asia Coprosperity Sphere had little staying power. At home, the government required greater and greater sacrifices from the Japanese people. The portion of the gross national product (GNP) devoted to the war effort increased from 31 percent in

1942 to 42 percent in 1943 and then to 51 percent in 1944. American ships dominated the Pacific and cut off the import of raw materials. Agricultural production was curtailed by the shortage of chemical fertilizers and by the loss of farm labor to war-related industries. American firebomb raids brought terrible suffering to the already undernourished and disease-prone urban population.

Surrender

Allied forces followed an island-hopping strategy, working their way north from the south Pacific toward Japan. The fighting became ever more destructive, desperate, and deadly. The battle for Saipan, a small island in the Marianas, in July 1944 was ferocious and fanatical. Ivan Morris, in his classic study of the samurai ethic in Japanese cultural tradition, describes how this ethic motivated a suicidal resistance to the indignity of capture on Saipan:

> When organized military resistance became impossible, some 3,000 Japanese soldiers, most of them armed with nothing but bayonets or sticks, charged into the concentrated machine-gun fire of the American marines and were mown down to the last man. At times the Japanese corpses were piled so high that the marines had to move their machine-gun emplacements into an open line of fire as new waves surged forward. A particularly macabre note was provided by a contingent of wounded soldiers, many of them swathed in bandages and leaning on the shoulders of their comrades, who staggered out of the hospitals and infirmaries to take part in the last suicide attack. Subsequently entire units of Japanese soldiers knelt down in rows to be decapitated by their commanding officers, who then in turn committed harakiri. . . . As the marines advanced through the blood-drenched island, they witnessed one mass suicide after another, culminating in the terrible last scene when hundreds of Japanese civilian inhabitants hurled themselves off the cliffs. . . . Less than 1,000 Japanese survived from the original 32,000, and hardly a single soldier remained to be taken prisoner.[2]

When Saipan fell in July 1944, the Japanese home islands came into bombing range of American land-based planes, and General Tōjō resigned as prime minister.

At this point it was clear to both sides that Japanese defeat was inevitable. The question was: How would the war be terminated? On the Allied side, U.S. President Roosevelt and British Prime Minister Churchill had announced unconditional surrender as their goal, and public opinion was in overwhelming support. On the Japanese side, the navy was prepared to negotiate surrender. Most Japan leaders recognized that their cause was lost.

An incendiary raid on Tokyo, March 9–10, 1945, killed more than 100,000 people. Cities across the country were laid waste through thousands of sorties by American bombers, often flying at chimney-top level. But the Japanese army determined that it must win one great battle, even risking an invasion of the home islands, before it could honorably sue for peace. Women and children were armed with spears and told to prepare for invasion.

The last great battle was fought over Okinawa, the final line of defense, seen as a citadel protecting the home islands. Its desperation and ferocity were even greater than the battle for Saipan. Kamikaze attacks were launched against U.S. ships preparing for the Allied invasion of Okinawa, which began on April 1, 1945. By the time the island fell on June 22, some 12,281 Americans had been killed, more than 110,000 Japanese soldiers, and tens of thousands of Okinawan civilians. It was the highest toll of any campaign in World War II.

The rush of events became swift and complex. On April 12, Roosevelt died and an obscure vice-president, Harry S Truman, succeeded him. Germany surrendered and on May 8 the war in Europe was over. On June 18 American leadership finalized plans for Operation Olympic, an invasion of the Japanese home islands to be launched with an assault on Kyushu, planned for November 1.

Churchill, Stalin, and Truman met at Potsdam in mid-July. Stalin confirmed that the Soviet Union was preparing to enter the war against Japan, assuming that it would recover its territorial concessions in Manchuria. Stalin had made clear that, in addition, the USSR wanted to occupy part of a defeated Japan, probably Hokkaido. During the Potsdam Conference, Truman learned of the successful testing of an atomic device in New Mexico, prompting him to issue a declaration that warned Japan to surrender or face "prompt and utter destruction." The Potsdam Declaration listed the Allies' objectives as dismantling the Japanese Empire, punishing war criminals, and establishing a democratic order—but partly because it did not clarify what would happen to the imperial institution, the Japanese rejected the declaration on July 28. Accordingly, the atomic bomb was dropped on Hiroshima on August 6, killing, by Japanese estimates, 87,150 civilians; three days later 38,000 died in the atomic bombing of Nagasaki. Tens of thousands more of these two cities' inhabitants died subsequently of radiation sickness and the effects of the bomb. Kyoto, hitherto virtually untouched by the war, had been proposed as a principal target but was spared through the intervention of U.S. Secretary of War Henry Stimson, who had long admired the city's cultural treasures and historic beauty.

In the wake of these shocking events and of the dramatic entrance of the Soviet Union into the war on August 8, an imperial conference was called at which the Emperor personally intervened to express his will that the Allies' demands be accepted, with the sole reservation that the prerogatives of the Emperor as sovereign ruler not be compromised. The Americans sent an ambiguous reply stating that the Emperor would be "subject to the Supreme Commander of the Allied Powers" and "the ultimate form of government of Japan shall be established by the freely expressed will of the Japanese people." Truman meantime ordered that there be no more use of the bomb without his permission—one more bomb was ready—and he wrote in his diary that the thought of destroying another city was too horrible. Japan was prostrate. The Japanese were a weary and demoralized people, living in silent desperation and resigned to defeat. General Curtis LeMay, who commanded the strategic bombing of Japan, said, "Another six months and Japan would have been beaten back into the Dark Ages."[3] On August 15, 1945, the Emperor broadcast a rescript enjoining the Japanese people to bear the unbearable and to surrender with decorum. The broadcast was met with an emotional combination of relief and anguish: the war was over, but Japan was to be occupied by enemy soldiers for the first time in its history.

A typical gathering of neighborhood people to hear the radio address by the Emperor announcing surrender, August 15, 1945. *Kyodo News Service of Japan*

The Controversy over the Atomic Bombing

We would do well to pause and consider the atomic bombing of Hiroshima and Nagasaki, because it brought World War II to an end, began the atomic age, exerted an incalculable effect on the postwar Japanese psyche, and remains one of the most controversial events in modern history. Controversy has involved many issues. What was the motive for using it? Was it necessary? Were there viable alternatives? Historians have come to no firm consensus on these issues. They have adopted radically different interpretations and views.

There is, first of all, what we may regard as the orthodox view, the interpretation adopted by most historians. In this view, the bomb was used to bring the war to an early end, saving both Allied and Japanese lives by avoiding an invasion of the home islands. In his memoirs, Truman wrote that he had been told by General George Marshall, U.S. Secretary of the Army, that it might cost half a million American lives to force the enemy's surrender on his home ground. Further, in light of the fanatical and suicidal Japanese resistance in the Pacific islands, it was necessary to shock Japan into surrendering. For that reason, a second bomb was speedily dropped, creating the impression that there could be many more. Stimson, who had been U.S. Secretary of War and Truman's advisor on the bomb, writing in 1947, asserted that an invasion was the only alternative at an estimated cost of "over a million casualties to American forces alone." Given this alternative, Stimson wrote, "no man, in our position and subject to our responsibilities, holding in his hands a weapon of such possibilities for accomplishing this purpose and saving those lives, could have failed to use it and afterwards looked his countrymen in the face." It was, he concluded, "our least abhorrent choice."[4] James B. Conant, the president of Harvard University, a leader of the Manhattan Project which built the bomb, and an advisor instrumental in the decision to target Hiroshima, responded to critics by saying that the bomb was "part and parcel" of the war effort and "it made no sense to condemn the A-bomb as morally more egregious than strategic bombing."[5] After all, the firebombing of Tokyo in one night, March 9–10, 1945, had killed as many as 100,000 people—more than the Hiroshima bomb.

Another view, adopted by a later generation of historians writing during the Vietnam War period, questioned the use of the bomb when Japan was already prostrate. They pointed out that prominent American military leaders such as Dwight D. Eisenhower felt it was unnecessary to use the bomb. These historians contended that its use was related to the beginning of the Cold War: it would end hostilities before the Red Army established its influence in East Asia, it would prevent having to share the occupation of Japan with Russia, and it would strengthen the U.S. diplomatic hand in negotiations with Stalin over the Soviet sphere in Eastern Europe.

Still another interpretation emphasizes the irrational impulses of domestic politics and public opinion as paramount in the decision. In particular, these scholars cite the influence of the policy of unconditional surrender as a war aim, enunciated early in the war by Roosevelt as a way of rallying morale and sentiment in the United States and in the alliance. As one scholar writes, "From its informal origins in the hyperbole of U.S. politics, unconditional surrender gradually became more than a propaganda slogan. Through frequent repetition it became policy . . . [and] it left Japan in the dark about the consequences of defeat."[6] It contributed to a powerful momentum for total all-out warfare. Four days after becoming president, in his first address to the U.S. Congress, Truman reaffirmed unconditional surrender as a policy and the entire chamber rose to its feet to applaud. In a poll taken on June 1, 1945, by a margin of 9-to-1 Americans supported an uncompromising stance on war aims even if it meant invasion of the Japanese homeland. In the face of such animus against Japan, any effort to modify war aims or means was greatly handicapped. The most important effort in this regard was made during the last year of the war by U.S. Under Secretary of State Joseph Grew, who had been U.S. ambassador to Japan from 1931 to 1941. He advocated a clear statement to the Japanese that the imperial institution would be maintained in a peace settlement. He argued that this would facilitate not only surrender without invasion, but also occupation and reform, and rehabilitation of Japan as an ally in a postwar struggle with the Soviet Union. He succeeded in winning considerable support within the government, but when the Potsdam Declaration was drafted, Secretary of State James Byrnes deleted a reference to keeping the imperial institution because, he said, the "terrible political repercussions" were too great to risk. Japanese rejection therefore was immediate. Many Japanese leaders opposed surrender as long as it was not clear what the fate of the imperial institution would be. Only when the Emperor himself intervened and expressed his will was the Gordian knot cut.

Finally, the historians' assessment of the use of the bomb has another dimension, which until recently has received relatively little attention. Especially since the death of Emperor Hirohito in 1989, as new memoirs and records have come to light, a number of historians, both Japanese and non-Japanese, have raised issues of his responsibility. If he could bring about surrender in August 1945, why not many months earlier when Japanese leaders recognized the cause was lost? It was not only historians who wondered. As the Emperor lay dying in 1988, the mayor of Nagasaki, Motoshima Hitoshi, a man of remarkable personal courage, responding to questions put to him in the city assembly and afterward by the media, asserted that the Emperor bore partial responsibility for the war and its calamitous termination. "It is clear," he said, "from historical records that if the Emperor, in response to the reports of his senior statesmen, had resolved to end the war earlier, there would have been no battle of Okinawa, no nuclear attacks on Hiroshima and Nagasaki." His statement ignited an immense media uproar and many demanded that the mayor, a Christian, retract his statement, apologize, and resign. He stood his ground, but eventually he was shot by a right-wing nationalist. He recovered, though, and was even reelected.

Until recently, the Emperor was generally portrayed by historians as a peace-loving man who had no sympathy with militarists but who, as a constitutional monarch, could not interfere with politics. Some, but by no means all, historians now see him as more supportive of the army and resistant to ending the war in early 1945 when political leaders came to him privately and urged him to take immediate steps to end the futile war effort. Some of these historians see him as sympathetic with the army; others see him as personally of weak character. The result, as one writes, was that "surrender was delayed, Tokyo was fire bombed, the battle of Okinawa was fought, and atomic bombs were dropped on Hiroshima and Nagasaki mainly because the emperor could not exercise the leadership to end the war."[7]

Returning to the American decision, we may see how complex the historical analysis has become. It is possible, as the theologian Reinhold Niebuhr wrote, to see "historic forces more powerful than any human decision" at work. "Since the Germans were at work on the bomb during the war, we [Americans] had to develop it too; once built it was bound to be used if it would shorten the war."[8] Seeing its use in the context of what Raymond Aron called "the century of total war," we can see how a powerful momentum built up toward the use of ever more destructive weaponry and the growing willingness to use this weaponry even against civilian populations. Edwin Reischauer, the leading figure in postwar American studies of Japan, concluded that the use of the bomb on Hiroshima was justifiable to shock the Japanese government into surrender, but that there was no justification for the second bomb on Nagasaki, "snuffing out some 70,000 lives almost inadvertently."[9]

The American Occupation

Although nominally the Allies occupied Japan, in fact the enterprise was overwhelmingly American. It was dominated by the personality of General Douglas MacArthur, who was appointed Supreme Commander of the Allied Powers (SCAP). Though he received general policy directives from Washington, MacArthur was given broad discretion in the implementation of reforms, and his personal dominance was so great that the acronym SCAP soon came to designate the entire

Occupation administration. Unlike Germany, where collapse of the wartime government compelled the occupying forces to assume direct control, Japan had a government still intact at the time of surrender, and so SCAP was able to govern indirectly as a supervisory organ above the existing government.

From the beginning, two fundamental beliefs underlay United States planning for the Occupation. In the first place, there was an insistent faith in the universality of American values and institutions. Those enduring results of the American experience, MacArthur wrote in 1947, "are no longer peculiarly American, but now belong to the entire human race." It was believed that the United States, with all its faults, was the most advanced of all nations; and because all societies had to develop along more or less the same lines, reforms in Japanese society should be modeled along American lines. Japan therefore became the subject of an extraordinary experiment in the transference of American ideals and institutions to an Asian setting.

The other fundamental tenet in the philosophy of the Occupation was the belief that the most effective way of curing the Japanese of their militarism was by creating a democratic society. If people were given control of their own destiny, they would by nature and out of self-interest choose a peaceful course. "War's genesis," wrote the Supreme Commander, "lies in the despotic lust for power. . . . Never has it originated in the voluntary action of a free people—never will a free people voluntarily associate itself with the proposition that the road to peace and well-being and happiness lies through the crucible of war."[10] Those two fundamental beliefs moved the Americans to undertake the most radical reforms ever made in Japanese society.

The reforms could not successfully have been imposed had there not been a warm receptivity to undertaking such changes. Many Japanese felt that their prewar leaders had led them astray and that sweeping reform of Japanese institutions was necessary. They often referred to the Occupation as the "second opening of Japan," similar to the period nearly a century earlier when the country had received new and rejuvenating influences from the outside. For the Japanese, the Occupation period was a time of intense self-criticism and introspection, of revulsion for much that was old and traditional. This mood fed on itself and created a disposition in favor of innovation. As a consequence, reform became the vogue and the Occupation's task was greatly facilitated.

Demilitarization

The initial task the Americans set for themselves was to destroy the military system that had been built up since the Meiji Restoration. That entailed disbanding the military and secret police forces and closing bases, arsenals, and munitions factories; it also meant punishing or dismissing the leaders held responsible for the system and discrediting the values they had sponsored. Only after the field was cleared in this fashion, it was believed, could democratic institutions be successfully implanted.

The months after surrender brought a confusing relocation of vast numbers of weary and uncertain people. More than 5 million troops, more than half of whom were overseas, had to be demobilized and disarmed. In addition, more than 3 million civilians who had held positions in Japanese overseas territories streamed back into the home islands, placing still more stress on the debilitated economy. Factories that had produced for the military were closed, their employees turned out, and machinery was shipped off to neighboring countries as part of a reparations policy.

One of the most controversial aspects of the Occupation was the International Military Tribunal for the Far East, which MacArthur created to try war criminals. The trials of the Japanese leaders dragged on for over two years, and eventually seven men, including former Prime Ministers Tōjō and Hirota Kōki, were sentenced to death by hanging. Sixteen leaders were sentenced to prison for life, one for twenty years, and former Foreign Minister Shigemitsu for seven years. The issues raised by these convictions, such as the principle of holding individual leaders responsible for acts of their government, and subjecting them to alien, ex post facto laws, have been the subject of continuing controversy. In addition to this retribution, hundreds of lower-ranking officers were executed for atrocities and thousands of others sentenced to various terms of imprisonment.

The determination of SCAP to revolutionize Japanese society was made clear right at the outset by a decision to remove nearly the entire stratum of prewar leadership. A "purge" directive was issued on January 4, 1946, which automatically removed from eligibility for political office anyone who had played a part in promoting "Japanese aggression or militant nationalism." Military officers, heads of overseas business organizations, colonial officers, and leaders of nationalist organizations were purged. In all, 220,000 persons were declared ineligible to hold office in the new political order. One prominent American writer visiting Japan was stunned by the policy: "This use of the word 'purge' was new to me; I had never heard it in political talk except in connection with Russia."[11] But SCAP felt no self-doubts, in the belief that if the former oppressive forces were swept clear then democratic forces would naturally grow and flourish. The purge was executed swiftly and mechanically with little time allowed for reviewing individual cases. A serious shortcoming in the policy was the exemption of the civilian bureaucracy from the purge. With some exceptions, SCAP left the bureaucracy intact, for it was needed to run the day-to-day business of government. As a consequence, the bureaucracy preserved remarkable strength of continuity from prewar days and became the major power in postwar politics—to the detriment of democratic forces.

A New Political Order

Once these measures—demobilizing the armed forces, destroying war-related industries, purging the prewar leadership, and trying war criminals—were accomplished, the Occupation was ready to turn to the creative tasks of building a new democratic order. The tone was set by proclaiming a "Japanese Bill of Rights," which abolished all restrictions on speech and assembly and threw open the gates to free about 2,500 political prisoners, many of whom were Communists. SCAP later regretted this enthusiasm, but the measure reveals the high idealism of the early Occupation days.

The thorniest problem MacArthur and his staff had to deal with was deciding the fate of the Emperor. In most of the Allied countries there was strong sentiment in favor of destroying the imperial institution and trying Hirohito as a war criminal. Months went by after surrender without any firm decision by the U.S. government. MacArthur himself was impressed with the Emperor at their first meeting, and the photograph of the two men taken at the time records one of the most poignant moments in Japanese history: the Supreme Commander, casual in his fatigues, hands on hips, towering over the nervous Son of Heaven, standing at attention in formal attire.

The Emperor's advisors worked shrewdly to try to change his image. It was their idea, apparently, that he make a formal renunciation of his "sacred and inviolable" status. On New Year's Day 1946, Hirohito made his so-called Declaration of Humanity, in which he stated that "the ties between Us and Our people . . . do not depend upon mere legends and myths. They are not predicated on the false conception that the Emperor is divine, and that the Japanese people are superior to other races and fated to rule the world."

MacArthur came to the conclusion that the imperial institution was necessary to maintain political stability and to sanction and facilitate reform. He wanted the Emperor kept as a constitutional monarch and therefore sought to convince Washington by predicting catastrophic consequences if the Emperor were removed: "The whole of Japan can be expected, in my opinion, to resist. . . . I believe all hope of introducing modern democratic methods would disappear. . . . It is quite possible that a minimum of a million troops would be required which would have to be maintained for an indefinite number of years. In addition a complete civil service might have to be recruited and imported, possibly running into a size of several hundred thousand."[12]

In the face of such determined advice the opposition in Washington withered, and the decision was made to preserve the imperial institution as the symbolic head of a new democratic state.

Scarcely less vexing was the problem of constitutional revision. There was general agreement among American planners that the Meiji Constitution would have to be wholly rewritten. It was seen as having blocked the development of democratic politics and as being partly responsible for the growth of militarism. Still, the hope in Washington

The first meeting of General MacArthur and the Emperor. *U.S. Army*

was that SCAP could maintain a low profile and allow the Japanese themselves to conduct the process of revision, lest knowledge that constitutional reforms had been imposed reduce the possibility of their acceptance and support by the Japanese people in the future. Therefore, MacArthur asked the new prime minister, Shidehara—SCAP had some confidence in him because of his liberal foreign policy during the 1920s—to undertake "liberalization of the constitution." The latter appointed a distinguished committee of legal scholars and bureaucrats for this purpose, and for three months the committee deliberated. On February 1, 1946, the proposals of the committee were presented to MacArthur.

They proved, however, to be highly conservative, amounting only to limited revisions of the Meiji Constitution. At this point MacArthur decided to intrude upon the constitutional revision. He clearly felt that if left to the Japanese the process would be too slow and painful. He wanted to get on with creation of a new political order, and nothing could be done until the basic document was written. MacArthur therefore pushed ahead and proceeded, behind the scenes, to impose his own version of a constitution. He ordered the Government Section of SCAP to draft a constitution that could serve as a "guide" for the Japanese cabinet. The head of the Government Section, General Courtney Whitney, was instructed that the document should provide for the Emperor as a constitutional monarch, "responsible to an electorate based upon wide representative suffrage," and should declare that "war and war-making would be forsworn."

As far as we know, the decision to insert a clause in the constitution renouncing war and a standing army grew out of a conversation that Shidehara and MacArthur had on January 24, 1946. In his *Reminiscences* the latter writes that Shidehara suggested to him that the constitution "prohibit any military establishment" so that "the rest of the world would know that Japan never intended to wage war again." This suggestion may well have come as part of the Japanese effort to improve the negative image of the Emperor. MacArthur writes that when he agreed with the suggestion, Shidehara's "amazement was so great that he seemed overwhelmed as he left the office. Tears ran down his face, and he turned back to me and said, 'the world will laugh and mock us as impracticable visionaries, but a hundred years from now we will be called prophets.'"[13]

In an almost Alice-in-Wonderland atmosphere Whitney assembled members of his Government Section, proclaimed them "a constitutional assembly," and directed them to draft a document. In six days (!) the task was complete, the product handed to MacArthur for his approval, and on February 13, 1946, it was presented to the Japanese cabinet at a meeting in the foreign minister's residence. The cabinet members were put under heavy pressure, with the implied threat to go

The Emperor visiting a repatriation center in early 1946. *UPI/Bettmann*

directly to the Japanese people if the document were not accepted. On March 5 the cabinet, after making some minor changes, approved the MacArthur draft and passed it on to the Emperor, who dutifully accepted it. The following day it was made public, and MacArthur gave a poker-faced statement to the press praising the Japanese for "such an exemplary document which so coincided with his own notion of what was best for the country." It was unlikely that many were misled to believe this was a Japanese product, for the language and concepts were patched together from the Anglo-American political tradition and had unmistakable echoes of the Declaration of Independence, the Constitution of the United States, and the Gettysburg Address.

The new constitution made a number of revolutionary changes in the Japanese political order:

1. It reduced the Emperor, formerly sacred and inviolable, to a position as "the symbol of the State and of the unity of the people with whom resides sovereign power."

2. It provided that "the Japanese people forever renounce war as a sovereign right" and declared that "land, sea, and air forces, as well as other war potential, will never be maintained" (Article 9).

3. It made the cabinet responsible to the Diet, as in the British system; and it made the legislature, which under the Meiji Constitution had been partly elective by male suffrage and partly appointive, entirely elective by universal suffrage.

4. It replaced the highly centralized structure of government under the Meiji system with one that allowed a much greater measure of local autonomy, by increasing the power of local officials and making their positions elective.

5. It created an independent judiciary with the right of judicial review.

6. It afforded protection for a wide variety of human rights: freedom of the press, freedom of assembly, academic freedom, equality of the sexes, and collective bargaining.

Economic Reforms

SCAP set out similarly to democratize the economy. Washington had ordered MacArthur to reform labor, business, and agriculture to accomplish "a wide distribution of income and of the ownership of the means of production." Occupation planners blamed the prewar concentration of economic power in the hands of the big business and landlord classes for creating the social environment in which militarism could take root. Moreover, because many of the planners had earlier worked for the New Deal programs of Franklin Roosevelt, they were predisposed in favor of economic reform that would alleviate the frustrations of industrial workers and tenant farmers.

The influence of the New Deal was particularly apparent in the reforms undertaken to promote the labor union movement and to break up the giant industrial combines. SCAP prodded the Diet to pass a trade union act in December 1945, which was patterned after the Wagner Act passed by the United States Congress ten years earlier. This "Magna Carta of Japanese Labor" guaranteed the rights of workers to organize, to bargain collectively, and to strike; and it prohibited various unfair practices by employers. Subsequent legislation provided for minimum acceptable working conditions, unemployment insurance, and procedures for resolution of labor disputes.

The Occupation enthusiastically promoted campaigns of unionization, and the number of members grew rapidly. During the prewar period only 420,000 of a total industrial labor force of 6 million workers were union members, in the peak year of membership. By June 1948, thanks to the prodding of SCAP, union membership soared to 6.5 million members. Yet the significance of this figure may be easily exaggerated, for the values underlying the union movement in Western democracies were frequently absent from a movement brought into being more by government initiative than by the voluntary action of laboring men and women themselves. It was not uncommon for the head of a firm to take the initiative in organizing a union in his own company.

Much controversy was generated by the Occupation's program to break up the zaibatsu, those vast economic combines such as Mitsui, Mitsubishi, Sumitomo, and Yasuda. Products of Japanese economic growth and of the need to concentrate capital, skilled labor, and technology, they were seen by the Americans as obstacles to economic democracy. An economics professor who had participated in antitrust actions during the New Deal and who was brought to Tokyo to advise the Occupation wrote that "concentration of economic control enabled [the zaibatsu] to continue a semifeudal relationship between themselves and their employees, to continue to suppress wages and to hinder the development of independent political ideologies. Thus the formation of the middle class, which was useful in opposing the militarist group in other democratic countries, was retarded."[14]

To bring about a deconcentration of economic power, the Occupation dissolved ten holding companies as well as the twenty-six largest industrial companies and the two largest trading companies. In addition, a "shareholding revolution" was carried out, which sought to diffuse the stocks of more than 600 companies into the hands of many. In less than two years nearly 1.4 million shares were sold to the public. In April 1947 the Diet was prodded into passage of legislation modeled on American antitrust laws, which established a Fair Trade Commission to police business and to prohibit monopoly practice.

The most successful of the economic measures engineered by the Americans was the program of land reform. It was an idea that captured MacArthur's imagination, perhaps because of Jeffersonian ideas that survived from his early days in Virginia—or perhaps because of his father's participation in land reform in the Philippines at the turn of the century. In any case, SCAP pressured the Japanese government into a far-reaching program that called for a complete dispossession of absentee landlords and for retention by other owners of up to 7.5 acres farmed by the owner himself and of an additional 2.5 acres more of tenanted land. (Somewhat larger plots were permitted in Hokkaido.) The government purchased all land in excess of these limits and sold it to the existing tenants on easy terms. The reform was an immense undertaking, involving the establishment of more than 11,000 local land commissions, which were composed of tenants and owners and which instituted changes in the property rights of some 6 million families and hence in the whole fabric of social relations. The amount of land under tenancy agreement was reduced from in excess of 40 percent to approximately 10 percent, transforming the countryside into a society of small independent farmers.

People line up for food rations in early postwar days. *UPI/Bettmann*

Social Reforms

MacArthur and many of the American policy planners believed that the fundamental success of the Occupation reforms would depend upon a transformation of society and its supporting values, which they believed were still basically feudal. "Supposedly," MacArthur wrote, "the Japanese were a twentieth-century civilization. In reality, they were more nearly a feudal society, of the type discarded by Western nations some four centuries ago."[15] The Occupation therefore set about liberalizing the entire social structure and converting Japan to a philosophy of democratic individualism.

The Americans took special pride in bringing about what they regarded as "the emancipation of the women in Japan." Female suffrage was one of their primary goals, and when the first general elections of the postwar period were held in April 1946, more than 13 million women voted for the first time and thirty-nine women were elected to the Diet.

The constitution explicitly provided that "equality of the sexes" should govern matters of property rights and inheritance, and it stated that "marriage shall be based only on the mutual consent of both sexes and it shall be maintained through mutual cooperation with the equal rights of husband and wife as a basis." These principles were incorporated into a new civil code, which came into effect on January 1, 1948.

Another important part of SCAP's effort to transform Japanese society and its supporting values was the reform of the education system. The U.S. Education Mission, a twenty-seven-member group of educators that made a whirlwind tour of Japan in the spring of 1946, recommended what proved tantamount to wholesale adoption of the U.S. education system and its philosophy. One of the first tasks recommended by the mission was to carry out a vast decentralization of the functions of the heretofore powerful Ministry of Education. The ministry's tight control over secondary education was to be superseded by popularly elected boards of education at the local level, which were given control of staff, curriculum, and choosing textbooks. Other structural reforms imitated the American pattern. In place of the former multitrack education system, which SCAP considered undemocratic and elitist, it established a single-track coeducational plan along American lines, with six years of elementary schooling, followed by three years of junior high school and three years of senior high school for all children. Similarly, at the postsecondary level, the old differentiation among technical schools, normal schools, and imperial universities was done away with, and all institutions of higher learning were reorganized as four-year universities. Many critics have argued that, as a consequence, Japanese education became homogenized in a way that diluted the strengths of the old differentiated and diverse system.

SCAP's education reformers also wanted to root out the nationalist orientation of the schools and replace it with a strong democratic and individualist philosophy. The Diet rescinded the Imperial Rescript on Education, which had been in effect since 1890 and which had set the nationalist tone of educational values. In its place, the Fundamental Law of Education of 1947 defined the purpose of the education system as contributing to "the peace of the world and the welfare of humanity by building a democratic and cultural state." As is always the case after a revolution, history had to be rewritten; in this instance new textbooks emphasized the themes of peace, democracy, and international cooperation. Also, as the teachers became organized into a powerful trade union dominated by left-wing politics, most history texts stressed such concepts as economic exploitation and the struggle of the people against the oppression of the ruling class. As a result, the education system became deeply enmeshed in partisan politics in the postwar era.

The "Reverse Course"

Occupation policy comprised two main phases. During the first two years, from 1945 to 1947, under the sway of postwar ideals that sought elimination of militarism and establishment of a democratic society, Americans consciously played the role of revolutionary. By 1947 there was a feeling within SCAP that the work of reform was nearly complete, and MacArthur, at a news conference in March, surprised reporters by suggesting that it was time to plan the end of the Occupation. But before his hopes could materialize, the onset of the Cold War began to transform the outlook and approach of policy planners. By 1948 the tension between the Soviet Union and the United States and the growing power of the Chinese Communist movement led the U.S. Department of State to rethink American objectives for Japan. George Kennan, the new director of the Department of State's Policy Planning Staff, recommended after a trip to Tokyo that "no further reform legislation should be pressed. The emphasis should shift from reform to economic recovery. . . . Precedence should be given . . . to the task of bringing the Japanese into a position where they would be better able to shoulder the burdens of independence."[16]

Accordingly, a marked shift in Occupation policy ensued, one that many dismayed Japanese intellectuals and writers subsequently termed "the reverse course." It seemed to them that Americans were going back on the principles and programs enunciated during the preceding two years. To a considerable extent, they were right. It is possible to exaggerate this change, but there was an unmistakable shift in the Occupation in 1948; the new tone became more pronounced with the success of the Communist Revolution in China in 1949 and the beginning of the Korean conflict the following year. SCAP now had less sympathy for the social reformers, the labor organizations, and the left-wing politicians. The purge, originally intended to eliminate prewar nationalists, was revived and directed at members of the left wing, particularly the Communists. The program of business deconcentration was abandoned and replaced by a harsher attitude toward organized labor. In July 1948 SCAP intervened to avert a general walkout by the railway and communication unions, compelling a revision of the National Public Service Law to prohibit government employees from striking.

A more important indication of the shift from reform to rehabilitation was the arrival in February 1949 of Joseph M. Dodge, a Detroit banker, brought to Japan as financial advisor to SCAP for the purpose of reviving the Japanese economy. By recommending a balanced national budget and establishing an official exchange rate, Dodge sought to curb inflation and to attract foreign investment. The recommendations, implemented in the summer of 1949, were strong medicine, requiring retrenchment by both government and business, and a stiffened resistance to the economic demands of labor. Owing to these measures as well as to the "red purge," which eliminated thousands of left-wing officials from government and union positions, union membership began to decline.

The most notable retreat from the idealism and the utopianism of the early Occupation was the revised thinking about Japan's defense. The preamble to the new constitution had emphasized "peaceful cooperation with all nations" and had announced the intention of preserving Japan's national security by "trusting in the justice and faith of the peace-loving peoples of the world." Article 9 had codified this intention. The heady atmosphere in which these ideals were unfurled had already passed by 1948 and MacArthur had cause to regret his earlier enthusiasm. Japan, rather than China, appeared the stable hope for an alliance in Asia, and the punitive aspects of the Occupation, which had largely run their course by this time, were now reversed. It no longer made sense to American policymakers to seek a weak and pacifist Japan. Therefore, shortly after the outbreak of the Korean War in June 1950, Japan was permitted to establish a 75,000-man paramilitary force, which was to take over from American troops responsibility for Japanese domestic security. It would not do, in light of the provisions of Article 9, to call it an "army" and so it was referred to as a National Police Reserve. Only later was it renamed the Self-Defense Force.

When World War II ended, American policymakers commonly thought in terms of occupying Japan for at least twenty-five years in order to maintain peace and security. But the Japanese proved much more tractable to reforms than was expected, friendly relations developed, domestic pressures in the United States called for bringing the soldiers home, and MacArthur by 1947 was ready to end the Occupation. Although changing perceptions of security requirements in East Asia prevented early termination, the Occupation lasted less than seven years. A peace treaty was signed in San Francisco on September 8, 1951, and the Occupation officially ended on April 28, 1952. Actually the de facto end had come earlier because SCAP ceased to play a major role within Japan after the Korean conflict began.

Though SCAP disappeared, American influence continued to dominate Japan long after the formal end of the Occupation. Together with the San Francisco Peace Treaty, the American-Japanese Security Treaty of 1952 was signed, leaving Japan in effect a military protectorate of the United States. That treaty provided for the retention of American bases and allowed the United States to use the American forces stationed there in any way that would "contribute to the maintenance of international peace and security in the Far East." It prohibited Japan from granting military bases to any other power without American consent.

This passive and dependent role was consonant with the confused and pacifist mood of postwar Japan. But it also suited its national self-interest. Adopting an essentially nonpolitical posture allowed Japan to define its national aims in narrow economic terms and thus to concentrate the energy of its people on the tasks of improving their material livelihood.

Notes

1. Quoted in Donald Keene, *Landscapes and Portraits: Appreciations of Japanese Culture* (Tokyo: Kodansha, 1971), 303.
2. Ivan Morris, *The Nobility of Failure: Tragic Heroes in the History of Japan* (New York: Holt, Rinehart, and Winston, 1975), 299.
3. Quoted in Peter Duus, ed., *The Twentieth Century,* vol. 6 of *The Cambridge History of Japan,* ed. John Whitney Hall (Cambridge: Cambridge University Press, 1988), 381.
4. Henry L. Stimson, "The Decision to Use the Atomic Bomb," *Harper's Magazine* (February 1947).
5. James Hershberg, *James B. Conant: Harvard to Hiroshima and the Making of the Nuclear Age* (New York: Knopf, 1994), 284–285.
6. Leon V. Sigal, *Fighting to a Finish: The Politics of War Termination in the United States and Japan, 1945* (Ithaca, N.Y.: Cornell University Press, 1988), 93.
7. Herbert P. Bix, "The Showa Emperor's 'Monologue' and the Problem of War Responsibility," *Journal of Japanese Studies* 18 (1992), 302.
8. Richard Fox, *Reinhold Niebuhr: A Biography* (New York: Harper and Row, 1985), 244.
9. Edwin O. Reischauer, *My Life Between Japan and America* (New York: Harper and Row, 1986), 101.
10. *Life* (magazine) (July 4, 1947).
11. John Gunther, *The Riddle of MacArthur* (New York: Harper, 1951), 149.
12. U.S. Department of State, *Foreign Relations of the United States: 1946,* vol. 8 (Washington, D.C.: U.S. Government Printing Office, 1971), 395–396.
13. Douglas MacArthur, *Reminiscences* (New York: McGraw-Hill, 1964), 303.
14. Corwin Edwards, quoted in Kozo Yamamura, *Economic Policy in Postwar Japan* (Berkeley: University of California Press, 1967), 2.
15. MacArthur, *Reminiscences,* 283.
16. George F. Kennan, *Memoirs: 1929–1950* (Boston: Little, Brown, 1967), 391.

13

Postwar Politics and Purpose

It is tempting to think of defeat and the American Occupation as constituting a sharp break in Japanese history. Postwar Japan, born amidst the most calamitous events in modern history, appeared to be embarked on a new and progressive course. A people broken in spirit by a conflict that had cost them nearly 3 million lives, including those first victims of the atomic age, embraced a new ethos of peace and democracy. The industry and empire for which the nation strove were destroyed. The country was an international outcast, occupied by foreign soldiers for the first time in its history. A new political and social structure, inspired by foreign values, was imposed to replace the old discredited institutions. A sharp break with prewar history seemed undeniable.

With greater perspective on postwar Japan, however, we can see unmistakable signs of continuity from presurrender days into the new era. Despite the wrenching changes, some leaders, values, and institutional practices survived the upheaval and served as central features of the postwar political system. This system underwrote the policies of economic growth that shaped postwar Japanese history. The conservative leaders who survived the reforms and the purge gave the postwar system an extraordinary stability and built a consensus for economic growth that gave the nation a clear purpose.

Among the surviving conservatives, the key figure in shaping postwar politics and the conception of Japanese national purpose was Yoshida Shigeru, who was prime minister for most of the first decade of the postwar period and who served concurrently as foreign minister during much of this time. Yoshida, who so dominated the postwar political scene that he was sometimes referred to as "One Man" Yoshida, gathered around him a powerful group of political disciples known as the Yoshida School. They became the dominant force behind the resurgent conservative influence in the postwar political system.

Formation of the Postwar Political System

On the surface, party politics in the early postwar period were marked by turmoil and confusion. Everything seemed new. The purge appeared to have wiped the slate clean to permit the emergence of a new political elite. The first postwar election, in April 1946, saw the participation of more than 200 parties. More than 2,700 were candidates for the Lower House, more than one-half of them independents or members of minor parties. More than 80 percent of the House members elected in 1946 were newcomers.

The discrediting of the prewar system and the reform ethos introduced by the Occupation's creation of new political institutions gave strong encouragement to the liberal currents in society. The Japan Socialist Party (JSP) became a contender for power, although it was often split between its liberal and moderate wings. The Japan Communist Party (JCP) also showed new strength, gaining as much as 10 percent of the vote in the early postwar elections. Most of the articulate sectors of the population were sympathetic with the progressive cause. The media, writers, teachers, students, labor leaders, and white-collar workers favored the new values of social reform, democracy, and pacifism.

In retrospect, we can see that the postwar years were the finest hour for the left-wing parties. Their ideas emerged out of wartime disillusion, revulsion from Japanese nationalism, and profound distrust of traditional state power. Progressives of all stripes held that prewar nationalism, which had been built on the extraordinary claims of the collectivist ethic, the Japanese family-state, and the emperor system had led them astray, blinded them to their real self-interest, overcome their best instincts, and reduced Japan to an international pariah. They passionately embraced the new values and institutions established by the Occupation. They took their stand in support of the new democratic order and above all in support of the role that the constitution in Article 9 envisioned for Japan in the world. They believed that Japan had a unique mission to usher in a new, peaceful international order, that as victims of the advent of atomic weapons, the Japanese people could convincingly argue that wars were ever more destructive, that a new age in international affairs was accordingly at hand, and that the sovereign prerogative to go to war must be renounced. In no other country was the progressives' hope for the future world order so high as in Japan, for no other nation's recent experiences seemed to bear out so compellingly the costs of the old ways.

In the face of such a strong progressive tide, it was remarkable that the conservatives were able to cling to power. The key to their success was an alliance with the bureaucracy, which provided a strong basis for the conservatives' staying power. The purge, it will be recalled, was not used extensively against the bureaucracy, owing to the decision of SCAP to keep the Japanese government intact and to rule through it. In the prewar days the bureaucracy had been one among multiple elites competing for power and influence in the political system. During the Occupation the other elites—the military, the party, and the zaibatsu leaders—were primary targets of the purge. The seasoned and experienced bureaucrats were left largely unscathed (aside from the Home Ministry) and in a dominant position.

As a consequence, after many of the former politicians were purged, veteran bureaucrats moved into positions of leadership in the conservative parties. Since the turn of the century, when Itō Hirobumi left the oligarchy to form the Seiyūkai, it had been common for the conservative parties to draw much of their leadership from former bureaucrats. That practice was all the more common in postwar Japan.

During the first decade of the postwar period the Liberal Party (Jiyūtō) emerged as the dominant conservative party. A descendant of the prewar Seiyūkai, it was led by Yoshida Shigeru, who was a veteran bureaucrat of the prewar Foreign Ministry. Yoshida served as prime minister from 1946 until 1954, except for a short period between 1947 and 1948 when the socialists and coalition government briefly held power. He brought many experienced bureaucrats into the Liberal Party and thus was able not only to form a strong party but also to fashion a close working relationship with the bureaucracy, on which the Occupation was relying to govern the country.

Yoshida is one of the most important figures in modern Japanese history. His likes had rarely been seen since the Meiji oligarchs passed from the scene. Shrewd and arrogant, brilliant and abrasive, scion of a prominent family, he rose through the ranks of the prewar Foreign Ministry, serving during the 1930s as ambassador to Italy and then to Great Britain. Devoted to the imperial cause, he believed it was best pursued by accommodation to and "making use" of the Anglo-American powers. In the 1930s he was often appalled, not by the goals of Japanese imperialism but by the way they were implemented, which he believed needlessly affronted the Anglo-American powers. During the war, his opposition to the militarists landed him in the custody of the Kempeitai, the military police, who held him under arrest for ten weeks after they discovered he was behind a secret but abortive attempt to bring about an early end to the war.

Although he was at heart a conservative, an elitist, and a nationalist, Yoshida's wartime opposition to the militarists made him acceptable to the Occupation as a leader of postwar Japan. His appointment as prime minister was sanctioned by the Occupation in May 1946, following the first postwar election. Despite his enmity toward the militarists, Yoshida was neither a liberal nor a democrat. He was a realist and a nationalist, determined to preserve as much as possible of the old imperial order and to set Japan on a path that would restore the nation as a great power.

More than any other person, Yoshida shaped the postwar political system, which functioned through close reciprocal relations among three entities—the conservative party, the bureaucracy, and the combined forces of big business and agriculture—in what is sometimes called the ruling triad. Each component of the triad contributed important elements to the coalition of conservative forces, and the system worked so well that it seemed, in the words of one scholar, like "a marriage made in heaven." Business and agricultural interests, as they began to recover, gave the Liberal Party and Yoshida their support in order to gain favors and preferential treatment and to counter the liberal tide represented by the left-wing parties. The most important component of the triad, however, was the bureaucracy. Yoshida installed his followers in both the bureaucracy and the party, and, it was these followers who became known as the *Yoshida gakkō,* or Yoshida School. A reporter once asked Yoshida how many "students" there were in his school. He replied in characteristically jocular fashion that he did not know because he did not charge tuition. In 1949 Yoshida recruited thirty elite bureaucrats to join the Liberal Party and run in the general election. Among their number were two future prime ministers: Ikeda Hayato (prime minister from 1960 to 1964) and Satō Eisaku (prime minister from 1964 to 1972). They were sometimes humorously referred to as the "honor students" of the Yoshida School because, as we shall see, they carried forward his purpose and program after he retired from politics.

The period from 1946 to 1955 was a formative time for the postwar political system. For nearly all this period the progressive forces were sufficiently splintered so that Yoshida and the Liberal Party were able to dominate the scene. At the end of 1954, however, the Liberal Party was ousted from power by another conservative party, a descendant of the prewar Minseitō party. Known as the Democratic Party (*Minshutō*), it too included many prewar bureaucrats and politicians. Confronted by the continuing strength of the conservative parties, the left-wing parties decided in 1955 to put aside their squabbling and join in a united party. Except for the JCP, which determined to continue its lonely struggle begun in 1922, the left wing came together in 1955 to form a unified JSP (*Nihon Shakaitō*). The JSP appeared to have the potential to take power, but the uniting of the progressives into a single Socialist Party with the purpose of taking power and instituting liberal reforms at home and a neutral role in international affairs at once sent shock waves through conservative ranks. The business community saw its interests jeopardized and brought pressure on the conservatives to cease their internecine warfare. Accordingly, also in 1955, the two conservative parties, the Liberal Party and the Democratic Party, joined to stave off the progressive challenge. The resulting Liberal Democratic Party (LDP) succeeded in establishing solid control of the postwar political system for nearly four decades.

When these new political alignments were created in 1955, it appeared there would be two parties, the LDP and the JSP, that would compete for power on opposing political agendas. In the long run, however, the JSP proved incapable of maintaining a united front; there was too much ideological distance between its left and right wings. They consumed their energies in ideological struggles to which a majority of the public was indifferent. The left-wing progressives adhered to what they called their "peace principles," which advocated unarmed neutrality in the Cold War. The notion of unarmed neutrality and the decidedly pro-Communist sympathy that characterized the left-wing progressives were too extreme for the remainder of the JSP. Splits in the ranks and defections soon occurred. In 1960, a right-wing group of the party broke away to form the Democratic Socialist Party (*Shakai Minshutō*). The socialist capacity to attract the votes of the moderately discontented was further undermined when in 1964 the political arm of the Buddhist organization *Sōka Gakkai* formed the *Komeitō* (Clean Government Party), which also drew support away from the socialists.

As a result of this fracturing of the progressives, the socialists became the perpetual opposition, while the most meaningful competition for power was fought out within the LDP, which continued to be dominated for the most part by its mainstream Yoshida School. After 1955 the ruling triad dominated the political system for two decades. The LDP's one-party rule depended on its close ties with business and agriculture; it needed the rural vote and the financial backing of the business community. Agricultural interests were in turn rewarded with subsidies, price supports, and the pork barrel. Business, working hand-in-glove with the LDP and the bureaucracy, gained legislative rewards in the form of cheap capital, a protected domestic market, and a wide array of high-growth policies. So smoothly functioning was this partnership that it came to be known abroad as "Japan, Incorporated."

Although the constitution provided that the Diet should be "the highest organ of state power and shall be the sole law-making organ of the state," in practice the bureaucracy initiated and drafted virtually all important legislation and possessed extraordinary administrative prerogatives in interpreting and implementing laws. Arrogantly, but with some justification, a former vice-minister on one occasion characterized the Diet as no more than an "extension of the bureaucracy."[1] In the two decades following the end of the Occupation, every prime minister was a former bureaucrat, and half of the cabinet seats were held by former bureaucrats.

In addition to the power of the bureaucracy, a key reason the triad model functioned so smoothly was that the conservatives succeeded in forging a strong national consensus in favor of economic growth as Japan's highest priority. The shaping of this new sense of national purpose was, above all, the achievement of Yoshida.

The Yoshida Doctrine

The essential themes of postwar Japanese history were the reestablishment of bureaucratic and business leadership of the nation, the single-minded pursuit of economic growth, and a passive role in international politics. To a considerable extent the withdrawal from international politics and the obsession with improving the national livelihood were the result of a popular pacifism shaped by the wartime trauma and the utter discrediting of the policies of the militarists. But it is important to stress that the postwar orientation toward economic growth and passivity in foreign affairs were also the product of the pragmatism of Japan's conservative political leaders and an opportunistic adaptation to the international political-economic environment in which they found themselves. Former U.S. Secretary of State Henry Kissinger concluded in his memoirs that "Japanese decisions have been the most farsighted and intelligent of any major nation in the postwar era."[2] Kissinger was referring to the shrewd, pragmatic way in which Japan pursued its national interest by concentrating on economic development while shunning involvement in international political-strategic issues, which would have diverted energies and attention from national recovery.

In the desolation and despair of the postwar days, when Japan was a virtual international pariah and the nation's fortunes were at the lowest point in history, Yoshida gradually put together a sense of national purpose that guided the country for the next four decades. His conception of national purpose far outlived his own career, in part because, as we have seen, he succeeded in installing a powerful group of followers in the conservative ruling party and in the bureaucracy to carry on his policies in the decades after he left office. Yoshida's influence also endured because of his extraordinary skill in perceiving world trends and in using them to Japan's special advantage. He had a clear sense of the strengths and potentialities, as well as the limitations, of the Japanese nation. From these insights he was able to fashion an enduring concept of the national interest as the nature of the postwar international order took shape.

Because he was a veteran diplomat and longtime student of diplomatic history, Yoshida had an unusual sense of the possibilities that changes in international politics might offer. When he formed his first cabinet in the spring of 1946, he observed to a colleague that "history provides examples of winning by diplomacy after losing in war."[3] That is, a defeated nation, by analyzing and exploiting the shifting relations among world powers, could contain the damage incurred in defeat and could instead win the peace. A Japanese scholar has recently suggested that Yoshida thought of himself like Talleyrand, the French foreign minister who went to the Congress of Vienna in 1815 "to win back with statecraft what his nation had lost in the disastrous Napoleonic War."[4] Yoshida sensed that disputes between victors over the postwar settlement might be used by the defeated nation to its own advantage. In fact, the Cold War offered just such an opportunity.

In the immediate postwar period, Yoshida's primary concern in foreign affairs was to restore Japan's reputation and to gain acceptance by the international community. This goal entailed convincing world opinion that Japan had changed and that the Japanese people were indeed committed to a new, peaceful course. In the prewar period, Yoshida had been an advocate of a close Anglo-Japanese relation. He now determined that Japan should associate itself as closely as practicable with the Americans, the new hegemonic power. But doing so did not mean sacrificing the national interest to the U.S. purpose. On the contrary, as he said, half seriously, "Just as the United States was once a colony of Great Britain but is now the stronger of the two, if Japan becomes a colony of the United States, it will also eventually become the stronger."[5] In other words, Japan could look to its long-range interest by assuming for the time being a subordinate role within the U.S. international order.

Negotiating an end to the Occupation and a bilateral military agreement with the United States to provide Japanese security after it regained independence compelled Yoshida to formulate in much greater detail and sophistication the nature of Japan's postwar national purpose. In the course of these negotiations he worked out a brilliant strategy—what we may call a Yoshida Doctrine—that served Japan for the next several decades.

The critical moment for the determination of Japan's postwar strategy arrived in 1950, with the dangers and opportunities that the Soviet-U.S. Cold War rivalry presented to Japan. The dangers were that Japan would be drawn into Cold War politics, expend its limited and precious resources on remilitarization, and postpone the full economic and social recovery of its people. Conversely, Soviet-U.S. rivalry offered certain opportunities. The Cold War made Japan strategically important to the United States and gave Yoshida bargaining leverage. He reasoned that Japan could make minimal concessions of passive cooperation with the United States in return for an early end to the Occupation, a long-term guarantee of Japan's national security, and an opportunity to concentrate on all-out economic recovery.

With the Communist Revolution in China in 1949 and the outbreak of the Korean War the following year, the United States sought to draw Japan into its regional defense system and to remilitarize it for purposes of the Cold War. As Vice-President Richard Nixon publicly admitted in 1953, U.S. leaders came to feel that imposition of Article 9 and the disarmament of Japan were "mistakes." When John Foster Dulles, special emissary of the Secretary of State, came to Japan in June 1950 to negotiate a peace treaty and the end of the Occupation, he urged Japanese rearmament. On this and subsequent occasions, Dulles sought to undo the MacArthur constitution by seeking to establish a large Japanese military force. He also wanted Japan to join a regional defense alliance similar to the North Atlantic Treaty Organization (NATO) in Europe that would facilitate Japanese rearmament but keep it under international control. This was the path Germany chose in Europe by joining NATO. The U.S. view in these years was that the Korean War represented a Soviet "invasion . . . to approach Japan," and that Japan was "the most desired prize" for the Communists, "a natural target for the desire to dominate the Far East." Japan must rearm to prepare for a Soviet and Chinese invasion.[6]

In his negotiations with Dulles, Yoshida refused to accede to these demands. He established his bargaining position by making light of Japan's security problems and intimating that Japan could protect itself through its own devices by being democratic and peaceful and by relying on the protection of world opinion. After all, he argued, Japan had a constitution that, inspired by U.S. ideals and the lessons of defeat, renounced arms, and the Japanese people were determined to uphold it and to adhere to a new course in world affairs.

Yoshida's bravado left Dulles (in the words of a colleague) "flabbergasted," embittered, and feeling "very much like Alice in Wonderland."[7] In succeeding meetings, Yoshida negotiated from this position. He skillfully argued that rearmament would impoverish Japan and create the kind of social unrest that radicals in Japan would exploit. He further pointed out to Dulles the fears that other Asian countries had of a revived Japanese military, and he enlisted MacArthur's support. MacArthur obligingly urged that Japan remain a nonmilitary nation and instead contribute to the free world through its industrial production. Yoshida's firmness spared Japan from military involvement in the Korean War and instead allowed Japanese business to profit enormously from procurement orders. Yoshida privately called the resulting stimulus to the economy "a gift of the gods." More such gifts appeared over the next decades.[8]

In the protracted negotiations with Dulles, Yoshida made minimal concessions; he consented to U.S. bases on Japanese soil and to limited rearmament, sufficient to gain Dulles's agreement to a peace treaty and to a post-Occupation guarantee of Japanese security. The Yoshida

Doctrine began to take shape in these negotiations. We may sum up its tenets as follows.

1. Japan's economic rehabilitation must be the prime national goal. Political-economic cooperation with the United States was necessary for this purpose.

2. Japan should remain lightly armed and avoid involvement in international political-strategic issues. Not only would this low military posture free the energies of its people for productive industrial development, it would avoid divisive internal struggles.

3. To gain a long-term guarantee of its own security, Japan would provide bases for the U.S. Army, Navy, and Air Force.

The Yoshida Doctrine became Japan's international strategy for the next forty years until the Cold War ended.

Yoshida's manipulation of domestic politics and U.S. pressure was both shrewd and cynical. He made minimal concessions to U.S. demands for Japanese contribution to their own defense. Initially he offered military bases and a commitment to gradual rearmament. He grudgingly agreed to upgrade the National Police Reserve, which MacArthur established in July 1950 with 75,000 men, to the status of National Security Force in January 1952 with 110,000 men. In a comment highly revealing of his method, Yoshida told a young associate (a future prime minister), Miyazawa Kiichi, at the time that: "the day [for rearmament] will come naturally when our livelihood recovers. It may sound devious, but let the Americans handle [our security] until then. It is indeed our Heaven-bestowed good fortune that the Constitution bans arms. If the Americans complain, the Constitution gives us a perfect justification."[9]

Yoshida, in short, was convinced that the Cold War would require the United States to maintain its presence in Japan, which alone would be sufficient to deter a Soviet attack. He would therefore give exclusive priority to pursuing Japanese economic recovery and maintaining political stability and would defer indefinitely the task of preparing the Japanese people for a return to the hard realities of international politics. It became an idée fixe of postwar Japanese diplomacy to avoid any collective security commitments.

His resistance to Dulles's pressure for participation in a regional collective security arrangement, however, had its price: Japan would have to become a subordinate to the United States in international affairs. On the same day that the San Francisco Peace Treaty was signed (September 8, 1951), Japan signed a security treaty with the United States that was highly unequal. It preserved many of the Occupation prerogatives of the U.S. military and in effect made Japan a military satellite of the United States. In addition to granting bases to the United States, it gave the United States a veto over any third country's military presence in Japan, the right to intervene to quell domestic disorder in Japan, the right to project military power from bases in Japan against a third country without consulting Japan, and an indefinite time period for the treaty. In addition, the United States insisted on extraterritorial legal rights for its military and dependents. At the same time, Yoshida was also compelled to recognize Taiwan as the legitimate government of China and thus to forswear normal relations with the mainland government. In sum, Dulles exacted a heavy price from Yoshida for his stubborn refusal to rearm and participate actively in the Cold War effort by joining a regional collective security alliance.

U.S. pressure on Japan to participate actively in its alliance system resumed after the signing of the peace and security treaties. The United States pressed Japan to accept military aid for a threefold expansion of its forces from the 110,000-strong National Security Force to an army of 350,000. Yoshida knew that increasing the size of the army, besides being controversial at home, would bring closer the day when the United States would press Japan to dispatch it for overseas conflict in the Cold War. Given the great pressure that Dulles, who was now Secretary of State, and the U.S. government brought to bear, Yoshida had to expand the armed forces. Still, Yoshida was able to temper U.S. demands. In 1954, the Diet passed legislation establishing the Self-Defense Force with a total of 152,000 men—substantially less than one-half of what the United States had demanded. Moreover, Yoshida and the Japanese government insisted that Article 9 would not permit the dispatch of these forces overseas. Dulles had once again met his match.

Elaboration of the Yoshida Doctrine

Yoshida fell from power in December 1954. In a sense it was the end of an extraordinary era, for Yoshida had dominated domestic politics during a formative decade. In another sense, the era was not over for Yoshida's influence continued for several more decades.

Initially, his conservative opponents held sway. In the year following his fall, the conservative parties united to form the LDP. For the next five years, from 1955 to 1960, conservatives within the LDP who opposed Yoshida's policies held power. These anti-Yoshida conservatives were frankly political nationalists who strongly opposed his exclusive concentration on economics and his dependence on American security protection. They adopted a wholly different approach to foreign policy. They wanted to revise the constitution, to carry out a forthright rearmament, to negotiate a more equal security treaty with the United States, and generally to pursue a more autonomous and independent course. This agenda proved bitterly divisive. The JSP was passionately committed to an ideological defense of the constitution and of unarmed neutralism in foreign affairs. The JSP had gained sufficient strength in the Diet to oppose the LDP, and its hold on public opinion through the support of the media, intellectuals, and the unions made constitutional revision virtually impossible.

The cabinet of Prime Minister Hatoyama Ichirō in 1956 tried to sign a peace treaty with the Soviet Union. Russia had refused to be part of the peace treaty negotiated in 1951 with America and other Western powers. The sticking point of negotiations in 1956 was the Japanese demand for return of the southern Kurile Islands, seized by Stalin at the end of the war. It appears that a compromise solution was torpedoed when U.S. Secretary of State Dulles indicated strong U.S. disapproval. The so-called Northern Territories issue therefore continued to prevent a peace treaty with Russia.

Japan and the United States, however, moved to revise and update their security treaty. Kishi Nobusuke, an anti-Yoshida conservative who served as prime minister from 1957 to 1960, proposed the elimination of the clause permitting U.S. intervention in domestic disturbances; he wanted a voice in the deployment of U.S. forces stationed in Japan and an explicit guarantee of U.S. protection in case of an attack on Japan. Kishi, who had served in the Tōjō cabinet and had been

Prime Minister Yoshida signing the U.S.-Japan Security Treaty in San Francisco, September 1951. At left is Ikeda Hayato, later prime minister. Third from left is John Foster Dulles, who negotiated the treaty. Fourth from left is Dean Acheson, U.S. Secretary of State. *Bettmann Archive*

indicted as a war criminal during the Occupation, aroused widespread distrust. The JSP mounted fierce public opposition to ratification of the new security treaty, but it was signed nevertheless in 1960. Ratification was rammed through the Diet, and the issue evoked the greatest mass demonstrations in Japanese history. As the final deliberations in the Diet were completed, hundreds of thousands of protesters gathered in front of the building and 6 million workers went on strike. When final ratifications were exchanged at the foreign minister's residence, beer crates were stacked by the fence so that the American ambassador could escape student activists, if necessary, by scaling the fence and running across neighboring gardens to a waiting limousine. Although such a humiliating conclusion to the ceremonies was avoided, the 1960 security treaty crisis was reminiscent of the Rice Riots of 1918 in the indelible impression it made on the ruling elite and the nation's political life.[10] A visit from President Eisenhower was cancelled, Prime Minister Kishi resigned, and the conservatives retreated to Yoshida's economics-first strategy.

This tumultuous outcome of the insistence by the anti-Yoshida conservatives on raising the divisive issues of rearmament gave a long-term advantage to the Yoshida School. The demonstrations of 1960 showed the strength of popular opposition to rearming. If conservatives continued to raise the issue of rebuilding Japan's military, they would subject the country to prolonged turmoil. For the next two decades, rather than weaken political stability, these divisive issues were shelved, and the conservatives turned again to the Yoshida wing of the party, which was acknowledged to be the mainstream.

Under the next two prime ministers, Ikeda Hayato (1960–1964) and Satō Eisaku (1964–1972), both closely associated with Yoshida, the Yoshida Doctrine was further consolidated into a national consensus. Ikeda, who had been Yoshida's key economic advisor and finance minister, suppressed the debates on political nationalism and instead reestablished stability by concentrating on policies of managed economic growth. Although he was Yoshida's understudy in the early postwar years, Ikeda was a strong personality. He knew what he wanted. He was forced to resign his post as Minister of International Trade and Industry in 1952 because of his blunt remark in the Diet that "it makes no difference to me if five or ten small businessmen are forced to commit suicide" as a result of his policies favoring heavy industry. A leading economic historian described Ikeda as "the single most important figure in Japan's rapid growth. He should long be remembered as the man who pulled together a national consensus for economic growth."[11] As the centerpiece of his administration, Ikeda announced a plan for doubling Japan's income within a decade. This plan was part of a systematic and well-coordinated effort to formulate policies that would avoid ideology, raise living standards, and improve housing and welfare. It concentrated exclusively on issues of economic nationalism on which the LDP, the bureaucracy, the political opposition, and the populace generally could achieve substantial agreement. Ikeda's plan envisaged a 7.2 percent growth rate that would double the GNP over a ten-year period. In actuality, by the latter half of the 1960s, the average growth rate climbed to 11.6 percent, far surpassing Ikeda's target set at the beginning of the decade. Almost imperceptibly the appeal of the political left was co-opted, and the country settled in for a long period of enthusiastic pursuit of high economic growth.

Under another Yoshida protégé, Satō Eisaku, who succeeded Ikeda and was prime minister longer (1964–1972) than any other individual in Japanese history, the Yoshida Doctrine was further elaborated in terms of nuclear strategy. In 1967 Satō enunciated three non-nuclear principles, which held that Japan would not produce, possess, or permit the introduction of nuclear weapons onto its soil.

In 1967 Satō added another building block to the structure of foreign policy that Yoshida had begun. To preserve Japan's low posture in international politics, he formulated a ban on weapons exports. At this time also, the practice began of constraining defense expenditure to less than 1 percent of the GNP.

In summary, we can see that the Yoshida Doctrine became a finely tuned set of policies to further Japan's postwar national interest. In addition to the three fundamental principles of the Yoshida Doctrine by which Japan permitted U.S. military bases on Japanese soil in return for a U.S. guarantee of Japanese security, while Japan remained as lightly armed as possible so that the nation could concentrate all its energies on economic growth, there were several important corollaries: Japan would not dispatch its Self-Defense Force abroad to be part of collective defense schemes; Japan would not become a nuclear power; Japan would not export arms; and Japan would limit its defense spending to 1 percent of the GNP.

The Yoshida Doctrine proved its worth by maintaining domestic political stability and avoiding involvement in regional security obligations. For example, during the Vietnam War South Korea was induced to dispatch more than 300,000 troops to fight alongside the Americans, but the Japanese avoided direct military involvement and battened on procurement orders. The Yoshida Doctrine worked well to provide a clear sense of direction and stability in both domestic and foreign affairs. At home, it served to maintain a balance among widely diverse views on foreign policy. It was a political compromise between the pacifism of opposition groups and the security concerns of the right-wing conservatives. Abroad, it attained the American guarantee of Japanese security without obligating Japan to become directly involved in the Cold War. This broad consensus in favor of a mercantile role in international affairs was widely accepted in the mainstream of political, bureaucratic, and business elites as a policy best suited to Japanese national interests. As one senior Japanese bureaucrat observed, "Postwar Japan defined itself as a cultural state holding the principles of liberalism, democracy, and peace, but these were only superficial principles (*tatemae*); the fundamental objective (*honne*) was the pouring of all our strength into economic growth."[12]

Notes

1. Chalmers Johnson, "Japan: Who Governs? An Essay on Official Bureaucracy," *Journal of Japanese Studies* 2 (autumn 1975), 11.
2. Henry Kissinger, *White House Years* (Boston: Little, Brown, 1979), 324.
3. See John W. Dower, *Empire and Aftermath: Yoshida Shigeru and the Japanese Experience, 1878–1954* (Cambridge, Mass.: Harvard University Press, 1979), 312.
4. Iriye Takanori, cited in *Journal of Japanese Studies* 19 (winter 1993), 227.
5. U.S. Department of State, *Foreign Relations of the United States: 1950*, vol. 6 (Washington, D.C.: U.S. Government Printing Office, 1966), 1166–1167.
6. See Dower, *Empire and Aftermath*, 461.
7. William J. Sebald, *With MacArthur in Japan: A Personal History of the Occupation* (New York: W.W. Norton, 1965), 257–258.
8. Dower, *Empire and Aftermath*, 316.
9. Miyazawa Kiichi, *Tokyo-Washington no mitsudan* (Tokyo: Jitsugyō no Nihonsha, 1956), 160. Also see Tetsuya Kataoka, *The Price of a Constitution: The Origin of Japan's Postwar Politics* (New York: Crane Russak, 1991), 118.
10. John Welfield, *An Empire in Eclipse: Japan in the Postwar American Alliance System* (London: Athlone, 1988), 138.
11. Takafusa Nakamura, *The Postwar Japanese Economy: Its Development and Structure*, trans. Jacqueline Kaminski (Tokyo: University of Tokyo Press, 1981), 80.
12. Amaya Naohiro, quoted in Kenneth B. Pyle, *The Japanese Question: Power and Purpose in a New Era* (Washington, D.C.: American Enterprise Institute, 1992), 36.

Economic Nationalism

Despite the wrenching changes that defeat and Occupation brought to the Japanese people, we can see that important characteristics of prewar Japan survived. Leaders such as Yoshida Shigeru were still devoted to the traditional goals of nationalism, although they recognized that these goals must be pursued in different ways. The survival of the bureaucracy as a powerful institution provided an extraordinary measure of the continuity from presurrender days.

Many of the characteristics and accomplishments of postwar Japan were rooted in the prewar period, especially in the decade and a half of militarism from 1931 to 1945. Not only was there continuity, the wartime years left a surprisingly important legacy that contributed to the nation's postwar emergence as a great economic power. From the standpoint of the triumphant emergence of Japanese capitalism in the 1960s and 1970s and its success in catching up with the West, the Pacific War can even be seen as a "useful war."[1]

This wartime legacy has many aspects to the subsequent economic growth. What first catches our attention in this regard is the continuity of personnel and the valuable experience that the bureaucracy, which survived the purge, had acquired in mobilizing and managing the wartime economy. The bureaucrats became adept at controlling trade and foreign exchange and guiding the fortunes of key industries. The lessons they learned in long-range planning were of incalculable value in the desperate economic chaos after the war, when they acquired even more power amidst the urgency of rehabilitating the national livelihood.

A second legacy of the militarist period was the industrial structure of the economy. The so-called second industrial revolution during the period from 1931 to 1945, when Japan shifted from light to heavy and chemical industrialization in building its military production, hastened Japan's postwar emergence as an economic leader in chemicals and heavy industry. Moreover, the second industrial revolution was accomplished through the formation of a network of small enterprises that served the needs of large companies. Production of parts was farmed out to subcontractors to hasten production increases. Tens of thousands of these small- and medium-sized firms sprang up, forging links with large parent companies; and they constituted much of the flexibility, resilience, and dynamism of postwar expansion. In the 1960s, for example, more than 40 percent of the subcontractors supplying parts to Toyota traced the origins of their links with the automaker to the war years.

An additional useful legacy of the wartime economic experience was the mastery of new skills and technologies by a rapidly expanded workforce to meet the needs of military production. Nearly 4 million new workers entered the industrial labor force during the fifteen-year period. Also from 1935 to 1945 the number of technical schools grew from 11 to 400. Engineers trained for providing the sinews of war now turned their skills to peacetime industry.

Nationalism and the desire to catch up with the West persisted in the postwar period, but efforts now focused on economic and industrial goals. For example, machine gun factories were converted to make sewing machines; optical weapons factories now produced cameras and binoculars. One diplomat reminisced in 1979: "The [mighty battleship] *Yamato* and [the fighter planes known as] Zeros—forerunners of the postwar Japanese technology—are still very much alive, so it is said among us Japanese, in mammoth tankers, excellent automotive engines, etc. which Japan turns out by the thousands and millions. They have served our nation in a manner never foreseen in their heyday."[2]

Since the early days of the Meiji Period, Japanese leaders had shaped the nation's values and institutions to achieve the goal of catching up with the advanced industrial nations. Fukoku-kyōhei, a wealthy country and a strong army, industry and empire, were the objectives. The postwar conservatives revived the end purpose of achieving national power, but they focused sharply on economic means.

A remarkably revealing anecdote about Ōkita Saburō, postwar Japan's leading economic planner, demonstrates the indomitable spirit of the Japanese people even in defeat. In the spring of 1945, as the last months of the war were unfolding, Ōkita visited an engineering professor at the Tokyo Imperial University. The two, knowing the war was lost, fell to talking about the lessons learned and Japan's postwar prospects. The engineer recorded in his diary that Ōkita felt that not all was lost if Japan drew the proper lesson from its tragic experience, namely that "Japan, poorly endowed with natural resources, must shape its future around developing precision engineering." In other words, Ōkita believed that Japan must concentrate its energies on taking imported resources and fashioning them into high-quality products for export:

> Ōkita made himself comfortable and we spoke for a long time. He told me this story from around 1882 which an Englishman—it might have been Bagehot—used to tell as a warning to the people of this time.
>
> A poor warrior wanted to buy a splendid suit of armor but had no money, so he cut down on the amount of food he ate and little by little saved enough to buy a fine suit of armor. A war broke out and courageously he left to fight, but because his body had become so weak from his years of semi-starvation, he could not bear the weight of his armor and was soon slain by the enemy.
>
> This was just what happened to Japan. He did not think that a defeated Japan would be allowed to rearm at all, but this would probably be a blessing in disguise. Japan did not have the qualities of a first-class power, but she could excel as a second-class power.
>
> I completely agreed with all he said. I will actually be happy if rearmament is completely prohibited. An army in uniform is not the only sort of army. Scientific technology and fighting spirit under a business suit will be our underground army.[3]

As it turned out, the postwar era favored this newly focused national purpose of building Japan into a great economic power.

High Economic Growth, 1950–1973

The Yoshida strategy was a brilliant adaptation to the conditions in Japan's international environment. Japan made its way in the post–World War II era by relentlessly pursuing its own narrowly defined self-interest and by frustrating all attempts to engage it in collective security arrangements. This strategy and the underlying foreign policy were a brilliant success because Japan could rely on the United States to guarantee its security and maintain the international order of free trade, leaving Japan free to follow policies of economic nationalism.

The Pax Americana after 1945 provided a liberal international economic order in which a defeated and outcast nation could take refuge, focus its sights on economic growth, and seek to rise again in a new form. Relying on U.S. preoccupation with the Cold War to provide military security and an open market, Japan intensified its bureaucratic controls and strengthened its mercantilist policies. Reversing many Occupation reforms and rebuilding many illiberal political-economic institutions, the country redoubled its efforts in a concentrated economic rather than political struggle. As two Japanese economists described it, "the banks and the economic bureaucracy functioned as general staff behind the battlefield in this second 'total war' called high economic growth."[4] Thus Yoshida and his successors determined to profit from the international order even while flouting its liberal norms. Economic nationalism became a way of enhancing Japan's international prestige, replacing the prewar approach based on military power.

More than any other country, Japan was the beneficiary of the postwar international order. It was not immediately apparent that Japan could prosper without its imperial possessions. John Foster Dulles, the architect of the San Francisco Peace Treaty, remarked in 1952 in an uncharacteristically flip vein, that "suicide was not an illogical step for anyone concerned about Japan's economic future."[5] Nevertheless, for more than twenty-five years after the end of World War II, Japan operated in extraordinary and uniquely favorable political-economic circumstances. In contrast to every other major power, it was spared the psychological and material costs of participating in international politics. Accordingly, the Japanese were able to concentrate their resources and energies on achieving economic growth. Until the late 1960s, Japan benefited from a special relationship with the United States under which the latter sponsored Japanese recovery and development by keeping the U.S. market open to Japan's goods while allowing Japan to limit severely the import of goods into its own economy. The expanding world trade that the United States was promoting through the International Monetary Fund (IMF) and the General Agreement on Tariffs and Trade (GATT) permitted a vigorous expansion of Japanese manufactured goods and the ready purchase of abundant and cheap raw materials. Moreover, Japan had easy access to new, inexpensive, and highly efficient Western technology, which it imported in large quantities. As one Japanese scholar commented, "The international environment of the 1960s looked as though heaven had created it for Japan's economic growth."[6]

At the time of surrender, output had been stumbling along at pre–World War I levels. Statistics show the remarkable pace of recovery: from 1946 to 1954 real national income grew at an average of 10.8 percent, an impressive rate, but this achievement merely returned the economy to prewar levels of productivity, national income, and personal consumption. Having regained its former level by 1954–1955, the economy then maintained an astonishing rate of growth for the next fifteen years: 9.1 percent for 1955–1960, 9.8 percent for 1960–1965, and 12.1 percent for 1965–1970. During the high-growth period of 1950–1973 the real growth rate averaged more than 10 percent—nearly three times the growth rate of the U.S. economy during the same period.

In the course of this remarkable expansion, the structure of the economy underwent a fundamental transformation. Inevitably the relative share of agriculture, forestry, and fishing declined rapidly, while manufacturing and construction experienced a sharp rise. Throughout the prewar period, although the importance of machinery and armaments was growing, cotton and silk textiles had continued to dominate the manufacturing sector. By the 1960s manufacturing output was more diversified and sophisticated, developing aggressively in a variety of areas such as shipbuilding, optics, iron and steel, chemicals, machinery, and consumer durables.

What were the dynamics of this rapid economic growth?

First, the productivity of the economy rose rapidly owing to extensive technological innovation. In part that was the unavoidable result of having to replace so much of Japan's industrial capacity, which had been destroyed by the wartime bombing. Since the beginning of the Pacific War, Japan had been cut off from most of its Western industrial contacts, and by the 1950s a large body of Japanese engineers and skilled technicians was ready and anxious to close the technological gap that had opened in the intervening years. As Yutaka Kōsai writes:

> This gap was soon closed by the massive introduction of technologies from foreign companies. . . . Because Japan did not encourage direct foreign investment after World War II, this introduction of foreign technology was achieved through technical cooperation without capital tie-ups, . . . avoiding foreign control of Japanese business. Many foreign firms were willing to sell their technology because the Japanese market was regarded as too small to be worth developing. . . . Technical innovations enormously increased the productivity of Japanese industry. The Japanese also tried to improve upon the technology that they imported, . . . thereby enhancing Japan's international competitiveness.[7]

A second driving force behind economic growth was the high rate of investment. A large share of the GNP was plowed back into new plants and equipment to achieve additional growth. Investment was particularly heavy in export industries and capital goods industries, where demand was strong and the market favorable. A critical factor permitting the unusual amount of investment was the high rate of savings achieved by the Japanese. In comparative terms, personal savings of Japanese during the 1960s averaged as much as 18 percent of disposable income, while Americans in the same period averaged between 7 and 8 percent. Many reasons are responsible for this high rate of savings including the semiannual lump-sum bonuses paid by Japanese companies, the relative underdevelopment of consumer-lending institutions, and inadequate retirement programs. Personal and corporate savings together permitted a high rate of investment.

The third important ingredient of postwar economic growth was Japan's ample supply of highly motivated and well-educated labor. Millions of Japanese returned from overseas to swell the ranks of labor, and by the mid-1960s the effects of the postwar baby boom were evident in the rising proportion of young men and women in the labor force. As a consequence, wages did not rise rapidly and did not outstrip productivity. Labor moved to more productive sectors of the economy. The number of agricultural workers declined between 1950 and 1965 by 4.6 million, and over the same period the percentage of the labor force employed in small firms experienced a similar decline. Furthermore, the motivation of the labor force—the willingness to work long and hard with a strong sense of loyalty to one's firm—caught the attention of labor economists in many other industrialized countries.

A fourth cause of added strength for the Japanese was the overall growth of international trade. In contrast to prewar times when protectionist sentiment prevailed in many countries, the postwar reduction of trade restrictions caused a rapid expansion of world trade. Between 1953 and 1965 Japanese exports grew an average of 17 percent each year. This impressive performance was the result of much careful and deliberate planning by both government and business to produce goods that had strong world demand and to achieve price competitiveness through efficient production. Accordingly, as we have noted, Japan abandoned its former concentration on textile exports and turned instead to such new goods as transistor radios, cameras, color televisions, and automobiles.

Finally, several other factors promoted rapid growth. The role of government is surely one of the more important. Government encouraged growth through a wide variety of measures, including tax concessions for the corporate sector, attractive loans to leading industries, and what is called "administrative guidance" exercised by the Ministry of International Trade and Industry (MITI). To strengthen Japan's competitive ability in the export market, promote technological change, and enforce efficient use of resources, MITI encouraged mergers and various kinds of collusive arrangements among the largest firms. Another factor, of course, was the small allocation for national defense—after the mid-1960s less than 1 percent of the GNP (as compared with 6 percent in the prewar days). Substantial resources were thereby freed for investment in more productive industries. Another fortuitous factor in Japanese growth was the stimulative effect of the Korean War. The war created a boom in textiles, cement, and iron and steel industries. Overall, it had the effect of priming the pump and injecting much-needed dollars into the economy, giving it a fast start on sustained, rapid growth over the next two decades.

Industrial Policy Debate

Among all the explanations for Japan's economic success in the high-growth period, the most controversial factor is the role of government and industrial policy. Many scholars have emphasized the leading role of the state, working cooperatively with business, in promoting growth. Chalmers Johnson, the leading proponent of this view, describes Japan as a "developmental state," with its elite bureaucracy serving as an "economic general staff" masterminding Japan's high-speed growth. MITI and the Ministry of Finance encouraged the rationalization of firms and industries and guided the structural transformation of the economy. MITI stimulated the movement of capital and labor out of declining industries such as coal and textiles and into promising new industries with high-growth potential—first into electronics, steel, petrochemicals, and automobiles, and later into computers, semiconductors, and biotechnology.

Johnson describes the formation of a high-growth system through a set of policies and institutions that were shaped by bureaucrats steeped in the experience of the prewar and wartime efforts to mobilize the economy. "This high-growth system," he writes, "was one of the most rational and productive industrial policies ever devised by any government."[8] The stage was set by the Occupation's reverse course, the determination to promote Japanese economic rehabilitation, and the measures undertaken in 1949 known as the Dodge Line. These draconian measures sought to curb inflation, stabilize the economy, and attract foreign investment. Almost unnoticed, the Japanese bureaucracy created MITI in 1949. In the same year, the Foreign Exchange and Foreign Trade Control Law gave the new ministry its first and most important tool to influence corporate decisions: the power to allocate all foreign exchange. If they were to grow and compete, Japanese firms had to import raw materials and foreign technology. MITI used its new law to influence the growth rate of various industries and their capacity to acquire new technology. Enactment of the Foreign Capital Law in 1950, the next step in constructing the high-growth system, gave MITI the power to limit, restrict, and control foreign investment, ownership, and participation in management of business ventures in Japan. Next, the Ministry of Finance together with MITI established the Japan Development Bank in 1951 with access to a huge investment pool known as the Fiscal Investment and Loan Plan (FILP), which comprised the nation's savings in the postal savings system. The system was a favorite place for individuals to save because their accounts were tax exempt. FILP thus amassed savings four times the size of the world's largest commercial bank. It became a powerful policy tool—Johnson calls it "the single most important financial instrument for Japan's economic development"[9]—which MITI used to provide low-cost capital to industries it favored for long-term growth. At the same time the Ministry of Finance was ensuring the availability of capital. By insulating the domestic capital market from the international capital market, it could ration and guide the flow of capital to large firms in industries such as steel, shipbuilding, automobiles, electronics, and chemicals that were adopting new technology and were central to increasing productivity and exports. In addition to allocating credit, the government used many other potent tools of industrial policy, including imposing high tariffs to protect industries critical to the growth strategy, establishing import quotas, reforming the tax system to favor growth, and giving direct and indirect subsidies to key industries.

Finally, as soon as the Occupation ended, MITI had the U.S.-inspired Anti-Monopoly Law revised and watered down. On September 1, 1953, the Diet amended the Anti-Monopoly Law so as to relax the Occupation-imposed restrictions on cartels, interlocking directorates, and mergers. To maximize the efficient use of resources, MITI preferred to have competition limited to a small number of very large corporations. The Fair Trade Commission's authority to prevent restraint of trade was constantly under attack from MITI. In one of the better-documented cases of collusive behavior that resulted from the changed rules, six Japanese firms manufacturing televisions joined forces, forming a market stabilization group in 1956 to control the domestic price of televisions. They maintained a high price level in the domestic market while government tariff policy kept the market closed to foreign producers. With high profit margins and an ensured market at home, the industry turned to exports, especially to the U.S. market. Through below-cost exports to the U.S. market, the Japanese firms were able to drive most of their U.S. competitors out of business. The Japanese government spurred and shaped the development of the television industry through "preferential credit allocation via large banks, lax antitrust enforcement, condoning of de facto recession cartels, MITI-guided investment coordination, and various forms of nontariff barriers."[10]

In sharp contrast to the scholars who have argued that the role of the developmental state was decisive in creating Japan's success during the high-growth period, many economists have held to a market approach. The market school argues that the factors responsible for Japanese growth were similar to those in other advanced capitalist countries. Rather than the role of the state, they stress such factors as technology; the rates of savings, investment, and taxation; the high level of skills and education in Japan; the huge stock of advanced Western technology; the unparalleled export opportunities created by expansion of world trade, and the availability of capital. They emphasize the role of private enterprise responding to market forces. Patrick and Rosovsky hold that "the main impetus to growth has been private—business investment demand, private saving, and industrious and skilled labor operating in a market-oriented environment."[11] They argue that Japan had an unusually well-educated labor force, that business invested heavily in new technology, that productivity grew rapidly as a consequence, and that new markets opened up internationally affording unique opportunities for economic expansion. Some observers point out that government policy was sometimes an obstacle to technological advancement and efficiency. They point to MITI's discouragement of Sony's transistor technology, its failed attempt to limit the automobile industry to Toyota and Nissan, and the government policies that created excess capacity in the steel industry.

Other economists of the market persuasion draw attention to a new entrepreneurial vigor in the postwar period, the role of corporate strategies and corporate culture. After all, write James Abegglen and George Stalk, two business economists, "companies, not societies, compete for markets; companies, not governments, trade; and in the end it is companies that prosper or stagnate—in Japan as well as in the United States or Europe."[12] A new aggressive breed of Japanese entrepreneur came to the fore. In place of the top management of major companies who had been purged in the Occupation and who had served the families that owned the zaibatsu with an emphasis on conservative strategies, reliability, and soundness, came a new set of young professional managers geared to fierce competition in adopting new technology, innovating, and acquiring an expanded market share. They were more inclined to take risks, even in the face of contrary advice from the bureaucracy. Self-made new entrepreneurs such as Honda Sōichirō, who succeeded in the motorcycle and automobile industry, are cited as examples.

In addition to the aggressiveness of new entrepreneurship, the uniqueness of Japanese corporate culture has attracted great interest abroad among management consultants and in business schools. The Japanese instinctively took pride in their corporate behavior patterns and business culture. Particularly noteworthy was the unique pattern of labor-management relations, whose origins in the early twentieth century we discussed in chapter 9. Features such as lifetime employment, seniority-based wages, company or enterprise unions, and extensive welfare provisions by the company developed in the interwar years and spread further through the workforce in large enterprises after World War II.

The organization of big business in Japan was also distinctive. New enterprise groups known as *keiretsu* emerged in the early 1950s to replace the zaibatsu dissolved by the Occupation. The keiretsu took different forms. Six great enterprise groups—Mitsui, Mitsubishi, Sumitomo, Fuyo, Dai-ichi Kangyō, and Sanwa—were organized horizontally. That is, each "horizontal keiretsu" comprised several dozen members including a main bank, large financial institutions, the largest manufacturing firms, and a large general trading company. Within each group, members held one another's shares. They had interlocking directorates and engaged in intragroup financing and joint R&D ventures. The presidents met monthly. These horizontal keiretsu helped to provide long-term stability, efficiency, reduced risk, and mutual support. There were also giant vertical keiretsu organized in the automobile, electronic, and other industries (Nissan, Toyota, Hitachi, Matsushita, Sony, and others). They served to organize huge numbers of subcontractors and suppliers of services. The vertical keiretsu provided efficient, long-term reciprocal benefits for a parent company and its suppliers, including coordination of planning and investment, sharing of technology and information, control of quality and delivery, and flexibility throughout the business cycles. Finally, the distribution keiretsu allowed manufacturers to control the mass marketing of products. These networks allowed manufacturers to prevent price competition among retailers, to maintain high profit margins in the domestic market, and so to permit cutthroat competition in the international market. In short, the distribution keiretsu became "an effective means to force Japanese consumers to subsidize the international competitiveness of large manufacturing firms."[13]

The Japanese also took pride in certain internal features of their firms that had developed in the postwar period, such as "management of the flow of parts through the factory; organization and tight control over inventory; engagement of blue collar workers in the design of production and quality control processes; cooperative interaction among engineers, marketing people, financial officers, and factory managers; new concepts in plant maintenance to reduce downtime and increase product quality; and aggressive reduction of the variety of parts in products."[14]

Postwar Japanese Capitalism

The controversy over industrial policy between the proponents of the state developmental school and the market school bears some resemblance to the contrasting interpretations of growth-from-above and growth-from-below schools that differed in their assessment of the role of government in initiating industrialization in the early Meiji Period (discussed in chapter 7). As in that case, we find no easy answer to this controversy either. Certainly the role of the state was more important in the high-growth period than subsequently. And to some extent the part played by bureaucrats in facilitating growth varied among industries. But some scholars are now taking a more complex view of the functions of industrial policy. In accounting for Japanese business success, they stress neither government nor the business sector but both working together in a close reciprocal and interactive relationship. According to this interpretation, Japanese industrial policy was less the creature of a strong and autonomous state than it was the product of "reciprocal consent" between business and government working cooperatively as a result of long-term and well-established networks of communication and negotiation. As one scholar describes it, "MITI responds to business interests and tries to help industries develop and sustain a consensus approach to common problems. When, after consultation with MITI a majority opinion ('consensus') forms within an industry as to what its interests are and what the basis of competition should be, MITI can help enforce compliance through provision of administrative guidance."[15] Because this interpretation emphasizes the consensual and inclusive nature of the elite networks, it is reminiscent of the characterization of the political system as Japan, Incorporated.

The high-growth period from 1950 to 1973, when the first oil shock occurred as a result of the abrupt quadrupling of oil prices by the international cartel, was a unique time in Japanese history in which a variety of important factors aided rapid economic growth. A strong political consensus supporting growth as the overriding national purpose served to mute political conflict. Business and government worked hand-in-glove to formulate long-term goals and policies. Labor as a political movement had little say about policy and was effectively co-opted in any case by the success of economic expansion and by such features of the employment system as lifetime employment and company unions. Administrative guidance by the government was effective because it resulted from long-term relations and mutual consultation between a ministry such as MITI or the Ministry of Finance and the industry affected. Moreover, industrial policy was successful because it enhanced market forces and was designed to make Japan competitive and efficient in international markets. For example, in electronics the purpose of policy was not to provide "permanent hothouse protection" but rather it was "aimed at enabling . . . firms to achieve economies of scale and to take maximum advantage of learning curve effects."[16] As a late developer regaining its pace after the interruption of wartime destruction, Japan saw many advantages to close collaboration between business and government.

How then can we characterize this capitalist system? One scholar describes it as a "brokered capitalism," dominated by the elites and dedicated to economic nationalism. The leaders of this system as well as many of its institutions, ideas, and practices were "formed in the crucible of war." He concludes that "the economic bureaucrats are indeed influential actors in this grand enterprise, but so also are big business and the conservative politicians."[17]

Another scholar has characterized it as a "bridled capitalism." The system was not one in which market forces were given free rein. Instead the historically formed system consisted of "policies and institutions, reflecting a shared ideology of 'catching up with the West,' [which] effectively performed the role of a bridle." The elite power groups guided the economy. Market forces were made more vigorous through incentives to encourage more saving, more rapid acquisition of new technologies, and more risk-taking so that firms would become productive, efficient, and competitive.[18]

The conservative elites in business, government, and society succeeded in creating an impressive commitment to growth, with a remarkable esprit de corps among them. In a memorable analogy, the economist William Lockwood once likened the elite relations to a "web of influences and pressures interweaving through government and business, rather than a streamlined pyramid of authoritarian control. . . . A web it may be but with no spider."[19]

The elites focused their consensus on an economic strategy of building the economy through international trade. Japan would become a processing trade nation. Because Japan was so resource poor, this strategy entailed limiting imports so far as possible to primary products (raw materials, fuel, and food) and exporting manufactured goods. By adopting new Western technology as rapidly as possible Japan would strive to produce and export increasing quantities of more technologically advanced, internationally competitive products. This export-led strategy was not new, but it was pursued with more single-minded vigor in the postwar period. The strategy bore fruit. Japan rode the waves of an unparalleled period of expanding world trade. Japanese exports increased nearly 25-fold between 1955 and 1970. Over a longer period, from 1955 to 1987, exports achieved a staggering 114-fold increase.[20]

Government policies directed cheap and plentiful capital to the lead industries in this strategy. Tax, monetary, and fiscal policies were all marshaled to minimize the long-term risks of adopting new technology and of boldly expanding productive capacity. The state was the guarantor. Laws to prod development of critical industries, such as machine tools, were enacted while the Anti-Monopoly Law pushed through during Occupation was emasculated through successive revisions. By 1971, thirty-six manufacturing cartels had been sanctioned by industry-specific laws.[21] At the same time imports were severely limited by stringent quota and tariff policies, inspection procedures, and product standard laws to discourage the entry of foreign manufactured products.

The high-growth period marked the flowering of postwar Japanese capitalism, but the achievements of this period owed much to the political-economic system built over the preceding century. It was shaped by Japan's late development and its determination, first articulated by the Meiji leaders, to catch up with and overtake Western countries. What was distinctive about the postwar period was the more intense and concentrated form that economic nationalism took. The Yoshida Doctrine and its institutionalization by Prime Minister Ikeda in his Income-Doubling Plan forged a remarkable national consensus that focused the energies of the society and the political system and helped dampen domestic divisions that would have flared had Japan been more actively engaged in the international politics of the Cold War. In the high-growth period, Japan's "brokered" or "bridled" capitalism functioned with a high degree of efficiency and effectiveness. A cohesive, elite coalition of political and economic leaders formulated and implemented policies that propelled Japan on the last leg of its campaign to catch up with the Western industrial powers.

Notes

1. John W. Dower, ed., *Japan in War and Peace: Selected Essays* (New York: New Press, 1993), 9–32.
2. Quoted in Michael A. Barnhart, *Japan Prepares for Total War: The Search for Economic Security, 1919–1941*, (Ithaca, N.Y.: Cornell University Press, 1987), 273.
3. Saburō Ōkita, *Japan's Challenging Years: Reflections on My Lifetime* (New York: George Allen and Unwin, 1985), 26.
4. Quoted in Kenneth B. Pyle, *The Japanese Question: Power and Purpose in a New Era* (Washington, D.C.: American Enterprise Institute, 1992), 42.
5. Quoted by Orville J. McDiarmid in Eleanor M. Hadley, *Antitrust in Japan* (Princeton, N.J.: Princeton University Press, 1970), 408.
6. Quoted in Pyle, *Japanese Question*, 44.
7. Yutaka Kōsai, "The Postwar Japanese Economy, 1945–1973," in Peter Duus, ed., *The Twentieth Century*, vol. 6 of *The Cambridge History of Japan*, ed. John Whitney Hall (Cambridge: Cambridge University Press, 1988), 520–521.
8. Chalmers Johnson, *MITI and the Japanese Miracle: The Growth of Industrial Policy, 1925–1975* (Stanford: Stanford University Press, 1982), 199.
9. Ibid., 210.
10. Kozo Yamamura and Jan Vandenberg, "Japan's Rapid Growth Policy on Trial: The Television Case," in *Law and Trade Issues of the Japanese Economy*, ed. Gary R. Saxonhouse and Kozo Yamamura (Seattle: University of Seattle Press, 1986), 266.
11. Hugh Patrick and Henry Rosovsky, eds., *Asia's New Giant* (Washington, D.C.: Brookings Institute, 1976), 47.
12. James C. Abegglen and George Stalk, Jr., *Kaisha, the Japanese Corporation* (New York: Basic Books, 1985), 5.
13. Kozo Yamamura, *Japan's Economic Structure: Should It Change?* (Seattle: Society for Japanese Studies, 1990), 36.

14. Edward J. Lincoln, "The Showa Economic Experience," in *Showa: The Japan of Hirohito,* ed. Carol Gluck and Stephen R. Graubard (New York: W. W. Norton, 1992), 199.
15. Gregory W. Noble, "The Japanese Industrial Policy Debate," in *Pacific Dynamics: The International Politics of Industrial Change,* ed. Stephen Haggard and Chung-in Moon (Boulder: Westview Press, 1989), 54.
16. George C. Eads and Kozo Yamamura, "The Future of Industrial Policy," in *The Domestic Transformation,* vol. 1 of *The Political Economy of Japan,* ed. Kozo Yamamura and Yasukichi Yasuba (Stanford, Calif.: Stanford University Press, 1987), 434.
17. Dower, ed., *Japan in War and Peace,* 26.
18. Kozo Yamamura, "The Success of Bridled Capitalism: Economic Development of Japan, 1880–1980," in *The Wealth of Nations in the Twentieth Century,* ed. R. Meyer (Stanford, Calif.: Hoover Institution Press, 1995).
19. William W. Lockwood, "Japan's 'New Capitalism,'" in *The State and Economic Enterprise in Japan,* ed. William W. Lockwood (Princeton, N.J.: Princeton University Press, 1965), 41.
20. Kozo Yamamura, "Bridled Capitalism" (forthcoming).
21. Ibid.

The New Middle-Class Society

Under their determined elite leadership, the Japanese people quietly pursued the newly sharpened goal of economic growth as a means of catching up with the world's leading industrial powers. Coming as a welcome respite from the deprivations of the war years, the concentration on improving their own livelihood evoked prodigies of effort. There were, as one economic historian observed, "few heroic achievements,"[1] only the steady hard work of the people and their cumulative efforts to enhance their living standard. Until the oil shock of 1973 ended Japan's cheap supply of energy, the growth rate was steady and achievements were continuous. Sheltered from the divisiveness of foreign policy entanglements, the Japanese people were convinced that if they limited consumption, saved, and worked hard their lot would improve. It was a renewal of the prewar culture of diligence but with more personal ends.

Postwar Japanese society was characterized by a high degree of stability, social order, and integration. This cohesiveness was reflected in the political sphere by the continuity of LDP rule, the efficiency of business organizations, the stability of labor-management relations, and low crime and divorce rates. For a time after the success of the 1960 Anti-Security Treaty demonstrations, the student movement provided public pyrotechnics, but by the 1970s it subsided and students too joined in the stoic ways of a burgeoning middle class, content with material progress.

The quiet emergence of mass middle-class society was the most important consequence of the high-growth period. The postwar reforms contributed to an evening out of personal income, and by 1970 Japan had the greatest equality of income distribution among all the advanced industrial nations. At the same time, nearly 90 percent of the Japanese people identified themselves as members of the middle class. Characteristic of this middle-class consciousness was a desire for consumer durables, a university education for the children, and home ownership. All this stimulated a high savings rate and in turn sparked economic growth. The result was a mass-consumption market, a homogeneous life-style, and a scramble to keep up with the purchases of one's neighbors: sewing machines, televisions, refrigerators, washing machines, vacuum cleaners, automobiles, air conditioners, and so on.

The remarkable social order and stability that accompanied this emergent middle-class consciousness was generated less by strong government than by the institutions of family and school. Although the Occupation imposed a set of public institutions based on belief in individual freedoms and a view of society as the sum of individual choices, these institutions functioned in ways quite different from what was originally intended.

Thomas Rohlen traces the high degree of order and cohesiveness in postwar Japanese society to childhood training and the early school years. Japanese teachers laid great store on inculcating order "by repeated practice of selected daily tasks (such as putting away shoes or cleaning the room) that socialize the children to high degrees of neatness and uniformity." By establishing a sense of routine, peer pressure, and social responsibility, Japanese teachers established order through indirect control in their classroom. Highly regimented routines instilled cooperation, conformity, an understanding of social necessities, and responsibility and attachment to a group. Consequently, "failure to follow directions, careless variance from group norms and standards in such matters as uniforms, etiquette, and practice, for example, create surprising levels of consternation centering on issues of the offending individual's connectedness to the group. The result of such pressure is very high levels of orderly conduct in the organized spheres of society that do not depend on authoritative action."[2]

Not only in early childhood training, but throughout life when one entered an organization or a group, the same pattern of regimented routines and learned social lessons were used to establish a working order. Japanese firms devoted much greater time and resources to training new employees through programs not dissimilar to what in the West would be considered boot camp training or induction into religious sects. Although Confucian traditions of respect for hierarchy undoubtedly contributed to these practices, the techniques to achieve group integration appear to be much more recent and more highly developed.

As a consequence of such pervasive practices, direct formal interventions by government authority were seldom necessary. The Japanese exhibited a strong tendency to avoid formal exercise of authority and instead to prefer compromise and consensual governance. Accordingly, power at the center of government tended to be diffuse, and identifying clearly a single controlling seat of authority was difficult. Japanese went to great lengths to avoid public confrontation or force to compel behavior and resolve disputes.

Growth of a Meritocracy

The education system revealed a great deal about the nature of postwar Japan. For the great middle mass of society it offered new opportunities for personal advancement, although the system itself was organized to serve the needs of business and the national goal of economic growth. Education was the focus of the nation's aspirations to such an extent that it was, as Rohlen points out, indicative of the Japanese national character. In the individual's scramble for success in school, "many important virtues—diligence, sacrifice, mastery of detailed information, endurance over the many preparatory years, willingness to postpone gratification, and competitive spirit—are tied together at a formative period and are motivated largely by a rather selfish individual desire to get ahead."[3]

Throughout their modern history, Japanese placed a high value on education, partly because it was one of the main means of social advancement. In the late Tokugawa Period, wealthy peasants often bought their sons an advanced education as a way of compensating for the restrictive class system. Reformers opposed the hereditary principle, arguing that rank should depend on merit as demonstrated in the fief schools. After the Meiji Restoration, when lower-ranking samurai came to power, the class restrictions were removed and education became a favored path of upward mobility. Fukuzawa Yukichi declared that a person's place in society should be determined by his mastery of the new practical learning taught in the schools. Whatever their family background, the best positions in government, business, and academia were open to university graduates. In Fukuzawa's day, a rush of talent rose from the lower orders, yet attendance at universities remained a limited phenomenon in the prewar period.

The years after World War II, more than ever before, saw an explosion of education opportunities and aspirations. By expanding the education system and reducing the inequality of income distribution, Occupation reforms created a more fluid society in which the incidence of social mobility between generations was much greater. Who was to advance in society came to be determined largely by academic success. Perhaps more than any other country at this time, Japan approached the ideal of a full-fledged meritocracy—that is, a society that "offers equal educational opportunity, makes it frankly competitive, and then uses the order of ability or merit produced to stratify individuals according to the many grades of work in society."[4]

As a result, education in preparation for the highly competitive university entrance examinations became a major preoccupation of both parents and children. "No single event, with the possible exception of marriage, determines the course of a young man's life as much as entrance examinations, and nothing, including marriage, requires as many years of planning and hard work."[5] Education dominated many aspects of Japanese social life because, more than any other factor, it was one's education that determined what share one was to have of the vastly increased national wealth. From 1952 to 1968 the number of students attending institutions of higher learning more than tripled, and by 1974 Japan had a higher percentage of the twenty- to twenty-four-year-olds attending school than any other major country except the United States. The driving force behind this almost universal desire for more higher education was the rapid growth of personal income and the ambition of parents and children for social advancement.

Competition for entrance into the best universities became extremely keen, based on the rigid standard posed by entrance examinations, which assumed special importance in Japan because a steep hierarchy of prestige was recognized among the universities. Employers with the most to offer recruited from the top universities, which were generally the old imperial universities. Those universities, able to offer the graduates superior careers, attracted the brightest students to take their entrance examinations. Owing to the ingrained pattern of lifetime commitment to one firm, which university one entered became critical, for that determined not only the kind of initial job one would have but also usually one's lifelong career.

The pressure on students taking their university entrance examinations became intense. They tried to get into as prestigious a university as possible. The period of *shiken jigoku* (examination hell) each year was accompanied by all kinds of manifestations of the anxiety and psychological burden imposed on both children and parents. One of the more bizarre cases was the discovery in 1975 of a father in woman's dress taking the examination for his daughter! Those students who did not succeed often tried again the following year, in the interim attending a special preparatory school. Only about two-thirds of the students succeeded on their first try.

Preparation for the examinations began very early in a child's life in the parents' efforts to gain admission to schools that were known as most successful in preparing students. Consequently, entrance examinations were given at every level of schooling—even in many kindergartens. (In one prekindergarten, officials unable to test two-year-olds decided to test the mothers instead!) Gaining admission to an elite kindergarten presumably would help in preparing for the examination to a leading primary school and subsequent successes in school. An increasing number of children at every level also attended private schools (called *juku*) after regular school hours. The juku (which were attended in 1975 by more than one-half of all sixth-grade students) specifically prepared children for entrance examinations at the various levels of schooling, and the success rates of the various juku were tabulated and widely discussed by the media. These cram schools were a flourishing, multibillion-yen business.

How students actually performed when they did enter the university was less important than the fact that they had arrived at one with a reputation well known by all prospective employers. The main function of the university system in Japanese society, in other words, was not so much to educate students as to rate them according to their ability and diligence, represented by success in the highly competitive entrance examinations. Employers found in those test results a measure of students' innate ability, their mastery of detailed knowledge, and above all, their degree of persistence in a lengthy process. After all, in gaining acceptance to a good university, students demonstrated that over a twelve- to fourteen-year period they had the kind of stamina and planning required to run a marathon or to conduct a protracted military campaign.[6]

Some observers, however, feel that the examination system did not offer the equality of opportunity that most Japanese supposed it did. They point to the fact that only better-off families were able to afford the private schools, tutors, and juku that would enhance the chances of success in the examinations. Other observers of the meritocracy feared that it posed future dangers for Japanese society, that because of the hereditary element in ability and because of the arranged marriage system, the bright would tend to intermarry with the bright and a rigid class system might develop. Dore wrote in 1970 that this "seems to me a danger that might well increase as the proportion of people getting to the top who were the sons of the people who got to the top increases. The danger will increase because, the more class position becomes hereditary, the greater the likelihood of sharp cultural differentiations occurring between the classes, and the greater the likelihood of antagonism resulting. In short, there seems to me a chance of Japan developing a class system with differentiations as sharp as in the class system which developed in Britain in the nineteenth century."[7]

However this may be, the surge of education aspirations in the postwar period has left its mark on Japanese society. It contributed to another important trend in the postwar period—the rapid decline in population growth. The immediate postwar years saw the restoration of family life and a baby boom of some proportions, but beginning in 1950 the birth rate began to drop sharply. By the mid-1950s Japan had one of the lowest birth rates in the world, and it still has. During the two decades from 1952 to 1972, the average number of children per nuclear family declined from 3.3 to 1.9. The changes wrought as a result in Japanese social life are many. One of the most important, for example, was the change in the life of the "typical" Japanese woman.

Statistical studies show that in 1940 she completed her education at the age of 14.5, married at the age of 20.8, and had almost five children between ages 23.2 and 35.5. In 1972 the average Japanese woman completed her education at 18.5, married at 23.1, and had two children between ages 25.3 and 27.9. Births, in other words, were concentrated to free the mother to work and thus contribute to the cost of educating her children.

Many other reasons may also be offered for the decline in the fertility rate. One group of reasons clusters around new concepts of family life. In prewar days it was a patriotic virtue to produce large families, but since the war the prevailing ethic has emphasized a smaller family. In 1948 the Diet passed the so-called Eugenics Protection Law, which aimed at disseminating information about birth control and contraceptives and which also legalized abortion. The desire to improve one's standard of living became a legitimate goal, pursued with such frenzy that it was sometimes criticized in the media as "My Homeism." When people sought consumer durables—color televisions, refrigerators, washing machines—and better housing, they had to make decisions about savings and consumption that, one way or another, affected the number of children wanted in the family. Similarly, it became less common to depend on one's children in old age, less common to have three generations under one roof, and so it became necessary to accumulate substantial savings for retirement. At the same time, the increased competition for quality education consumed a very large part of a family's budget and, at the very least, reinforced the propensity to limit the number of children in each family. Surveys of the reasons for Japan's high rate of individual savings showed that one of the two most important reasons influencing family saving was the desire to provide for the children's education.

The Position of Women

Some observers have said that Japan more closely approximates the ideal of a meritocracy than any other society. One glaring exception, despite the great expansion of middle-class society, however, was the limited number of new opportunities accorded to women—not by the force of law but by the influence of social customs and expectations. For example, despite the fact that the Occupation's Fundamental Law of Education guaranteed equality of education and prohibited discrimination on the basis of sex, women did not have the same opportunities because of a lag in attitudinal change. The percentage of women finishing high school and proceeding to higher education was roughly the same as males, but they did not advance to the same quality of higher education and therefore generally could not compete for the more desirable positions in the workforce. In 1980, men comprised 82 percent of all four-year college students, whereas women made up 90 percent of all two-year college students. That is, two of every three female high-school graduates continuing their education entered junior college; nine of every ten males continuing went on to a university or four-year college. Junior colleges emphasized home economics and had the reputation of being schools for brides.

Occupation reforms were seemingly revolutionary in their implications for women, and MacArthur had taken special pride in "the emancipation of the women of Japan." In addition to the suffrage, the 1947 constitution went further than the U.S. Constitution in explicitly guaranteeing women equality before the law. The new civil code passed in the same year provided women with an equal right to own and inherit property and to seek divorce, and ended all legal distinctions based on gender that had deprived females of equal rights. In actual practice, however, due to the persistence of traditional attitudes and behavior, women often refused to accept their inheritance from their parents, and they often acquiesced in divorces sought by their husbands. Family court records show that more than twice as many women as men refused their share of a parent's estate. Relatively few divorces were judicial. In 1900 virtually all divorces were by consent; in 1980 the figure was still almost 90 percent. As Robert Smith observes, "In this statistic lies one more bit of evidence of the glacial character of fundamental change in the conjugal relationship. Divorce by consent, it is well known, makes it notoriously easy for a husband or his family to *force* a woman to agree to an action that she does not seek. . . . The high percentage of divorcees by consent may be taken as a handy index of female powerlessness in Japanese society."[8]

The position of women was also slow to change in the world of paid employment. Although far more women were in the labor force in the postwar period and most women held down a job at some time in their lives, relatively few pursued a lifetime career outside the home. Women's compensation was less than 60 percent of men's, and they generally did not qualify for the age-seniority system that tied pay to length of service. Women's work was usually regarded as temporary in that they would leave when they married, bore their first child, or reached age thirty. Even if they later returned to the same firm, they would start at the beginning so far as accrual of time was concerned. Women's work was generally a means of supplementing the family income and, in this sense, as Smith aptly puts it, "work is not an alternative to homemaking; it is an extension of the home role."[9]

From a frequently offered Japanese perspective, however, adherence to the American-imposed values in the constitution and civil code would have led to a weakening of the family, a rise in the divorce rate, juvenile delinquency, and other social ills—what is frequently called "the American disease." For most Japanese the family, rather than the individual, was the fundamental unit in society. They preferred to see the role of husbands and wives as complementary and mutually dependent. The wife ordinarily had a great deal of power and autonomy in managing the household and raising the children and was often the caretaker of elderly parents. Frequently, the middle-class husband turned over his entire paycheck to his wife, who was responsible for budgeting, saving, and managing the finances in the domestic realm. Robert Smith cites results of recent Japanese surveys that "ask women and men whether they would prefer to have been born as a member of the opposite sex. Between 1958 and 1980 the percentage of women replying that they are content to have been born female has risen from 27 percent to 67 percent. For men who are content to have been born male, the percentage has held steady at about 90 percent. These results may mean that today's women have more to be content with; it may also mean that they have come to see that the lot of men is less enviable than their predecessors thought."[10] In either case, the results suggested the growing satisfaction with the affluence and stability of middle-class life.

Evolution of the Political System

The continuous years of steady economic growth in the postwar period came to an unexpected end with the 1973 oil crisis. For the preceding two decades the economy had been growing at an average real rate of almost 10 percent. One of the factors that had facilitated this prosperity was the ready availability of cheap energy. But in October 1973 war broke out in the Middle East, and the Organization of Petroleum Exporting Countries (OPEC), the international oil cartel, announced a fourfold price hike. Japan, which depended on imported oil for three-fourths of its energy needs, was stunned. Double-digit inflation resulted; industrial production fell 20 percent; the high-growth period was over.

We may think of the early 1970s as constituting a watershed in postwar Japanese history. It was not simply the end of high growth. It was a time when popular discontent with policies of high growth began to show up in changed voter behavior. The solid consensus favoring growth began to erode as more and more people realized the costs that growth exacted. Special-interest groups arose, seeking enhanced portions of the national wealth. Initially opposition parties seemed to benefit from this discontent, but eventually the LDP responded in ways that changed the political system and made its workings more complex and diffuse.

Until the early 1970s the postwar Japanese political system had developed a great deal of coherence and unity of purpose. The conservatives dominated the system through an elite triad model consisting of the LDP, the bureaucracy, and big business. The opposition socialist parties had joined together in 1955, prodding the conservatives to unite. It at first appeared that a genuine two-party system might emerge. But the socialists proved inept from start to finish, and opposition to LDP rule soon fractured. This fracturing made it evident that the LDP was in control, and real competition for power occurred among its factions rather than within the party as a whole. In local government as well, during the 1960s, the LDP monopolized the governorships and the prefectural assembly positions.

This smooth-working political system was challenged by myriad new developments in the early 1970s. Partly these developments were domestic in origin, springing from pressures generated by a burgeoning middle-class society, and partly they came from abroad where the new size of Japan's economy was creating problems for its trading partners. In fact, serious trade friction and foreign affairs were beginning to intrude into the hitherto sheltered political-economic system.

The most dramatic indication that something was wrong in what had been a "conservatives' paradise" was the rise of an environmental and consumer protest over the social costs of rapid growth. By the end of the 1960s Japan had become the most highly polluted industrial society in the world. Four major lawsuits, filed on behalf of pollution victims, "became the focus for an antipollution movement that soon grew to be national in scope and threatened the LDP's local and national legislative majorities and the triumvirate's informal and closed method of policymaking and implementation."[11] The citizens' movement struck fear in the elite coalition because it generated a popular excitement comparable to the civil rights movement in the United States[12] and threatened the leadership with a loss of mastery over social change. This fear spurred the government to action, and the so-called pollution Diet of 1970 enacted legislation that effectively made Japan a leader in pollution control.

The antipollution citizens' movement was indicative of the new interest groups springing up and of the limits to the progrowth consensus that had knit the country together behind the conservative coalition. The opposition parties capitalized on these new concerns, especially at the local level. They took up the middle-class cause of more attention to quality of life (sewers, parks, and housing), urban crowding, welfare, and social security. As the number of independent urban voters grew, many of them signaled their concerns with votes that brought the smaller parties, including the Communist Party, to office in local government. The LDP grip on its Diet majority began to slip.

The conservatives clearly would have to reach out to new voters and broaden its electoral base. The key politician in transforming the LDP was the colorful and anomalous Tanaka Kakuei, who served as prime minister from 1972 to 1974. Although he led the transformation of the political system, he was an exception to its elitist ways. The son of a cattle broker, he alone among Japan's modern prime ministers never received a university education. He fought his way up the political ladder of the LDP by dint of a forceful personality and shrewd political instincts, serving in the key posts of Minister of Finance and then Minister of International Trade and Industry. As he rose through the ranks he mastered the use of the pork barrel to further his career; that is, he rewarded his supporters and allies with spending on public works projects; he also mastered the manipulation of contributions from business intended to influence the political process—although this practice ultimately brought his demise. Whatever one may say of the unsavory side of this "money politics," it prepared Tanaka for prodding the LDP toward a flexible politics more responsive to the middle class.

To broaden the electoral base of the LDP, it was necessary to bring together the politicians with the interest groups and the bureaucrats who controlled the ministries with jurisdiction over the resources needed to respond to the special interests. Tanaka and other politicians like him sought to become masters of the bureaucracy. This did not necessarily entail confrontation but rather gaining the technical knowledge that bureaucrats had hitherto monopolized, capitalizing on divisions and jurisdictional infighting within the bureaucracy, and recruiting political leadership from pure politicians rather than from former bureaucrats as had been the common practice. It all added up to more influence for professional party politicians. In the cabinet that Tanaka appointed in 1972, for example, only one-third of the ministers were former bureaucrats. Diet members built up special expertise through many terms in office in a particular area of public policy—agriculture, education, defense, construction, or whatever might be of special interest to the member's constituency. These cliques (*zoku*) of Diet members with expertise became valuable to the bureaucrats who needed legislation passed. Thus triangular relationships of bureaucrats, special-interest groups, and Diet members formed, and the LDP was able to acquire a greater role in the political system, which had hitherto been overwhelmingly dominated by the bureaucracy. The bureaucrats retained immense power, greater than in other advanced industrial countries, but the process was now more complex.

This change in the political system was a result of the LDP's need to broaden its electoral base by responding to the needs of the new middle class and thereby co-opting independent voters who supported opposition parties. The LDP, once largely dependent on the support of farmers, merchants, and the self-employed, now tried to attract the support of urban white- and blue-collar workers. It became a catch-all party seeking to respond to the interests of the broad masses. The government greatly expanded its spending on urban infrastructure (streets, parks, sewers) and especially on medical care and pension plans. The resort to deficit spending to meet the needs of a far more diverse constituency paid off as the LDP won back independent voters and rebuilt its control of the Diet and important local and prefectural posts. Increasingly, the electorate became wedded to the status quo, and citizen and consumer movements that had appeared to threaten the conservative ascendancy at the beginning of the 1970s sank into disuse.

Japanese Democracy

Did the rise of the middle class and the new responsiveness of the conservative elites to its interests succeed in establishing a more genuinely democratic political system? The issue is intensely debated among political scientists. We have seen that the Occupation's intention of establishing democracy was undercut by its failure to purge the bureaucracy and instead to depend on it and leave it in an even stronger position than it had held in the prewar period. Thus the distinction between the formal principles and institutions enshrined in the constitutional order and the reality of how the political system in fact operated was extreme indeed. Nevertheless, as the well-being and education of the citizenry increased and as postwar party politicians gained experience, the question remained: was the system in fact being democratized and was the gap between principle and reality being closed?

Critics of Japanese democracy argue that the elites dominate and distort the formal institutions, that it, like Japanese capitalism, "has been brokered, in ways that respect the form but frequently kill the spirit of democracy."[13] These critics point out that, as in the case of the Meiji Restoration, reforms in the postwar period were instituted "from above." Although they had experienced tutelage in democratic values, the Japanese people had never on their own achieved a democratic revolution. Democracy was therefore a fragile blossom. Its values, while given lip service, had not been instilled in the lifeblood of the people by their historic and cultural experience. The Japanese were instinctively more comfortable with collectivist than individualist values, with respect for hierarchy than equality, with productionist than consumerist values, with nationalist sentiment than universalist principles.

The critics of Japanese democracy made many telling arguments. First, they stressed the cultural limitations on democracy as a decision-making process. Democracy is majority rule, but Japanese values continued to stress group consensus and collectivist principles. As Rohlen wrote, "At the small group level there is a definite reluctance to call a vote if the outcome might be divisive (which in most cases means not unanimous). Voting makes public the fact of dissensions and creates winners and losers. In small groups, fraternal organizations, and many other intermediate scale entities, the Japanese preference is to avoid majority rule. One wonders, as a result, about the social foundations of democracy in Japan. Qualities of group maintenance take precedence over expeditious use of rules."[14]

Second, critics stressed the elitist domination of the political system. The web of personal ties, based on school, family, and marriage, that interrelate the leaders of government, business, and bureaucracy exercise unusual sway over political institutions. Furthermore, the continuity in elite domination was demonstrated by the fact that seats in the Diet are increasingly "inherited" by sons or relatives of retiring members. Nearly 40 percent of the LDP Diet members in 1992 were sons or sons-in-law, or other close relatives of former Diet members.

Third, the LDP controlled a majority of seats in the Lower House for nearly four decades, from the party's formation in 1955 to the summer of 1993. When there is no alternation of parties in power how, critics asked, could a truly democratic politics emerge? Factional politics within the LDP determined who would be prime minister, and differences in political philosophy or an agenda of change rarely determined the outcome.

Fourth, the bureaucracy, which was not accountable to the electorate, held the real power in the political system. As many analysts have said, the Diet served to buffer the bureaucracy from the wishes of the electorate. Japan's laws were normally drafted by the bureaucrats, and Japanese cabinets changed so frequently that a minister appointed from the LDP had no time to make a difference on the prevailing bureaucratic power. Furthermore, Diet members lacked sufficient staff assistants to formulate or adequately study legislative issues. The role of the Diet, Johnson argued, was "to fend off the numerous interest groups in the society" and "create space for bureaucratic initiative unconstrained by political power."[15]

Although the doubters about the influence of the new middle class on the quality of Japanese democracy were many, other observers believed that owing to the evolutionary changes in the political system that took place in the early 1970s Japan came closer to becoming a full-fledged democracy. Japanese democracy had distinctive characteristics, they admitted, but nonetheless it was similar in its workings to the democratic systems in other advanced industrial nations. Much stress was placed on two developments: first, the rise of special-interest groups and the role of the state in responding to their demands, and second, the growing power and influence of elected officials relative to the bureaucracy. It was argued that the LDP's need to accommodate the interests of the new middle mass of voters made it more assertive in its relationship with the bureaucracy, which while still very powerful could not act against the wishes of the Diet and the LDP. One political scientist concluded in 1989: "Even if the Japanese bureaucracy exercises a good deal of influence over policy formation, its influence is not significantly greater than in other parliamentary democracies where, unlike the United States, the civil service is immune to changes in the executive. The same is true in Great Britain, France, Sweden, and most European parliamentary systems. . . . On balance, therefore, Japanese governmental institutions are weighted to ensure popularly elected officials a strong and predominant voice in policy-making comparable to other democracies."[16] Those who emphasized Japan's democratic features pointed to the trend of outside forces penetrating bureaucratic autonomy. Japan was democratizing. It was not a perfect democracy but where, after all, they said, does the perfect democracy exist?

Notes

1. Takafusa Nakamura, *The Postwar Japanese Economy: Its Development and Structure,* trans. Jacqueline Kaminski (Tokyo: University of Tokyo Press, 1981), 49.
2. Thomas Rohlen, "Order in Japanese Society: Attachment, Authority, and Routine," *Journal of Japanese Studies* 15 (winter 1989), 5–40.
3. Rohlen, *Japan's High Schools* (Berkeley: University of California Press, 1983), 109.
4. Ibid., 135.
5. Ezra Vogel, *Japan's New Middle Class* (Berkeley: University of California Press, 1971), rev. ed., 40.
6. Rohlen, *Japan's High Schools,* 108.
7. Ronald P. Dore, "The Future of Japan's Meritocracy," *Bulletin of the International House of Japan* (October 1970), 49.
8. Robert J. Smith, "Gender Inequality in Contemporary Japan," *Journal of Japanese Studies* 13 (winter 1987), 13.
9. Ibid., 16.
10. Ibid., 24.
11. Frank Upham, *Law and Social Change in Postwar Japan* (Cambridge, Mass.: Harvard University Press, 1987), 29.
12. Ibid., 54.
13. John W. Dower, *Japan in War and Peace: Selected Essays* (New York: New Press, 1993), 67.
14. Rohlen, "Order in Japanese Society," 16.
15. Chalmers Johnson, *MITI and the Japanese Miracle: The Growth of Industrial Policy, 1925–1975* (Stanford: Stanford University Press, 1982), 315–316.
16. T. J. Pempel, "Prerequisites for Democracy," in *Democracy in Japan,* ed. Takeshi Ishida and Ellis S. Krauss (Pittsburgh: University of Pittsburgh Press), 31–32.

End of an Era

Beginning in the late 1970s it became clear to a growing number of Japanese that their nation was coming to the end of a centurylong era in their history. Many of the forces that had shaped modern Japanese history were being fundamentally transformed. The challenges that Japan had confronted since the mid-nineteenth century had either been met or no longer seemed pressing. Japan therefore needed to rethink not only the values, policies, and institutions that had guided national life since the Meiji Period; it also needed to reassess its goals and reorient its national purpose in the light of new conditions.

The awareness of these issues gained national attention during the administration of Prime Minister Nakasone Yasuhiro from 1982 to 1987. Nakasone, an LDP member who had always opposed the Yoshida Doctrine with its emphasis on economic growth and a low international profile, tried to reshape the national purpose, but with only limited success. Making the proposed changes in light of the extraordinary achievements of Japanese policies and institutions in the postwar period proved exceedingly difficult.

Nevertheless, after Nakasone left office, the Cold War came to an end in 1989 and the international system changed in ways that inevitably affected Japan. The result was increased urgency to change old ways and try to prepare for a new era in the nation's history.

The End of Late Development

Probably the most important theme running through Japan's history in the modern era was the effect that the timing of Japan's industrialization had in shaping all its institutions and policies. Japanese national life was influenced by an awareness of being a latecomer. Japan's economic and technological backwardness in comparison to the West had dominated Japanese national consciousness for more than a century. As we have seen, this awareness set in motion an intense drive to overtake the West. The arrival of the Western imperial powers in the mid-nineteenth century offered Japan a challenge to bridge the gulf between themselves and the early industrializers and to overcome Japan's backwardness. Japan's leaders in the 1860s began an intense search for ideas and techniques that could close the gap. Looking for shortcuts out of their predicament, intellectuals and government leaders in Japan studied the institutions and technical innovations of the economically advanced countries to determine which aspects should be adopted in order to catch up with the early industrializing countries.

Other non-Western countries were aware of their backwardness but nowhere else was this consciousness so intense and so pervasive that it drove a people with such single-minded determination. From the beginning of its modern history in 1868, Japan struggled to achieve national power. Unlike other modern revolutions, the Meiji Restoration did not give rise to universal values or an ideology of universal appeal. Instead, it generated a nationalist struggle to gain equality with the West. National power was to be achieved by unremitting hard work, unity, and sacrifice. The Japanese were a driven people.

For most of its modern history the nation pursued the twin goals of industry and empire. A wealthy country and a strong military, fukoku-kyōhei, would make Japan the equal of the West. When the quest for empire ended in military defeat, Japan's postwar leaders focused their sights on catching up economically and redoubled the national effort.

By the end of the 1970s, both in Japan and—more important for Japanese self-esteem—overseas it was readily acknowledged that Japan had advanced to the front rank as a global economic power. In the judgment of a chorus of contemporary observers, the nation had mastered the skills of organizing a modern industrial society with greater success than any other people, causing a Harvard University sociologist to rate it simply number one in the world. Ezra Vogel's book *Japan as Number One* (1979) became a runaway best-seller in Japan. The Japanese had been working and waiting for a century to hear that message. Vogel's book was followed by a succession of other books by foreigners praising Japanese achievements and analyzing the distinctiveness of Japan's industrial organization. The popular French writer Jean-Jacques Servan-Schreiber, in his book *The World Challenge* (1981), asserted that "Japan stands as a model to all the world."

A new national pride was palpable in the early 1980s. The *Asahi* edition of November 17, 1984, reported that a majority of Japanese now regarded themselves as superior to Westerners. This conclusion was based on the 1983 *Survey of Japanese Character,* which the government conducts at five-year intervals. The *Asahi,* announcing the results of the 1983 survey, observed that one of the most striking changes of attitude over the thirty years since the first survey was the response to the question, "Compared to Westerners, do you think, in a word, that the Japanese are superior? Or do you think they are inferior?" In 1953, 20 percent answered that the Japanese were superior. In 1983, 53 percent answered that the Japanese were superior.

These new attitudes toward the West developed as Japan's economic progress became apparent. As early as 1967, a Kyoto University professor described Europe as an object for sightseeing but no longer useful as a model. He wrote of the "relative decline in status of the European countries in the postwar world" and held that "we are either moving shoulder to shoulder with Europe or are already out in front." He concluded that the "Japanese today cannot fail to perceive the bankruptcy of Europe." By the late 1970s, Japanese periodicals widely discussed *Eikokubyō* (the British disease) which one writer defined as "a social disease which, upon the advancement of welfare programs, causes a diminished will to work, overemphasis on rights, and declining productivity."

Nor was the United States exempt from such patronizing attitudes. After the Vietnam War and the Watergate crisis, discussion of America's "fading glory" was not infrequent. An editorial writer for the *Asahi* wrote, "Watching the United States suddenly losing its magnificence is like watching a former lover's beauty wither away. It makes me want to cover my eyes." Articles about the "American disease" also appeared, particularly in light of the Japanese conquest of the American automobile industry in the 1980s. The American disease referred to a wasteful, inefficient society, bereft of its work ethic, no longer able to maintain the quality of its goods, crime- and divorce-ridden, suffering social disintegration.

Above all, confidence mounted that Japan was overtaking the West in technological capacity. A survey conducted by the government's Economic Planning Agency in 1985 found that among Japan's 1,600 leading firms, 90 percent believed that they had caught up with or surpassed the technological capacity of U.S. firms. By this time, most Japanese no longer believed that the nation should emulate foreign models. There was a pervasive belief that Japan had fulfilled the goal of the Meiji Restoration of absorbing what the West had to offer.

No one captured the national mood of the 1980s better than Nakasone Yasuhiro, the most colorful prime minister since Yoshida. On the eve of assuming office in 1982 he wrote, "The first necessity is a change in our thinking. Having 'caught up,' we must now expect others to try to catch up with us. We must seek out a new path for ourselves and open it up ourselves."

Nakasone was a nationalist who had always opposed the Yoshida Doctrine's exclusive emphasis on economic growth and on avoidance of an international political-strategic role. Instead he favored constitutional revision, an autonomous defense capacity, and greater nationalist content in education. He was feared by the progressives as an old-style nationalist. But Nakasone, influenced by a circle of conservative intellectual advisors, concluded that the achievement of catching up with the West meant that Japan needed a new and broader definition of national interest. Japan must no longer adhere to the narrow mercantilist policies of the past: they had been the means of Japan's catch-up struggle. Japan must increasingly play the role of a leader in the international system.

Nakasone argued the need for sweeping institutional reforms to underwrite a new role in the world. During his five years in office, he pressed for change on many fronts. The centurylong pursuit of equality with the West had left its mark on all of Japan's institutions. They were designed to promote a uniform and disciplined national effort to achieve this goal. They were also designed to insulate Japan from direct influence by foreign companies and individuals. To play the new role of an international leader, Japan's economic, social, and educational institutions had to be made more open, flexible, tolerant of diversity, and responsive to the international expectations associated with Japan's new status.

Nakasone turned his attention first to reform of economic institutions. The economy included many institutions that from a Western perspective constituted an illiberal way of conducting affairs: government industrial policy, cartels and other forms of collusion, a closed distribution system, enterprise groups (keiretsu), forced placement of government debt, noncompetitive public-sector procurement, tax preferences, and encouragement of savings to promote exports—in short a system that had facilitated policies of economic nationalism. Nakasone and his advisors argued that, having caught up in so many areas, it was no longer in Japan's own interest to maintain these policies. These distinctive institutional arrangements, which were defended by an array of powerful domestic interests, had become the subject of intense foreign criticism because of Japan's mounting trade surpluses.

In 1985 Nakasone appointed an advisory group, chaired by the former governor of the Bank of Tokyo, Maekawa Haruo, to recommend measures to deal with the trade imbalances. The so-called Maekawa Report the following year proclaimed that "the time has come for Japan to make a historic transformation in its traditional lifestyle." The report recommended restructuring the economy away from policies of short-term national interest to measures that would lessen economic friction with other countries: removal of barriers to trade in a number of industries, increased imports, changes in preferential tax treatment for savings, reduction of the workweek to five days, and reform of the distribution system that had kept Japanese consumer prices high. This effort to loosen the reins on the economic structure and to shift to a leadership role in the global economy proved difficult to implement because of vested interests and the successes that traditional policies had achieved. Nakasone ultimately had to admit that restructuring the economy was a long-term goal that he could not achieve in his term.

Reform of the education system, another of Nakasone's priorities, likewise proved difficult. In this case, the absence of external pressure deprived the process of useful stimulus. Education reform was a key part of Nakasone's desire to overhaul institutions and to prepare Japan for a new role of international leadership. In 1984 he established an advisory council on education reform to recommend changes. Nakasone and his advisors believed that during the long years of catching up with the West the school system had become so highly centralized and rigid, so intent on rote memory work and test scores, so focused on meeting company hiring policies and a mass-produced supply of workers for Japanese industry that it stifled qualities of creativity and diversity that Japan would need in the future. Many business leaders were coming to the conclusion that standardization and

Prime Minister Nakasone raises his arms as he shouts "banzai" cheers at the conclusion of a Liberal Democratic Party convention in 1985. *Reuters/Bettmann*

regulation of education had become a dead weight inhibiting the development of the more diverse and creative workforce that the economy would need in the twenty-first century.

In 1987, the education council recommended changes to liberalize and loosen up the rigid system, introduce greater latitude into the curriculum, and establish a wider range of criteria for judging achievement than simple test scores. What the council wanted to encourage was greater individuality and creativity so that Japan could provide the new ideas and creativity required to succeed in the future.

Nakasone and his advisors also wanted the schools to take the lead in the "internationalization" of Japan. They wanted to open schools to international influences, remove obstacles to hiring foreign teachers and enrolling foreign students, improve foreign language instruction, and enhance Japanese understanding of other cultures. The desired product of a reformed education would be a newly self-confident Japanese, at home in the world, not clinging to other Japanese when abroad, but rather communicating easily with foreigners and understanding their mores.

The education council stimulated a lively debate about the shortcomings of the education system and the needs Japan would have in its future international role, but the impetus for reform soon petered out because implementation of the council's recommendations was left to bureaucrats in the Ministry of Education who were generally wedded to the old ways and reluctant to loosen their control on the system.

The End of the Yoshida Doctrine

Japan was at the end of an era in the 1980s not only because the catch-up goals had been achieved, but also because the international environment was abruptly transformed with the end of the Cold War. The Cold War had provided Japan with a unique opportunity to recover from World War II. Avoiding any collective security commitments became an idée fixe of postwar diplomacy. Yoshida and his successors built an elaborate set of policies to prevent Japan's being drawn into overseas involvement. After the Japanese Self-Defense Force was organized in 1954 because of U.S. pressure, the government adopted the fixed position that their overseas dispatch or any kind of collective security arrangement were unconstitutional. Other policies maintaining Japan's determination not to become a nuclear power, not to export weapons or military technology, and not to spend more than 1 percent of GNP on defense reinforced Japan's low posture. Without these policies and their seemingly incontestable constitutional sanction, the pressure on Japan to contribute to the Cold War effort would have been close to irresistible. Although it permitted the Japanese to pour all their efforts into improving the nation's livelihood, the Yoshida Doctrine had an Achilles' heel. It was in a sense destructive of the national self-esteem. Japanese were sometimes referred to as workaholics and "economic animals." French President Charles de Gaulle once dismissed Prime Minister Ikeda as a "mere transistor salesman," and U.S. Secretary of State Henry Kissinger privately derided Japanese diplomats as "little Sony salesmen." Japanese themselves became increasingly aware that they were, as one writer said, economic giants and political pygmies on the international scene. Another writer, Yoshida Mitsuru, observed, "High economic growth is not bad in itself; what is bad is that the Japanese have no sense of the ends to which they wish to apply the power brought about by high economic growth."[1]

Nakasone wanted to change all that. From the time he took office in 1982 he set out to restore national pride and self-confidence and to adopt an active role in international politics. A century of borrowing Western culture together with the experience of defeat and occupation had undermined self-respect. To restore pride in Japan's modern history, Nakasone attached importance to the Yasukuni Shrine in Tokyo, the Shintō shrine established in the prewar era to honor Japan's modern war dead. Japanese could not agree whether it was acceptable for prime ministers and cabinet ministers to worship formally at Yasukuni Shrine, because it would seem to honor Japan's imperialist past and infringe on the postwar constitutions's separation of religion and the state. For Nakasone, the issue assumed great symbolic importance because it offered a way of putting aside World War II as a source of national shame and embarrassment and returning to traditional reverence for the spirits of the war dead. Just as other nations had war memorials such as the Arlington National Cemetery, so the Japanese should acknowledge the Yasukuni Shrine and show the gratitude of the people for the sacrifices of their forbears. It was time, Nakasone said, to achieve a consensus on this issue so that "approaching the twenty-first century, the Japanese state and the Japanese people can walk proudly in the world." On August 15, 1985, he became the first prime minister to offer prayers at the Yasukuni Shrine in his official capacity on the day commemorating the end of the war. He also made a contribution from official funds. Fifteen cabinet ministers and 172 LDP Diet members joined Nakasone. His worship precipitated immense controversy. Both at home and in China and Korea noisy protests were evoked by the suspicion that he intended to revive prewar nationalism. Responsibility for Japan's imperialist expansion and wartime invasion of other Asian countries were still deeply felt. So serious was this reaction that he did not visit the shrine a year later and, brooding about the persistent international distrust of Japan, he wrote:

> Other countries, especially those against whom we committed aggression and our neighboring countries whom we victimized, see little difference between Germany and Japan. I think a century must pass before the suspicion and distrust of our neighbors will dissipate. Of course Hitler's philosophy and methods were fundamentally different from those of Japan. . . . Moreover, not only is Japan economically and technologically powerful, as a people we have strong solidarity, our labor and management cooperate, and we have a remarkable sense of public order. In these circumstances, and because we are a population of 120 million, neighboring states inevitably fear us.[2]

Despite this discouragement, Nakasone used the diplomatic responsibilities of his office to promote an activist foreign policy. He wanted to undo the impression, left by the Yoshida Doctrine, that Japan was passive, dependent on others for its security and unwilling to shoulder international responsibilities. Forty years after the end of World War II Japan still had 45,000 American soldiers stationed on its soil. He talked about revision of Article 9 of the constitution and he tried to change policies that limited Japan's defense spending. But more was required than the words of this colorful prime minister to change a doctrine and a system that had been so successful in the recent past. The balance of power in Japanese politics was still with the adherents of the Yoshida strategy who wanted to continue to concentrate exclusively on economic and technological advancement. Nakasone left office in 1987 with a wry remark that the outcome of his hope to transform Japan's international role was yet to be seen.

In the years after Nakasone left the prime ministership, however, the international system changed dramatically. The Berlin Wall was toppled, East European countries freed themselves of the Russian yoke, and the Soviet Union disintegrated. The Yoshida Doctrine, which had been a Japanese response to the Cold War, was thrust into a new context. The Soviet-American confrontation that had stifled the activities of the United Nations gave way to a period of multilateral efforts to maintain and restore peace in the world's trouble spots. Japan, because of its great economic power and its stake in the international economy, was suddenly expected to adopt a more active role in such international peacekeeping activities.

The Persian Gulf Conflict which broke out in 1990 when Iraq invaded Kuwait was the first great international crisis of the post–Cold War period. Politics in Japan was thrown into turmoil. When an international coalition to restore peace was organized under a United Nations resolution, many countries expected that Japan, as a great economic power dependent on the Middle East for two-thirds of its energy needs, would take an active part in supporting the coalition. Public opinion in Japan was perplexed. Should members of the Japanese Self-Defense Force participate in the multinational effort? If not, should Japanese doctors, nurses, or engineers assist? The debate that ensued in Japan over its proper role revealed a mixture of self-complacency, isolationism, and reluctance to abandon the status quo. Decades of withdrawal from international politics immobilized the Japanese political scene. Eventually, the political leaders decided to send no personnel but instead to make a $13-billion contribution to support the coalition. This sizable sum was scorned in many foreign quarters as "checkbook diplomacy" and as a failure of Japan to meet the responsibilities of a country so deeply dependent on the stability of the international system.

Stung by such criticism, the Diet passed the United Nations peacekeeping operations (PKO) legislation in June 1992, which ended the ban on sending the Self-Defense Force abroad. It limited troop deployment to logistical and humanitarian support of United Nations missions, monitoring elections, and providing aid in civil administration. The law did not permit the Self-Defense Force involvement in armed United Nations missions, such as monitoring cease-fires, disarming combatants, and patrolling buffer zones. Although a small step, the PKO legislation began to erode support for the Yoshida Doctrine. After passage of the legislation, in September 1992 the government dispatched a contingent of several hundred personnel to join the United Nations peacekeeping mission in Cambodia. Most were engineers helping to rebuild roads and bridges. Although the steps initiated by Nakasone and after him the PKO legislation were small and incremental, it was clear that most Japanese leaders were preparing for a more active role in international politics.

Internationalization

It was more than the end of an era that Japan experienced as it entered the 1990s. Japan was undergoing a historic transformation unique in its history that required a redefinition of Japan's national interest and national purpose. Not only was the catch-up period over, but the Yoshida Doctrine was outmoded. Powerful forces were propelling the Japanese nation into a new global role for which little in its 2,000-year history had prepared it.

These forces were primarily economic. The growth of the Japanese economy was at the root of these changes. Japanese household savings, which as we have seen were extraordinarily high throughout the postwar period, amounting to 18 percent of disposable income in 1980 as opposed to less than 5 percent in the United States, underwrote Japan's rise as an international investor over the course of the 1980s.

Surplus savings so great that they could no longer be absorbed at home were exported to the rest of the world. Year after year, during this decade, Japan amassed trade and current account surpluses. Japan's net external assets rose from $10.9 billion in 1981 to $383 billion a decade later. By 1990 Japan had become the largest net creditor in the world, "the greatest creditor nation the world has ever known."[3] In 1970 the cumulative value of Japanese overseas investments was $3.6 billion, in 1980 $160 billion, and in 1991 $2.0 trillion.[4]

The message of these and similarly stunning statistics was that Japan and individual Japanese were being drawn into international affairs to a degree unprecedented in Japan's history. Earlier Japanese trade contacts had kept foreigners at arm's length. Imports and exports were usually handled through large general trading companies that involved relatively little real personal interaction. But the new investment patterns required genuine economic intimacy with other peoples. As Edward Lincoln observes:

> Even portfolio investments in foreign stock and bond markets require extensive and continuous knowledge of local economic trends and corporate behavior to be financially successful. But the strongest impact comes with direct investment. To put the matter at an elemental level, managing workers in Tennessee requires far more interaction or meaningful understanding of economic, political, and social aspects of the United States than exporting cars from Japan. Successful direct investments require an understanding of foreign cultures, legal systems, idiosyncratic conditions in local financial and real estate markets, political systems, labor supply conditions, labor law or customary work conditions, and a tolerance and acceptance of diverse ethnic and racial groups.[5]

The implications for the Japanese people were overwhelming. International investment on such a massive scale led to a rapid growth in the number of Japanese managers and their families living abroad. In 1970, some 267,000 Japanese lived abroad; in 1980, 445,000; in 1990, 620,000. In 1985, a total of 23,830 Japanese went abroad for education or training; in 1990 the figure was 121,645.

Many other factors associated with economic growth including financial deregulation, yen appreciation, and technology transfer promoted greater direct involvement in the world. One of the most perplexing new factors was brought on by demographic changes, which we discussed in chapter 14. In 1990 the birthrate hit a historic low of 1.5 children over a woman's childbearing span, indicating the onset of labor shortages. Japanese became reluctant to accept undesirable, unskilled jobs which they described as *kitanai, kiken,* and *kitsui* (the three k's), which we may translate as (the three d's) dirty, dangerous, and difficult. Accordingly, a homogeneous and insular nation was struggling for the first time with an influx of foreign workers, numbering upwards of 300,000 at the beginning of the 1990s whereas in 1970 there had been virtually none.

These many new interactions with foreigners led the Japanese to think of the 1990s as a time of *kokusaika* or internationalization. It was not a development that came easily to the Japanese people, who harbored widespread ambivalence toward foreigners. As the editor of Japan's most prominent economic journal wrote in 1986, reflecting on derogatory remarks Prime Minister Nakasone had made about the United States and its minorities:

> The Japanese belief in their own superiority seems to be more deeply ingrained than ever because of their ability to produce superb industrial products and high technology. . . . Japanese are a people of great contradiction. While the Japanese appear to have been prostrated before America, deep in their hearts they have a certain enmity toward Americans. They look down on fellow Asians, but cannot abandon an obligatory feeling of affinity toward them.[6]

Achieving a closer relationship with Asia was one of the significant challenges brought on by this period of internationalization. For four decades Japan had remained aloof from Asia, concentrating on investment and production at home and trade with the West. But economic forces radically changed this situation. An international agreement in 1985 to increase sharply the value of the yen suddenly made it profitable to shift production and assembly of many Japanese manufactures offshore to other Asian countries that had much lower wage scales. Japanese interest in the development of other Asian economies dramatically increased. By the end of the 1980s Japan was not only the world's largest creditor nation, it was also the world's largest donor of official development assistance. Nearly two-thirds of this aid went to Asian countries. Japan acquired an impressive array of economic tools that made it possible to establish economic leadership in the region, and it offered other Asian countries a persuasive set of economic inducements to follow its leadership: foreign aid, commercial loans, technology transfer, direct investment, and preferential access to the Japanese market.

At the same time, for Japan to exert political leadership in Asia was impossible because of the legacy of World War II. Japan's postwar conservative leaders had not dealt forthrightly with the Japanese role in Asia during the war. Although many Japanese were severely self-critical in assessing Japan's wartime role, mainstream conservative leaders were not. Prime Minister Yoshida had dismissed the Pacific War as a "historic stumble," when military and diplomatic blunders had deflected the Japanese from their legitimate goals pursued since the Meiji Restoration. A continuing series of episodes confirmed the persistence of this conservative view. Only grudgingly and after international outcry did education bureaucrats permit high school social studies texts to mention Japanese invasion of China. Repeatedly, only international protests had forced the dismissal of cabinet ministers who argued that colonization of Korea had been legitimate or that the rape of Nanking was a fabrication. Only reluctantly, when confronted with undeniable evidence, did the government admit that hundreds of thousands of Asian women had been compelled to serve as comfort women providing sexual services to the Japanese army. Such continuing incidents made the formal, carefully scripted apologies that Japanese leaders periodically offered seem inadequate and incomplete.

The Struggle to Reorient Japanese Purpose

In 1989 Emperor Hirohito died and the Shōwa Period (1926–1989) came to an end. It was a moment when the fulfillment of the drive to catch up with the industrialized West was fully recognized. It was also a time when the international system, transformed by the end of the Cold War, made the postwar Yoshida strategy with its concentration on inward-looking self-interest seem increasingly outmoded. Finally, it was the beginning of a new era of trying to adapt to the forces of internationalization, which represented a wholly unprecedented challenge to the Japanese people.

As we have noted, growing recognition took hold in the 1980s that Japan must adopt a wholly new vision of its role in the world. As a nation that had largely achieved its goal of catching up with the Western industrial nations, Japan now needed to define for itself a new national purpose and to replace the institutions and policies established to "catch up." The first Japanese to recognize this need were the advisors to Prime Minister Nakasone during his administration from 1982 to 1987. These advisors, confident that Japan had at last caught up with the Western industrial economies, began to define a broader conception of Japanese national interest than that represented by the Yoshida strategy. As Japanese economic power burgeoned in the 1980s, and overseas interests and investments mounted, many Japanese leaders became acutely aware that Japan's own interests would no longer be best served by mercantilism and by a reactive and passive foreign policy. So great had Japan's stake in international stability grown, because of its export of goods and capital, that a fundamental revision of strategy was required. These internationalists wanted to define Japan's interests in broader terms because of changed conditions in the international system and particularly because of Japan's rapid rise in the system.

There were three essential beliefs that these internationalists came to recognize. First, it was in Japan's national interest to give support and leadership to the institutions of a liberal international economic order. Japan had become an economic power, and free trade is the ideology of the strong. As a MITI report concluded in 1986, "Japan cannot expect to grow or prosper unless the rest of the world grows and prospers."[7] Second, the internationalists believed that Japan must, in its own interest, reform its institutions to bring them into harmony with international norms and expectations and demonstrate that Japan was not a closed market, not a nation engaged in unfair trade practices. For more than a century, Japan had built institutions and political structures that could most efficiently mobilize and allocate resources. The government had suppressed domestic consumption to invest heavily in productive new industries. These policies had succeeded in generating huge trade surpluses, but they were the source of persistent trade friction with Japan's trading partners, and protectionist sentiment against Japan was mounting. In 1992, the chairman of the Sony Corporation, Morita Akio, admitting that "Japan might well be called a 'fortress' when seen from outside," concluded that "if Japan cannot on its own initiative, liberalize its markets, reform its political and administrative systems, and improve the structure of its economy, then the nation could find itself isolated from the global community now being shaped in the post–Cold War era."[8] Third, the internationalists believed that the Japanese people had to develop a new global consciousness, a more liberal nationalism, that would be respectful of other national traditions and that would provide popular support for a more active and responsible role in the United Nations and other international organizations. Especially, Japanese must develop new and friendly cultural relationships with other Asians to provide legitimacy for Japanese political-economic leadership in the region. In sum, among many Japanese political leaders, bureaucrats in major ministries, and leaders of businesses heavily involved in international trade, there was a dawning recognition that Japan's stake in the stability of the international political-economic order had grown so great that now, more than ever in the past, to be a Japanese nationalist was to be, in a certain sense, an internationalist.

To achieve such a major transformation of its national purpose and of its international role was a formidable challenge. Consensus on a new foreign policy and on restructuring and reforming domestic institutions was constrained by what we may call, in general, the burdens of history. The legacy of the centurylong forced march to catch up with the West became a barrier to internationalist consensus. The past policies and institutions were so successful that it was difficult to abandon them. Many politicians believed that concentration on economics and staying out of international power politics was the safer course for the Japanese state. Bureaucrats were reluctant to give up their immense powers of regulation. Business was reluctant to change such institutional arrangements as keiretsu, and lax enforcement of the Anti-Monopoly Law, and other unique aspects of Japanese management practices. The notion of reforming Japanese institutions to harmonize with Western institutions provoked an instinctive cultural nationalism. Cultural nationalists opposed reform of the Japanese economic system. For example, the nationalist politician Ishihara Shintarō opposed the belief expressed "both at home and abroad that the difference between Japan and Western Europe in the operation of their economies and business management stems entirely from the late-developing character of Japanese society." For Ishihara the distinctive features of the Japanese political system were not the product of a transitory historic phase that should now be reformed. On the contrary, "the decisive factor has been the distinctive character of Japanese culture," which he and other cultural nationalists argued constitute a superior Japanese system that should not be sacrificed.[9] Japanese business leaders held a similar widespread belief that rather than trying to harmonize their institutions with Western practice, Japan's institutions themselves should be a model for other countries to emulate.

If Japan was to make the changes required of the new age of internationalization, then the question of finding able political leadership was critical. In the summer of 1993 the Japanese political world experienced a stunning upheaval. In the wake of major scandals that angered the Japanese voting public, the LDP lost control of the Lower House of the Diet. For the first time since its founding in 1955, the LDP lacked a majority to form a government. Instead, a coalition of seven parties formed a new government headed by a reformist prime minister committed to sweeping changes in Japanese politics. The new prime minister, Hosokawa Morihiro, the grandson of the prewar leader Konoe Fumimaro, stayed in office only a few months. He fell from power in early 1994 as the tumult in the political world continued.

The proximate causes of the political turmoil that began in the summer of 1993 were the political corruption and failed attempts at political reform. But more fundamentally, Japan had entered a new era that made the old political alignments outmoded. The major issues reshaping the political scene were the issues of the new internationalism—that is, the degree to which Japan should play an active political-strategic role in the world, how far Japan should go in reforming its institutions to meet international expectations, and how open Japan should be with regard to a host of issues from education to foreign labor.

At the end of the twentieth century, Japan reminds one of Janus, the Roman god who was the guardian of portals and the patron of beginnings and endings. He is depicted with two faces, one looking forward, the other backward, symbolizing his powers. So with Japan. One face looks forward to the new century: it is fresh, young; its features are still not fully formed. It is a Japan still in the making, preparing for the future, impelled by a robust self-confidence, open to the world, assessing new policies, intent on reordering its society and government to meet new challenges. The face of the other Japan is strong, with clear though weatherworn features, looking back over a century-long struggle to achieve world power. It is a Japan still insecure, inward looking, satisfied in its proven ways; a Japan clinging to the past order and discipline of its national life, less hospitable to reform, less tolerant of new ways, reluctant to part with the values and institutions that have brought success.

In the past Japan had demonstrated an extraordinary capacity to institute reforms. In the aftermath of the Meiji Restoration and in the post–World War II period, Japan changed with astonishing rapidity. But these periods of change came in the wake of policy failures, institutional collapse, and national disaster. At the end of the twentieth century, however, Japan was trying to change after succeeding in its catch-up goals. Success made change and the development of new policies and institutions to meet the challenge of internationalism enormously difficult.

Notes

1. Quoted in Kenneth B. Pyle, *The Japanese Question: Power and Purpose in a New Era* (Washington, D.C.: American Enterprise Institute, 1992), 95.
2. Ibid., 7.
3. Edward J. Lincoln, *Japan's New Global Role* (Washington, D.C.: Brookings Institution, 1993), 59; Edward J. Lincoln, "Japanese Trade and Investment Issues," in *Japan's Emerging Global Role*, eds. Danny Unger and Paul Blackburn (Boulder, Colo.: Lynn Rienner, 1993), 135.
4. Lincoln, *New Global Role*, 62.
5. Ibid., 58.
6. *Japan Economic Journal* (October 11, 1986).
7. Quoted in Pyle, *Japanese Question*, 80.
8. Akio Morita, "Japan Should Globalize on Its Own Initiative," *Nikkei Weekly* (January 4, 1993).
9. Ishihara Shintarō, "Sakujitsu no tomo: Morita Akio hihan," *Bungei Shunjū* (June 1992).

Glossary

Bakufu originally a term meaning military government, it came to designate the central administration of the country, headed by the shogun.

Bummei kaika civilization and enlightenment; the adoption of Western science and institutions in the early Meiji period.

Daimyo a lord possessing a han with an assessed productivity of at least 10,000 koku of rice.

Fudai daimyo a house daimyo, retainer of the Tokugawa house; most were vassals of the Tokugawa prior to the Battle of Sekigahara.

Fukoku-kyōhei wealthy country and strong army; the goals of the Meiji leaders to achieve industrial and military power.

Genrō the elder statesmen who acted as imperial advisors and took responsibility for designating prime ministers from the 1890s to the 1930s.

Genroku Period strictly speaking, 1688–1704; sometimes more broadly used to designate the half century from 1680 to 1730, an epoch of brilliant flowering of Japanese culture.

Gōnō the class of wealthy peasants in the Tokugawa Period.

Han the domain of a daimyo.

Heisei Period era of the reign of the Heisei emperor who acceded to the throne in 1989.

Jōi a slogan at the time of the Meiji Restoration, demanding "expulsion of the barbarian."

Kaikoku a school of thought at the time of the Meiji Restoration favoring "opening the country" to trade with the Western world.

Keiretsu groups of affiliated business enterprises in the postwar period after the dissolution of the zaibatsu.

Kenseikai Constitutional Association; a political party founded in

1916 that gained power in the 1920s; renamed the Minseitō in 1927.

Koku a measure of grain: 1 koku = 4.96 bushels.

Kokugaku National Learning or nativism, a literary movement that interpreted ancient Japanese texts in the Tokugawa Period and that assumed an ideological character.

Kokutai a nationalist term denoting Japan's unique polity with its unbroken imperial line and the concept of the state as a family.

Kōmeitō the Clean Government Party founded in 1964 as the political arm of the Sōka Gakkai, a Buddhist lay organization.

LDP the Liberal Democratic Party founded in 1955 with the merger of two conservative parties.

Meiji Period era of the reign of the Meiji emperor, 1868–1912.

Minseitō Democratic Party. The Rikken Minseitō, its official name, was founded in 1927 to replace the Kenseikai.

MITI the Ministry of International Trade and Industry; established in 1949.

Rangaku Dutch studies; Western knowledge entering Japan in the Tokugawa period through the Dutch trading station in Deshima.

Sakoku closed country; the seclusion policy of the Tokugawa bakufu.

SCAP Supreme Commander of the Allied Powers; General Douglas MacArthur's title in the Occupation. The term came to refer to the Occupation administration.

Seiyūkai Friends of Constitutional Government, a political party organized in 1900.

Shimpan daimyo a related daimyo; member of a branch of the Tokugawa family.

Shishi "men of spirit"; political activists in the period of the Meiji Restoration.

Shogun generalissimo; originally a term designating the highest military office, it came to mean the head of the central administration in the Tokugawa Period.

Shogunate the bakufu.

Shōwa Period era of the reign of the Shōwa emperor, 1926–1989.

Sonnō-jōi revere the emperor and expel the barbarian; a slogan at the end of the Tokugawa period.

Taishō Period era of the reign of the Taishō emperor, 1912–1926.

Tokugawa Period 1600–1868.

Tozama daimyo an outer daimyo; one who had pledged loyalty to the Tokugawa only after the decisive battle of Sekigahara in 1600.

Warring States Period 1467–1568.

Zaibatsu industrial and financial combines that emerged after World War I and were dissolved by the Occupation.

Zoku cliques of Diet members that emerged in the 1970s having expertise of importance to interest groups and bureaucrats.

Suggestions for Further Reading

General Works

The literature in English on modern Japanese history has grown substantially over the past twenty-five years. Space does not permit mention of the scores of important articles. Here we can suggest only some of the important books. For a complete bibliography, the reader is referred to John W. Dower and Timothy S. George, *Japanese History and Culture from Ancient to Modern Times: Seven Basic Bibliographies* (Marcus Wiener, 1995). *The Concise Dictionary of Modern Japanese History*, compiled by Janet E. Hunter (University of California, 1984), is a useful aid. Also helpful are the *Kodansha Encyclopedia of Japan*, 9 vols. (Kodansha, 1983), and an updating and revision of its contents: *Japan: An Illustrated Encyclopedia*, 2 vols. (Kodansha, 1993).

The Journal of Japanese Studies, which began publication in 1974, can be regarded as the journal of record for the field. Its index in volumes 11, 15, and 21 should be consulted for important articles. Most important books in the field are reviewed in *JJS*. Among other journals containing valuable articles and book reviews on modern Japanese history are *The Journal of Asian Studies*, *Monumenta Nipponica*, and *Japan Forum*.

A number of general survey histories can be recommended. John Whitney Hall, *Japan: From Prehistory to Modern Times* (University of Michigan, 1991), is useful for its treatment of the pre-1868 background. An authoritative and detailed textbook is Edwin O. Reischauer and Albert M. Craig, *Japan: Tradition and Transformation* (Houghton Mifflin, 1989). Other reliable accounts are W. G. Beasley, *The Rise of Modern Japan* (St. Martin's, 1990); Mikiso Hane, *Modern Japan: A Historical Survey* (Westview, 1992); and Janet E. Hunter, *The Emergence of Modern Japan* (Longman, 1989). Marius B. Jansen, *Japan and China: From War to Peace, 1894–1972* (Rand McNally, 1975), traces Sino-Japanese relations in the context of the modern development of the two countries. John Hunter Boyle, *Modern Japan: The American Nexus* (Harcourt, 1993), is the most recent of several useful surveys of the U.S.–Japan relationship.

The field of modern Japanese history is well served by the six-volume *Cambridge History of Japan,* which contains useful chapters by leading authorities on most of the major historiographical issues. Readers' attention is particularly directed to *Volume 4: Early Modern Japan*, edited by John W. Hall (1991); *Volume 5: The Nineteenth Century*, edited by Marius B. Jansen (1989); and *Volume 6: The Twentieth Century*, edited by Peter Duus (1988).

An earlier generation of scholarship included in a series known as "Studies in the Modernization of Japan" (Princeton University Press) remains useful. Individual volumes in the series include: Marius B. Jansen (ed.), *Changing Japanese Attitudes Toward Modernization* (1965); William W. Lockwood (ed.), *The State and Economic Enterprise in Japan* (1965); R. P. Dore (ed.), *Aspects of Social Change in Modern Japan* (1967); Robert E. Ward (ed.), *Political Development in Modern Japan* (1968); D. H. Shively (ed.), *Tradition and Modernization in Japanese Culture* (1971); and James W. Morley (ed.), *Dilemmas of Growth in Prewar Japan* (1971). A critical discussion of modernization historiography is offered in John W. Dower's introduction to *Origins of the Modern Japanese State* (Random House, 1975). Included in the latter is Norman's classic work, *Japan's Emergence as a Modern State* (1940), which is still worth reading for the problems of interpretation it poses.

A number of other books that treat major themes in modern Japan should be called to the reader's attention. Two volumes have sought to correct the overall impression of consensus as a pattern in modern Japan by examining the place of conflict (rebellion, assassination, suicide, strikes, riots): *Conflict in Modern Japanese History: A Neglected Tradition*, edited by Tetsuo Najita and J. Victor Koschmann (Princeton, 1982), and *Conflict in Japan*, edited by Ellis S. Krauss, Thomas P. Rohlen, and Patricia Steinhoff (Hawaii, 1984). Tetsuo Najita, *Japan* (Prentice Hall, 1974), analyzes the dynamic tension in modern Japanese politics between bureaucratic expertise and idealistic protest. Ivan Morris, *The Nobility of Failure* (Holt, Rinehart and Winston, 1975), explores the Japanese attachment to tragic heroes in history who chose defeat and death rather than compromise their ideals. *Personality in Japanese History*, edited by Albert M. Craig and Donald H. Shively (Michigan, 1995), is also of related interest. Marius B. Jansen, *Japan and Its World: Two Centuries of Change* (Princeton, 1980), is a literate essay on Japan's relationship with the outside world from the 1770s through the 1970s.

Several books on Japanese society and culture are of broad interest for the student of history. The classic is Ruth Benedict, *The Chrysanthemum and the Sword* (Houghton Mifflin, 1946). An authoritative book by Robert J. Smith is *Japanese Society: Tradition, Self, and the Social Order* (Cambridge, 1983). R. P. Dore's *City Life in Japan* (California, 1958), is still important and can be supplemented by Theodore C. Bestor, *Neighborhood Tokyo* (Stanford, 1989). Edward Seidensticker's engaging two-volume history of Tokyo is useful: *Low City, High City* (Knopf, 1983) and *Tokyo Rising* (Harvard, 1991). The origins and destiny of Japan's modern aristocracy are analyzed in Takie Sugiyama Lebra, *Above the Clouds* (California, 1993).

For the reader wishing to survey the development of modern Japanese literature, a remarkable study by Donald Keene is recommended: *Dawn to the West: Japanese Literature of the Modern Era, Volume 1: Fiction* and *Volume 2: Poetry, Drama, Criticism* (Holt, Rinehart and Winston, 1984).

Sources of Japanese Tradition, edited by Ryusaku Tsunoda, et al. (Columbia, 1958), is a valuable collection of historical documents.

Tokugawa Government and Society

The reader would do well to begin with essays in volume 4 of *The Cambridge History of Japan* already mentioned. A survey of Tokugawa history is Conrad Totman, *Early Modern Japan* (California, 1995). During the last twenty-five years a great deal of significant research on the Tokugawa Period has continued to deepen our understanding of the highly complex government and the dynamic society that took shape after 1600. To grasp the historical influences that brought about the establishment of the Tokugawa Bakufu, the reader is directed to John W. Hall, *Government and Local Power in Japan, 500–1700* (Princeton, 1965); *Japan Before Tokugawa: Political Consolidation and Economic Growth, 1500–1650*, edited by John W. Hall et al. (Princeton, 1981); and Mary Elizabeth Berry, *Hideyoshi* (Harvard, 1982).

The critical role of foreign affairs in the bakufu's establishment is subject to revisionist treatment in Ronald P. Toby, *State and Diplomacy in Early Modern Japan: Asia in the Development of the Tokugawa Bakufu* (Stanford, 1991). Also relevant is George Ellison, *Deus Destroyed: The Image of Christianity in Early Modern Japan* (Harvard, 1988), and Marius B. Jansen, *China in the Tokugawa World* (Harvard, 1992).

Workings of the Tokugawa system of government are described in a number of works, including *The Bakufu in Japanese History*, edited by Jeffrey Mass and William Hauser (Stanford, 1985); Harold Bolitho, *Treasures Among Men: The Fudai Daimyo in Tokugawa Japan* (Yale, 1974); and Conrad Totman, *Politics in the Tokugawa Bakufu, 1600–1843* (Harvard, 1967). Two related case studies of local government are James L. McClain, *Kanazawa: A Seventeenth-Century Japanese Castle Town* (Yale, 1982), and Philip C. Brown, *Central Authority and Local Autonomy in the Formation of Early Modern Japan: The Case of Kaga Domain* (Stanford, 1993).

Studies of economic and social change in the Tokugawa Period are essential for understanding the background of industrialization. No scholar has made a greater contribution to this understanding than Thomas C. Smith, whose essays have been collected in the book *Native Sources of Japanese Industrialization, 1750–1920* (California, 1988). Readers' attention is called to two particularly important works: Thomas C. Smith, *The Agrarian Origins of Modern Japan* (Stanford, 1959), and R. P. Dore, *Education in Tokugawa Japan* (California, 1965). The latter should be supplemented by Richard Rubinger, *Private Academies of Tokugawa Japan* (Princeton, 1982). A useful collection of essays is J. W. Hall and M. B. Jansen (eds.), *Studies in the Institutional History of Early Modern Japan* (Princeton, 1968). The evolution of Tokugawa law is ably traced in Dan Fenno Henderson, *Conciliation and Japanese Law* (Washington, 1965), and Carl Steenstrup, *A History of Law in Japan until 1868* (Brill, 1991). The economic impact of social change on the samurai class is the subject of Kozo Yamamura, *A Study of Samurai Income and Entrepreneurship* (Harvard, 1974). The importance of demographic change in the Tokugawa Period for understanding Japanese industrialization is explored in two works: Susan B. Hanley and Kozo Yamamura, *Economic and Demographic Change in Preindustrial Japan* (Princeton, 1977), and Thomas C. Smith, *Nakahara: Family Farming and Population in a Japanese Village, 1717–1830* (Stanford, 1977). Ann Bowman Janetta, *Epi-*

demics and Mortality in Early Modern Japan (Princeton, 1986), is an important addition to this literature.

Books particularly helpful in understanding the cultural currents of the period are Howard Hibbett, *The Floating World in Japanese Fiction* (Tuttle, 1975), and two books by Donald Keene: *The Japanese Discovery of Europe* (Stanford, 1969; rev. ed.) and *World Within Walls* (Holt, Rinehart and Winston, 1977).

For many years, the study of the role of ideas in Tokugawa history lagged, partly because of its complexity and the difficulty of the materials that must be mastered. It has, however, become one of the liveliest fields of study, beginning with Mikiso Hane's translation of the pathbreaking *Studies in the Intellectual History of Tokugawa Japan* by Masao Maruyama (Princeton, 1974) and the efforts of a number of scholars who published *Japanese Thought in the Tokugawa Period, 1600–1868: Methods and Metaphors* (Chicago, 1978), edited by Tetsuo Najita and Irwin Scheiner. In *Tokugawa Ideology: Early Constructs, 1580–1679* (Princeton, 1985), Herman Ooms offers a new interpretation of the ideological sources of legitimation upon which the bakufu drew. Kate Nakai, *Shogunal Politics* (Harvard, 1988), is a study of attempts to reform the bakufu. The diverse currents of late Tokugawa thought are the subject of several important works. Tetsuo Najita, *Visions of Virtue in Tokugawa Japan,* is a study of a "discourse on political economy" among merchants in Osaka. Nativism or national learning is treated in Harry Harootunian, *Things Seen and Unseen* (Chicago, 1989), and Peter Nosco, *Remembering Paradise* (Harvard, 1990). Other works on late Tokugawa political thought are Bob Wakabayashi, *Anti-Foreignism and Western Learning* (Harvard, 1986), and J. Victor Koschmann, *The Mito Ideology* (California, 1987).

The Meiji Restoration

The Restoration is surely one of the most complex and problematic events in modern history. Volume 5 of the *Cambridge History of Japan,* already mentioned, is a valuable source of essays on the causes and consequences of the Restoration. The research on Tokugawa intellectual history, just cited, has helped to clarify the place of new ideas in bringing on the Restoration. In addition, Harry Harootunian, *Toward Restoration* (California, 1970), studies the growth of political consciousness that was an essential ingredient of the Restoration movement.

The role of social protest in the onset of the Restoration can be examined in several works on the peasant class: Herbert P. Bix, *Peasant Protest in Japan, 1590–1884* (Yale, 1986); William W. Kelly, *Deference and Defiance in Nineteenth Century Japan* (Princeton, 1985); Stephen Vlastos, *Peasant Protests and Uprisings in Tokugawa Japan* (California, 1986); Anne Walthall, *Social Protest and Popular Culture in Eighteenth-Century Japan* (Arizona, 1986); and the same author's *Peasant Uprisings in Japan* (Chicago, 1991). A challenging work exploring more broadly the role of "the crowd" is George M. Wilson, *Patriots and Redeemers: Motives in the Meiji Restoration* (Chicago, 1992).

The more immediate circumstances surrounding the Restoration are demystified in a number of excellent works. The reader would do best to turn first to W. G. Beasley, *The Meiji Restoration* (Stanford, 1972), which has the virtues of synthesizing much of the voluminous research up to that time and offering an overview that carries the story through to 1873. Various aspects of the Restoration are analyzed in several other excellent works. Albert M. Craig, *Chōshū in the Meiji Restoration* (Harvard, 1961), approaches the event from an analysis of one of the two leading anti-Tokugawa domains. Thomas G. Huber, *The Revolutionary Origins of Modern Japan* (Stanford, 1982), contests many of Craig's conclusions. Marius B. Jansen, *Sakamoto Ryōma and the Meiji Restoration* (Princeton, 1961), builds its account around one of the leading activists. Conrad Totman, *The Collapse of the Tokugawa Bakufu, 1862–1868* (Hawaii, 1980); William G. Beasley, *Selected Documents on Japanese Foreign Policy, 1853–1868* (Oxford, 1955); and Peter Frost, *The Bakumatsu Currency Crisis* (Harvard, 1970), are also useful accounts of the denouement.

Japan's Cultural Revolution

There are many good books on the remarkable period of "civilization and enlightenment." G. B. Sansom, *The Western World and Japan* (Knopf, 1950), is still a good read, but much has been done since its publication. One might start by mentioning Masao Miyoshi, *As We Saw Them: The First Japanese Embassy to the United States* (California, 1979). Fukuzawa, of course, is the central figure in this period. The interested reader will want to consult the study of his ideas by Carmen Blacker, *The Japanese Enlightenment* (Cambridge, 1964), as well as *The Autobiography of Yukichi Fukuzawa* (Madison Books, 1992) and the translations of his important works: *An Encouragement of Learning* (Sophia, 1969), *An Outline of a Theory of Civilization* (Sophia, 1973), and *Fukuzawa Yukichi on Women* (Tokyo, 1988). Also useful is William R. Braisted, *Meiroku Zasshi: Journal of the Japanese Enlightenment* (Harvard, 1976). Earl H. Kinmonth, *The Self-Made Man in Meiji Japanese Thought* (California, 1981), and Donald Roden, *Schooldays in Imperial Japan* (California, 1980), are essential to an understanding of the ethos of this era.

The role of foreign models and advisors has received attention in several works: Hazel Jones, *Live Machines* (British Columbia, 1980); F. G. Notehelfer, *American Samurai: Captain L. L. Janes and Japan* (Princeton, 1985); and D. Eleanor Westney, *Imitation and Innovation: The Transfer of Western Organizational Patterns to Meiji Japan* (Harvard, 1987).

There are many dimensions to the cultural revolution. Kenneth B. Pyle, *The New Generation in Meiji Japan* (Stanford, 1969), examines the problems of cultural identity created for the educated by the importation of Western ways. Stefan Tanaka, *Japan's Orient* (California, 1993), and Joshua Fogel, *Politics and Sinology* (Harvard, 1984), are excellent studies of how Japan's academic view of Asia was formed. Irokawa Daikichi, *The Culture of the Meiji Period* (Princeton, 1985), on the other hand, looks at the everyday life of the common people. Carol Gluck, *Japan's Modern Myths* (Princeton, 1985), analyzes the formation of ideology. Religious turmoil is explored in James Ketalar, *Of Heretics and Martyrs in Meiji Japan: Buddhism and Its Persecution* (Princeton, 1993); Helen Hardacre, *Shintō and the State, 1868–1988* (Princeton, 1989); and Irwin Scheiner, *Christian Converts and Social Protest in Meiji Japan* (California, 1970). The emergence of newspapers is described in James L. Huffman, *Politics of the Meiji Press* (Hawaii, 1980).

An excellent study, James R. Bartholomew, *The Formation of Science in Japan* (Yale, 1989), explains how a scientific research tradition was developed in the years 1868–1921. A biography of a leader in Meiji educational policy is studied in Ivan Parker Hall, *Mori Arinori* (Harvard, 1973). Byron Marshall, *Academic Freedom and the Japanese Imperial University, 1868–1939* (California, 1992), traces the *cause-célèbre* conflicts between the academic elite and government leaders.

Political Developments

An important work of broad scope is *Japan in Transition from Tokugawa to Meiji*, edited by Marius B. Jansen and Gilbert Rozman (Princeton, 1986), which provides an interdisciplinary perspective on the decades of transition from the 1850s to 1880s. Michio Umegaki, *After the Restoration* (New York, 1988), deals with the establishment of the modern state during the first decade of the Meiji Period. The way in which the transition was achieved at the regional level is traced in Neil L. Waters, *Japan's Local Pragmatists: The Transition from Bakumatsu to Meiji in the Kawasaki Region* (Harvard, 1983), and James C. Baxter, *The Meiji Unification through the Lens of Ishikawa Prefecture* (Harvard, 1995).

The origins of Japanese constitutionalism have been the subject of much controversy. Three standard works are George M. Beckmann, *The Making of the Meiji Constitution* (Kansas, 1957); Nobutaka Ike, *The Beginnings of Political Democracy in Japan* (Johns Hopkins, 1950); and Robert A. Scalapino, *Democracy and the Party Movement in Prewar Japan* (California, 1953). Their interpretations were challenged by George Akita, *Foundations of Constitutional Government in Modern Japan, 1868–1900* (Harvard, 1967). Further useful reading would include Roger F. Hackett, *Yamagata Aritomo in the Rise of Modern Japan* (Harvard, 1971); Joseph Pittau, *Political Thought in Early Meiji Japan* (Harvard, 1967); Roger W. Bowen, *Rebellion and Democracy in Meiji Japan* (California, 1980); and Richard Minear, *Japanese Tradition and Western Law* (Harvard, 1970).

The rise and fall of political parties after the turn of the century can be traced in three fine books: Tetsuo Najita, *Hara Kei in the Politics of Compromise, 1905–1915* (Harvard, 1967); Peter Duus, *Party Rivalry and Political Change in Taishō Japan* (Harvard, 1968); and Gordon M. Berger, *Parties Out of Power in Japan, 1931–1941* (Princeton, 1977). Frank O. Miller, *Minobe Tatsukichi* (California, 1965), relates the thought of one of the parties' major ideologues; and Sharon Minichiello, *Retreat from Reform* (Hawaii, 1984), traces the career of Nagai Ryūtarō, a leading politician in the interwar period. For the development of the modern bureaucracy, see Robert M. Spaulding, *Imperial Japan's Higher Civil Service Examinations* (Princeton, 1967).

Industrialization and Its Social Consequences

Economists write fewer books than historians and the reader is urged to refer to a number of important articles that I have cited in the text by Crawcour, Landes, Patrick, Rosovsky, Saxonhouse, and Yamamura that relate to the role of the state and private enterprise in initiating industrialization. An early account of the beginnings of Japanese industrialization, Thomas C. Smith, *Political Change and Industrial Development in Japan: Government Enterprise, 1868–1880* (Stanford, 1955), is still useful. An important foray into Meiji business history is William D. Wray, *Mitsubishi and the N.Y.K., 1870–1914* (Harvard, 1984). Also of interest is Johannes Hirschmeier, *The Origins of Entrepreneurship in Meiji Japan* (Harvard, 1964). Teruko Craig has provided a graceful translation of the *Autobiography of Shibusawa Eiichi* (Tokyo, 1995), a Meiji entrepreneur par excellence.

There are a number of broad accounts of the development of the modern Japanese economy by economists, including Takafusa Nakamura, *Economic Growth in Prewar Japan* (Yale, 1983), and Ryōshin Minami, *The Economic Development of Japan* (St. Martin's, 1993). Aspects of the role of business are treated in Byron K. Marshall, *Capitalism and Nationalism in Prewar Japan* (Stanford, 1967), and William Miles Fletcher III, *The Japanese Business Community and National Trade Policy* (North Carolina, 1989).

The social issues raised by industrialization receive increased attention. Michael Lewis, *Rioters and Citizens* (California, 1990), is a careful study of the Rice Riots. Several important studies of labor relations and the government's reaction are Sheldon Garon, *The State and Labor in Modern Japan* (Princeton, 1987); Andrew Gordon, *The Evolution of Labor Relations in Japan: Heavy Industry, 1853–1955* (Harvard, 1955); W. Dean Kinzley, *Industrial Harmony in Modern Japan* (Routledge, 1991); and Ronald P. Dore, *British Factory–Japanese Factory: The Origins of National Diversity in Industrial Relations* (California, 1990). The political role of workers is examined in Andrew Gordon, *Labor and Imperial Democracy in Prewar Japan* (California, 1991).

The left-wing reaction to social problems is dealt with in a number of books: George M. Beckmann and Genji Okubo, *The Japanese Communist Party, 1922–1945* (Stanford, 1969); Gail Lee Bernstein, *Japanese Marxist: A Portrait of Kawakami Hajime* (Harvard, 1976); Henry D. Smith II, *Japan's First Student Radicals* (Harvard, 1972); Fred Notehelfer, *Kōtoku Shūsui: Portrait of a Japanese Radical* (Cambridge, 1971); Stephen S. Large, *Organized Workers and Socialist Politics in Interwar Japan* (Cambridge, 1981); Miriam Silverberg, *Changing Song: The Marxist Manifestos of Nakano Shigeharu* (Princeton, 1991); Germaine Hoston, *Marxism and the Crisis of Development in Prewar Japan* (Princeton, 1987); Germaine Hoston, *The State, Identity, and the National Question in China and Japan* (Princeton, 1995); and Atsuko Hirai, *Individualism and Socialism: Kawai Eijirō's Life and Thought (1891–1944)* (Harvard, 1987). Tatsuo Arima, *Failure of Freedom* (Harvard, 1969), analyzes the attitudes of intellectuals in the interwar years. Gary D. Allinson, *Japanese Urbanism: Industry and Politics in Kariya, 1872–1972* (California, 1975), describes the social and political effects of the Toyota factory on its locality. *Japan in Crisis: Essays on Taishō Democracy*, edited by Bernard S. Silberman and H. D. Harootunian (Princeton, 1974), and Koji Taira, *Economic Development and the Labor Market in Japan* (Columbia, 1970), also contain useful analyses of the interwar years.

The effects of industrialization on Japanese agriculture are examined in Ann Waswo, *Japanese Landlords: The Decline of a Rural Elite* (California, 1977); Penelope Francks, *Technology and Agricultural Development in Prewar Japan* (Yale, 1984); and Richard J. Smethurst, *Agricultural Development and Tenancy Disputes in Japan, 1870–1940* (Princeton, 1986). Thomas R. H. Havens, *Farm and*

Nation in Modern Japan (Princeton, 1974), traces the rise of agrarian nationalism. The role of government in mobilizing nationalism in the countryside is analyzed in Richard J. Smethurst, *A Social Basis for Prewar Japanese Militarism* (California, 1974). Ann Waswo's translation of Nagatsuka Takashi's novel *The Soil* (California, 1993) gives a picture of late Meiji village life.

The Role of Women

The effort to make up for past neglect of women's role in modern Japanese history is under way. One of the first books in this effort was Sharon L. Sievers, *Flowers in Salt: The Beginnings of Feminist Consciousness in Modern Japan* (Stanford, 1983). *Recreating Japanese Women, 1600–1945*, edited by Gail Lee Bernstein (California, 1991), is a splendid collection of studies on the definition of women's roles. Also, see Dorothy Robins-Mowry, *The Hidden Sun: Women in Modern Japan* (Westview, 1983). E. Patricia Tsurumi, *Factory Girls: Women in the Thread Mills of Meiji Japan* (Princeton, 1990), examines the exploitation of women in the textile factories. Mikiso Hane, *Reflections on the Way to the Gallows* (California and Pantheon, 1988), is an absorbing study of rebel women with political causes in prewar Japan. Barbara Rose, *Tsuda Umeko and Women's Education in Japan* (Yale, 1992), and Yoshiko Furuki, *The White Plum* (Weatherhill, 1991), are biographies of the pioneer founder of Tsuda College. A collection of Tsuda's correspondence edited by Furuki is also available: *Attic Letters* (Weatherhill, 1991). Regarding wifehood and motherhood see Takie Lebra, *Japanese Women: Constraint and Fulfillment* (Hawaii, 1984); Shidzue Ishimoto, *Facing Two Ways* (Stanford, 1984); Etsu Sugimoto, *A Daughter of the Samurai* (Doubleday, 1935); and Robert J. Smith and Ella Lury Wiswell, *The Women of Suye Mura* (Chicago, 1984).

For the postwar period, full-length works treating womanhood include *Women in Changing Japan*, edited by Joy Paulson and Elizabeth Powers (Stanford, 1976), and the eloquently written *Haruko's World* (Stanford, 1983) by Gail Lee Bernstein. Also see Anne Imamura, *Urban Japanese Housewives: At Home and in the Community* (Hawaii, 1987). Mary C. Brinton, *Women and the Economic Miracle* (California, 1994), is a major contribution on gender and work in postwar Japan. Of related importance is *Japanese Women Working*, edited by Janet Hunter (Routledge, 1993), and the "Symposium on Gender and Women" in the winter 1993 issue of *The Journal of Japanese Studies*. The views of a prominent Japanese social psychologist are found in Sumiko Iwao, *The Japanese Woman: Traditional Image and Changing Reality* (Free Press, 1993).

Imperialism and War

Perhaps the place to start on this major topic is with essays in Volume 6 of the aforementioned *Cambridge History of Japan*. The best comprehensive treatment of Japanese imperialism is found in two books: *The Japanese Colonial Empire, 1895–1945*, edited by Ramon H. Myers and Mark R. Peattie (Princeton, 1984), and *The Japanese Informal Empire in China, 1895–1937*, edited by Peter Duus, Ramon H. Myers, and Mark R. Peattie (Princeton, 1989). Also see William G. Beasley, *Japanese Imperialism, 1894–1945* (Oxford, 1987). For the first phase of Japanese imperialism, from 1895 to 1914, one would do well to begin with Peter Duus, *The Abacus and the Sword: The Japanese Penetration of Korea, 1895-1910* (California, 1995); Hilary Conroy, *Japan's Seizure of Korea* (Pennsylvania, 1960); and Akira Iriye, *Pacific Estrangement: Japanese and American Expansion, 1897-1911* (Harvard, 1972), which analyze the motivations of Japanese foreign policy in this period. Other useful studies include E. Patricia Tsurumi, *Japanese Colonial Education in Taiwan, 1895–1945* (Harvard, 1977); Mark R. Peattie, *Nan'yō: The Rise and Fall of the Japanese in Micronesia, 1885–1945* (Hawaii, 1988); Marius B. Jansen, *The Japanese and Sun Yat-sen* (Harvard, 1954); Ian Nish, *The Anglo-Japanese Alliance* (London, 1966); Shumpei Okamoto, *The Japanese Oligarchy and the Russo-Japanese War* (Columbia, 1970); and Ian Nish, *Origins of the Russo-Japanese War* (Longman, 1985). The reorientation of Japanese foreign policy after World War I is ably analyzed in Akira Iriye, *After Imperialism* (Harvard, 1965). Specific problems of diplomacy are treated in Roger Dingman, *Power in the Pacific: The Origins of Naval Arms Limitation, 1914–1922* (Chicago, 1976), and James W. Morley, *The Japanese Thrust into Siberia* (Columbia, 1957).

The international relations of the decade 1931–1941 has been the subject of many excellent works—many more than can be mentioned here. The reader would do well to turn first to a comprehensive thoughtful essay: Akira Iriye, *The Origins of the Second World War in Asia and the Pacific* (Longman, 1987). A multivolume Japanese study "Japan's Road to the Pacific War" has been partially translated, published by Columbia, and edited by James W. Morley: *Deterrent Diplomacy* (1976), *The Fateful Choice* (1980), *The China Quagmire* (1983), *Japan Erupts* (1984), and *The Final Confrontation* (1994).

The best treatment of the Manchurian Incident is still Sadako Ogata, *Defiance in Manchuria* (California, 1964). Ian Nish, *Japan's Struggle with Internationalism* (Kegan Paul, 1993), details the circumstances surrounding Japan's withdrawal from the League of Nations. Robert J. C. Butow, *Tōjō and the Coming of the War* (Princeton, 1961), and James B. Crowley, *Japan's Quest for Autonomy* (Princeton, 1966), offer contrasting interpretations of Japanese foreign policy. Stephen E. Pelz, *Race to Pearl Harbor* (Harvard, 1974), considers the influence of naval competition in the Pacific. The events leading to the Japanese-American conflict are the subject of many works, including Waldo Heinrichs, *American Ambassador* (Oxford, 1966); Jonathan Utley, *Going to War with Japan* (Tennessee, 1984); John Stephan, *Hawaii Under the Rising Sun* (Honolulu, 1984); Robert J. C. Butow, *The John Doe Associates* (Stanford, 1974); *Pearl Harbor As History*, edited by Dorothy Borg and Shumpei Okamoto (Columbia, 1973); *Japan's Decision for War*, edited by Nobutake Ike (Stanford, 1967); and Roberta Wohlstetter, *Pearl Harbor* (Stanford, 1962). *Pearl Harbor Reexamined*, edited by Hilary Conroy and Harry Wray (Hawaii, 1990), is a collection of diverse scholarly views of the outbreak of war.

Japanese politics as related to the onset of war still needs a great deal of study. An important and underrated study is Michael A. Barnhart, *Japan Prepares for Total War* (Cornell, 1987). Essays by Japan's leading postwar intellectual are stimulating: Masao Maruyama, *Thought and Behavior in Modern Japanese Politics* (Oxford,1969). We do have several important biographies of key figures: Yoshitake Oka, *Konoe Fumimaro* (Tokyo, 1983); Mark R. Peattie, *Ishiwara Kanji and Japan's Confrontation with the West* (Princeton, 1975); and George M. Wilson, *Radical Nationalist in Japan: Kita Ikki, 1883–1937* (Harvard, 1969). The young officers' uprising in 1936 is described in Ben-Ami Shillony, *Revolt in Japan* (Princeton, 1973).

The difficult and ambivalent position of intellectuals in the mounting crisis is discussed in Andrew Barshay, *State and Intellectual in Imperial Japan* (California, 1988); Kevin Doak, *Dreams of Difference: The Japan Romantic School and the Crisis of Modernity* (California, 1994); and Miles Fletcher, *The Search for a New Order* (North Carolina, 1982). Three books by Richard H. Mitchell deal with government suppression: *Censorship in Imperial Japan* (Princeton, 1983), *Thought Control in Prewar Japan* (Cornell, 1976), and *Janus-Faced Justice: Political Criminals in Imperial Japan* (Hawaii, 1992). Of related interest are Patricia Steinhoff, *Tenkō: Ideology and Societal Integration in Prewar Japan* (Garland, 1991); Elise Tipton, *Japanese Police State* (Hawaii, 1991); and Gregory J. Kasza, *The State and the Mass Media in Japan, 1918–1945* (California, 1988).

The role of the Shōwa emperor is the subject of continuing controversy. Three scholarly studies deal with the relevant issues: Nakamura Masanori, *The Japanese Monarchy: Ambassador Joseph Grew and the Making of the "Symbol Emperor System," 1931–1991* (M. E. Sharpe, 1992); Stephen S. Large, *Emperor Hirohito and Shōwa Japan* (Routledge, 1992); and Takeda Kiyoko, *The Dual-Image of the Japanese Emperor* (New York, 1988). David Titus, *Palace and Politics in Prewar Japan* (Columbia, 1974), is a study of the imperial institution and of bureaucratic decision making.

The literature on wartime Japan has been devoted primarily to battles, military figures, and strategy. But there are several important books that must receive the attention of serious students. The first, John W. Dower, *War without Mercy* (New York, 1986), analyzes the significance of race hate through contemporary propaganda and documents. Haruko Taya Cook and Theodore F. Cook, *Japan at War* (New Press, 1992), presents the oral histories of 68 men and women who recall their wartime experiences. Akira Iriye examines the Japanese-American war from the cultural perspectives of both countries in *Power and Culture* (Harvard, 1981). Other works are Ben-Ami Shillony, *Politics and Culture in Wartime Japan* (Oxford, 1981); Thomas R. H. Havens, *Valley of Darkness* (Norton, 1978); and John H. Boyle, *Japan and China at War, 1937–1945* (Stanford, 1972).

The atomic bombing of Hiroshima and Nagasaki stimulated more writing than any other aspect of modern Japanese history. The bulk of this writing is scattered in articles and memoirs rather than in full-length books. The interested student should therefore go first to bibliographic and historiographical essays: Barton J. Bernstein, "The Atomic Bomb and American Foreign Policy, 1941–1945: An Historiographical Controversy," *Peace and Change* 3 (Spring, 1974): 1–14, and J. Samuel Walker, "The Decision to Use the Bomb: A Historiographical Update," *Diplomatic History* 14 (Winter 1990): 97–114. The spring 1995 issue of *Diplomatic History* contains an important symposium, "Hiroshima in History and Memory." The seminal work on the end of the war is Robert J. C. Butow, *Japan's Decision to Surrender* (Stanford, 1954). Among other important full-length studies are Gar Alperovitz, *Atomic Diplomacy* (Penguin, 1985); Herbert Feis, *The Atomic Bomb and the End of World War II* (Princeton,

1979); Martin J. Sherwin, *A World Destroyed* (Vintage, 1977); and Leon V. Sigal, *Fighting to a Finish* (Cornell, 1988). Much remains to be done with Japanese sources to explain Japan's delayed surrender. John W. Dower, *Japan in War and Peace* (New Press, 1993), includes an account of Japan's own nuclear project.

Postwar Japan

Publication of a collection of sixteen essays entitled *Postwar Japan as History* (California, 1993), edited by Andrew Gordon, is an indication that historians will be directing increased attention to events since 1945 that had hitherto been largely left to other social scientists.

Study of the Occupation period is underway. General accounts include *Democratizing Japan* (Hawaii, 1988), edited by Robert E. Ward and Sakamoto Yoshikazu; Michael Schaller, *The American Occupation of Japan* (Oxford, 1985); Theodore Cohen, *Remaking Japan—the American Occupation as New Deal* (Free Press, 1987); Roger Buckley, *Occupation Diplomacy* (Cambridge, 1982); Howard B. Schonberger, *Aftermath of War* (Kent State, 1989); and Kazuo Kawai, *Japan's American Interlude* (Chicago, 1960).

Various dimensions of the Occupation are treated in a variety of books. Among them are Kyoko Inoue, *MacArthur's Japanese Constitution* (Chicago, 1991); R. P. Dore, *Land Reform in Japan* (Schocken, 1985); and Gary H. Tsuchimochi, *Education Reform in Postwar Japan* (Tokyo, 1993).

The conduct of the war crimes trials receives critical treatment in Richard Minear, *Victor's Justice* (Princeton, 1971). See also Arnold C. Brackman, *The Other Nuremberg* (Morrow, 1987), and *The Tokyo War Crimes Trial*, edited by C. Hosoya (Kodansha, 1986). Aspects of the legal reforms are discussed in Chalmers Johnson, *Conspiracy at Matsukawa* (Stanford, 1972), and Alfred Oppler, *Legal Reform in Occupied Japan* (Princeton, 1976). Kozo Yamamura, *Economic Policy in Postwar Japan* (California, 1967), analyzes the vicissitudes of economic reforms. Michael M. Yoshitsu, *Japan and the San Francisco Peace Settlement* (Columbia, 1982), studies the treaty that ended the occupation.

John Dower's masterful biography of Yoshida Shigeru, the key political figure of the time, *Empire and Aftermath* (Harvard, 1979), is an important source for postwar history. Kenneth B. Pyle, *The Japanese Question: Power and Purpose in a New Era* (AEI Press, 1992), traces the influence of the so-called Yoshida Doctrine in Japanese politics and foreign policy. Donald C. Hellmann, *Japanese Domestic Politics and Foreign Policy* (California, 1969), remains a valuable study of the peace agreement with the Soviet Union. George Packard, *Protest in Tokyo* (Princeton, 1966), is a study of the security treaty crisis in 1960. Works on postwar politics are numerous, and the interested reader should consult a bibliographic essay by Richard J. Samuels, "Japanese Political Studies and the Myth of the Independent Intellectual" in *The Political Culture of Foreign Area and International Studies*, edited by Samuels and Myron Weiner (Brassey's, 1992).

The role of the bureaucracy, the formation of industrial policy, and their prewar origins are analyzed in the seminal work Chalmers Johnson, *MITI and the Japanese Miracle* (Stanford, 1982). Marie Anchordoguy, *Computers, Inc.* (Harvard, 1989), is an excellent empirical study of Japan's industrial policy. Laura

Hein, *Fueling Growth: The Energy Revolution and Economic Policy in Postwar Japan* (Harvard, 1990), is of related interest. An important study of Japan's ideology of technological development is Richard J. Samuels, *"Rich Nation Strong Army"* (Cornell, 1994).

For a survey of the development of the postwar economy the reader should consult the second edition of Takafusa Nakamura, *The Postwar Japanese Economy* (Tokyo, 1995).

There are many commendable works on postwar society. Among them, Thomas P. Rohlen, *Japan's High Schools* (California, 1983), discusses the nature of Japan's so-called meritocracy; Frank K. Upham, *Law and Social Change in Postwar Japan* (Harvard, 1987), examines how law is used by elites to manage social change; and Norma Field, *In the Realm of a Dying Emperor* (Pantheon, 1991), presents a sensitive portrait of individuals who stand up for unpopular beliefs in contemporary society.

Finally, some of the most interesting scholarship on contemporary Japan is found in the three-volume series published by Stanford Press, *Political Economy of Japan: Volume I: The Domestic Transformation*, edited by Kozo Yamamura and Yasukichi Yasuba (1987); *Volume II: The Changing International Context*, edited by Takashi Inoguchi and Daniel Okimoto (1988); and *Volume III: Cultural and Social Dynamics*, edited by Shumpei Kumon and Henry Rosovsky (1992).

Index